Introduction to Microsoft® WINDOWS NT® Cluster Server

Programming and Administration

Introduction to Microsoft® WINDOWS NT® Cluster Server

Programming and Administration

Raj Rajagopal

MITRE Corporation

CRC Press

Boca Raton London New York Washington, D.C.

Library of Congress Cataloging-in-Publication Data

Rajagopal, Raj
Introduction to Microsoft Windows NT Cluster Server : programming and administration / by Raj Rajagopal.
p. cm.
Includes bibliographical references and index.
ISBN 0-8493-1866-1
1. Microsoft Windows NT Server. 2. Microsoft Windows NT. 3. Operating systems (Computers) 4. Client/server computing. I. Title.

QA76.76.063 R35 1999
005.4'4769—dc21

99-043496
CIP

International Standard Book Number 0-8493-1866-1
Library of Congress Card Number 99-043496
Printed in the United States of America 1 2 3 4 5 6 7 8 9 0
Printed on acid-free paper

Preface

Many businesses would like to be able to provide 24 x 7 customer access without having to shut down for maintenance. Most system administrators would prefer a method whereby they can perform routine maintenance and upgrades without having to wait for late evenings or weekends. Clustering technology permits these possibilities.

This book is meant for programmers, system administrators, and managers who are interested in better understanding clustering and applying it to their own situation. Highly available and manageable solutions using clustering and similar technologies have been around for a while. However, prior to Microsoft's Windows NT Cluster Server, organizations that needed clustering solutions had to implement proprietary solutions that were not widely available and come up with ways to interface those solutions with the organization's other data processing functions.

Chapter 1 begins with an introduction to clustering and covers terminologies unique to clustering, which are covered in detail in later chapters. The chapter also discusses how redundancy increases availability and the different ways of increasing redundancy both within a computer and across computers.

Chapter 2 discusses the benefits of clusters including improved scalability, configuration flexibility, integrity, availability, manageability, and performance.

Chapter 3 provides a detailed introduction to the subject of this book—Microsoft's Cluster Server (MSCS). It covers MSCS building blocks such as node, resource, and group. It covers how the building blocks perform clustering functions such as failover and failback. It discusses how heartbeat communications between nodes help cluster nodes keep track of each other and how shared data on a common quorum resource helps one node to take over the functions of another node. It also covers the MSCS architecture within the cluster service, including the different managers that make up the service such as the membership manager and database manager.

Chapter 4 covers setting up the Microsoft Cluster Server. It starts with the preparatory steps required, including determining if clustering is appropriate, and when it is the portions of the overall environment for which clustering is appropriate. The chapter then covers selecting the correct clustering configuration type such as hot spare configuration, static load balancing, etc. The chapter then covers licensing considerations such as per-seat licensing, per-server licensing, etc. After the preparatory steps, the chapter discusses the requirements for cluster setup including administration requirements such as determining the accounts and policies, hardware requirements, software requirements, and network requirements. The chapter then covers cluster setup steps including a pre-setup checklist, setting up the domain, setting up shared SCSI buses, installing the first node, connecting the second node to the first node. The chapter then covers post-setup activities such as verifying the cluster installation, ongoing cluster administration, etc.

Chapter 5 covers the unique functionalities of clusters: failover and failback. It provides an overview of the processes and concepts of pushing and pulling a group.

Chapter 6 covers Microsoft Cluster Server Communications including protocols, remote procedure calls, cluster heartbeats, name resolution, etc. The chapter also covers communication between the different cluster components including node-to-node communication, communication using the quorum resource, cluster-to-client communication, cluster service and resources communication, and cluster service and applications communication.

Chapter 7 covers cluster programming basics including APIs, entry point and callback functions, cluster control codes, and cluster properties. This chapter also covers cluster structures, resource DLLs, and cluster utility functions.

Chapter 8 builds on the programming basics introduced in Chapter 7 and covers the primary tool that Microsoft provides for building applications that take advantage of clusters — the Microsoft cluster server SDK. The chapter covers installing the SDK, an overview of using the cluster server SDK, programming resource DLLs, programming cluster administrator extension DLLs, programming applications, and programming custom resource types

Chapter 9 covers Microsoft cluster server administration including prerequisites for a cluster server administrator, installing the cluster administrator, administration, optimization, and tuning considerations. It also covers installing Windows NT Service Packs on Cluster Nodes and Administering Clusters from the command prompt.

Chapter 10 covers MSCS-based clustering solutions and case studies. It starts with a discussion of cluster support in Microsoft products such as SQL Server and Microsoft Exchange. It then covers cluster solutions from other vendors such as LifeKeeper for Windows NT and solutions from Compaq and HP. The chapter concludes with case studies of real-life cluster implementations including BlueCross/BlueShield of Oregon, First Union Capital Markets Group, IBM World Registry Division, John C. Lincoln Hospital, and others.

This work reflects the opinion of the author, and is not intended to represent the opinion of MITRE Corporation.

About the Author

Mr. Rajagopal has more than 19 years of professional experience covering all phases of software development— requirements, architecture, high-level design, low-level design, coding, testing, maintenance, and both project and line management. Currently, he is a Principal Scientist at MITRE Corporation. Prior to that he was a Senior Computer Scientist at Illinois Institute of Technology Research for four years and an Architect at IBM for nine years. He is a co-author of multiple patents in computer software.

Mr. Rajagopal has published many books and articles. His articles have been published by such magazines as *Application Development Trends*, *Computer Technology Review*, and *PC Today*. He is also a technical editor for major book publishers. He has reviewed *Windows NT Programming from the Ground Up*, published by McGraw-Hill and *Windows NT Registry Troubleshooting*, published by New Riders Publishing. As an adjunct professor, he teaches or has taught computer science and management courses at the University of Maryland, Johns Hopkins University, and the University of the District of Columbia. He has an MBA and an MS (Computer Science) in addition to undergraduate degrees in electronics, communications, and mathematics. Some of the books for which he is the author or co-author or editor are

Windows NT, UNIX, NetWare: Migration and Coexistence, published by CRC Press LLC;

Advanced Windows NT Programming, published by Osborne/McGraw-Hill;

Handbook of Heterogeneous Computing: Living with NetWare, UNIX, and Windows NT (1999), published by Auerbach Publications;

Handbook of Heterogeneous Computing: Living with NetWare, UNIXX, and Windows NT (2000), published by Auerbach Publications.

Contents

Chapter 6 Microsoft Cluster Server Communications

Chapter 7 Cluster Programming Basics

Chapter 8 Programming with the Cluster Server Software Development Kit

Chapter 9 Microsoft Cluster Server Administration

Chapter 10 Microsoft Cluster Server-Based Clustering Products and Case Studies

Appendix A

Appendix B

1 Review of Clustering Technologies

CLUSTERING TERMINOLOGY

Let us start with a definition of *cluster*. A cluster is a set of multiple, independent computer systems that project a single system image for access and management to most entities, such as human users and client applications, that are outside the cluster.

Figure 1 shows a schematic of a cluster made up of two computer systems and accessed by five clients. Each computer that is part of a cluster is called a node. The nodes of a cluster have network links between them that are used to communicate with each other. In addition to their own hard drives, the nodes also have a connection to a shared hard drive that stores shared cluster data. Figure 1 shows a Small Computer System Interface (SCSI) shared hard drive.

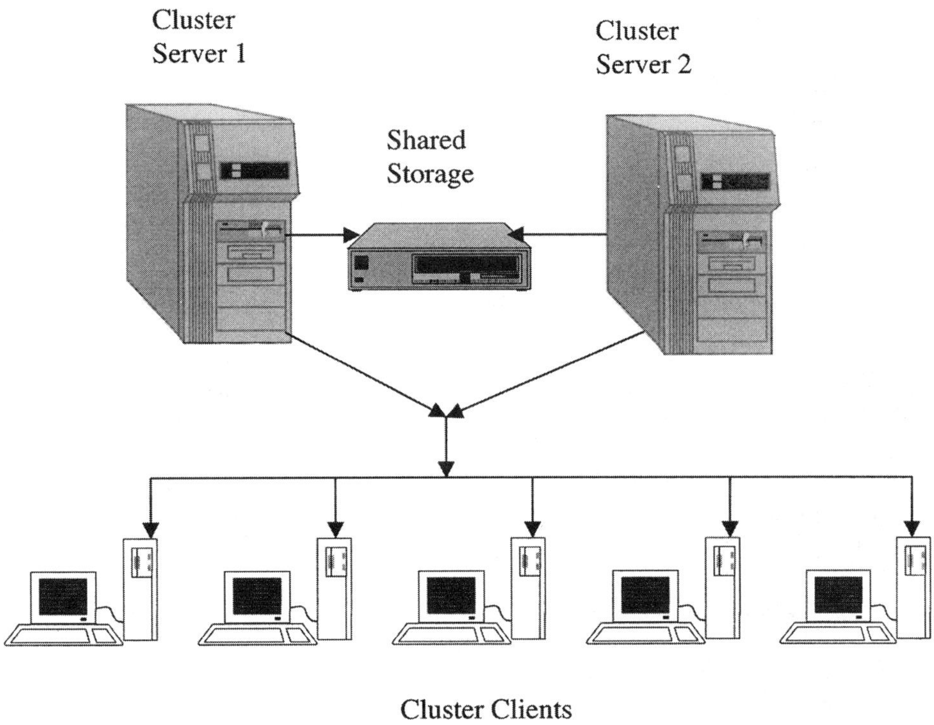

FIGURE 1 A cluster schematic.

Clustering is not a new technology and has been used by customers such as financial institutions and others for whom continuous availability of computer systems is essential. However, prior to Windows NT Cluster Server (formerly code named Wolfpack), customers who wanted the benefits of clustering for a particular business function had to buy a complete solution of clustering hardware and software from the clustering solution vendors. The customers then had to find ways to interface the business function using the clustering solution with other business functions that used general-purpose nonclustered solutions.

Clustering is a technology whose time has come for mass implementation. Windows NT Cluster Server is an attempt by Microsoft to make clustering available on the same general-purpose systems that run Windows NT today, including Intel-, Alpha-, and Reduced Instruction Set Computer (RISC) based systems. Besides the processors, disks, networking, and other cluster components are also standard off-the-shelf products. The price differential between a clustered Windows NT solution and a nonclustered solution is at such a price point that most business customers are likely to be able to justify the additional cost of clustered Windows NT solutions with the added benefit that customers do not have to worry about introducing vendor-unique hardware or software just for clustering.

At the rate of current technology evolution, chances are that the next major computer project you are likely to encounter will use a cluster. This is an introductory book that helps you understand the basics of clustering. We use the Microsoft Windows NT Cluster Server as the basic reference. We start with a review of clustering technologies, next look at benefits of clustered solutions, and then examine the architecture of Windows NT Cluster Server. In addition, we cover how clustering works, in particular, what happens at a *failover* (when one computer fails and another one takes over). Also we will look at programming considerations as well as setup and administration considerations, and conclude with a brief discussion of some recent cluster offerings from different vendors.

AVAILABILITY

One of the most important benefits of a cluster is its ability to provide high availability. Availability is when a system provides an acceptable level of service for a specific period of interest. When a system is not available, the condition is referred to as system outage, this outage is measured by downtime, or the time period for which the system is unavailable.

HIGH AVAILABILITY

A highly available system is one that provides an acceptable level of service for an extended period of time. Note that the duration of an extended period varies. For some companies, the extended period may be 16 h a day for 5 days a week, while for some other companies it may be 24 h a day for 5 days week. Highly available systems are designed and operated to have minimal planned or unplanned downtime. If a highly available system is down, it is expected to be brought back up relatively quickly.

CONTINUOUS AVAILABILITY

Continuous availability, as the name implies, is when the system is not expected to have any planned or unplanned downtime. Typically required in financial transaction and real-time processing applications, continuously available systems are designed to be serviced when the system is up.

AVAILABILITY MEASURES

Availability is commonly measured as a percentage. The percentage measure is computed as follows:

$$\%\text{Availability} = (\text{Total elapsed time} - \text{sum of downtimes})/\text{Total elapsed time}$$

The higher the percentage is the higher the availability of the system. Many computer systems have availability in the high 90s and some even have requirements in the 99.9xx range. Another measure that is related to availability is reliability. Reliability is commonly measured by computing the time between failures. The mean time between failures (MTBF) is computed as follows:

MTBF = (Total elapsed time – sum of downtimes)/Number of failures

FAULT TOLERANCE

Fault tolerance is a mechanism to achieve high and continuous availability through the use of redundant components in a system. The system is designed so that the redundant components take the place of components that fail so that the system is able to continue to provide service. However, no system is downtime proof. While the use of fault-tolerant designs and components increases availability, there is no way to ensure that a system will not undergo outage. As shown in Figure 2, there are multiple causes for system downtime and use of duplicate components addresses only some of the causes.

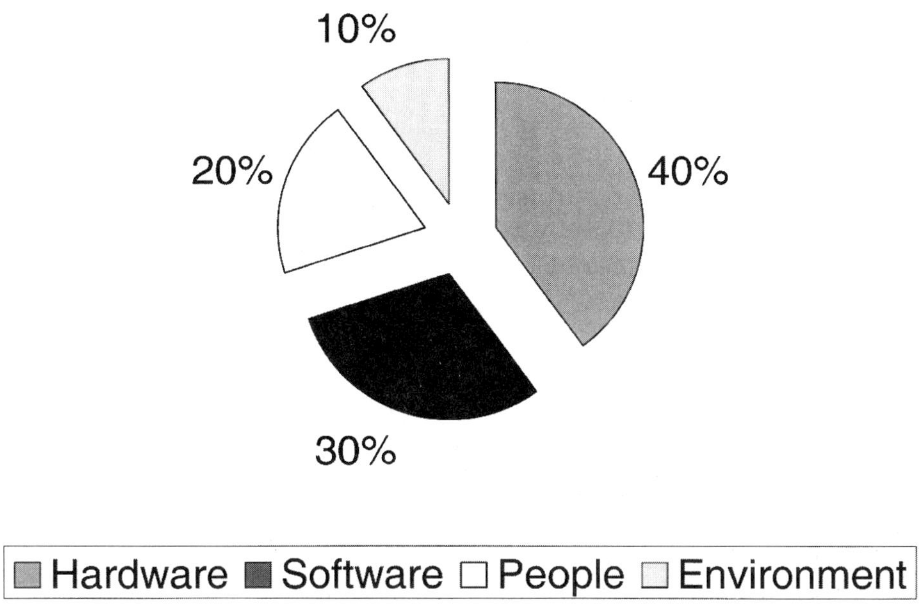

FIGURE 2 System downtime causes.

CLUSTER ORIGINS

Computer systems, like other human-built systems, can and do fail. The reliability of hardware components has increased a great deal and that of software components has also improved, but much less compared with hardware improvements. However, the number of components that make up a computer system has also increased and the components have also become increasingly complex. The net result is that computer systems are still prone to failure.

The traditional approach to increasing reliability is to build in redundancy and this approach is not new to computers. We have aircraft and ships with multiple engines. Redundancy can be applied to computer systems at two levels — within a single computer system and across computer systems. Within a single computer system, we have multiple central processing units (CPUs), an array of hard disks instead of a single hard drive, and so on. We also have one computer component backing up another component, for example, volatile memory backed by disk. Redundancy is also enhanced using fault-tolerant techniques. For example, the file system identifies bad sectors on disks and bypasses the bad sectors, thus permitting continued usage of the disk. Communication software have built-in checks to verify the data received (using check digits and so on) and errors are corrected by retransmissions of data.

Redundancy can also be setup across computer systems. We can have two systems, for example, one functioning as the main system and the other functioning as a backup of the main system. If the main system goes down, the backup system is activated and continues processing. The number of computer systems does not need to be restricted to two. We can have an arrangement where a number of computers function together and project an image of a single system. Such an arrangement is a cluster. Each computer system within a cluster has its own disk controller and memory; runs an independent copy of the operating system (OS) and applications; and also has its own power supply.

Note that redundancy within and redundancy across computer systems are not mutually exclusive. You can have multiple computers in a cluster, with individual computers having multiple processors.

REDUNDANCY WITHIN A COMPUTER SYSTEM

Redundancy within a computer system is achieved by having redundant components. For example, you can have two or more CPUs. You can also have multiple disk drives and multiple paths (buses) to connect the multiple CPUs and multiple disk drives. Let us look at each of these components in more detail.

PROCESSOR — MULTIPROCESSING

Until recently, most computing at the desktop and server level used machines that had only one CPU. *Multiprocessing*, where multiple processors exist on the same physical machine, has been used in the mainframes for some time. With the advent of cheaper processors and OSs that support multiple processors, multiprocessing is becoming more commonplace in servers and even on desktops.

When there is more than one processor within a computer system, there are different ways to split the computing work across the processors. The OS is the single most important piece of software to run in the computer system because it is required for other software to run and the computer system does not function without it. The way in which the OS and other software are allocated to use the different processors determines whether the computer system is using *symmetric multiprocessing* (SMP) or *asymmetric multiprocessing* (ASMP).

Asymmetric Multiprocessing

Asymmetric multiprocessing (ASMP) is when the two processors are not symmetric (or similar). The most common way in which the similarity between the processor fails is when the OS uses one or more processors for itself and schedules and runs the application programs in the remaining processor or processors. The significant consequence of this dissimilarity is when the processors running the OS fail and the other processors are up. In this case the system is not usable, even though one or more processors are up. Other ways in which the processors could be different are when one or more processors are dedicated to handle input/output (I/O) or when one or more processors have some extra hardware features, such as private memory, that the other processors do not have. While ASMP systems are a little easier to build because they are somewhat less complex than SMP systems, the benefits of SMP systems far outweigh the additional complexity. As a consequence, most multiprocessor systems tend to be SMP instead of non-SMP.

Symmetric Multiprocessing

SMP does not impose such restrictions on processors and lets all the processors be completely symmetric or identical. The difference between symmetric and asymmetric multiprocessing is illustrated in Figure 3. The smallest unit of execution of either the OS or an application is a thread. The OS has a number of threads running at any given time and so do all currently executing application programs.

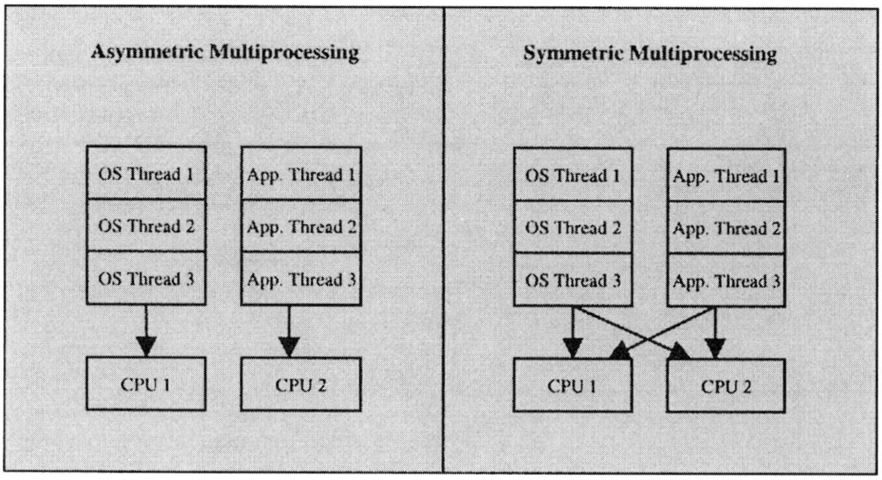

FIGURE 3 Symmetric and asymmetric multiprocessing.

The ability to run any program on any processor provides better load balancing (in ASMP, the processor that runs the OS may be idle while applications are waiting to use the other processors). Fault tolerance is also improved in SMP because the failure of a processor dedicated to the OS in ASMP means the machine is not operational, even though other processors may be operational. The price to pay for improved load balancing and fault tolerance is complexity. SMP OSs are more complex to build and maintain. Windows NT and many UNIX OS support SMP. SMP support is usually transparent to applications.

Microsoft Windows NT Server is designed to use up to 32 processors. Windows NT Server, Enterprise Edition is currently licensed by Microsoft for use on SMP servers with up to eight processors. Vendors selling original equipment manufacturer (OEM) versions of Windows NT Server, Enterprise Edition provide systems with up to 32 processors.

Disks

Redundant Array of Inexpensive Disks

Just as increasing the number of CPUs improves redundancy and availability, the hard disk storage on a machine can also include redundancy. Instead of one hard drive with one read/write mechanism, a disk unit can contain multiple hard disks and read/write heads. Such a unit can be set up so that the data written to a portion of a hard drive is automatically replicated elsewhere within the unit. If there is a problem accessing the data, then the duplicate copy of the data is accessed, thereby improving availability.

Buses

Buses are the data paths within the computer that carry data between components such as CPU, memory, etc.

Dual Bus Architectures

Just as we can have multiple CPUs, disks, etc. we can also have multiple buses. The most common form of multiple bus architecture is one involving the use of two buses. The same notion of redundancy and increased reliability also applies to dual bus architectures.

REDUNDANCY ACROSS COMPUTER SYSTEMS

While we can add processors, redundant disks, multiple buses, and an uninterruptible power source (UPS), there are limitations to what can be accomplished within the confines of one physical computer. For really scalable highly available solutions, the redundancy has to be designed and built in across physical computer boundaries. This concept is not new; there has been a lot of theoretical work and some working proprietary solutions have been available for a while. While there are other ways of connecting multiple computers together, we focus on clusters in this book.

Clusters

A cluster is a group of independent systems that work together and portray the image of a single system. A client interacts with a cluster just the same as if the client were interacting with one server.

Hot Standby and Active Backup

In a two-machine cluster, there is more than one way in which one machine can back up another. One way is to keep one of the machines idle but in a ready-to-start mode. The idle machine starts switches from ready-to-start mode to active mode when the other machine fails and takes over all the resources of the failed machine. This mode of operation is also called *hot standby*. Another way is not to keep one machine idle, but to have both machines up and running. When one machine fails, the other takes over some or all resources being managed by the failed machine. In the hot standby mode, the users should not see any performance degradation (except during transition time) if the two machines are configured in the same manner (i.e., they use the same processor or processors, same amount of memory, and so on). The obvious downside to hot standby is that one of the machines and its resources are idle. In the active backup mode, there could be performance degradation depending on the load on the system and the system configurations. The hot standby and active backup mode features are summarized in Table 1.

TABLE 1
Comparing Hot Standby and Active Backup Configurations

Feature	Hot Standby	Active Backup
Workload distribution	Static load balancing is not used	Static load balancing is used
Second server status	Inactive when the first or primary server is up	Active whether or not the first or primary server is up
Second server capacity	Typically is identical to the primary	Does not need to be identical to the primary
Resources failover	All resources of failed first or primary server are handled by the second server	Only those resources configured by the administrator failover to the second server

We discuss other ways for machines to back each other up later.

Tip: Although it may appear that one unit is wasted most of the time in hot standby mode while both units are being used productively in the active backup mode, keep in mind that each unit in the active backup mode is normally configured to have excess capacity (RAM, CPU, and so on) to run all attached resources.

Shared Disk, Mirrored Disks, and Shared Nothing Models

In a shared disk model, each server in a cluster can access every disk in the cluster. Some models permit common memory access in addition to common disk access.

In the mirrored disk model, each server has its own disks, and special software duplicates every write/update of the data on one server disk to a copy of the data on one or more other server disks.

In a shared nothing model, disks are not shared across servers in the cluster and each server exclusively owns its own disks as in the mirrored disk model. However, there is no mirroring and when a server fails, the cluster software automatically detects the failure and transfers ownership of a disk from one server to another. The three models are summarized in Table 2.

TABLE 2
Comparing Shared Disk, Mirrored Disk, and Shared Nothing Models

Model	Characteristics	Product Examples
Shared disk	Requires synchronization and serialization mechanisms, such as Distributed Lock Manager (DLM), to ensure regulated access to the disks when multiple servers are trying to access the disks; applications enhancements required to take advantage of shared disks	Digital VAX Cluster and Oracle Parallel Server
Mirrored disk	Possible load balancing using mirrored copy of data; mirrored copy of data could be disaster recovery solution, particularly if the mirror is not on the same site as the primary data; there are windows of time (times when mirrored data are written) during which the mirrored copy is not identical to the primary data	NSI, Octopus, Veritas, and Vinca
Shared nothing	Provides high availability, scalability, and manageability; no special application enhancements required	Tandem NonStop, Informix Online/XPS and Microsoft Cluster Server

Note: You also can have a combination of the models in a cluster. You can have some systems that share some resources and other systems that do not share any.

CLUSTERING SOLUTIONS AVAILABLE

There are a number of clustering solutions available from different vendors. Some of them are proprietary solutions that provide all the required hardware, software, and network connectivity. These are not addressed in this book. There are clustering solutions from vendors that are built using Windows NT and the Microsoft Cluster Server (MSCS). Chapter 9 contains a brief review of some of these solutions.

The rest of this book focuses on MSCS, the basis for Microsoft's clustering solution.

MSCS is a clustering mechanism implemented in software that enables applications to provide high availability on Microsoft Windows NT Server network OS platforms. Cluster Server handles directing client requests to the system within the cluster that is capable of handling the service request. If that system is unavailable, the request is redirected to a system that can handle the request. This redirection can be transparent to the client.

MSCS is implemented as an add-on product that operates on top of the Windows NT Server OS and is packaged with Windows NT Server, Enterprise Edition. MSCS does not work on other editions of Windows NT such as the Windows NT Workstation. MSCS supports all clients that can connect to Windows NT Server using Transmission Control Protocol/Internet Protocol (TCP/IP) such as MS-DOS, Windows 3.x, Windows 95, Windows NT, Apple Macintosh, and UNIX. MSCS does not require any special software on the client for its functions.

Tip: While the clustering functions provided by MSCS work only with Windows NT Server, Enterprise Edition, it is possible to install and administer the cluster administrator component on any computer running Service Pack 3 with version 4.0 of either Windows NT Workstation or Windows NT Server. Thus it is possible to administer an MSCS cluster from a cluster server, from a nonclustered Windows NT Server, or from a computer running Windows NT Workstation.

The initial release of MSCS supports clusters with two servers/nodes. A follow-on version is planned to support clusters with more than two servers/nodes and to include enhanced services to simplify the creation of highly scalable, cluster-aware applications.

MSCS provides the following major functions:

- Automatic detection of failures in cluster components such as servers and applications
- Automatic recovery from such failures
- A graphic administration mechanism to manage all the servers in a cluster as a single environment
- A standard set of clustering services on many different hardware platforms when running on top of Windows NT (just as Windows NT runs on different hardware platforms)
- A standard, cross-platform application programming interface (API) for developing and supporting cluster-aware applications

2 Benefits of Clusters

In the previous chapter, we looked at the cluster basics. Clustering technology provides a number of benefits. This chapter covers the benefits of Clustering. The book covers the Windows NT Cluster Server and all the following benefits apply to Windows NT Cluster Server. Keep in mind, however, that most of the benefits also are applicable to other clustering solutions):

Clustering provides a great many benefits such as:

- Improved scalability
- Improved availability
- Improved manageability
- Configuration flexibility
- Improved integrity
- Improved performance
- No special training required for administrators or end users
- Layered applications

The term *improved* in the preceding list refers to the improvement compared with a nonclustered environment.

We look at each of these benefits in detail. Before doing that, however, it should be noted that while most of these benefits are available in many clustering solutions, there are some additional benefits with the Windows NT Cluster Server. Windows NT Cluster Server combines the ease of configuring and maintaining the Windows NT operating system together with the economy of using industry-standard hardware and a standard application programming interface (API) that permits the development of cluster-enabled applications across many different environments that can run Windows. The standard API makes it cost-effective for third-party application developers to develop cluster-enabled applications, compared with developing cluster-enabled applications for proprietary cluster solutions. Table 1 compares Windows NT clustering and other clustering solutions.

The significance of clustering, however, goes well beyond the benefits listed in Table 1. The real significance is that clustering opens many new avenues for Windows NT. Windows NT is already well known for the ease of use, primarily by virtue of the user-friendly Windows interface. Businesses need more than a user-friendly interface. The deployment of Windows NT in major businesses required data center type capabilities and performance that businesses had come to rely on. Clustering technology brings data center type capabilities and performance to Windows NT Server. Thus clustering makes it possible for Windows NT to be used in a wider range of customer installations.

SCALABILITY

Another benefit of clustering is the ability to add systems on demand in an incremental manner. Because the cluster is made up of a number of systems and you can add (or remove) systems, the cluster can be scaled to meet requirements.

TABLE 1
Comparing Windows NT and Other Clustering Solutions

Windows NT-Based Clustering Solutions	Other Currently Available Clustering Solutions
Improved scalability, availability, integrity, and performance	Improved scalability, availability, integrity, and performance
Industry standard hardware — Windows NT clustering can be implemented using PCs that use Intel and other vendors' chips as well as on other machines such as Alpha and RISC that can run Windows NT	Typically, these clustering solutions require that proprietary hardware such as computers and networking mechanisms be used
Besides the ease of use of the Windows user interface, cluster administration functions such as cluster configuration are an extension to the regular Windows NT system administration functions and make it easy for the Windows NT System Administrator to learn cluster administration	These clustering solutions provided their own system administration functions, which commonly required that the administrator be specially trained in the administration of the proprietary hardware, software, and networking functions
Windows NT-based clustering is typically less expensive due to the availability of industry standard PCs available in high-volume	These clustering solutions tend to be more expensive as the proprietary hardware tend to be more expensive due to the low volume of such computers compared to industry-standard personal computers (PCs).
Due to the popularity of Windows-based applications, it is easier to integrate a clustering environment based on Windows NT with the remainder of the computing environment in an enterprise	It is more difficult to integrate a proprietary clustering environment with the remainder of the computing environment in an enterprise
It is easier to develop cluster applications as the cluster APIs are an extension to the Win32 APIs many programmers already use to develop applications	Developing cluster applications requires special training for programmers

The need for scalability typically arises when an existing computer system starts to be overutilized. Clustering permits the combining of the existing overutilized computer with a new computer to balance the workload. Once the cluster is created, resources on the overutilized computer are split across both nodes of a two-node cluster. The same concept of load sharing can be similarly extended to clusters with more than two nodes.

Once a cluster is created and operational, the cluster as a whole may start to be overutilized as well. This is when the real benefits of clusters become evident. It is a lot easier to upgrade or replace existing components such as memory or hard drives or even complete computers in a cluster compared with a stand-alone environment. Not only can the upgrade or replacement be performed with virtually no downtime; the penalty for not being able to perform the upgrade or replacement is not as bad as in a stand-alone environment.

In addition, applications can use the cluster APIs to access Microsoft Cluster Server (MSCS) services for dynamic load balancing and scaling across multiple servers within a cluster. Administrators can perform manual load balancing by moving workload between different servers within the cluster

CONFIGURATION FLEXIBILITY

The configuration flexibility that clusters provide is best understood by comparing it with nonclustered solutions.

In a nonclustered environment, an increase in workload is often handled by increasing the capacity of the server. In many instances this means replacing the current server with a bigger and better server that can handle the increased workload. Once the server upgrade is complete, some use would have to be found for the replaced server or it must be disposed. In a clustered environment, the current server does not need to be replaced. An additional server can be added to share the increased workload. The capacity of the additional server can be tailored to meet the workload needs and does not need to be related to the capacity of the existing server.

Clusters with both servers operational and active also offer configuration flexibility over hot standby configurations. When a hot standby configuration needs to be upgraded to meet increased workload, often the backup server has to be upgraded in an identical manner to that of the primary server, because a performance degradation would occur otherwise. If the primary and the backup servers are replaced, then some use would have to be found for both the replaced servers or they must be disposed. In a two-node cluster environment with both servers operational, upgrading of one server does not necessarily imply that the other server must be upgraded in an identical manner. The only requirement is that the second server have sufficient capacity to handle the cluster components that are failed over, when the first server fails, with adequate performance.

In addition to upgrades due to a permanent increase in workload, there are many instances in organizations where there is a temporary increase in workload. This may happen due to normal business cycles. This may also be due to the need to train a group of employees. In these instances, it is a lot easier to add additional capacity to a cluster to meet the temporary increase in workload.

Besides the configuration flexibility provided by clusters to increase the base capacity to meet workload, clusters also provide the ability to balance workload across servers within the cluster. The administrator can manually move resources from one server within the cluster to another, while the cluster is operational, to meet variations in workload. This load balancing ability is not available in nonclustered systems and hot standby systems.

INTEGRITY

Compared with nonclustered systems, clustered systems have improved error detection, error isolation, and error recovery mechanisms built in. Clustered systems exchange "heartbeat" messages and a system failure is automatically detected. The failed system is automatically isolated and the workload handled by the failed system is distributed to other systems in the cluster. The return to the original state prior to failure is also automatic once the failed system is fixed. Improved error detection, error isolation, and error recovery mechanisms occur for the most part without human intervention, which lets clustered systems have improved availability.

AVAILABILITY

Even if a business does not anticipate growing and benefiting from scalability, it still benefits by using clusters due to the increased availability of clusters (compared with nonclustered systems). Improved availability means reduced downtime. System downtime is estimated to cost U.S. businesses $4.0 billion per year with the average downtime event resulting in a $140,000 loss in the retail industry and a $450,000 loss in the securities industry.*

Clustering is designed to provide high resource availability to clients by ensuring that if a node fails, the cluster server automatically detects the failure and switches cluster resources to another node. Although some users may notice a momentary pause during switching (the pause is typically less than a second in most cases), resources continue to be available to clients.

Even if an entire node does not fail, but one or more applications on a node fail, the applications are automatically restarted. If the applications are unable to be restarted, then the applications are started on another node in the cluster and processing continues.

Clustered systems have, by design, a better uptime than nonclustered systems have. Let us take a simple example. Let us say that the uptime when you use one computer system is 90%. If you

* From FIND/SVP Strategic Research Division Report, 1992.

configure two of these in parallel (one takes over from another when one fails and the transition is so fast that we ignore transition time here), then what is the uptime of the overall system?

The uptime of the overall system is 99%, which is significantly better than 90%.

The overall uptime is figured in the following manner. The overall system is up at least 90% of the time (one of the two systems is up). In the 10% chance that one system is down, the other system is up 90%. Thus we need to add 9% (10% of 90%) to the overall uptime. Looking at it another way, the only time the whole system really fails is the 10% window of the second computer within the 10% window of the first one having failed already. Thus the overall uptime goes to 99%, without any increase in the basic uptime of one computer system. This illustrated in Figure 1.

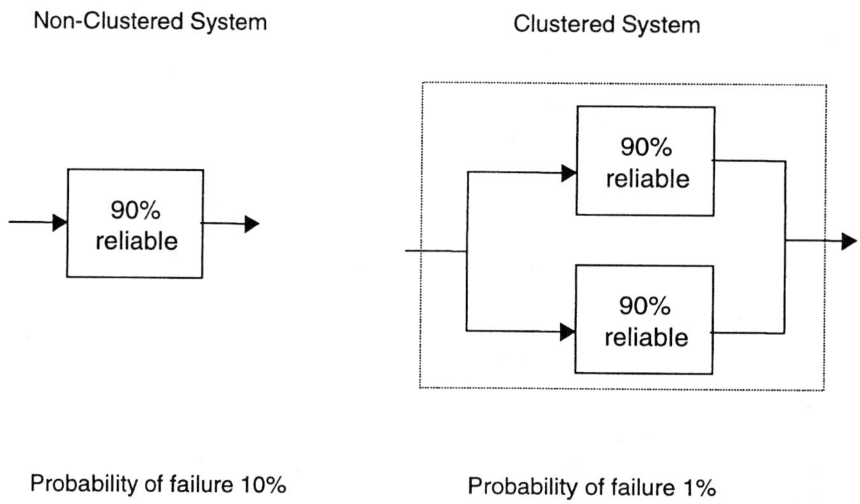

FIGURE 1 Comparing reliability of clustered and nonclustered systems.

The preceding example involved two systems. In clustered systems with more than two systems, the overall availability is even higher.

So far we have discussed how clustering improves availability when a cluster node or a cluster component within a node becomes unavailable for unplanned reasons. Clustering also helps improve availability even for planned downtimes such as when an administrator wants to perform hardware and/or software maintenance. Cluster availability during hardware and software maintenance is covered further in the section on manageability (later in this chapter).

Availability Scenarios, Measures, and Tools

The simplest scenario is one of a stand-alone system that goes down. The system is restarted and backups are reloaded if required and the system becomes operational again. In this scenario, one measure of availability is mean time between failures (MTBF). MTBF is defined as the ratio of the number of units of operating time to the number of times the computer is down (planned and unplanned). For example, if a computer system is used 365 days in the year, 7 days in the week, and 24 h a day and if it is down 10 times during the year, the MTBF is 6132 (24 × 7 × 365/10). Availability often is measured as the ratio of the time the computer was up to the total elapsed time. In the preceding example, if the computer was down for a total of 5 h in the 10 times it was down, the availability is more than 99.9% ((61320-5)/61320).

Note that due to wide variations in configurations and processes across companies there is no single industry standard for application availability. Also note that applications failure is only one cause for overall system downtime. Other causes for system downtime include user/operator errors and hardware/equipment errors. Clustering, by itself, can improve only application availability.

MANAGEABILITY

Managing Cluster Server is a welcome relief to both administrators and end users. When an administrator manages one or more nonclustered servers, routine administrative tasks that have to be performed would make a server unavailable to users. These tasks include

- Restarting a server due to a failure
- Backup server data
- Upgrading hardware such as adding disk or memory capacity
- Installing upgrades to software such as operating system patches
- Installing new software that requires a system restart to complete installation

With Cluster Server, the second node continues to make the server resources available to users. The availability of the second node enables the administrator to perform the tasks listed earlier without warning and stopping users from accessing the server. The administrators do not have to wait for nonpeak hours or weekends to perform the preceding tasks.

As mentioned earlier, the cluster projects a single system image to entities interacting with the cluster. For example, Cluster Server provides the means for an administrator to manage both nodes of the cluster as though the administrator is managing a single node. In addition, the administrator can administer the servers in the cluster from a single desktop, even though the cluster nodes are physically separate. For example, the administrator can move applications from one server to another for load balancing using simple Windows Graphic Users Interface (GUI) mechanisms such as point-and-click.

Besides administrators, network client systems and users using the network clients connect to the cluster resources the same way they connect to the same resources when they are not in a cluster. This means that no additional training or education is required for end users and administrators to use the Cluster Server. This feature significantly improves manageability.

PERFORMANCE

One major problem since the mass adoption of personal computers (PCs) has been that they are rarely fully utilized and there has been no simple way to pool the resources of underutilized ones. Clustering provides a way for pooling the PC resources, at least at the server level. This improves performance as a whole. Thus a two-server Windows NT cluster in most cases provides better performance than the performance obtained using the two servers independently, in spite of the overhead involved in clustering. Performance is measured by whatever is appropriate for how the servers are being used. For database/transaction servers, the performance may be measured in throughput; for application/file servers, the performance may be measured in response time.

LAYERED APPLICATIONS

Microsoft application development tools are being enhanced to develop cluster-aware applications. While more and more applications are likely to become cluster aware, it is not necessary for all applications that run on the server to be cluster aware to realize the benefits of clustering. Applications that are built on top of cluster-aware subsystems (such as a database application on top of

Microsoft Structured Query Language [SQL] Server) automatically benefit from the cluster enhancements to the underlying subsystem. Many applications including those commonly used in Web publishing and file/print services benefit from clustering without application changes.

COMMON USES OF MICROSOFT CLUSTER SERVER

According to a survey by Microsoft, the use of MSCS mirrors that of Windows NT, and MSCS is commonly used for the following types of applications:

- Mission critical database management
- File/intranet data sharing
- Messaging
- General business applications

Note: MSCS clustering solutions using Small Computer System Interface (SCSI) for shared storage connections may not be good candidates for off-site disaster recovery due to distance limitations of standard SCSI (which is usually 25 m without extenders and 1000 m with extenders). However, there are third-party remote disaster recovery solutions including those from N.S.I., Octopus, Veritas, and Vinca, and these solutions support MSCS clusters.

3 Microsoft Cluster Server Basics

INTRODUCTION

We saw a brief history of clustering and its role among different attempts to increase overall computer throughput and availability in Chapter 1. After having established clustering as a viable technology, the benefits of clustering are discussed in Chapter 2. In this chapter, we look at the product that is the focus of this book, the Microsoft Cluster Server (MSCS). As mentioned earlier, the code name Wolfpack was used by Microsoft for MSCS when it was still under development.

MSCS is implemented as an add-on that operates on top of the Windows NT Server operating system. MSCS is packaged with Windows NT, Enterprise Edition. MSCS does not work on other editions of Windows NT such as Windows NT Workstation. MSCS supports all clients that can connect to a Windows NT server using Transmission Control Protocol/Internet Protocol (TCP/IP) such as Windows NT, Windows 95, Windows 3.x, MS-DOS, Apple Macintosh, and UNIX. MSCS does not require any special software or setup on the client for its functions.

Tip: While the clustering functions provided by MSCS work only with Windows NT Server, Enterprise Edition, it is possible to install and administer the Cluster Administrator component of MSCS on any computer running Service Pack 3 with version 4.0 of either Windows NT Workstation or Windows NT Server. The Cluster administrator component provides cluster administration functions. Thus it is possible to administer an MSCS cluster from a cluster server, from a nonclustered Windows NT Server, or from a computer running Windows NT Workstation.

The initial release of MSCS supports clusters with two servers/nodes. The functions provided by MSCS include

- Automatic detection of failures in cluster components such as applications and servers
- Automatic recovery from such failures
- A graphic administration component to administer the entire cluster as a single entity
- Clustering functions that are available on a number of hardware platforms (not unique to MSCS; a logical extension from the fact that the Windows NT operating system is capable of running on multiple hardware platforms)
- A standard application programming interface (API) for developing cluster-aware and/or cluster management applications that is part of the Cluster Server Software Development Kit (SDK)

Future versions are expected to support clusters with more than two servers/nodes and to include enhanced services to simplify the creation of highly scalable, cluster-aware applications. Some of the major functions planned for the future releases include

- Clusters that support more than two servers/nodes
- Faster cluster interconnects

- Distributed storage
- True distributed applications
- Load balancing, and so on

CLUSTER SERVER CONCEPTS AND TERMINOLOGY

Let us begin with a review of definitions of some common clustering terms. A complete list of clustering terms is included in the Glossary.

Cluster

We started with a generic description of a cluster in Chapter 1 as "a set of multiple, independent computer systems that project a single system image for access and management to most entities, such as human users and client applications, that are outside the cluster." Microsoft provides a more product-specific definition of a cluster. As defined by Microsoft Cluster Server, "a cluster is a loosely coupled collection of two or more independent Microsoft Windows NT Server systems." Network clients and administrators view this collection as a single system. A cluster is made up of a number of components.

The following table briefly describes the cluster-related components.

TABLE 1
Cluster-Related Components and Descriptions

Cluster-Related Component	Description
Cluster administrator	Graphic Windows application used by administrators to control Cluster Server
Cluster database	Part of the Windows NT registry that contains information about the cluster such as nodes and resources
Cluster network driver	Provides communications between cluster nodes
Cluster node	A computer system that is a member of a cluster
Cluster resource	A unit or entity that is hosted by a cluster node; a resource being the basic unit managed by the Cluster Service; a resource started, stopped, or moved to another node
Cluster Service	Windows NT service for managing cluster operations; the service made up of a number of "managers" (see section on Cluster Service later in this chapter)
Group	A collection of resources that run together on a node and are failed over as a single unit
Network	A network across which a cluster node communicates with other cluster nodes
Network interface	A network adapter that is installed in a cluster node used for communications
Quorum resource	A special resource in a cluster that maintains cluster membership and resolves communication problems between nodes
Resource DLL	Can be more than one resource dynamic link library (DLL) in a cluster
Resource Monitors	Interface between Cluster Service and cluster resources; each resource handled by a resource monitor; can be more than one Resource Monitor in a cluster
Resource type	A category of resources, such as physical disks

We cover each of the cluster components in greater detail.

Cluster Node

Each computer that is a member of a cluster is called a cluster node. The terms node, server, and system are often used interchangeably to refer to a cluster member. You can also consider a cluster node as a Microsoft Windows NT Server system that is running the MSCS. The nodes of a cluster communicate between themselves using a network link. Cluster nodes and the communication links between them make up the cluster. Using redundant network paths for communication across nodes enhances cluster availability.

A cluster is similar to a general distributed system, which has multiple nodes. A cluster provides additional functions:

- Every node has full connectivity and communication with the other nodes in the cluster. Communication between nodes can be through either a shared storage device or using networks. Communications are effected through the following:
  - One or more Small Computer System Interface (SCSI) buses are shared between cluster nodes. Each shared SCSI bus attaches one or more physical disks. Multiple nodes in the cluster can access the same storage. Writing important status and tracking information to shared storage helps another node read that information and take over from another node, if the other node fails.
  - A private network, or interconnect, carries only internal cluster communication such as the communication between cluster nodes.
  - One or more public networks serve as backup for a private network and can be used both for internal cluster communication and for host client applications. Network adapters, known to the cluster as network interfaces, attach nodes to networks.
- Every node in the cluster is aware when another node joins or leaves the cluster.
- Every node in the cluster is aware of the resources that are available locally at that node as well as the resources that are available on the other nodes in the cluster.

A node can be an active or inactive member of a cluster. An active cluster member is a full-fledged cluster member that is currently online and in communication with the other cluster nodes and performing all cluster functions. An inactive member is not a full-fledged member and does not perform all the cluster functions.

A cluster has its own unique identity in addition to and distinct from the identities of its nodes. This is the identity that is used by network clients to access the applications and services running on the cluster, instead of the identities of the individual nodes. This cluster identity is also the one used by administrators to manage the cluster. Maintaining a unique identity allows the Cluster Server to perform cluster functions that are transparent to the clients such as:

- Moving applications
- Moving related resources between nodes
- Replacing a failed node
- Adding a new node

Network clients continue to communicate using the same cluster identity (IP address of virtual server; see later section on the Virtual Server). The network clients are normally not aware that the actual node they have been communicating with has been switched.

Cluster nodes and the communication links between them make up the cluster. The nodes of a cluster communicate between themselves using a network link. To enhance availability, the nodes communicate across redundant network paths.

When the cluster service starts, a choice is made as to whether the system should form its own cluster or join an existing cluster. During startup, the cluster service, by default, always attempts to join an existing cluster. To join an existing cluster, Cluster Server validates the node's name, password, and cluster database. If the name and password are valid and the data in this cluster database are consistent with the data in other cluster databases residing on the other nodes in the cluster, the node joins and becomes an active cluster member.

A node may not be able to join a cluster. The most common reason for this to happen is that the node cannot locate another active node. In this instance, the node attempts to form its own cluster. To form its own cluster, the node needs to synchronize its cluster database with the recovery log information. The recovery logs are used by the Cluster Service to keep the cluster databases residing on each cluster node consistent. The recovery log information is stored in the cluster quorum resource. The node attempts to access the quorum resource and if access is granted, the node verifies whether or not its cluster database has information that is consistent with the recovery logs. After the cluster database and recovery logs are synchronized, the node is able to form a new cluster.

Cluster Resources

A resource is a physical or logical entity that is owned by a cluster node. Applications such as database applications and Web servers, printers, and disk file shares are examples of resources. Resources provide a service to clients. A resource is the basic unit managed by the node Cluster Service. Cluster nodes host cluster resources. A resource can only be hosted on a single cluster node at any given time. Resources can be brought online and taken offline. Cluster Server can manage as a resource any entity that can be taken offline, brought online, and moved to another node if a failure occurs. A cluster resource has the following characteristics:

- It can be brought online and taken offline.
- It can be managed in a cluster.
- It can be hosted by only one node at a time.
- It can be moved between nodes.

A cluster resource can exist in a number of states. Before we look at the different states in which a cluster resource can exist, it is important to note that the different components that make up the Cluster Server have a number of states and/or substates each, as shown in the Table 2.

TABLE 2
Cluster Component States and Substates

Cluster Component	States and/or Substates
Cluster Service	Offline, online, paused
Cluster resource	Offline, online, starting, failed, onlinepending, offlinepending
Event processor substates	Initializing, exiting
Membership manager substates	Member search, Quorum disk search, dormant, forming, joining (see Table 8 later in this chapter)

We look at cluster resource states next, and at the states and substates of other components later in this chapter.

Cluster Resource States

A cluster resource can exist in one of four “stable” states or in one of two “pending” states. A stable state is one in which the resource can exist for an indefinite amount of time. A pending state is one in which the resource is in for a very short time and is normally in transition between stable states.

The four stable states are

- Offline — The initial state for any resource is the offline state.
- Starting — Once a resource is ready to participate in the cluster, the Resource Monitor (see section on Resource Monitor later in this chapter) attempts to bring the resource online.
- Online — If the resource succeeds in coming online, it is in the online state.
- Failed — If a resource fails, the resource immediately transitions to the failed state.

The two pending states are

- Onlinepending – The resource is in the process of coming online.
- Offlinepending – The resource is in the process of going offline.

The typical resource state transition is as follows:

All resources start in the offline state during which they are unavailable for use by a client or another resource. Then resources go into onlinepending and starting states when they are in the process of being brought online. When a resource is online, its state is online and it is available for use. When a resource is about to be taken offline, its state is offlinepending. Finally, the resource goes offline and its state is offline.

If the resource cannot be brought online or taken offline after a specified amount of time, the resource is set to the failed state. The administrator can specify the amount of time that MSCS waits before failing the resource by setting its *pending time-out* value to synchronize its cluster database with the recovery log information.

Resource state changes can occur either manually by an administrator using the Cluster Administrator to make a state transition or automatically during the failover process by MSCS.

Cluster Dependencies

Dependency is the relationship between two resources. Examples of dependencies are an application resource that is dependent on a disk resource for its data or a file share resource that is dependent on a disk resource for a shared folder. The relationship between the resources dictates that the resources belong to the same group run in the same node. The relationship also dictates the order in which the resources are taken offline and brought back online.

The following rules apply to dependencies between resources:

- The dependency relationship can be transitive. A resource (R1) can be dependent on another resource (R2), which in turn can be dependent on yet another resource (R3). In this case, R1 is dependent on both R2 and R3. This can extend to more than two levels.
- There is no (practical) limit on the number of resources on which a resource may depend.
- A resource should be taken offline before any resource on which it depends is taken offline.
- A resource and its dependents must failover together.
- A resource can be brought online only after all the resources on which it depends have been brought online.
- Two resources have a *direct* dependency between them when there are no intermediary resources between the two. When the relationship is transitive through an intermediary resource, the relationship is said to be *indirect*. In the preceding example, R1 is directly dependent on R2 and indirectly dependent on R3.

Dependency Trees

As mentioned earlier, a resource can be dependent on another resource, which in turn can be dependent on yet another resource. Because there can be many levels of this relationship dependency, there is a need for a mechanism to visualize the different levels. Such a mechanism is the dependency tree.

A dependency tree pictorially represents the dependency relationships between resources (including ones at multiple levels). The administrator can use a dependency tree to determine how resources interact. For example, if a resource needs to be taken offline for an administrative task, the dependency tree shows the other affected resources across multiple levels.

A multilevel dependency tree with direct and indirect relationships is shown in Figure 1.

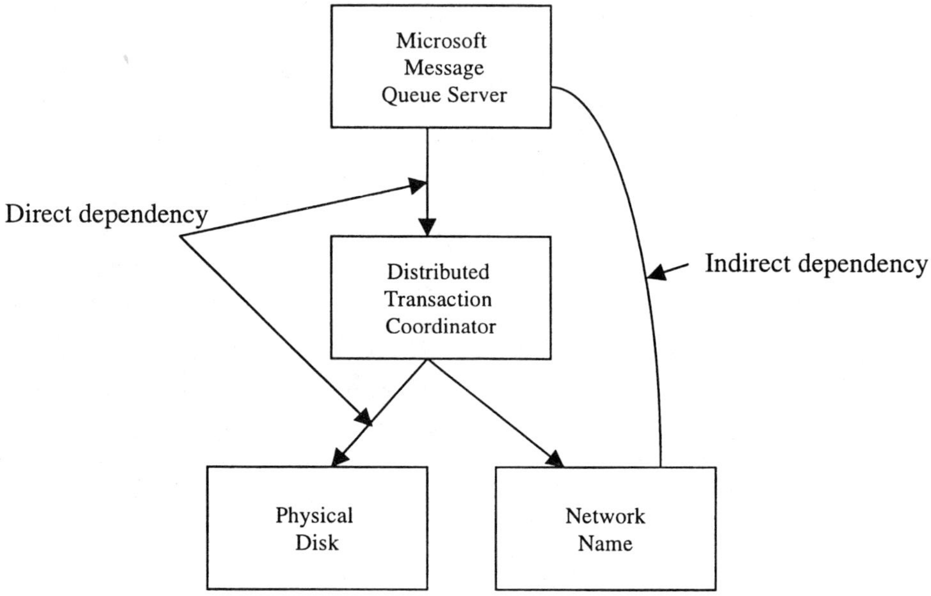

FIGURE 1 Dependency tree.

Figure 1 shows Microsoft Message Queue Server as a resource directly dependent on Distributed Transaction Coordinator (DTC), which in turn is directly dependent on physical disk and network name. Microsoft Message Queue Server is indirectly dependent on physical disk and network name.

Table 3 identifies each resource type that Microsoft Cluster Server supports and the required dependencies for each resource type.

Resource Types

Cluster resources are organized by type. Resource types are associated with a set of control codes. The control codes describe operations that all resource types can perform, such as returning or updating property values. To invoke a particular operation, applications call the Cluster Application Programming Interface (API) function ClusterResourceTypeControl and pass the control code that represents the specific operation. Cluster API functions are covered in greater detail in Chapter 7.

Resource types also are associated with a set of properties, or attributes. There are common properties (or attributes) that apply to all resource types, and private properties (or attributes) that apply only to resources of a particular type. Only some resource types define private properties.

TABLE 3
Resource Types and Dependencies

Resource Type	Description	Required Dependencies
Distributed Transaction Coordinator (DTC)	Microsoft DTC for cluster installation	Physical disk and network name
File share	File shares that are network accessible	Physical disk on which the shared folder is located
Generic application	Any application such as a network or client desktop application	None
Generic service	A Windows NT service	None
IIS virtual root	Internet information server virtual roots for FTP, WWW, and Gopher	TCP/IP address
IP address	IP network address	None
Network name	Network name for a computer or service on the network	TCP/IP address
Microsoft Message Queue Resource	Microsoft Message Queue Server product setup for cluster install	Physical disk, network name, Structured Query Language Server, and DTC resources
Physical disk	Disk that provides required storage, such as shared folders	None
Print spooler	Printer queues	Physical disk and network name
Time service	Service that helps consistency of time across cluster nodes	None

Cluster Server defines several types of resources and provides resource dynamic link libraries (DLLs) to manage those types. Third-party developers are encouraged to create new types to fit the specific needs of their cluster-aware applications and services. By creating a new resource type, a developer can have more control over how Cluster Server manages his or her application or service.

Cluster Server defines the following types of resources:

- Distributed Transaction Coordinator (DTC)
- Generic application
- Generic service
- Physical disk
- Print spooler
- File share
- IP address
- Internet Information Server (IIS) virtual root
- Message queue
- Network name
- Time service

The DTC resource type supports the Distributed Transaction Coordinator. DTC is the Microsoft Transaction Manager. Every DTC resource has a required dependency on both a network name resource and a storage class device. There can only be one DTC resource on each node of the cluster.

The generic application resource type is used for two purposes:

- To provide basic management of cluster-unaware applications
- To manage cluster-aware applications not associated with custom resource types

Generic application resources provide very little function and have very little failure detection or recovery. These resources are normally taken offline by terminating the associated process. You can use the absence of the processes as an indication of the failure or nonavailability of the resources in resource DLLs.

The generic service resource type manages Microsoft Windows NT services as cluster resources. The generic service resource type is very similar to the generic application resource type and both provide only the most basic functionality and virtually no failure detection or recovery. You can detect if a generic service resource is available by querying the Windows NT Service Controller. If the service is running, it is presumed to be online. If you need additional functionality other than that the basic functionality provided, you can define a custom resource type and provide the code for the additional functionality required.

The physical disk resource type describes a shared disk connected to two or more nodes in a cluster. In a typical cluster, the physical disk is included as a dependency for resources of various other types. Physical disk resources are the only type of resource defined by Cluster Server that can operate as a cluster quorum resource.

The print spooler resource type describes a network printer that applications access using a network IP address instead of an individual name. Every group can have only a single print spooler resource.

The file share resource type is used to manage a file share that applications can access using a network path.

The IP address resource type is used to manage IP network addresses. To access a group as a virtual server by network clients, include an IP address resource for the group along with a Network Name resource. Administrators configure an IP address resource by providing values for the address, subnet mask, and network name. See Chapter 9 for more details about configuring IP address resources.

The IIS virtual root resource type manages IIS virtual roots that support the WWW, FTP, and Gopher services. See IIS virtual root resource later in the chapter.

The message queue resource supports the Microsoft Message Queue Server. This resource depends on a network name resource and a DTC resource. Only one message queue resource can be running on a node at any point in time.

The network name resource type is used for naming and ease of access. This resource provides an alternate computer name for a cluster object that exists on the network. The network name resource in combination with an IP address resource provides a unique identity to a group, allowing the group to be accessed by network clients as a virtual server (see virtual server in this chapter).

The time service resource type is a special resource type in a cluster that functions as a "master clock" to ensure that time remains synchronized across all nodes in a cluster. The time service is unlike other resource types. Only one node runs the time service in a cluster at a time. That node is selected automatically to host the time service resource and to provide the correct time to the other nodes in the cluster. The information about the selected node is maintained in the cluster database. If the selected node fails or is to be brought down, an alternate node must be used to ensure that the time service is maintained. In this case, the time service is stopped and restarted to ensure that time is kept consistent across all nodes of the cluster.

Resource Properties

Properties are attributes that describe a cluster object. Most cluster objects including resources have properties. Properties are of two types:

- Common properties
- Private properties

A common property is an attribute that exists for every instance of the type of cluster object for which it is defined. For example, the common resource property RestartAction exists for every resource in the cluster. Another example is the local restart policy for a resource, which defines the desired actions in the event that the resource cannot continue on the current node. Common properties are stored in the cluster database.

A private cluster property is an attribute that exists only for specific instances of the type of object for which it is defined. For example, the signature of a physical disk resource is a private property. Thus a given cluster object may or may not have a private property. Table 4 provides a summary of private properties. Private properties can be stored in the cluster database or an alternate location. They can also be generated dynamically. We look at resource properties in more detail in Chapter 7.

Table 4 summarizes the private properties for the resource types we looked at earlier.

TABLE 4
Resource Types and Properties

Resource Type	Private Properties
Distributed Transaction Coordinator (DTC)	No private properties
File share	Many private properties of which some are mandatory and others are optional; mandatory properties include the share name and the resource path
Generic application	Many private properties including a command line for running the application and a reference directory
Generic service	Three private properties including the name of the service and startup parameters
IIS virtual root	Many private properties including the physical location of the resource, the security information, an alias for client access, and the name of the related Web service
IP address	Private properties include the address, subnet mask, and network name
Network name	The only private property for this resource is the name of the resource; the name when used in a group provides an identity for a group
Microsoft Message Queue Resource	No private properties
Physical disk	There are two private properties — drive designator and disk signature of which only one (can be either one) is mandatory
Print spooler	There are two private properties — a default spool directory and a time-out value
Time service	No private properties

GROUP

A group is a collection of resources to be configured and managed as a single unit. A cluster operation performed on a group is performed on all resources within the group. For example, when one resource in a group fails, and it is necessary to move the resource to an alternate node, all the other resources in the group are moved to the alternate node as well. A resource is owned by a single group and a group is owned by a single node at any point in time.

While the first release of MSCS restricts a cluster to two nodes, there can be any number of groups in a node and any number of resources within a group. The relationship of cluster, node, group, and resources is shown in Figure 2.

Figure 2 shows a cluster with two nodes. Node 1 has two groups, group 1 and group 2. Group 1 has one resource, resource 1, while group 2 has two resources, resource 1 and resource 2. Similarly, node 2 has two groups, one group with one resource and the other group with three resources.

It is important to use resource dependencies in forming groups. Resources dependent on each other must be part of the same group. For example, a group that contains the file share must also

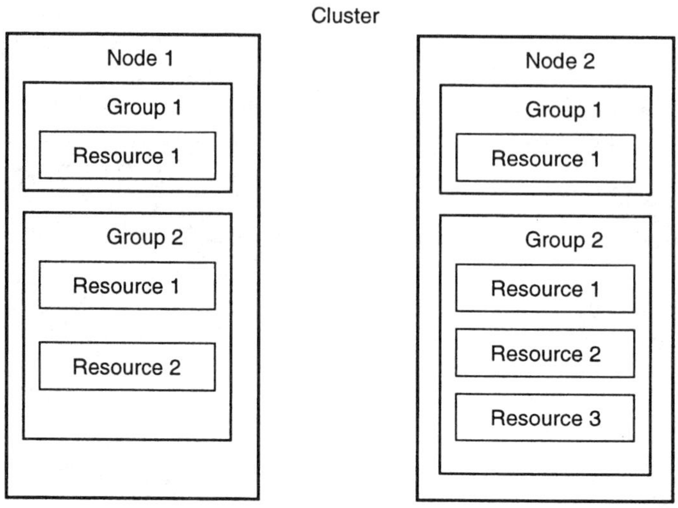

FIGURE 2 Relationship between cluster, nodes, groups, and resources.

contain a disk resource and preferably a network name resource as well. As another example, if a group is set up to provide a virtual server function, then the group should contain all necessary resources such as a network name resource and an IP address resource. An active cluster node can act as host to one or more cluster groups. All resources within a group must be online on the same node in the cluster. When a group is failed over, the state of each resource is altered according to its dependency relationships with the other resources in the group. Although groups are typically formed from related or dependent resources, groups can also be established with resources that are unrelated and not dependent to balance the load or to enable other administrative conveniences.

Besides dependency constraints, resource grouping is also determined by the needs of the organization. Resources that are associated with a single department or task can be grouped for administrative convenience. For example, one of the groups in the cluster can provide file and print services to one department and another group can provide similar services to another department. Administrators could establish at least as many groups as there are nodes in the cluster. This spreads the resources around the cluster and provides greater flexibility in cluster configuration and load balancing.

When a group is made up of an application, it normally includes all the application-related peripherals and data. When a group includes a network name resource and an IP address resource, the group is referred to as a virtual server. (See virtual server later in the chapter.)

Similar to resources, groups have properties as well. Each group maintains many common properties in the cluster database that describe the group and dictate how and when the failover and failback processes should occur. In addition, every group maintains a list of the nodes that are eligible to host the group. The list of preferred nodes for a group is generated from the lists maintained by the resources that are members of the group. This list includes the node or nodes on which the group/resource prefers to run and the nodes that the group/resource prefers to move to during a failover.

Typical clusters include one group for each independent application or service that runs on the cluster. Typical cluster groups contain the following types of resources:

- IP address
- Network name
- Physical disk
- Application or service

Cluster Database

The cluster database contains information about the cluster such as member nodes, resources, resource groups, and so on.

The cluster database is a part of the Windows NT registry at each node. However, your applications should not use the regular Windows NT registry functions to access the cluster database. You can access the cluster database from your application or resource DLL by using either control code functions or database management functions. The database management functions are meant to supplement the control code functions. The database management functions are similar to the registry functions, except that changes are propagated to other cluster nodes to keep the cluster consistent. Even if a node is offline, cluster changes are tracked through a log file stored on the quorum resource and subsequently synchronized when the node comes back online. This is part of the log synchronization performed at node startup.

Internet Information Server Virtual Root

While most of the other resource types such as disk, spooler, and file share do not need to be described, the Internet Information Server (IIS) virtual root may not be very familiar. The IIS virtual root resource type is used to provide failover (see section on failover later) capabilities for IIS virtual directories. A virtual directory is a directory that is outside of the home directory and appears to browsers as a subdirectory of the home directory. It is automatically created in IIS when an IIS virtual root resource is created in Cluster Administrator (see Chapters 4 and 8 for more details about the Cluster Administrator), eliminating the need to create the virtual directory in IIS before creating the resource. An IIS virtual directory that is accessed over the network must be in the same domain as the IIS server. IIS virtual root resources are closely related to other Cluster Server resources such as IP address resources, network name resources, and physical disk resources.

Interconnects

Interconnects are the connections between cluster nodes. Nodes in a cluster are connected in two ways:

- Using shared storage
- Using network connections, also called interconnects

The interconnects provide an alternate path for communication between the cluster nodes. The interconnects are either private or public. Private interconnects are private networks that carry internal cluster communications such as the status communications between cluster nodes. When clients are also included, the interconnect is typically a public network.

Although MSCS can function with just one interconnect, using two interconnects is recommended to increase redundancy and to reduce the risk of communication failures. Private networks are recommended, but not required.

Failover

Failover is the essence of clustering. Failover is the process of relocating services and resource/group of resources from a node that fails to another node that is operational. For example, a cluster may have two nodes, node 1 and node 2. The IIS may be running on node 1 and providing Internet services. When node 1 fails, IIS will failover to node 2 and Internet services are continued.

Failover is a two-step process. First, the resource/group/service becomes offline in the first node. Then the resource/group/service becomes online in the second node. The offline and online transitions between resources occur in a predefined order. Resources that have other resources dependent on them are taken offline after the dependent resources are taken offline. Similarly, dependent resources are brought online first before resources that are dependent on them are brought online.

A number of additional failover-related terms such as failover object, failover policy, and failover time are defined in the Glossary. Failover is covered in more detail in Chapter 5.

FAILBACK

Failback is the reverse of failover. While failover occurs when a node fails, failback occurs when a node comes back online. Failback is the process of migration of one or more resources, groups, etc. back to a primary node when the primary node returns to operational status after a failure. In the prior example, IIS failback to node 1 occurs. Note that the administrator can control what resources, groups, etc. failback. The fact that a resource or group failover occurs does not necessarily mean that the resource or group failback automatically occurs.

VIRTUAL SERVER

As mentioned in Chapter 1, the cluster projects a single image to the entities interfacing with it. A client may interface with a cluster and obtain services from an application running on node 1 of the cluster. After a failover, the client may access the same application, which is now running on node 2. This switch is transparent to the client. The transparency is achieved by the client not directly accessing node 1 or node 2 servers, but a virtual server instead.

A virtual server is a group that contains an IP address resource, a network name resource, and other required resources. The group, which is the virtual server, appears as any other individual server to clients and hence the name virtual server. Users access applications or services on the virtual server in the same way they would access the application or service on a physical (nonvirtual) server. Besides the transparency for programmatic access from a client, this transparency also avoids the need for any special training to use clusters. End-user menus dealing with servers such as the Explorer menu list the virtual server in the same manner as a physical server.

QUORUM

Quorum is a voting mechanism that is used to guarantee that specific data necessary for recovery can be maintained consistently between all cluster members. This mechanism involves a special resource called the quorum resource, described next.

Quorum Resource

The quorum resource stores recovery data on shared storage. The quorum resource is typically a SCSI disk or fault-tolerant disk set that can be owned by one cluster node at any point in time. When the node that owns the quorum resource fails, the surviving nodes negotiate to take over the ownership of the quorum resource. Negotiating for the quorum resource is an orderly process to settle potentially chaotic situations. Chaotic situations can arise, for example, when all the servers are up on the network but some of the network connections are very slow or lost. In this situation, all servers are active and think the other servers are down and attempt to take ownership of the quorum resource.

The Cluster Service Membership Manager maintains the quorum mechanism. Each quorum resource receives one vote and that vote is transitively passed to the node that currently owns the resource. By default there is only one quorum resource per cluster. We cover the quorum resource in more detail later in this chapter.

CLUSTERING MODELS

There are two main clustering models used in clustering:

- Shared device
- Shared nothing

Let us take a closer look at both these models.

Shared Device Model

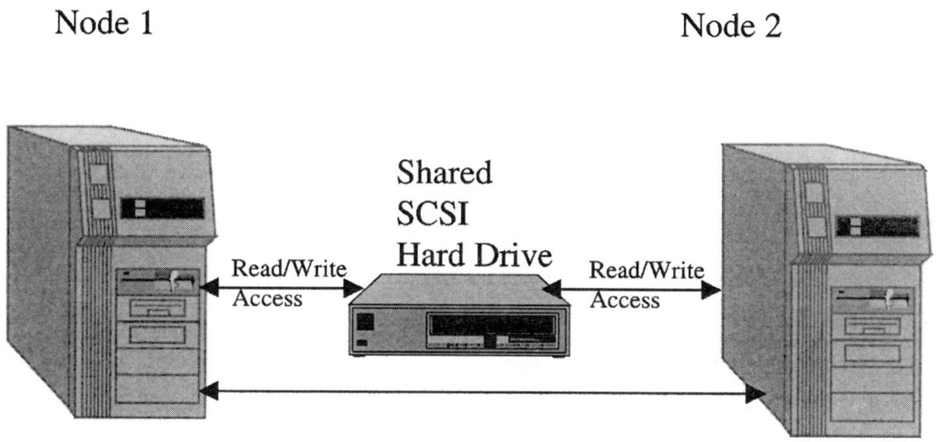

FIGURE 3 Shared device model.

In the shared device model, applications running on any node in the cluster may access any hardware device, such as a hard disk, connected to any other node in the cluster. Two or more applications can read or write the same data on the common disk. If two or more applications need to read the same data, the data must be read multiple times from the disk. While the read is a problem of redundant access, updating the same data poses even greater problems.

When two or more applications can update the same data, there must be a mechanism to ensure that changes by one application are not overlaid by another. The mechanism must also ensure that the applications do not get into a deadlock situation where each application is waiting for another one to release a lock forever. This problem is very similar to the common data access problem even on a single computer with multiple processors (as in an symmetric multiprocessing [SMP] system). The mechanism that permits multiple applications regulated access is called distributed locking.

The distributed locking synchronization mechanism is handled by a component called a Distributed Lock Manager (DLM). The DLM is typically a service provided to applications running on the cluster that keeps track of references to hardware resources that are part of the cluster. When multiple applications attempt to reference a single hardware resource, the DLM recognizes and resolves the conflict by serializing the access to the hardware resource. While this accomplishes the objective of enabling regulated access, using a DLM has some disadvantages as well. DLM introduces overhead into the system due to the need for additional message traffic between nodes of the cluster. Using DLM also results in the performance degradation due to serialized access to hardware resources compared with nonserialized parallel access.

The shared disk model is useful when expensive or specialized peripheral devices need to be shared. This model is also useful when individual applications running on different nodes need to access data stored in a shared-disk database management system. However, access to the shared device can limit system scalability. Shared-disk databases, for example, cannot grow beyond a certain size because of the overhead needed to coordinate access to the shared disks from many processors.

Shared Nothing Model

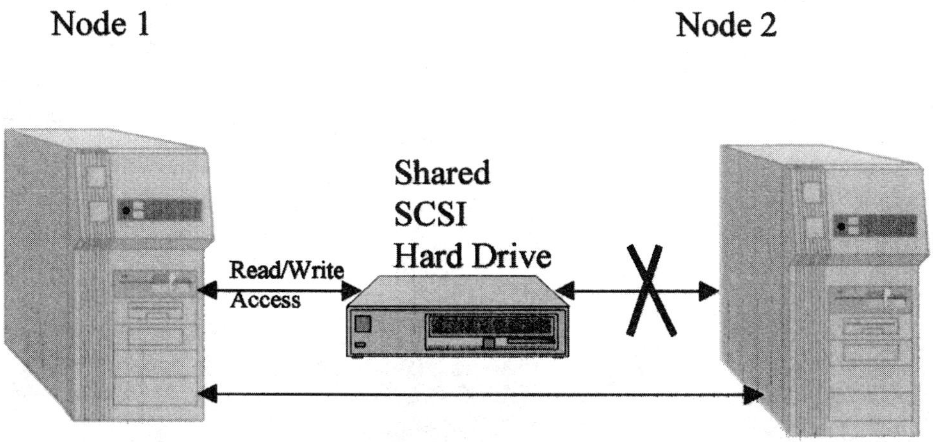

FIGURE 4 Shared nothing model.

The shared nothing model is designed to avoid the overhead used by the DLM in the shared device model. In this model, each node of the cluster owns a subset of the hardware resources of the cluster and the nodes do not share any resources such as memory or disk. Only one node owns and controls the access to a hardware resource at any given time. When a failure occurs, another node takes ownership of the hardware resource and enables the continuity of access to that hardware resource.

In the shared nothing model, each system has its own memory, operating system, and subset of the cluster resources. Only one system owns and manages any given resource at a time. This avoids the need for distributed locking synchronization mechanisms and associated overhead. If the system that owns the resource fails, another system can take ownership of the resource. Requests from clients are automatically routed to the system that owns the resource. After a failure, the client requests are again routed automatically to the new owner of the resource.

In this model, requests from applications are automatically routed to the system that owns the resource. For example, if an application needs to access a database on a hard drive owned by a node other than the one it is running on, the node passes the request for the data to the other node. This allows the creation of applications that are distributed across nodes in a cluster.

Typically, applications that require only limited shared access to data work the best in the shared device model. Applications that require maximum scalability benefit from the shared nothing cluster model. The two clustering models are compared in Table 5.

Next, let us look at the cluster architecture that depicts how the building blocks and other cluster components interact in the formation and execution of the cluster.

TABLE 5
Comparing Shared Device and Shared Nothing Models

Shared Device Model	Shared Nothing Model
Enables direct access of applications on different nodes to a resource	Access to a resource is through one controlling node only
Needs distributed locking synchronization	Does not need locking synchronization
Scalability limited due to need for synchronization	Scalability is not limited
Suitable for applications requiring limited shared database or the need to directly access a resource	Suitable where scalability is important and where access through a controlling node is acceptable

CLUSTER SERVER ARCHITECTURE

Figure 5 shows an overview of the Cluster Server architecture. This architecture shows the interaction between different Cluster Server components as well as how the Cluster Server components relate to applications of various types.

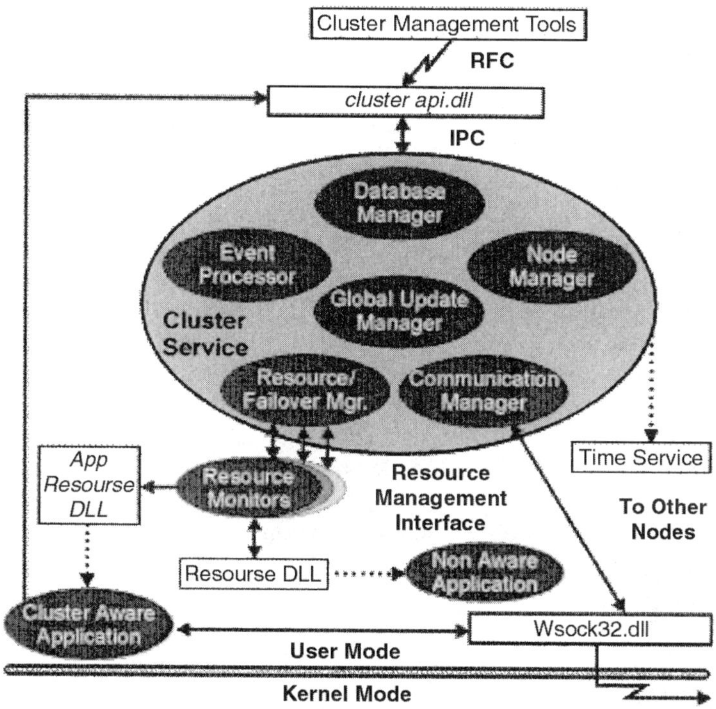

FIGURE 5 Cluster Server architecture. (Reproduced with permission from Microsoft.)

The Cluster Server architecture is made up of the following software components:

- Cluster Service, which in turn is made up of the following:
  - Database Manager
  - Checkpoint Manager
  - Communication Manager

    - Node Manager
    - Global Update Manager
    - Resource Manager
    - Event Log Manager
    - Failover Manager
    - Membership Manager
- Cluster Network Driver
- Cluster Administrator
- Resource Monitors
- Resource DLLs

Let us look at the cluster architecture and its components in greater detail.

The Cluster Service is the "brains" of a cluster. There is one instance of the Cluster Service running on every node in a cluster. The Cluster Service manages resources and coordinates with other instances of the Cluster Service in the cluster. The Cluster Service is made up of a number of dependent interconnected components called managers. We look at the Cluster Service in greater detail later in this chapter.

The Cluster Network Driver is part of the communications infrastructure in a cluster. The Cluster Network Driver maintains configuration information provided by the Cluster Service. It provides communication between cluster nodes. This communication includes the internal cluster status messages that are crucial in maintaining cluster membership. When the Cluster Network Driver detects a communication failure, it notifies the Cluster Service.

Resource Monitors act as an interface between the Cluster Service and cluster resources. Each resource is handled by a resource DLL that is loaded into the Resource Monitor process. Resource Monitors isolate the Cluster Service from failures in a resource DLL. There can be multiple Resource Monitors in a cluster. In fact, it is prudent to isolate resources that are suspected or expected to fail, so that their failure does not impact the remainder of the cluster.

Resource DLLs are used to manage cluster resources of a particular type. Each resource DLL is written to manage one or more resource types. The sequence of events that happen when the Cluster Service issues a request to a resource is as follows:

- The Cluster Service issues a request that is targeted to a resource.
- That request is passed to the Resource Monitor.
- The Resource Monitor looks up a table containing pointers to entry point functions contained in the resource DLL (this table is available to the Resource Monitor when the resource DLL gets loaded).
- Using the table of pointers, the Resource Monitor calls an entry point function in the resource DLL responsible for the resource.
- The resource DLL handles the request and interfaces with the resource.

The entry point functions are part of the resource API. Programming using resource APIs is covered in more detail in Chapter 7 and Chapter 8. A list of resource APIs is included in Appendix B.

Cluster Server includes resource DLLs for standard resource types such as the IP address and physical disk. It is possible for third-party developers to develop custom resource types. As part of creating custom resource types, developers should create the associated resource DLLs to replace or augment the Cluster Server resource DLLs. Cluster Administrator is a graphic application used by administrators (see Cluster Administrator later in the chapter).

While the Cluster Administrator supports standard cluster objects by default, it is possible to extend the functionality of the Cluster Administrator by writing extensions. Extensions may be required, for example, for custom resource types.

Note: Cluster Administrator is the name of the MSCS tool used to manage the Cluster Server. Sometimes in cluster-related literature this term is also used to refer to the human being who is responsible as a system administrator to administer a cluster. However, it should be obvious from the context what is referenced.

Besides these Cluster Service components, other components of the overall cluster environment include applications that execute in the cluster environment and a Cluster Administrator who uses cluster management tools to administer the cluster.

Applications in a Cluster Environment

Figure 5 shows three types of applications:

- Cluster management
- Cluster aware
- Cluster unaware

Figure 5 also shows the different ways in which a cluster-aware and a cluster-unaware application interface in the cluster environment. Let us look at each of the different cluster applications in more detail.

Cluster management applications are used for cluster administrative tasks such as:

- Adding and remove resources, groups, and other cluster objects
- Establishing resource dependencies
- Configuring clusters
- Establishing failover policies
- Changing the membership of groups
- Moving a group from one node to another, etc.
- Initiating failover to perform maintenance
- Manually moving resources for load balancing
- Handling routine maintenance
- Monitoring cluster activity

Microsoft provides cluster management applications as part of MSCS. The most popular cluster management application is the Cluster Administrator. Microsoft also provides a command line cluster management application with Cluster Server called CLUSTER.EXE. Both these tools are covered in more detail in Chapter 9. Administrators use these applications for the cluster administrative tasks mentioned earlier. The one administrative function that cannot be done through the cluster management applications is adding a new node to a cluster. A new node is added to a new or existing cluster by installing Cluster Server on the node and bringing up the Cluster Service on that node.

Both cluster-aware and cluster-unaware applications run on a cluster node and can be managed as cluster resources. However, the resource types used for cluster-aware and cluster-unaware applications are different. In addition, only cluster-aware applications can take advantage of features offered by Cluster Server through the Cluster API. For example, cluster-aware applications can:

- Report status on request to the Resource Monitor
- Respond to requests to be brought online or taken offline gracefully

A cluster-aware application is typically managed by the Cluster Service as a custom resource type. Custom resource types are typically created by third-party developers in connection with their custom applications. Custom resources can be managed by the Cluster Server, but they require the creation of a cluster administration extension DLL. This DLL and the resource DLL are created by the third-party developer who created the custom resource.

Almost all Windows applications that exist today are cluster unaware. Obviously, these applications should be capable of being executed in clusters. MSCS typically manages a cluster-unaware application as a generic application resource. Unlike the custom resource, the generic application resource is one of the standard resource types defined by MSCS. Generic application resources can be administered with Cluster Administrator and do not require special administration extension DLLs. These applications can also failover to an alternate node when a failure occurs.

Figure 6 shows how these Cluster Server components relate to applications of various types and to each other within a single Windows NT Server network operating system.

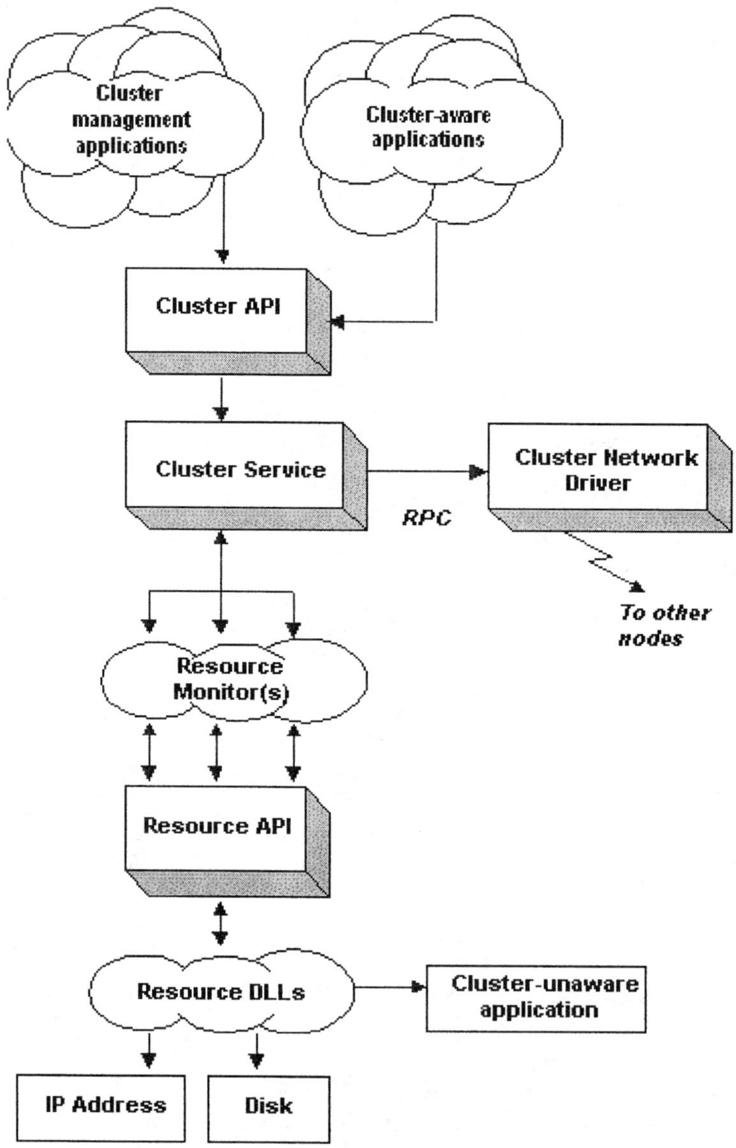

FIGURE 6 Cluster components and relationships. (Reproduced with permission from Microsoft.)

Cluster Service

The Cluster Service is a new service that has been added to the list of Microsoft Windows NT services to provide clustering functions. Each node in a cluster must run its own Cluster Service. Cluster Service controls cluster-related activities and provides all the cluster functions. The functions provided by the Cluster Service include

- Coordinating event notification
- Facilitating communication between other software components
- Handling failover operations
- Managing configuration, etc.

Cluster Service States

There are three distinct states in which a node in the cluster may exist based on the state of the Cluster Service. These states are summarized in Table 6.

TABLE 6
Cluster Service States and Description

Cluster Service State	State Description
Offline	The node is not a fully active cluster member and does not perform all the cluster-related functions; there is not enough status information about an offline node; the node may not be up or may be running noncluster-related services; the Cluster Service may have started but failed, or the Cluster Service may not have been started
Online	The node is a fully active member of the cluster; it performs all cluster-related functions such as cluster database updates, sends and receives heartbeats, and participates in owning and running groups
Paused	The node is a fully active member of the cluster and is very similar to the online state; it performs cluster database updates and sends/receives heartbeats; it does not participate in the owning or running of groups

The offline state is the state when the Cluster Service is not running on a node or the computer itself is powered off.

The online state is the state of normal cluster operation. As noted earlier, the online and paused states are basically the same with the major exception that no groups or resources can be online on a node when the Cluster Service on that node is in the paused state.

The paused state is primarily used for performing routine maintenance functions such as upgrading a cluster application.

The Cluster Service is made up of several closely related interdependent components called managers. Table 7 describes the function of each Cluster Service Manager.

The Event Processor along with the Membership Manager manages the transitions of the Cluster Service from one state to the next. The states are visible to other nodes outside the local Cluster Service.

While the Cluster Service has the three states listed in Table 6, the Cluster Service managers listed in Table 7 may have their own states (called substates) as well. However, unlike the Cluster Service states, the states of the Cluster Service Managers are not visible outside the Cluster Service.

TABLE 7
Cluster Service Managers and Description

Manager	Interfaces with	Description of Functions
Checkpoint Manager	Windows NT Registry Quorum resource	Saves data from the cluster database in the quorum resource; saves other necessary portions of the system registry in the quorum resource
Database Manager	Cluster database	Maintains the cluster configuration database; controls access to the cluster configuration database
Event Log Manager	Event logs	Replicates the Windows NT event log records across the cluster nodes
Failover Manager	Resource Manager	Starts and stop resources; transfers groups and resources from one node to another; manages resource dependencies
Global Update Manager	Database Manager	Works with Database Manager to propagate cluster changes to all nodes; handles cluster configuration changes; handles cluster state changes
Log Manager	Recovery log quorum resource	Writes changes to the recovery log on the quorum resource when any of the cluster nodes are down; takes checkpoints when necessary to ensure that the local cluster databases are kept consistent across the cluster
Membership Manager	Node Manager Cluster Network driver	Works with the Node Manager and the Cluster Network Driver; maintains cluster membership; provides membership information to other components in the Cluster Service; tracks active and inactive nodes
Node Manager	Cluster Network driver	Maintains node and network configuration; maintains state information
Resource Manager	Failover Manager	Initiates the transfer of cluster groups to other nodes; interfaces with the Failover Manager; determines redistribution of group ownership

Database Manager

The Database Manager provides two major functions:

- Maintains the cluster database
- Provides an interface that other cluster components can use to access the cluster database

The Database Manager is the component of the Cluster Service that maintains the cluster database. The cluster database is physically stored as part of the registry on each node of the cluster. This database contains information about all the entities in the cluster, such as the cluster itself, resource types, groups, and resources. One instance of the Database Manager runs on each node in a cluster. The Database Managers communicate with each other to maintain consistent cluster configuration information.

In addition, the Database Manager also provides an interface to the configuration database that is used by the other components of the Cluster Service. Cluster Services coordinate updates to the registry to maintain consistency and provide atomic updates across the nodes in the cluster.

Node Manager

The Node Manager maintains the "pulse" of the cluster. One instance of the Node Manager runs on each node in a cluster. The Node Manager on one node is in constant communication with the

Node Manager on the other node to detect node failures in the cluster. This is accomplished by sending heartbeat messages between the nodes.

If the Node Manager on a node does not respond, it is presumed that the node not responding has failed. The active resources on the failed node must be transferred to the node that is still running. The Resource/Failover Manager handles the actual failover.

If the Cluster Service fails on a node, all the resources on the node failover even if the resources are still all online and functioning. This is because there is no way to figure out the state of the resources in a cluster when the Cluster Service fails. The order in which the resources are failed over and failed back depends on resource dependency relationships.

Quorum resource interaction

An interesting situation arises when both nodes are still up, but the communication link or links between the nodes fail. Each node thinks that the other node has failed. However, because both nodes are still functioning, the Node Manager on each node would try to failover the resources to the node on which the Node Manager was running and bring all the resources back online.

To prevent this situation, the Cluster Server relies on the quorum resource to ensure that only one node has a resource online. If communication between nodes fails, the node that has control of the quorum resource then brings all resources online. The node that is unable to communicate and access the quorum resource takes all the resources that it has offline.

Event Processor

The Event Processor performs the following functions:

- Handling requests to open, close, or enumerate cluster objects
- Maintaining cluster objects
- Delivering events to cluster-aware applications and other components of the Cluster Service

The Event Processor is the communications center of the Cluster Service. It is responsible for connecting events to applications and other components of the Cluster Service. The Event Processor starts the Cluster Service and brings the node to the offline state. After completing initialization, the Event Processor calls the Membership Manager to join or form a cluster.

Event Processor substates

The Event Processor maintains the following substates. As mentioned earlier, these states are independent of the Cluster Service states and are not visible outside the Cluster Service:

- Initializing — This occurs when the Cluster Service is in the process of starting.
- Exiting — This occurs when the Cluster Service is in the process of cleaning up prior to exiting.

Membership Manager

The Membership Manager is called by the Event Processor after the Event Processor starts the Cluster Service and completes initialization. The Membership Manager handles the task of the node joining or forming a cluster. Typically, the Membership Manager returns when it has either joined or formed a cluster. Occasionally, the Membership Manager may fail to do either. The Membership Manager may fail due to different reasons:

- The current cluster node (that is up) rejects the request to join the cluster.

- It fails to find other cluster members.
- It fails to locate the quorum disk.

The Membership Manager maintains cluster membership by keeping track of active cluster nodes and nodes that are configured to be part of the cluster, but not yet active. A node becomes active when it starts its cluster service and synchronizes with other active nodes. One instance of the Membership Manager runs on each active node. Cluster membership is initially set up by the administrator.

Membership Manager substates

The process of joining or forming a cluster is complicated and requires multiple steps involving several state transitions. The Membership Manager maintains these states (listed in Table 8) and as mentioned earlier, these states are independent of the Cluster Service states and are not visible outside the Cluster Service.

TABLE 8
Membership Manager Substates and Description

Membership Manager Substate	Substate Description
Member Search	The node is trying to find an online cluster member in its cluster
Quorum Disk Search	The node is trying to find a quorum disk; locating the quorum disk helps the synchronization of the node cluster configuration and forming a cluster
Dormant (sleeping)	The node has been unable to find either an online cluster member or the quorum disk and is dormant
Forming	The node was unable to find an online cluster member, but found the quorum disk and is in the process of forming a cluster
Joining	The node has found an online cluster member and is negotiating to join the cluster; if the negotiation fails, the Membership Manager will signal a failure to the Event Processor

Global Update Manager

The Global Update Manager provides a common mechanism for all cluster components of the Cluster Service to perform updates such as effecting state transitions (e.g., online/offline of resources). In addition, the Global Update Manager also handles notification of cluster state changes to all active nodes in the cluster.

Resource/Failover Manager

The Resource/Failover Manager is responsible for:

- Managing resource dependencies
- Starting and stopping resources, by directing the Resource Monitors to bring resources online and offline
- Initiating failover and failback

The Failover and Resource Managers perform these tasks based on resource and system state information received from Resource Monitors and Membership Manager. The Failover and Resource Managers handle all failures including resource failures, node failures, etc.

Failover

If a resource fails, the Resource Manager attempts to restart the resource in the current node where the resource was operational prior to failure. If the restart attempt does not succeed, the Resource Manager invokes the Failover Manager, which moves the resource (and the group the resource belongs to) to an available node in the cluster.

If an entire node fails, the Resource Manager moves all resource groups from the failing to an available node.

When all resources and groups have been successfully transferred, all remaining active cluster members update their cluster databases to reflect the new state of the cluster.

Failback

When a node that has failed comes back online, the Resource/Failover Manager on the returning node initiates any configured failbacks. The Resource/Failover Manager on the returning node contacts the Resource/Failover Manager on the node that currently has the resources online.

Failback is administrator configurable. All resources/groups that failover need not failback automatically. The administrator can specify which resources/groups should be failed back. In addition, the failback does not need to occur as soon as the failed node comes back online. There is a failback option that can be configured to control the time of day during which failback can occur. If a failback window has been configured, the Resource/Failover Manager waits for the designated time before initiating failback.

Cluster Network Driver

The Cluster Network Driver, CLUSNET.SYS, is responsible for:

- Providing cluster communication
- Monitoring the status of all network paths between nodes
- Routing messages over the optimal path
- Detecting the failure of nodes

The Cluster Network Driver is part of the communication path between cluster nodes and helps to maintain cluster membership. The Cluster Network Driver maintains configuration information and communicates this information with the other nodes in the cluster. When a communication failure is detected, the Cluster Network Driver notifies the Cluster Service.

Heartbeats are sent to every node in the cluster. When there are multiple communication links between nodes, heartbeats are exchanged using all network paths between nodes. Heartbeats sent to a node or across a communication link that are not received signal a failure of the node and/or the communication link.

If a node fails to respond to a heartbeat message or voluntarily leaves the cluster, the Cluster Network Driver notifies the Membership Manager and Node Manager. These Cluster Service components initiate "regrouping" to take the inactive node offline and to cancel its membership in the cluster. When the Failover Managers on the surviving nodes are notified that a node has failed, they exchange messages to redistribute any groups that were hosted by the inactive node.

Cluster Networks

Cluster networks serve the following functions:

- Carrying internal cluster communication
- Providing client systems with access to cluster application services
- Connecting client systems to cluster application services
- Carrying traffic unrelated to cluster operation

Cluster Server relies on the availability of network paths to ensure that the nodes of a cluster can communicate. If one network path fails, another network path must be able to maintain and to continue the communications. Therefore, maintaining accurate information about network topology is critical to the functioning of a cluster.

To perform cluster communications, Cluster Server maintains configuration information about network topology. The configuration information includes

- Data about all the networks that are available to the cluster
- Status information about a particular network or networks and current usage
- IP address resources

Internal cluster communication includes cluster control messages. IP address resources are created on networks to provide clients with access to cluster services. While the Cluster Server authenticates all internal communication, organizations particularly concerned about security can restrict internal communication to physically secure networks.

Figure 7 provides an example of these four roles. The key below the diagram lists the values that are stored in a network Role property. The private network, or interconnect, is used only for internal communication between the cluster nodes. The Internet, due to its widespread usage, is only used to connect client systems to the cluster. The corporate network is used for both client connections and internal communication. Network X is an example of a network that, for whatever reason, cannot be used by the cluster.

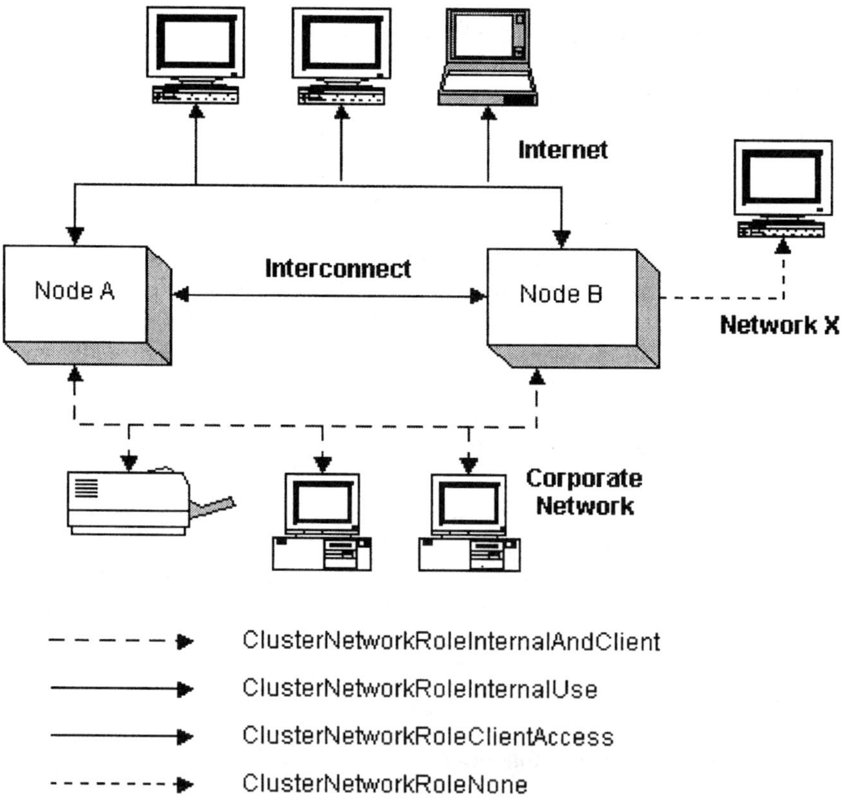

FIGURE 7 Cluster network interconnect. (Reproduced with permission from Microsoft.)

Typically, Cluster Server attaches to every available network, storing property information for each in the cluster database. However, an administrator can prevent the Cluster Service from attaching to a network by assigning the value ClusterNetworkRoleNone to its role property. Only the first three roles listed in Figure 7 identify a network as one that should be utilized by the Cluster Service.

Networks used by the Cluster Service expose their behavior through Cluster API functions. One of the functions, **ClusterNetworkControl**, is used to initiate a variety of operations that are network related. The operations are defined by a set of control codes. Several of the operations involve accessing network data stored in the cluster database. Chapter 7 and Chapter 8 cover the Cluster API functions, including **ClusterNetworkControl** in more detail.

Resource Monitor

Resource Monitor is a Cluster Server component that acts as an intermediary between the Cluster Service and cluster resources. More specifically, the Resource Monitor acts as an intermediary to handle two-way communications between the Cluster Service and a resource DLL that is responsible for a resource.

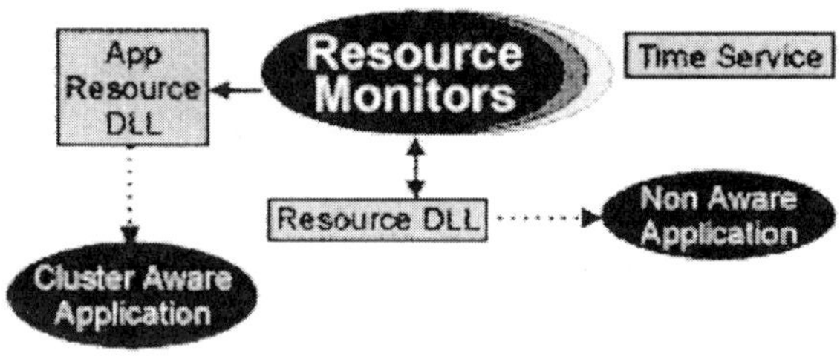

FIGURE 8 Resource monitor interaction. (Reproduced with permission from Microsoft.)

As shown in Figure 8, when the Cluster Service makes a request of a resource, the Resource Monitor transfers that request to the appropriate resource DLL. If not already loaded, a Resource Manager loads a resource DLL when the Resource Monitor begins processing a resource. When a resource DLL reports status or wants to notify the Cluster Service of an event, the Resource Monitor ensures that the information is passed back to the Cluster Service.

A DLL that is loaded into the Resource Monitor process exposes and provides the means to access the capabilities of each resource. The primary role of a Resource Monitor is its ability to isolate the Cluster Service from failures in a resource DLL. This ability permits the Cluster Service to provide uninterrupted service in spite of resource-related failures. Multiple Resource Monitors can be used to isolate resources from one another.

The default for the Cluster Service is to start a single Resource Monitor for all resources on the node. However, it is possible, and in many cases desirable, for each node to have multiple Resource Monitors. Each of the Resource Monitors can monitor one or more resources. Taking this idea to the limit, it is possible to configure each resource to have its own Resource Monitor. While such a configuration is possible, the isolation is commonly limited to problematic resource DLLs. Configuring a problematic resource DLL to run in its own Resource Monitor ensures that it does not affect other resources using the common Resource Monitor.

Each Resource Monitor runs as a separate process and a Resource Monitor is not run in the same process as the Cluster Service. The Resource Monitor runs in a process separate from that of the Cluster Service for two reasons:

- To protect the Cluster Service from resource failures
- To allow the Resource Monitor to take action if the Cluster Service fails (the Resource Monitor detecting Cluster Service failure and responding by taking all the resources and groups on the affected node offline)

Resource Monitors do not make decisions or set policies. Resource Monitors simply carry out the commands of the Cluster Service.

One of the functions provided by Resource Monitors is the monitoring of the state of a resource (such as whether or not the resource is online/offline). The Resource Monitor notifies the Cluster Service of any changes in the state of the resource.

Each Resource Monitor contains a "poller" thread, a thread used exclusively for polling resources. Poller threads are the means by which the Resource Monitors determine the online/offline state of resources. To determine if a resource has failed, the Resource Monitor thread makes calls to the resource DLLs. There is one poller thread for every 16 resources.

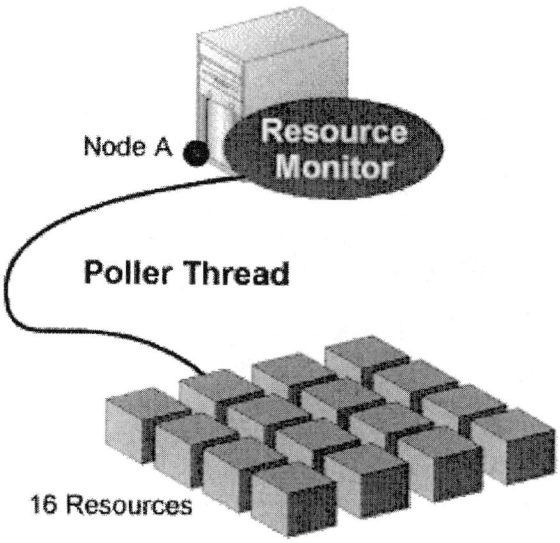

FIGURE 9 Resource Monitor threads. Reproduced with permission from Microsoft.)

Each resource is polled based on two different polling intervals:

- LooksAlive — With a frequency based on this interval, the Resource Monitor checks to determine if the resource is still active. The check performed by the resource DLL is a quick, cursory check to see if the resource is still running.
- IsAlive — With a frequency based on this interval, the Resource Monitor performs a more thorough check to determine if the resource is behaving as expected. The frequency of this check is less than the frequency based on the LooksAlive interval.

The administrator can set the two polling intervals. If the poller thread detects a failure, the Cluster Service is notified. Detection of failure does not cause the polling to be stopped. The IsAlive polling is still performed on the resource. This is for a reason. If the resource is able to recover and start working again with polling continuing to monitor the resource, this allows faults that the resource recovers from to be detected, and the Cluster Service to be notified that the resource is working again.

The Resource Monitor does not attempt to bring the failed resource back online unless told to do so by the Cluster Service. It is up to the Resource/Failover Manager to attempt to restart the resource or cause failover to occur.

Resource Monitors and Resource States

In addition to monitoring the state of resources, the Resource Monitor is also responsible for managing the resource state transitions in response to Cluster Service commands and resource DLL responses to IsAlive/LooksAlive polling mentioned earlier. The states in which a resource can exist are covered earlier in this chapter.

Offline

The initial state for a resource is the offline state. In this state the resource is not available to clients. To transition out of the offline state, the Cluster Service can call the Resource Monitor with a ResourceOnline command.

When a resource needs to be taken offline for maintenance or to be failed over to another node, the Cluster Service can issue the ResourceOffline or ResourceShutdown command to the Resource Monitor. The Resource Monitor calls the resource DLL offline/shutdown entry point function. It also unloads the resource DLL.

Starting

Once a request has been received to start a resource, the Resource Monitor attempts to bring the resource online. If the resource succeeds in coming online, its state transitions to the online state. If the resource fails to come online within a specified time interval, it will revert back to the offline state.

Online

As mentioned earlier, the Cluster Service brings a resource online by issuing the ResourceOnline command to the Resource Monitor. The Resource Monitor calls the Online entry point of the resource DLL and returns the result of the call to the Cluster Service. If the resource comes online, the resource state transitions to the online state and the resource is added to the Resource Monitor list. Polling (IsAlive/LooksAlive) is started for the resource. If the Online call fails, the resource state returns back to the Offline state.

Failed

If a resource being polled by a Resource Monitor fails, its Cluster Service is notified and the resource immediately transitions to the failed state. As mentioned earlier, the Resource Monitor continues to poll the resource and if the resource recovers, the Resource Monitor brings the resource back online (unless the Cluster Service explicitly requests that the Resource Monitor takes the failed resource offline).

In addition to the stable states, there are two states known as pending states. These pending states are

- Onlinepending
- Offlinepending

These states are expected to be very short — typically less than a few seconds. If the resource DLL does not complete the transition from a pending state to a stable state within a fixed period of time, approximately 3 min, then the Resource Manager terminates the resource and tries again according to the policies defined for the resource.

The pending states are entered whenever the Online or Offline entry point functions report an error. Once in the pending state, the resource DLL moves the resource into the expected stable state, or the failed state. However, if the resource DLL does not move the resource into a stable state within the predefined period of time, the Resource Monitor fails the resource, and then calls the Terminate entry point function.

Resource DLLs

Let us take a closer look at resource DLLs. When the Cluster Service issues a request to a resource, that request is passed to the Resource Monitor. The Resource Monitor in turn calls an entry point function in the resource DLL responsible for the resource. When a resource DLL is loaded, it passes table pointers to the Resource Monitor. This table contains the pointer to each of the entry point functions. The Resource Monitor uses these pointers when it calls the entry point functions.

MSCS provides resource DLLs for the management and monitoring operations for standard resource types such as the IP address and physical disk resources. The name of the resource DLL that is included with MSCS for the standard resource types is shown in Table 9. As mentioned earlier, third-party developers can create custom resource types and associated resource DLLs to replace or augment the resource DLLs provided by MSCS.

TABLE 9
Resource Types and Associated DLLs

Resource Type	Cluster Server DLL
Generic application	Clusres.dll
Generic service	Clusres.dll
IIS virtual root	Iisclus3.dll
Physical disk	Clusres.dll
File share	Clusres.dll
Network name	Clusres.dll
Print spooler	Clusres.dll
TCP/IP address	Clusres.dll
Time service	Clusres.dll
Distributed Transaction Coordinator (DTC)	Clusres.dll
Microsoft Message Queue Server	Clusres.dll

The following are characteristics of resource DLLs:

- Resource DLLs included with MSCS for standard resource types run in a single process. They are loaded into the Resource Monitor process.
- They run in the system account.
- They are treated as privileged code.
- Resource DLLs communicate with their resources using interprocess communication mechanisms.

Cluster Component Properties

We looked at resource properties earlier in the chapter. The concept of properties applies to all other cluster components just as for resources. As for resources, the other components also have common and private properties.

Time Service

The time service (Timeserv.exe) is responsible for maintaining a consistent view of time on all nodes in the cluster. The Node Manager component of the Cluster Service elects a node as the time source for the cluster. The time source node provides the time to the other members of the cluster.

The requirement for the nodes to have consistent time is necessary to provide applications the ability to function correctly when a failover occurs. This is done using a time stamp, or some other object, which is maintained with files. If a consistent time were not maintained and a failover took place, an erroneous situation could occur; for example, it could appear that the file or other object was created in the future.

Cluster Security

Windows NT Cluster Server uses built-in Windows NT security features for securing communication between nodes; joining of nodes; and controlling authentication and access, including client access to the cluster and shared resources. For example, Windows NT functions let a Cluster Administrator specify which users or groups can:

- Administer the cluster
- Access files or folders on file share resources

Table 10 lists the Windows NT security features you can use to control client access to the various types of resources supported by MSCS.

TABLE 10
Security by Resource Type

Resource Type	Windows NT Security
DHCP server	Controlled by DHCP
File share	NT File System (NTFS) share-level security
Generic application	Windows NT Network authentication and NTFS security applied to the shared SCSI file system
Generic service	Determined by Windows NT Service configuration
IIS virtual root	Windows NT Network, IIS, and NTFS file-level Security
IP address	N/A[a]
Distributed Transaction Coordinator (DTC)	Controlled by MS DTC
Microsoft Message Queue Server	Controlled by MSMQ
Network name	N/A[a]
Physical disk	NTFS file-level security
Print spooler	Windows NT Network and print-level permissions
Time service	N/A[a]

[a] N/A, not applicable

Quorum Resource

We have had a brief look at the quorum resource. Now, let us look at this important cluster component in more detail. Every cluster contains a special resource called the quorum resource. The quorum resource plays a very crucial role in the cluster. It maintains cluster membership and resolves communication problems between nodes in the cluster. The quorum resource must provide physical storage that can be accessed by any node in the cluster and must also provide a means of *persistent arbitration.* When one of the cluster nodes fails, the quorum resource logs the changes to the cluster database.

In every cluster, a single resource is designated as the quorum resource. A quorum resource can be any resource if it satisfies the following conditions:

- Offers a means of persistent arbitration — Persistent arbitration means that the quorum resource must allow a single node to gain physical control of it and to defend its control. For example, SCSI disks use their Reserve and Release commands for persistent arbitration.
- Provides physical storage that can be accessed by any node in the cluster — The quorum resource stores data that are critical to recovery when there is a communication failure between cluster nodes.

To maintain a cluster's membership, the Cluster Service relies on the frequent, timely exchange of messages with its peers on other nodes. Although unlikely, it is possible for a failure to occur of all possible networks connecting the cluster nodes. Such a failure could cause the cluster to divide into two or more sets of active nodes that can communicate within the set but not between sets. Each set would assume that nodes in the other sets have failed and would attempt to take control of their resources. To prevent this scenario, the node that gains access to the quorum resource is the node that is granted the ability to form the cluster. The quorum resource thus guarantees that only one set of active, communicating nodes operates as the cluster, acting as a tie-breaker in the unlikely event that cluster nodes are running, but cannot communicate.

When a cluster node fails, changes to the cluster database are written to the quorum resource. To realize the importance of this function, consider the situation where node 2 in a two-node cluster fails. If node 1 goes down before node 2 is brought back online, node 2 must gain control of the quorum resource to be made aware of node 1 changes. Node 2 must update its private copy of the cluster database with the changes from the recovery log maintained by the quorum resource. When the quorum resource is out of disk space, all changes to the cluster database are prevented. The quorum resource thus maintains access to the most current version of the cluster database and essential recovery data.

When a cluster node is started, it first tries to gain control and take to ownership of the quorum resource. If the quorum resource does not already have an owner, the node takes ownership of the quorum resource. In this case, the node has formed a cluster. If another node owns the quorum resource, the starting node joins the cluster.

As other nodes join the cluster, control of the quorum resource can be traded among them, as long as they remain in communication. If communication with the node that controls the quorum resource fails, then the surviving nodes must arbitrate for control. The node that gains control of the quorum resource and the nodes with which the controlling node can communicate continue to operate as the cluster. Nodes that were previously active and now cannot communicate release all their resources and halt operation immediately.

The only type of resource defined by Cluster Server 1.0 that can be a quorum resource is the physical disk. Third-party developers can create their own resource types to be quorum resources. Hardware manufacturers may also supply other resource types capable of storing the quorum resource. In any case the resource performing the role of the quorum resource must be able to perform arbitration and act as storage devices as mentioned earlier. Microsoft recommends that clusters use a stripe set of disks.

The quorum resource stores log data in the cluster log. The clustering software maintains these data. If the nodes in the cluster cannot communicate with each other, only one of them is allowed to continue operating. In this situation, the quorum resource, which can be owned by only one node, is used to determine which node can continue operating.

You specify an initial quorum resource when you install the first node of a cluster. You can use Cluster Administrator to change the quorum resource to a different storage resource.

If the quorum resource fails or becomes corrupted, or if the quorum log becomes corrupted, the Cluster Service cannot start. To correct this situation, you must modify the Cluster Service to start with a different quorum resource.

4 Setting Up Microsoft Cluster Server

Setting up a cluster using Microsoft Cluster Server (MSCS) involves two major tasks — planning and setup. Do not equate setting up a cluster with that of installing the MSCS. Installing MSCS is only a very small part in setting up a cluster using MSCS.

PLANNING FOR THE MICROSOFT CLUSTER SERVER

Planning is the first phase in implementing a Windows NT Server clustering solution. The importance of good planning cannot be overemphasized. A good plan helps avoid many problems in the later phases.

The typical planning cycle for setting up a Windows NT cluster contains the following steps:

- Determine if clustering is appropriate. Do not implement clusters unless it makes good business to do so.
- If clustering is appropriate, determine the critical portions of the overall system that can benefit from clustering.
- Select the type of cluster configuration to be employed such as high availability clustering or hot standby clustering, etc.
- Select appropriate licensing for the cluster.

Determining if Clustering is Appropriate

The determination of whether or not clustering is appropriate is actually performed at two levels.

The first is at the global application level. Many applications, which involve a lot of end-user interaction and systems dealing with financial transactions typically cannot tolerate downtime. For such applications, clustering is almost a necessity. Batch applications, which can be rerun in the event of failure, may not need clustering.

The second level is within the application system itself. Even if clustering is appropriate for an application and can improve the overall availability, it is important to note that clustering cannot guarantee availability and clustering helps availability of only selected portions of the overall system. For example, while clustering can help with the failure of hardware or software components in a server, clustering does not help if the failure occurs in parts not controlled by the Cluster Server such as a power failure or dial-up connection failure or a dedicated wide area network (WAN) connection failure. Thus by looking at the nature of the application and the hardware, software, and network components of an application, one can determine if clustering is appropriate for an application.

Unless the nature of the application warrants clustering at any cost, a trade-off analysis is usually performed to compare the cost of implementing clustering with the benefits of implementing clustering. Even if the trade-off study concludes that clustering is not cost justified for your application, you can increase availability of your application using the nonclustering methods listed next (note that some of these can also be used in addition to clustering):

- Use uninterruptible power supply (UPS) to minimize the impact of failures due to power outage or fluctuations.
- Use redundant array of inexpensive disks (RAID) to minimize the impact of disk errors and failures.
- Use redundant WAN communication connections to minimize the impact of a WAN connection failure to one or more remote sites.
- Use multiple modems/modem pool to minimize the impact of modem failures for dial-up access.

Identifying the Clustering Appropriate Portions

After establishing that clustering is appropriate, the next step is to identify the portions of the system that will benefit from clustering. While clustering improves the availability of server functions to clients, not all portions in an application system may need to be part of a clustered environment. This step identifies the specific portions within the application where clustering can help the overall availability. When there are multiple portions in the application that can benefit from clustering, this step can help in the prioritization of the portions to help select those portions that can benefit the most from clustering.

The portions of a system that frequently benefit from clustering are those that provide access to critical data and where loss of access can adversely affect the ability to do business. Examples include

- Applications that perform business transactions such as order entry whose failure would cause stoppage in the entering of orders into the system
- When critical business output functions have to be performed such as printers that print statements, checks, invoices, and so on
- File servers that store business critical data accessed and updated by business applications
- Internet Information Server (IIS) Web Sites that permit access to critical business functions

The most common benefit from clustering is improved availability. Availability requirements dictate which IIS Web sites, file shares, printer shares, and services should be moved to a cluster. Besides availability requirements, there are some functions that the applications should perform to fully benefit from clustering. The applications should:

- Use Transmission Control Protocol/Internet Protocol (TCP/IP) for network communications. Cluster Server cannot failover applications that do not support TCP/IP.
- Be capable of storing data on the shared remote storage. If the data were stored on a nonshared storage, then the data would be unavailable after failover.

Selecting the Clustering Configuration Type

Having established a need for clustering and having identified the portions of the overall system that would benefit from clustering, the next step is to decide on the cluster configuration type. There are four configuration types for implementing Cluster Server clusters:

- Hot spare configuration
- Static load balancing configuration
- Partial cluster configuration
- Hybrid configuration

Let us look at each of the configuration types in more detail.

Hot Spare Configuration

Hot spare configuration provides maximum availability and performance of the different cluster configurations. This functionality comes with a price. The price paid is that the capacities of both the cluster nodes are never fully utilized. One of the cluster nodes makes all the resources available, while the other node is idle and waiting, ready to be used, in case the primary cluster node fails. The idle node is a dedicated "hot spare." If the primary cluster node fails, all the resources are moved to the hot spare node.

The performance level during failover operation may be the same or lower than the performance level during normal operation depending on the capacity (central processing unit [CPU], memory, etc.) of the hot spare compared with the capacity of the other node. If both capacities are the same, the performance is the same. However, if a business is willing to tolerate degraded performance during failovers, then the business can save some money by making the hot spare node of lesser capacity than the other node. This configuration is conceptually the same as providing a spare (fifth) tire (that is not designed to handle the same load and speed as the regular tires in a car), which gets used in an emergency.

Static Load Balancing

In static load balancing, both the nodes in the cluster support cluster resources. No node is idle, and balancing of resources across both nodes provides a higher performance/cost trade-off compared with the hot spare configuration. Because each node must be able to run its own resources and the resources of both nodes in the event of a failover, performance may degrade when a failover occurs, depending on the resources and the capacity of the nodes. Static load balancing is a high-availability solution (as opposed to maximum availability with the hot spare configuration solution).

Partial Cluster Configuration

Partial cluster configuration is somewhat similar to the hot spare configuration in that a primary server performs more functions than the other server does. The main difference between this configuration and the hot spare is that the primary server also runs cluster-unaware applications. When implementing Cluster Server, chances are that existing legacy applications may have one or more of the following characteristics:

- The application is not cluster aware.
- The application does not require high availability.
- The application may not be configurable for failover, perhaps because it:
  - Does not use TCP/IP for network communications. The application can use high level protocols such as Named Pipes or Remote Procedure Call (RPC), but the underlying protocol for network communications must be TCP/IP. Applications that use non-TCP/IP protocols such as NetBEUI cannot take advantage of the MSCS failover feature.
  - Does not use the shared Small Computer System Interface (SCSI) drive to store data.

Note: Applications that cannot be failed over can still be installed and used on either cluster node. However, if the node in which an application runs fails, the application becomes unavailable. Because only some of the applications are moved over to the other node, this configuration is termed partial cluster configuration (unlike the hot spare configuration where all the applications are moved).

Applications that can be failed over can be further divided into two groups: those that support the MSCS API and those that do not. Applications that support the MSCS application programming interface (API) are defined as MSCS aware. These applications can register with the Cluster Service to receive status and notification information, and can use the MSCS API to administer MSCS clusters. The application can use the status and notification information and the MSCS API to perform application level functions that supplement cluster functions already built into MSCS. Applications that do not support the MSCS API are defined as MSCS unaware. If MSCS-unaware applications meet the TCP/IP and remote-storage criteria, they can still be used with MSCS and often can be configured to failover. However, MSCS-unaware applications cannot perform application level functions that take advantage of clustering. Applications that keep significant state information in memory are not the best applications for clustering because information that is not stored on disk is lost at failover.

Hybrid Configuration

The hybrid configuration is a hybrid of the previous models, which combines the advantages of the other models into a single cluster. While the previous configuration types showed the different variations possible, this configuration is the one that is likely to be used by many users, particularly those with a combination of resources that require failover, resources that do not require failover, and cluster-unaware applications. This solutions permits all the previously mentioned scenarios to coexist. This configuration permits the coexistence of:

- Resources that require failover, for example, static load balancing for two database shares
- Resources that do not require failover, for example, file and print shares in one node not requiring failover ability and being in logical groups, or virtual servers (see virtual servers later)
- Noncluster-aware applications, for example, executing on a node, operating as usual without any failover protection

There is another configuration possible, which is called virtual-server-only configuration. This is not really a clustering configuration because there is only one node (and hence failover is not possible). Virtual servers are logical groups set up for user and administrative convenience.

Table 1 compares the four configuration types.

TABLE 1
Cluster Configuration Types

Type	Suitability	Availability	Failover Considerations
Hot spare	Best suited for mission critical applications and resources	Highest of all configuration types	Configure groups to failback to the higher performance node (if the hot spare has lesser capacity)
Static load balancing	Best suited for file and/or print sharing	High	Configure all groups with one preferred server
Partial cluster	Suited when there are both Cluster Server-unaware applications and cluster-aware resources	High for clustered resources; normal for Cluster Server-unaware applications	Configure groups to failback based on if one node has more capacity than the other
Hybrid	Best suited for organizations that require a combination of resources that require failover, resources that do not require failover, and cluster unaware applications	High to very high for clustered resources; normal for Cluster Server-unaware applications	Groups to be set up to let the different servers share the load appropriately

Tip: Once you have decided to implement clustering in some portion of your overall system, do not forget its impact on the rest of the system. The cluster relies on networking over TCP/IP. Many installations have some problems running with TCP/IP and such problems are best addressed before installing clustering. In addition, you may need to take additional steps such as configuring your existing NT servers and clients to use Windows Internet Name Service (WINS) and Domain Name System (DNS). Make sure you have identified these additional steps and plan for them in your overall cluster setup.

Licensing Considerations

The next step in the planning process is to ensure that the licensing arrangement is the right one for your business environment.

Licenses are required for

- Cluster operating systems software
- Cluster applications software
- Cluster client software

The cluster operating systems software consists of Windows NT Server and Cluster Server. Both of these must be licensed separately for each of the machines in the cluster they run on.

Cluster application licensing terms for applications that run on clustered servers are set by the application vendor. For Microsoft applications, Microsoft requires that the application must be separately licensed for each server on which the application is installed. Most applications have components of the application that run on the server and other components that run on clients. Many applications charge a license fee based on either the number of clients that are attached to the server or the number of clients that are active at any given time. See per-seat licensing and per-server licensing later.

Cluster client software is typically the operating system that runs on the clients attached to a Windows NT Server running MSCS and the portion of applications that run on the clients. Examples of client operating systems include Windows NT Workstation and Windows 95/98.

Per-Seat Licensing

If the customer is using per-seat client access licenses for the application, then those licenses apply when a client is accessing the application on either server in the cluster.

Per-Server Licensing

If the customer is using per-server (or concurrent use) client access licenses for the application, then each computer in the cluster should have a sufficient number of per-server client access licenses for the expected peak load of the application on that computer. Client access licenses on a failed node do not failover to the other node in the cluster.

Cluster Server Licensing

In a Cluster Server cluster, if an application is run on both servers, then the application must be licensed for both servers. This licensing requirement is true even if the application runs only on one server at a time but must be installed on both servers to permit failover.

CLUSTER SETUP REQUIREMENTS

Once planning is complete, the next step involved in setting up a cluster using MSCS is the actual setup of hardware and software. Before a cluster can be set up, there are administration, hardware, and software requirements that must be met.

The next step in setting up a cluster is to ensure that you have met all the requirements. These requirements can be classified as Administration requirements, hardware requirements, software requirements, etc. Let us look at each of the requirements in more detail.

ADMINISTRATION REQUIREMENTS

Cluster administration requirements include setting up the domain accounts, deciding on group failover policies, and ensuring that cluster capacity is planned correctly.

Domain Accounts

Both cluster nodes should have computer accounts on the domain and should be members of the same domain. To be able to install MSCS, you must log on to both nodes under a domain account that has administrator permissions on both nodes.

Tip: It is not enough if both accounts belong to a work group. They should be members of the same domain as well.

The administrator permission is required only for the installation. The domain user account, under which the Cluster Service runs, does not require any special account privileges. Keep in mind, however, that this user account is unlike a regular user account and does not need to be logged into on a regular basis. As such, password policies, such as requiring password changes and change password on next logon, should be turned off.

When you install MSCS on a member server, MSCS Setup gives cluster administrative permissions to the local administrators group. When you install MSCS on a Primary Domain Controller (PDC) or Backup Domain Controller (BDC), MSCS Setup gives cluster-administrative permissions to the domain administrators group.

When you administer a cluster from a remote location, such as from another server or a computer running Windows NT Workstation, you must also have administrative permissions on both nodes of the cluster, or you must have specific permissions to administer the cluster. By default, the local administrators group on both nodes has permission to administer the cluster. To give permission to administer the cluster from domain accounts that do not belong to the administrators group on both nodes, in the cluster Properties dialog box, click Permissions on the General tab.

If you have administrative permissions on both nodes of the cluster, you can fully administer the cluster. However, if you have only specific permissions to administer the cluster, you cannot change the cluster description or change cluster security.

Group Failover Policy

MSCS lets you bunch resources into a group and specify settings that apply to all resources that belong to the group. These settings or policies determine exactly how a group behaves when failover occurs. For example, the policies let you specify whether a group must failover immediately when a resource fails or restart attempts should be made first. The policies also let you specify your preferences for specific nodes and/or times. You can vary your policies as appropriate for each resource group you set up.

Failover policies for groups include three settings:

- Failover timing — This setting lets you set a group for immediate failover when a resource fails; alternately, you can instruct MSCS to try to restart the group a number of times before failover occurs. If it is possible that the resource failure can be overcome by restarting all resources within the group, then set MSCS to restart the group.

- Failback timing — This setting lets you set a group to failback to its preferred node as soon as MSCS detects that the failed node has been restored; alternately, you can instruct MSCS to wait until a specified hour of the day, such as before or after peak business hours.
- Preferred node — This setting lets you set a group so that it always runs on a designated node whenever that node is available. This is useful, for example, if one of the nodes has better hardware and/or software to host the group.

Setting Up Groups

As mentioned earlier, MSCS lets you bunch resources into a group, which provides a convenient way to handle a collection of resources. There are four steps you can take to organize your applications and other resources into groups:

- Listing all resources
- Listing all dependencies for each resource
- Making preliminary grouping decisions
- Making final grouping assignments

Let us look at each step in more detail.

List all resources

List all your resources to determine which applications, hardware, connections, and operating system software MSCS can protect in your network environment. Besides critical business applications, MSCS can failover other important software such as print spoolers that protect client access to printing services and file servers that maintain client access to files.

List all dependencies for each resource

Resources have dependencies and resources cannot provide a useful function if the dependent resources are not available. For example, if a Web-server application fails over, the Web addresses and disks on the shared SCSI buses containing the files for that application must also failover if the Web server is to function. When you create this list, make sure that you include all dependent resources. All the dependent resources must be located in the same group as the resource that is dependent on them. This ensures that MSCS keeps interdependent resources together at all times.

Two guidelines for listing resources are

- A resource and its dependencies must be together in a single group.
- A resource cannot span groups.

For example, if several applications depend on a particular resource, you must include all those applications with that resource in a single group.

Make preliminary grouping decisions

Another factor in the way you assign groups is administrative convenience. For example, you might put several applications into one group because viewing those particular applications as a single entity makes it easier to administer the network.

A common use of this technique is to combine file-sharing resources and print-spooling resources in a single group. All dependencies for those applications must also be in the group. You can give this group a unique name, for example, based on the department or part of your organization it serves. Whenever you need to administer the department or part, you would look for this group in Cluster Administrator.

Another common practice is to put applications that depend on a particular resource into a single group. For example, suppose a Web-server application provides access to Web pages, and that those Web pages provide result sets that clients access by querying a Structured Query Language (SQL)-database application through the use of Hypertext Markup Language (HTML) forms. By putting the Web server and the SQL database in the same group, the data for both core applications can reside on a specific disk volume. Because both applications exist within the same group, you can also create an IP address and network name specifically for this resource group.

Make final grouping assignments

After you list the resources that you want to group together, assign a different name to each group, and create a dependency tree. A dependency tree is useful for visualizing the dependency relationships between resources.

To create a dependency tree, first write all the resources in a particular group. Then draw arrows from each resource to each resource on which the resource directly depends.

A direct dependency between resource A and resource B means that there are no intermediary resources between the two resources. An indirect dependency occurs when a transitive relationship exists between resources. If resource A depends on resource B and resource B depends on resource C, there is an indirect dependency between resource A and resource C. However, resource A is not directly dependent on resource C.

Capacity Planning

After you assess your clustering needs, you are ready to determine how many server computers you need and with what specifications (Random Access Memory [RAM], hard disk storage, real memory, etc.). This is capacity planning. The following steps help in your capacity planning effort:

- List all your applications, regardless of whether on not you plan to use them with MSCS.
- Sort the list of applications based on whether or not you want the applications to failover.

Let us look at each of these steps in more detail.

List All Your Applications

Most groups contain one or more applications. Make a list of all applications in your environment, regardless of whether or not you plan to use them with the MSCS. Include in this list applications that reside on MSCS nodes but that do not use the failover feature because it is either impossible or unnecessary to configure the applications for failover. Although you do not set failover policies for non-failover applications or arrange them in groups, the applications still use a portion of the server capacity.

Sort the List of Applications

Determine which of your applications can benefit by using the MSCS failover feature. Remember that the applications you want to benefit from MSCS failover feature must qualify for failover by the two criteria described in the previous section — support for TCP/IP and ability to store data in shared storage.

Hardware Requirements

After you choose a cluster model, determine how to group your resources, and determine the failover policies required; then you are ready determine the hardware capacity required for each server in the cluster. The sections explain the criteria for choosing computers for use as cluster nodes:

- Hard disk storage requirements — Each node in a cluster must have enough hard disk capacity to store permanent copies of all applications and other resources required to run all groups. Calculate this for each node as if all these resources in the cluster were running on that node, even if some or all those groups run on the other node most of the time. Plan these disk space allowances so that either node can efficiently run all resources during failover.
- CPU requirements — Failover can strain the CPU processing capacity of an MSCS when the server takes control of the resources from a failed node. Without proper planning, the CPU of a surviving node can be pushed beyond its practical capacity during failover, slowing response time for users. Plan your CPU capacity on each node so that it can accommodate new resources without unreasonably affecting responsiveness.
- RAM requirements — When planning your capacity, make sure that each node in your cluster has enough RAM to run all applications that may run on either node. Also, make sure your Windows NT paging files are set appropriately for the physical memory of each node.

As an example, MSCS runs on top of the Windows NT Server, Enterprise Edition and the minimum requirements for a single server to run Windows NT Server, Enterprise Edition are

- Pentium 90 MHz or higher processor for Intel or compatible systems or a system with Alpha processor for Reduced Instruction Set Computer (RISC) systems (although MSCS supports Alpha processors, it cannot mix different processor architectures in the same cluster)
- 64 MB of memory (RAM)
- 500 MB of available hard disk space
- VGA, Super VGA, or video graphics adapter compatible with Windows NT Server 4.0
- Compact disc read-only memory (CD-ROM) drive
- Microsoft Mouse or compatible pointing device

Keep in mind that this is a "minimum requirements" list, below which NT Server does not run. However, as always, to get a decent performance, you need a much better machine. For best clustering results, choose similar — if not identical — hardware for both nodes. The two computers should preferably be the same brand, and preferably even the same model. The SCSI adapters used in both nodes must be identical to ensure that the adapter basic input/output system (BIOS) and other firmware in both nodes are fully compatible. The network adapters used in each node need not be identical.

One hardware detail you should pay attention to is the number of expansion slots. Depending on your cluster configuration, hardware choices, and fault tolerance requirements, you may not have enough expansion slots in your computers. For example, if each node has a local SCSI bus, three network adapters, and three SCSI adapters for three shared SCSI buses, each node requires seven expansion slots plus slots for video, sound, and other devices that require adapters. One way to overcome the potential shortage of slots for adapter cards is to use dual- or quad-SCSI adapters and network adapters. These adapters put the hardware for two or four separate adapters on one physical adapter. While this does conserve on expansion slot use, you do lose some hardware redundancy.

Note: The hardware requirements discussed in this book are generic. For specific information about supported hardware, see the MSCS Hardware Compatibility List (HCL), which is available online at http://www.microsoft.com/hwtest/hcl. For specific information about MSCS original equipment manufacturer (OEM) configurations that have been verified by Microsoft, check with your hardware vendor. Please see the Bibliography for additional details about the MSCS HCL.

Clusters and RAID

While MSCS can work with simple hard disk drives, it makes more sense to use redundant array of inexpensive disks (RAID) in clustering solutions because the use of RAID improves availability even more compared with non-RAID clustering solutions. Even if you do not plan to use RAID, try to use two disk drives in a mirroring arrangement where one disk mirrors the other. This improves availability.

The MSCS hardware–software bundles validated by Microsoft use many different hardware RAID configurations. Because many hardware RAID solutions provide power, bus, and cable redundancy within a single cabinet, as well as track the state of each component in the hardware RAID firmware, they provide data availability with multiple redundancy, protecting against multiple points of failure. Hardware RAID solutions also use an onboard processor and cache to provide outstanding performance.

Windows NT (and therefore MSCS) can use these disks as standard disk resources.

Although Windows NT Server includes support for software fault-tolerant disk sets, this option is not supported within MSCS.

Tip: Although NT works with Integrated Drive Electronics (IDE) and Enhanced Integrated Drive Electronic (EIDE), use SCSI whenever possible if you are concerned about fault tolerance. Some fault-tolerant features, such as cluster remapping, are available with SCSI but are not supported with IDE or EIDE.

You need the following SCSI hardware:

- SCSI cables
- SCSI terminators (facilitating high availability use of the shared bus, by disabling the internal termination on your SCSI controllers and using external termination on the shared bus)
- A SCSI adapter in each cluster server to provide a shared external bus between the nodes

Note: You cannot use the default adapter IDs because both adapters share the same bus. In addition, Microsoft recommends that you need to disable the BIOSs of some SCSI adapters to prevent the possibility of one node resetting the bus as it boots while the other node is attempting to use the bus.

- At least one disk drive in a storage enclosure on the shared bus

Each physical disk or fault-tolerant disk set on the shared SCSI bus is owned by only one node of the cluster. The ownership of the disks moves from one node to another when the disk group fails over or moves to the other node. Therefore, if you intend to share resources from both nodes of a cluster, you need at least two shared storage disks.

If you are using a hardware RAID solution, you need at least two shared volumes, regardless of whether they are mirrored disks, striped sets with parity, or non-fault-tolerant volume sets.

The disk resources on the shared SCSI bus must have the same drive letter on both nodes. Keep in mind that a typical NT system reassigns drive letters at startup based on the order in which it discovers disks. This is a problem for MSCS. To prevent reassingment of drive letters, you can use the Windows NT Disk Administrator after installing Windows NT. Use Windows NT Disk Administrator to manually assign drive letters only on the first node. NT Server stores drive assignments in each node registry. MSCS setup copies this configuration when you install MSCS on the second node. Because assignment of drive letters varies from computer to computer and MSCS makes all drive assignments permanent during setup, you should assign drive letters to all disk resources on the shared SCSI bus before installing MSCS.

Tip: Because the drive assignments must be the same on different computers, start using letters closer to the end of the alphabet series, such as the letter S. By starting your assignments from X and working back toward C/D, you give yourself enough room to add additional internal CD-ROM and other drives to a cluster member without running the risk of interfering with the shared cluster drive assignments.

Although you can partition drives that are used on the shared SCSI bus, there are some restrictions imposed by MSCS:

- You must partition and format all disks you use with MSCS before running MSCS setup.
- Partitions of a single physical disk cannot be members of different fault-tolerant disk sets.
- All partitions on one disk are managed as one resource, and move as a unit between nodes.
- All partitions must be formatted with NT File System (NTFS) (they can be either compressed or uncompressed). This requirement is for shared storage only. The drives of the nodes themselves can use either File Allocation Table (FAT) or NTFS.

Another detail to keep in mind with respect to shared storage is that your system and shared storage must exist on different buses. This means that you need two controllers (or a multichannel controller) to support your external shared storage. This controller can be a SCSI, a Differential SCSI, or a Fibre Channel controller. However, Microsoft plans to support the clustering of more than two nodes in the future using only Fibre Channel controllers.

Software Requirements

The following are required software for setting up a cluster:

- Microsoft Windows NT Server, Enterprise Edition for the servers
- Client software such as Windows NT Workstation (client being one supported by Windows NT Server)
- Optionally, perhaps other software as needed such as Microsoft SQL Server 6.5 required for running Microsoft Message Queue Server

Network Requirements

The nodes of an MSCS cluster must be connected by one or more physically independent networks (sometimes referred to as interconnects). Although MSCS clusters can function with only one interconnect, two interconnects are strongly recommended and are required for the verification of MSCS OEM systems that include both hardware and MSCS software.

Redundant, independent interconnects eliminate any single point of failure that could disrupt communication between nodes. When two nodes are unable to communicate, they are said to be partitioned. After two nodes become partitioned, MSCS automatically shuts down one node to guarantee the consistency of application data and the cluster configuration. This can lead to the unavailability of all cluster resources. For example, if each node has only one network adapter, and the network cable on one of the nodes fails, each node (because it is unable to communicate with the other) attempts to take control of the quorum resource. There is no guarantee that the node with a functioning network connection can gain control of the quorum resource. If the node with the failed network cable gains control, the entire cluster is unavailable to network clients.

A network that connects cluster nodes can support one of four types of communication:

- Only node-to-node communication
- Only client-to-cluster communication

- Both node-to-node communication and client-to-cluster communication
- No cluster-related communication

Networks that support only node-to-node communication are referred to as private networks. Networks that support client-to-cluster communication (either with or without supporting node-to-node communication) are referred to as public networks. Typically, your servers need two Peripheral Component Interconnect (PCI)-based Network Interface Cards (NICs) (or a multiported NIC), one of which is used for cluster interconnect. The cards should support one of Ethernet, Token Ring, or Fiber Distribution Data Interface (FDDI).

Tip: The "autosense" mode of some 10/100 Ethernet adapters causes problems in clusters. This is because packets cannot be handled by the adapter during the detection process and must be queued. Some adapters may inadvertently trigger the autodetection process to reoccur, resulting in queued and delayed communications. The cumulative effect may cause cluster nodes not to receive critical packets in a timely fashion and may lead to premature failover of cluster resources. Microsoft recommends that you configure such adapters manually (see Knowledgebase article Q174812 for more details).

Before you install the MSCS software, you must configure both nodes to use the TCP/IP protocol over all interconnects. Also, each network adapter must have an assigned static IP address that is on the same network as the corresponding network adapter on the other node. Therefore, there can be no routers between two MSCS nodes. However, routers can be placed between the cluster and its clients. If all interconnects must run through a hub, use separate hubs to isolate each interconnect.

Tip: MSCS does not support the use of dynamic IP addresses assigned from a Dynamic Host Configuration Protocol (DHCP) server for the cluster administration address, the address associated with the cluster name (or any IP Address resources). You can use either static IP addresses, or IP addresses permanently leased from a DHCP server, for the Windows NT Network configuration on each node.

Installing MSCS on computers with logically multihomed adapters

A logically multihomed adapter is one that has two IP addresses assigned to it. These adapters can be used only for node-to-node cluster communication if their primary addresses are on the same IP subnet. (A logically multihomed adapter primary address is the one that appears when you run Control Panel, double-click Network, click TCP/IP on the Protocols tab, and click Properties.)

If the primary addresses on both nodes are not on the same IP Subnet, reorder the IP addresses assigned to the adapter by clicking Advanced on the IP Address tab, and then removing and adding the IP addresses again. Add the IP addresses with the matching subnet first, and then add the other IP addresses.

CLUSTER SETUP STEPS

PRESETUP CHECKLIST

Before installing MSCS, make sure you have the following:

- Appropriate permissions to install a cluster
  - You must log on to each node under a domain account that has Administrator permissions on the node.

  - Both nodes must be configured as members of the same domain (not a work group) and have computer accounts on that domain.
  - You must also supply the user name, password, and domain for the account under which the Cluster Service can run. This account requires no special account privileges, but password restrictions, such as requiring password changes and change password on next logon, should be turned off.
- The name of a folder that stores the cluster files on each node (the default folder being %WinDir%\cluster, where %WinDir% is your Windows NT folder)
- A cluster name (when running MSCS Setup and installing the second node, connecting to the first node by specifying the cluster name [or the computer name of node 1]; the cluster name also able to be used to connect to a cluster in Cluster Administrator [as can either node name]; the cluster name not able to be the same as the computer name of either node and not able to conflict with any other computer name [printer, server, cluster, domain, and so forth] in use on your network; the cluster name able to be changed using Cluster Administrator)
- A static IP address and subnet mask for the cluster (the static IP address and associated subnet mask you give your cluster being a floating address that is paired with the cluster name)
- The connectivity being in place (can test for TCP/IP connectivity by pinging one node from the other using the TCP/IP addresses; after confirming TCP/IP connectivity, can test NetBIOS name resolution over TCP/IP using the NBTSTAT command line program)

SETTING UP THE DOMAIN

We mentioned earlier that both cluster nodes must belong to the same domain. However, even within a domain there are still more choices to be made. These choices pertain to the configuration of the cluster nodes as member servers or domain controllers. The following combinations are possible:

- Both nodes are member servers within a domain and neither is a domain controller (PDC/BDC).
- Both nodes are BDCs within an existing domain.
- One node is a PDC and the other is a BDC within a self-contained domain.
- One node is a domain controller (PDC/BDC) and the other node is a member server.

Note: MSCS documentation does not explicitly specify this combination.

There are a number of considerations involved in deciding the domain model and these are covered later. It is important to decide on the model up front because changing the role of a Windows NT machine from being a member server to a domain controller requires the reinstallation of Windows NT.

In general, it is preferable to install MSCS on machines that are just member servers and not domain controllers. This is because domain controllers tend to have more overhead and it is better that MSCS is not affected by the domain-related functions a PDC/BDC must perform. If you install MSCS on member servers or on two BDCs in an existing domain, you preserve your existing domain model. If you create a new domain and install MSCS on a PDC and a BDC, you must establish domain trusts with your existing domains so users can access the MSCSs. These can be either two-way trusts or one-way trusts with your existing domains, depending on your domain model.

If you install MSCS on a PDC–BDC pair, install the first node on the PDC. This allows the service account to be accessed and modified without complicating domain security. The second node of the cluster should be the BDC. If the PDC fails, the BDC functions in its stead. However, clustering is not involved in this procedure. The roles of PDC and BDC cannot be made a failover resource. MSCS is concerned only with the services provided by the domain controllers, not the domain roles themselves.

If you plan to install MSCS on either PDC–BDC or BDC–BDC node pairs, review the hardware choices you made in capacity planning. You should account for the additional overhead that is incurred by the domain controller services. In large networks running on Windows NT, substantial resources can be required by domain controllers for performing directory replication and server authentication for clients. For this reason, many applications, such as Microsoft SQL Server and Microsoft Message Queue Server, recommend that you not install the application on domain controllers for best performance. However, if you have a very small network in which account information rarely changes and in which users do not log on and off frequently, you can use domain controllers as cluster nodes.

The simplest and most efficient server configuration has all MSCS nodes installed on domain controllers in one domain that contains only MSCS nodes. This configuration provides the following benefits:

- Because all groups and accounts have a domain scope, access-control problems with local users and local groups are eliminated.
- Similarly, on nondomain controllers, you should not specify local accounts and groups when setting access permissions for files and folders that reside on any disk on the shared SCSI bus. This is not a problem on domain controllers because the local accounts and groups have security context on all domain controllers in the domain.
- Minimal resources are required to support logon requests and replication because (1) cluster nodes typically do not log on and log off frequently, and (2) few user-account changes will require little replication.
- Because you are adding only one domain to your existing domain structure, minimal trust-relationship changes are required.

Setting up Shared Small Computer System Interface Buses

Setting up the shared SCSI bus involves connecting and configuring the shared SCSI bus and assigning drive letters. This step must be done before you can install MSCS on either node.

To connect the shared SCSI buses and assign drive letters:

1. Install Windows NT Server, Enterprise Edition on both nodes, following the instructions provided in the Windows NT Server documentation. The contents of the Windows NT Server, Enterprise Edition base CD are shown in Figure 1. The contents of the Windows NT Server, Enterprise Edition component CD are shown in Figure 2.
   Tip: If you attempt to run the Cluster Setup program on a system that does not have NT Server Enterprise Edition installed, MSCS lets you install only the Cluster Administrator program.

2. Prepare and install the SCSI controllers for the shared SCSI bus, following the instructions in your SCSI bus owner's manual. Ensure the SCSI controllers for the shared SCSI bus are using different SCSI identifications (IDs). Do not connect the shared SCSI buses to both computers while configuring the two systems. Install the controllers but do not connect them to the shared SCSI bus. Connection is done in step 4.

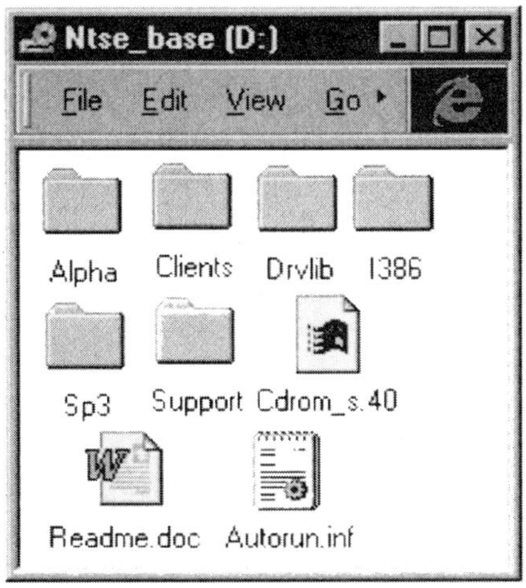

FIGURE 1 Contents of the Windows NT Server, Enterprise Edition base CD-ROM.

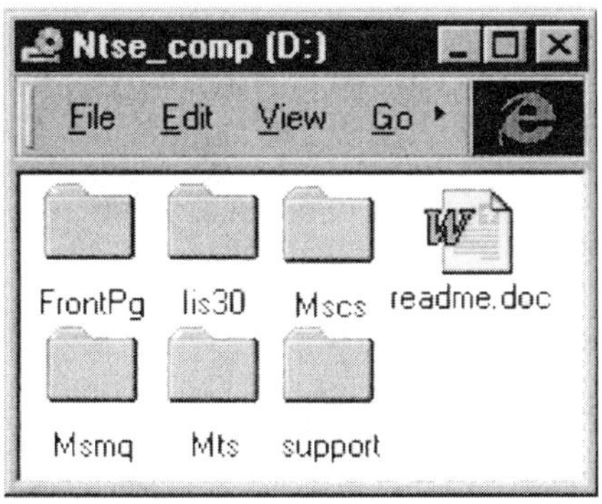

FIGURE 2 Contents of the Windows NT Server, Enterprise Edition component CD-ROM.

3. Install and configure all network cards to use TCP/IP, following the manufacturer instructions. Verify you have connectivity (using ping and NBTSTAT as mentioned earlier) on all networks.
4. Connect the shared SCSI devices to the shared buses, and then connect the shared SCSI buses to both nodes. (Install MSCS on at least one node before you run Windows NT Server, Enterprise Edition simultaneously on both nodes.)

   Tip: You have to be extra careful if you access the shared storage through noncluster mechanisms. NTFS, by itself, is not a cluster-aware file system and data corruption can occur if multiple nodes access the shared storage simultaneously. MSCS takes care of this problem by providing a special disk driver that limits disk access to one node at a time.

5. You can make drive letter assignments in the same manner as you did for internal drives (Log on with an administrative account, invoke Disk Administrator from Administrative Tools, create partitions (if needed), assign drive letters, and NTFS format the shared drives). Because MSCS can only failover at the physical disk level, you do not benefit

by having multiple partitions on a disk. Start the drive assignments toward the end of the alphabet series and work backward as mentioned earlier.

6. Start Windows NT Server, Enterprise Edition on the first node on which you intend to install MSCS. Turn on the second node, but do not allow Windows NT Server, Enterprise Edition to start. You can do this by pressing the SPACEBAR when the OS Loader screen appears, allowing you to select an operating system.

You are now ready to install MSCS on the first node.

For a two-machine cluster, you set up a cluster by configuring each machine to be the failover or secondary server of the other machine. After you connect and configure your shared SCSI bus and assign drive letters, you install MSCS in two phases. First, you install MSCS on one node, setting up all the basic information for the cluster. Then, you install MSCS on the second node, and most of the configuration settings from the first node are automatically detected. You can install either node first, as long as you prepare the SCSI controllers and disk resources on the shared SCSI bus as described in "assigning drive letters," earlier in this chapter.

Installing the First Node

If you are not installing the first node on a PDC, the PDC of the domain to which the server belongs must be online. If it is not, you cannot install MSCS. If you have not yet installed Service Pack 3 (SP3) as part of your Windows NT Server, Enterprise Edition installation, install it on both nodes before you begin installing MSCS.

Note: You must reapply SP3 each time you add new software or hardware components to your configuration.

To install MSCS on the first node:

1. Start Windows NT Server, Enterprise Edition, and log on using a domain account that has administrator permissions on the node. If you previously disabled the Installer, click Start, click Run, and type: nhloader.exe.
2. In the Microsoft Windows NT Server, Enterprise Edition Installer dialog box, click Continue; then, select the MSCS check box, and click Start Installation.
3. If you are installing from your network, establish a network connection to the MSCS Setup files; then switch to the Cluster\I386 or Cluster\Alpha folder (depending on your platform), and run Setup.exe. (see the MSCS welcome screen)
4. At the welcome screen, close any open applications and click Next. The setup program shows a hardware compatibility confirmation reminder screen.
5. Ensure your MSCS hardware configuration is compatible with MSCS, click I Agree, and then click Next.
6. Because this is the first node in the cluster, Click Form a New Cluster, and then click Next. (For the second node, you select the Join option — see step 6 in the next section.)
7. Type the name of the new cluster in Enter the name of the cluster to join or form, and then click Next. The name you enter here is used to create an MSCS network name resource that is a part of the default MSCS group named Cluster Group. This name is limited to 15 characters, because it serves as the NetBIOS name for the cluster. Microsoft recommends that you use this name to administer the cluster. If you want to change this name later, use the Cluster Administrator program.
8. Enter the path to the folder you want to contain the MSCS files, or click Browse to specify the path, and then click Next.

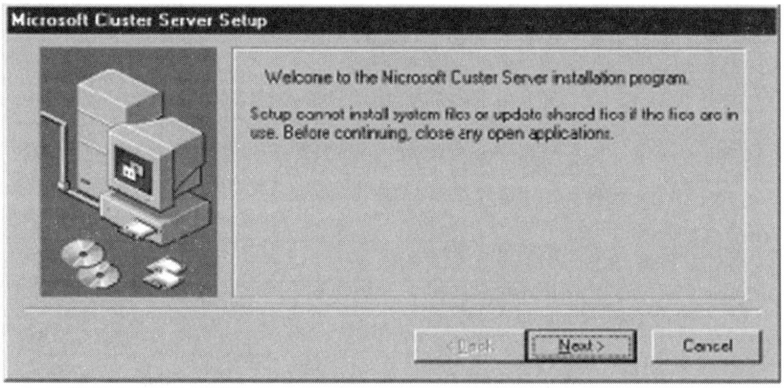

MSCS welcome screen

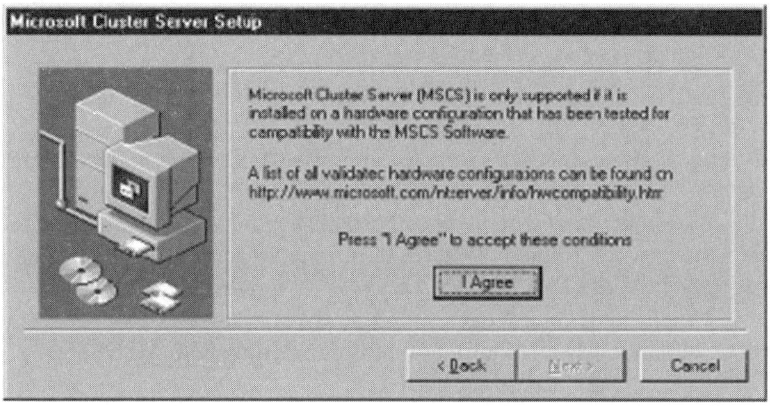

Confirmation reminder screen

9. By default, MSCS installs the files in a \cluster folder within the Windows NT folder (typically C:\Winnt\Cluster).
10. In the domain name selection dialog shown next (see Figure 3), enter the user name, password, and domain for the account the Cluster Service will run under; and then click Next. The MSCS service must run under an account on the domain. If at a later time, you want to change the account name, use startup properties in the control panel.
11. This account requires no special account privileges, but ensure that the password never expires (for obvious reasons) and turn off Change password on next logon.

Connecting the Second Node to the First Node

After you install MSCS on the first node, you are ready to install MSCS on the second node.

Make sure that the following prerequisites have been taken care of before installing MSCS on the second node. To install MSCS on the second node of a cluster, the first node must be online. Also, the PDC of the domain to which the server belongs must be online. If either server is not online, you cannot install MSCS.

If the nodes use NTFS for the file system, NTFS permissions can be set on the folder and files being shared. When setting NTFS permissions, you must ensure that the user account used by the Cluster service to log on has at least Read access to the directory. (Otherwise the Cluster Service is unable to bring file shares online.) Also, the permissions for the resources must be the same for both nodes.

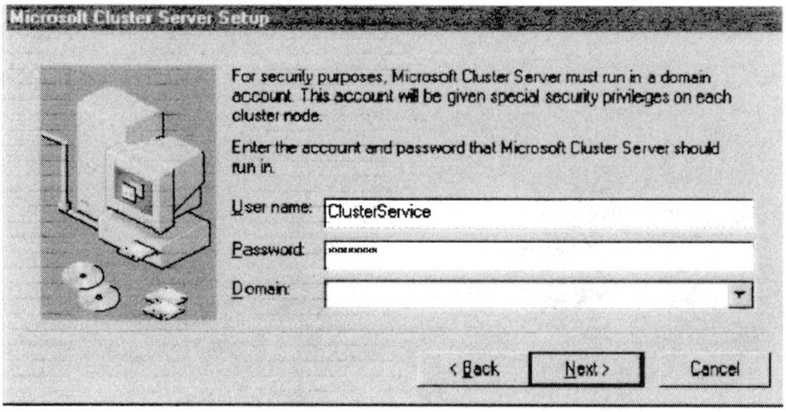

FIGURE 3 Domain name selection dialog.

To install MSCS on the second node:

1. Start Windows NT Server, Enterprise Edition and log on, using the same domain account that you used to install MSCS on the first node.
2. In the Microsoft Windows NT Server, Enterprise Edition Installer dialog box, click Continue; then, select the MSCS check box, and click Start Installation.
3. If you are installing from your network, establish a network connection to the MSCS setup files; then switch to the Cluster\I386 or Cluster\Alpha folder (depending on your platform), and run Setup.exe.
4. At the welcome screen, click Next.
5. Ensure your MSCS hardware configuration is compatible with MSCS, click I Agree, and then click Next.
6. Click Join an existing cluster, and then click Next.
7. Type the name of the cluster you established on the first node (in step 6 of the previous procedure) in Enter the name of the cluster to join or form, and then click Next.
8. Enter the path to the folder that you want to contain the MSCS files, and then click Next.
9. By default, MSCS installs the files in a \cluster folder within the Windows NT folder (typically C:\Winnt\Cluster).
10. Enter the password for the domain user account you specified when installing the first node, and then click Next.
11. Click Finish.
12. Microsoft includes a utility for backing up your cluster configuration. For more information, see the MSCS release notes.

Verifying Cluster Installation

You can verify the installation of your cluster by starting Cluster Administrator and checking that both nodes in your cluster are detected.

To start Cluster Administrator:

- On either node, click Start, point to Programs, point to Administrative Tools (Common), and then click Cluster Administrator.
- In Cluster or Server Name, type the name of the cluster (or type either the name or IP address of one of the nodes).

If installation is successful, the computer names of both nodes appear on the left side of the Cluster Administrator window.

ONGOING CLUSTER ADMINISTRATION

Now that you have setup a cluster, there are some rules that Microsoft provides for smooth running of the cluster. Most of the rules are fairly obvious and intuitive, and are

- Do not reassign system drive letters.
- Do not start nodes under operating systems that let utilities make low-level writes to physical disks.
- Do not change cluster node computer names or TCP/IP addresses. Note that a typical cluster uses at least five TCP/IP addresses — two addresses are used for intracluster communications (cluster node to cluster node communications), two addresses are used for connecting the cluster to your client network, and one address is for cluster management. In addition, you need an additional static TCP/IP address for each group of applications or services for which you want to provide failover capability and one TCP/IP address for each virtual server you want to set up.
- You must delete disk resources in the Cluster Administrator program before you repartition disks on the shared storage bus.
- You must reapply service packs after software or hardware additions. While this rule may seem redundant and not intuitive, strange and complicated problems can arise if this rule is not followed.
- You must restart cluster nodes if you change the partitions of disks on the shared bus.

UNINSTALLING A CLUSTER SETUP

You can uninstall the node of a cluster at any time. Before uninstalling a node, you should take all groups offline or move them to the other node. You should also close Cluster Administrator:

To uninstall MSCS:

1. Click Start, point to Settings, and click Control Panel.
2. In Control Panel, double click Add/Remove Programs.
3. On the Install/Uninstall tab, click Microsoft Cluster Server, and then click Add/Remove.

INSTALLING CLUSTER ADMINISTRATOR ONLY

You can install Cluster Administrator on any computer running SP3 with version 4.0 of either Windows NT Workstation or Windows NT Server. You can also install Cluster Administrator on any computer running Windows NT Server, Enterprise Edition (which includes SP3).

Note: When you install Cluster Administrator, Cluster.exe is also installed (in the Windows NT\System32 folder). For more information on Cluster.exe, see administering clusters from the command line in Chapter 9.

Follow the steps listed next to install the Cluster Administrator:

1. Run MSCS Setup from the Microsoft Windows NT Server, Enterprise Edition 4.0 Components CD (in the MSCSs\Cluster\I386 or MSCS\Cluster\Alpha folder, depending on your platform). Alternatively, if you are installing from your network, establish a network

connection to the MSCS Setup files, switch to the Cluster\I386 or Cluster\Alpha folder (depending on your platform), and run Setup.exe.
2. If prompted, click Install Cluster Administrator.
3. Specify the folder you want to contain the MSCS files, and click Next. By default, MSCS installs the files in C:\Winnt\Cluster.
4. Click Finish.

Tip: If you have installed only Cluster Administrator, you cannot uninstall it. You must manually delete the cluster folder within the Windows NT folder (typically C:\Winnt\Cluster), remove Cluster Administrator from the Administrative Tools (Common) folder (typically C:Winnt\Profiles\All Users\Start Menu\Programs\Administrative Tools [Common]).

SETUP CONSIDERATIONS

There are a number of precautionary steps you should be aware of when setting up a cluster. Observing these precautions can save you potential problems down the road.

- When you install MSCS, MSCS creates a cluster group as part of the installation. This group contains the IP address and network name for cluster administration. Do not add additional resources to this group because this may interfere with the ability to administer the cluster. For example, failure of a resource you add to the group may trigger failover resulting in the inability to successfully administer the cluster. When you need additional resources (as you undoubtedly will), create groups for the additional resources, or place the resources in other groups within the cluster.
- Two-disk subsystems exist in a clustered environment: those relevant to the shared SCSI bus and those that support Windows NT. These two systems should be kept separate. Do not put Windows NT system files on the shared SCSI bus. The Windows NT system files can reside on either FAT or NTFS drives, but the shared SCSI bus must contain only NTFS-formatted drives.
- Do not modify the access permissions on the disk that contains the quorum resource. MSCS must have full access to the quorum log. (The quorum log file is used to write all cluster state and configuration changes that cannot be committed to the other node.)
- Do not restrict the access of either node to the folder on the quorum disk containing the quorum log (\MSCS by default) for the same reason as stated earlier.
- Make sure that clients use the network name associated with the group in which shared resources belong. If a group failover to another cluster node occurs, shared resources are only available through the group network name. Thus, if a client uses the wrong network name, it may not reestablish network connections after failover.
- If you create shares on the server, create them as a resource within the cluster software. If not, the share is not be able to failover to another node, because the share is considered a local share.
- Do not use the MSCS Permissions dialog box to give local users or local groups permission to administer the cluster. The single exception to this rule is the local administrator group. Local users and local groups have security context only on the local computer. If these groups were allowed to have cluster administration permissions, the security context would be meaningless when failed from one node to another.
- Do not specify local accounts and groups when setting access permissions for files and folders that reside on any disk on the shared-SCSI bus.

5 Failover and Failback

There are two instances when a failover from one machine to another is necessary. You may have a planned failover so that one server can be brought down (and perhaps has some maintenance or upgrade performed). The other instance is an unplanned failover.

For a two-machine cluster, you set up a cluster by configuring each machine to be the failover or secondary server for the other machine. The two servers keep tab of each other to see if the other machine is up using heartbeats. When one machine fails, its resources move to the failover machine and the processing continues. When the failed machine comes back online, the resources are moved back. The process of moving resources back to the original server is failback.

Unlike some other clustering solutions, Windows NT Cluster Server is not a cold standby clustering solution. Both machines are up and running until the time one of the machines fails or is brought down. Windows NT Cluster Server includes resource dynamic link libraries (DLLs) to allow the following resources to be moved to a cluster:

- File shares
- Printer queues
- Microsoft IIS Web sites
- Generic services or applications (a service/application that does not include a resource DLL but meets the requirements to be used in a cluster)
- Distributed Transaction Coordinator
- Message Queue Server

The primary Microsoft Cluster Server (MSCS) component that handles failover and failback is the Resource/Failover Manager.

RESOURCE/FAILOVER MANAGER

The Resource/Failover Manager is responsible for:

- Managing resource dependencies
- Starting and stopping resources, by directing the Resource Monitors to bring resources online and offline
- Initiating failover and failback

The Failover and Resource Managers perform these tasks based on resource and system state information received from Resource Monitors and Membership Manager. The Failover and Resource Managers handle all failures including resource failures, node failures, etc.

FAILOVER

If a resource fails, the Resource Manager attempts to restart the resource in the current node where the resource was operational prior to failure. If the restart attempt does not succeed, the Resource Manager invokes the Failover Manager, which moves the resource (and the group to which the resource belongs) to an available node in the cluster.

If an entire node fails, the Resource Manager moves all resource groups from the failing to an available node.

When all resources and groups have been successfully transferred, all remaining active cluster members update their cluster databases to reflect the new state of the cluster.

FAILOVER PROCESS OVERVIEW

Let us take the cluster example introduced in Chapter 2. Let us say that the administrator has set up so that group 3 failover to node 1 occurs in the case of node 2 failure and group 4 does not failover as shown in Figure 1.

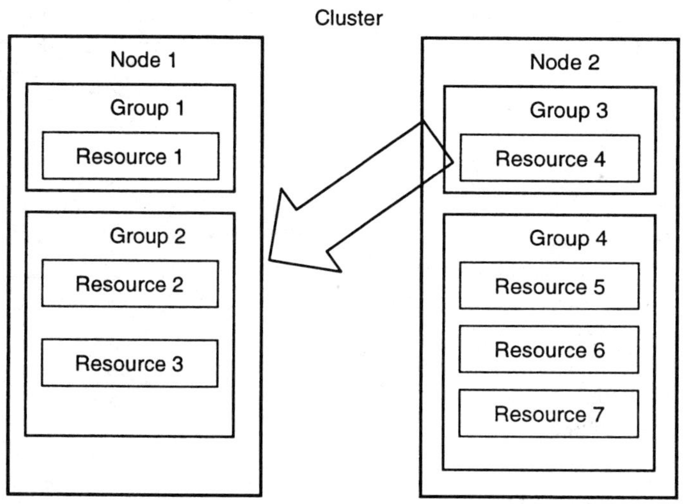

FIGURE 1 Failover of group 3 from node 2 to node 1.

After the failover process is complete, the relationship between cluster, nodes, groups, and resources is shown in Figure 2.

FAILOVER PROCESS FLOW DIAGRAM

An overview of the failover process is shown in Figure 3. Failover is automatic and no manual intervention is required.

FAILOVER FROM THE SERVER PERSPECTIVE

The following is a quick overview of one possible sequence of events when a server A fails and server B takes over:

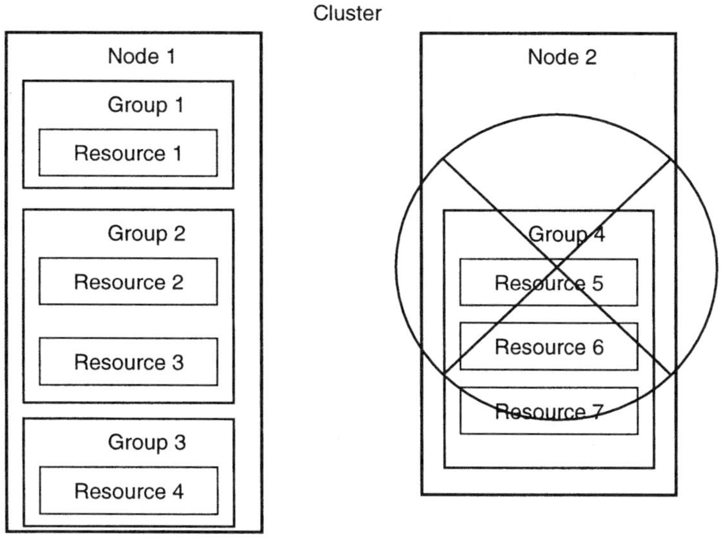

FIGURE 2 Relationship between cluster, nodes, groups, and resources.

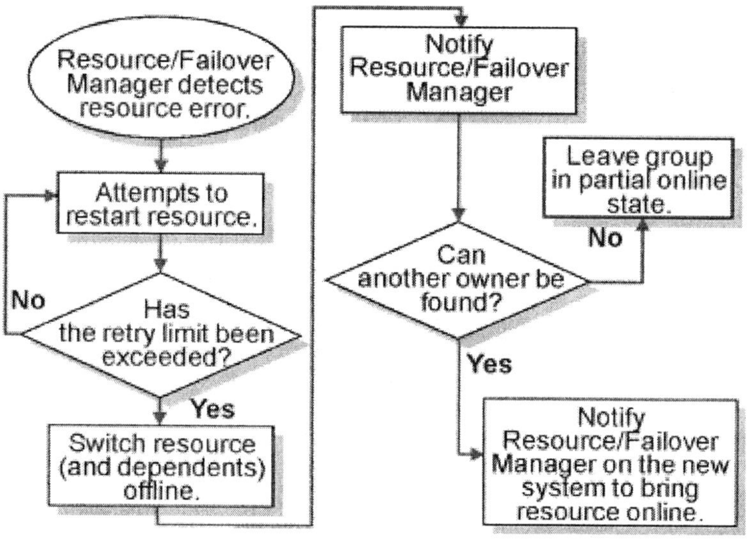

FIGURE 3 Overview of failover process steps. (Reprinted with permission from Microsoft.)

1. Server B does not receive a status message (heartbeat) from server A within a specified time interval (default is 30 s).
2. Server B starts failover.
3. Server B informs users of server A of failure.
4. Windows NT file server is dismounted.
5. Disks are taken offline.
6. Server B takes control of Small Computer System Interface (SCSI) bus and disks.
7. Windows NT file server is remounted.

8. Resource recovery including application recovery occurs. Resource recovery involves pushing and pulling groups (pushing and pulling are discussed later). Application recovery scripts are executed. If an application or service stores volatile information in specific registry keys, then the application or service registry information can be carried over to the new server as part of failover. Registry recovery is a configurable feature that is available to the generic application and generic service resource types. Applications restart using the same physical disks that were used by server A and restart using the last known application state information.
9. Database recovery is performed.
10. Server A users are reconnected to server B, automatically or manually.
11. Some users are reconnected to the applications on which they were working and other users need to log back on. This may happen to ensure security and some applications are designed to require the user to log back on if the client to server connection is broken.

Tip: Note that any state information other than the information stored in the registry must be managed and restored by the application itself (because the application is restarted on the new server).

Pushing a Group

When the Resource/Failover Manager is notified that one of its online resources has become unavailable, depending on the failover settings, it may choose not to restart the resource and instead take the resource offline along with any dependent resources. After the resource is taken offline, a failover is initiated, and then the group of resources are pushed to another node in the cluster. This is referred to as pushing a group to another node.

The steps that occur when pushing a group are as follows:

1. All resource objects in the failed resource dependency tree are enumerated, including all resources that depend on the failed resource and the resources on which the failed resource depend.
2. The Resource/Failover Manager takes all resources in the dependency tree offline. The resources are taken offline based on their dependencies, sequentially and synchronously.
3. Failover is initiated. The Resource/Failover Manager on the node that previously owned the resource notifies the Resource/Failover Manager on the destination node. The destination node is notified that a failover is occurring.
4. The destination Resource/Failover Manager begins to bring the resources online, in the opposite order from which they were taken offline.

Failover from the Client Perspective

The client may have a stateless connection with a cluster server (such as a regular Web browser client accessing a Web server) or the client may have had a connection that included state information (as in many business client server applications). In addition, the client may have been actively communicating with the server while the failure occurred or may have been between communications. The consequences at the client side of a failover depend on the type of connection and whether or not it was actively communicating at the time of failure as summarized in Table 1.

Other Failover Considerations

The administrator can set failover and failback policies and MSCS uses the policies in performing failover and failback. For example, the administrator can set a failover threshold and failover period.

TABLE 1
Failover at the Client

State Information Usage	Actively Communicating	Not Actively Communicating
Client not using state information	User may see a standard error message indicating that a failure occurred; simple retry reestablishes communications with a new node in the cluster	Failure is transparent; a new node in the cluster handles the next client communication
Client using state information	User may need to log back on; the transaction being performed when failure occurred may need to be recovered or reentered	User may need to log back on; automated logging back on using cached data may be possible in some instances

Failover threshold is the number of times the group can fail (within the number of hours specified by the failover period) and MSCS attempts to bring the group back online. When the threshold is exceeded within the failover period, MSCS stops attempting to bring the group back online. Even though the group itself is online, the resources within the group may be online, because MSCS attempts to leave the resources in their current state when dealing with the group. Resources also have threshold and period values as groups.

Typically, the failover process is underway within 5 s and applications are available within 30 s of a node failure. Note that the application availability depends on the application restart time, which varies by application.

Tip: MSCS uses a shared SCSI bus for shared storage. Some SCSI host adapters may provide termination only while a computer has power. When a cluster node with such a SCSI adapter is powered off, termination may be lost. If the shared SCSI bus loses termination, the surviving node may not have access to the shared SCSI devices. This situation may also happen when a standard SCSI terminator is used with a Wide SCSI bus because the standard terminator may not terminate the high bits on the wide SCSI bus.

Failover Times

The time interval required to bring a resource online on another node after the node in which the resource is running fails depends on the following factors:

- Type of resource
- Resource properties
- Group properties
- Dependent resources
- Other factors

Let us look at the factors in more detail.

Type of Resource

The amount of time a resource takes to come online depends on the amount of work the resource has to do as part of its initialization. A resource such as an Internet Protocol (IP) address may come online quickly, while a resource such as a database server or a network name may take several seconds. The database may check integrity of data files as part of its initialization. A network name needs time to be registered on the network and to check for duplicate network names.

Resource Properties

Resources may be configured to stay offline after a specified number of failures. They may also be restricted from running on specific nodes within the cluster. You can use Cluster Administrator to modify these properties.

Group Properties

Groups may have a preferred owner and may be configured to failback automatically if the preferred owner node is available. Groups may be configured not to failback to another node or to failback only during a specific time window.

Resource Dependencies

Resources may also be dependent on other resources in their group. The dependent resources may not come online until the resources they depend on have come online.

Other Factors

If a node fails, surviving cluster nodes must arbitrate for access to the quorum disk resource. The time required for quorum disk arbitration depends on the performance of hardware and attached devices on the shared SCSI bus. Hardware and network performance can impact the times of a number of resource functions including startup and failover time requirements.

FAILBACK

When a node has failed and then comes back online, the Resource/Failover Manager on the returning node initiates any configured failbacks. Contacting the Resource/Failover Manager on the node that currently has the resources online does this.

There is a failback option that can be configured to control the time of day during which failback can occur. If a failback window has been configured, the Resource/Failover Manager waits for the designated time before initiating failback.

Failback Process Overview

When node 2 is back online, MSCS follows the failback process to restore the configuration. By assuming that the administrator has specified that group 2 should be failed back to node 2, the cluster configuration after failback is as shown in Figure 4.

Failover Process Flow Diagram

An overview of the failover process is shown in Figure 5.

Failback from the Server Perspective

The following is a quick overview of one possible sequence of events when server A recovers from its failure and server B relinquishes the load it had taken over from server A. Failback, like failover, is automatic and no manual intervention is required.

1. Server A boots and as part of the boot-up procedure brings up MSCS automatically.
2. MSCS checks the network to locate server B.
3. Server A rejoins the cluster.

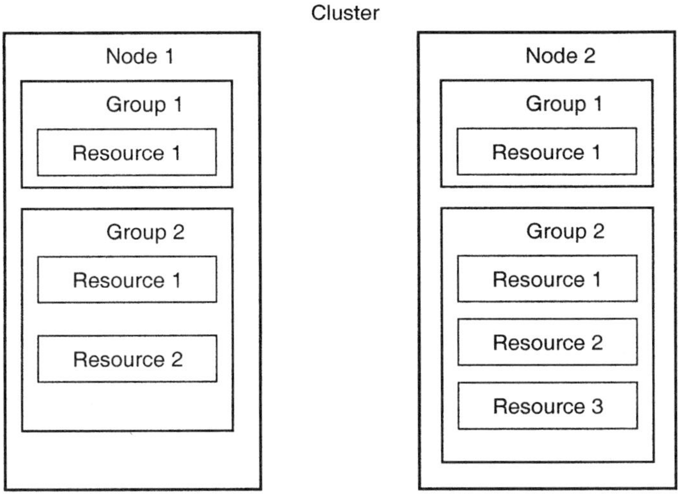

FIGURE 4 Cluster configuration after failback.

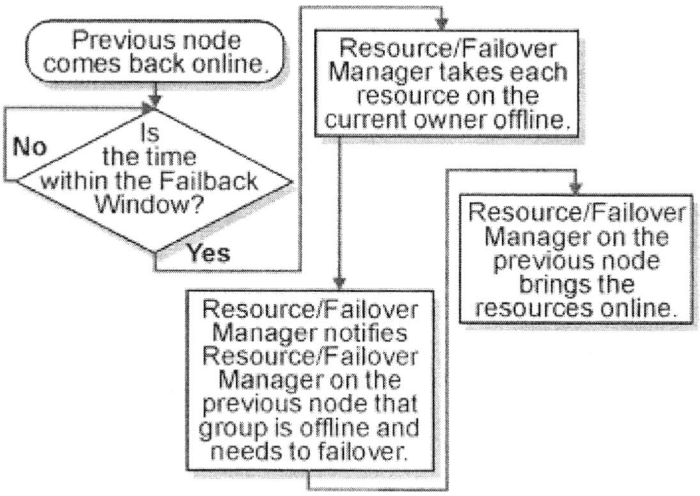

FIGURE 5 Overview of failback process steps. (Reprinted with permission from Microsoft.)

4. Server B updates server A with current cluster status information.
5. Server A then initiates failback procedures to move back failed-over workload from server B back to itself. Server A follows the administrator's set up in deciding which groups should be failed back.

Tip: When setting up a group for file share, a disk resource must be included in the group because the file share is dependent on the disk. In addition, the administrator should also include a network name resource to access the file share, instead of the cluster name of the group containing the file share and disk resource. This ensures that if a failover occurs for the disk and file share group, but not the cluster name group, users still are able to gain access to the file share.

Pulling a Group

When a cluster node fails, the resources on the failed node must be pulled from the failed node to the surviving node. This is referred to as pulling a group. This process is very similar to pushing a group, with the exception of not having any resources to take offline because the node failed.

CONCLUSION

It is important to note that while MSCS can significantly reduce planned and unplanned downtime, it is not a guarantee for zero downtime. The cluster is not available under the following conditions:

- Both (or all) the servers in a cluster require maintenance at the same time. This condition may be due to a very short time window available for maintenance and performing maintenance on one server at a time does not complete maintenance within the available window.
- There is a window (usually very small) when MSCS switches failed resources from one server to another. Switching a failed application to another server may not start until MSCS attempts to restart the failed application on the same server multiple times (the number of attempts is specified by the administrator).
- Some applications require that data created by a prior version of the application be converted to a new format before installing the later version of the application. Conversion of existing application data typically requires that the application is not running. Such instances make the application unavailable to clients, whether the application runs in a clustered environment or not.
- Irrecoverable failures of disk, power, or major natural disasters occur.

6 Microsoft Cluster Server Communications

INTRODUCTION

Microsoft Cluster Service (MSCS) takes advantage of much of the networking inherent in Windows NT Server, Enterprise Edition. It is crucial that certain specific features are configured correctly if your deployment of MSCS is to be successful. In an MSCS cluster, Windows NT networking is used for both node-to-node communication and client-to-cluster communication.

MSCS COMMUNICATION BASICS

The basic components of any communication are protocols and addressing or name resolution. Let us look at protocols and name resolution in more detail.

PROTOCOLS

MSCS requires and supports only one protocol suite — Transmission Control Protocol/Internet Protocol (TCP/IP) suite for all its internal and client communications. TCP/IP is an industry-standard suite of protocols, providing communications in a heterogeneous environment. TCP/IP is the most common protocol used for access to the Internet and Internet resources, where a variety of computer systems are involved. This feature also makes TCP/IP very well suited as an enterprise networking protocol because it provides interoperability between different types of computer systems.

NAME RESOLUTION

Cluster clients use name resolution services to find cluster resources (just as clients in Windows NT networking use the name resoultion services to find resources in a Windows NT network). MSCS also uses these services when a node joins another node to form a cluster.

Name resolution is the process of translating computer names that can be set up by users and are user friendly to IP addresses (which are sets of numbers). For name resolution, you can use the Windows Internet Name Service (WINS), the Domain Name System (DNS), or both.* There is another option - use of IP broadcast name resolution. However, you should avoid IP broadcast name resolution whenever possible, since IP broadcasts increase network traffic and are ineffective in routed networks.

MSCS does not require any special configuration of either WINS or DNS. If you use WINS, all cluster resource names that have associated IP addresses are registered with WINS. If you use DNS, you can specify pertinent DNS record entries for the cluster resources. In general, you should treat each cluster group as a separate entity and manage names and addresses accordingly.

NODE-TO-NODE COMMUNICATION

MSCS handles communication between nodes using the underlying communication support available through Windows NT network services. MSCS secures all node-to-node communications using built-in Windows NT security services.

Nodes in a cluster communicate using their Cluster Services. The Cluster Service keeps track of the current state of the nodes within a cluster and determines when a group and its resources should failover to an alternate node. Typically, node-to-node communications are the highest when a cluster is forming, when failover occurs, and whenever configuration changes are made to the cluster. During cluster formation, node-to-node communication occurs for the purpose of synchronizing the cluster databases that reside on each node (the cluster database stores configuration information about the cluster resources).

During the normal operation of a cluster, communications occur between the nodes of a cluster to detect node failures and status changes, and to manage the cluster as a single entity. This communication takes the form of messages (called heartbeats) that are sent regularly between the Cluster Services of the two nodes. In general, the network overhead required during normal operations is very small compared with the data traffic between nodes. Communication sessions can be multiplexed over multiple networks to eliminate a single point of failure.

There are three methods used for communication between the nodes of a cluster:

- Remote procedure calls (RPCs) between the Cluster Server service on each node
- Cluster heartbeats
- Quorum resource

Let us look at each of these communication methods.

REMOTE PROCEDURE CALLS

When both nodes in the cluster are running, the Cluster Server service uses RPCs for communication between nodes. The RPC communication happens much like the communication between other Windows NT services. For example, when a group or resource is deleted on one node, RPC is used to communicate the change to the other node in the cluster. When both nodes are not running, the

---

* This book presumes that you are familiar with WINS and DNS and does not go into detail about these services except for the following brief summary.

WINS is a NetBIOS name service used to translate computer names to IP addresses. WINS significantly reduces the number of IP broadcasts that are used by Microsoft network clients. If a client needs to resolve a name to an IP address, the client sends a packet to the WINS server, requesting the corresponding IP address. WINS keeps a database of all the IP addresses on your network, each of which is mapped to a unique NetBIOS name.

Client computers that use WINS are configured with one or more IP addresses of WINS servers. When a client starts up, it communicates directly with a WINS server and registers its computer name and corresponding IP address. When a WINS client needs to resolve a computer name to an IP address, the WINS client sends a request to the WINS server for the IP address of the computer name being used.

DNS works similarly to WINS and is another option for maintaining IP address databases on your network. Unlike WINS, DNS resolves host names to IP addresses. These names are organized hierarchically instead of equally on levels, as in WINS. DNS name registration is static and must be done manually, unlike WINS registration, which is done dynamically and automatically.

In Windows NT, the Microsoft implementation of DNS is tightly integrated with WINS. This allows non-WINS clients to resolve NetBIOS names by querying a DNS server. Administrators can safely remove any static entries for Microsoft-based clients in legacy DNS server-zone files in favor of the dynamic WINS–DNS integration. However, the major difference between WINS and DNS is that while WINS supports the Dynamic Host Configuration Protocol (DHCP), DNS does not. MSCS does not support the use of IP addresses assigned from a DHCP server for the cluster administration address, the address associated with the cluster name, or any IP address resources. However, you can use either static IP addresses or static IP addresses assigned from a DHCP server for the Windows NT network configuration on each node.

existing node then uses the quorum resource to store any changes for later communication to the other node.

Cluster Heartbeats

Each node in a cluster periodically exchanges datagrams with the other node in the cluster to determine if both nodes are up and running correctly. This process is referred to as sending heartbeats. If a node does not respond to the heartbeat, the node is seen as having failed.

The first node of the cluster to come online is the node that is responsible for sending out the heartbeats. The first node starts sending the heartbeats when it is notified that the second node has come online. The second node must respond to each heartbeat.

The first node sends heartbeats approximately every 0.5 s. The second node will typically responds to each heartbeat within 0.2 s. Each of these heartbeat datagrams is 82 bytes in size.

Use of Heartbeats to Determine Node Failure

How heartbeats are used to determine the failure of a node depends on which node has failed.

When the Second Node to Come Online Fails

If the second node of the cluster to come online fails, the first node to come online sends 18 heartbeats after the last response from the second node. If no response is received from any of these heartbeats, it is determined that the second node has failed. The timing of the heartbeats is as follows:

1. Four heartbeats at approximately 0.7-s intervals
2. Three heartbeats within the next approximately 0.75 s
3. Two heartbeats at approximately 0.3-s intervals
4. Five heartbeats within the next approximately 0.9 s
5. Two heartbeats at approximately 0.3-s intervals
6. Two heartbeats approximately 0.3 s later

As a result, it takes approximately 5.3 s for the first node to determine that the second node has failed.

When the First Node to Come Online Fails

If the first node of the cluster to come online fails, the second node to come online starts the process defined in the preceding section when it has not received a heartbeat within approximately 0.7 s.

Communication Using the Quorum Resource

A quorum resource is a resource that stores cluster management data and is accessible by all nodes of the cluster. Cluster Server currently only supports NT File System (NTFS) formatted SCSI drives as the quorum resource.

The cluster management data stored on the quorum resource consist of a log of cluster configuration changes, which is called the quorum log. The quorum log, quolog.log, is stored by default in the \MSCS folder on the quorum resource. By default, the maximum size for the quorum log is 64 KB.

There is a log of cluster configuration changes on the quorum resource because it is possible that both nodes may not be online at the same time. For example, node B is offline and an administrator makes cluster configuration changes on node A. If node A then goes offline and node B comes back online, node B would be unaware of the configuration changes without the log on the quorum resource. Therefore, node B would bring the cluster online using the old configuration state. Because the log exists on the quorum resource, the node checks the log for any configuration changes before the cluster is brought online.

When all nodes have processed the changes they need from the change log, the entries are removed from the log.

Verifying Quorum Resource Access

Use Windows NT Explorer to verify that a node can access the quorum resource. The node that currently has the group containing the quorum resource should have the drive letter of the resource listed in Windows NT Explorer and the user should be able to access the drive. If the drive is not listed or cannot be accessed, the Small Computer System Interface (SCSI) cabling and termination should be examined for problems.

CLUSTER-TO-CLIENT COMMUNICATION

Clients typically access network applications and resources through network names and IP addresses. When these network applications and resources are hosted within an MSCS cluster, clients can continue to find and access the resources, even though they may move between nodes. MSCS enables this by the failover of both the IP address and network name for a given resource.

Figure 1 illustrates the Cluster Service involvement in client communications.

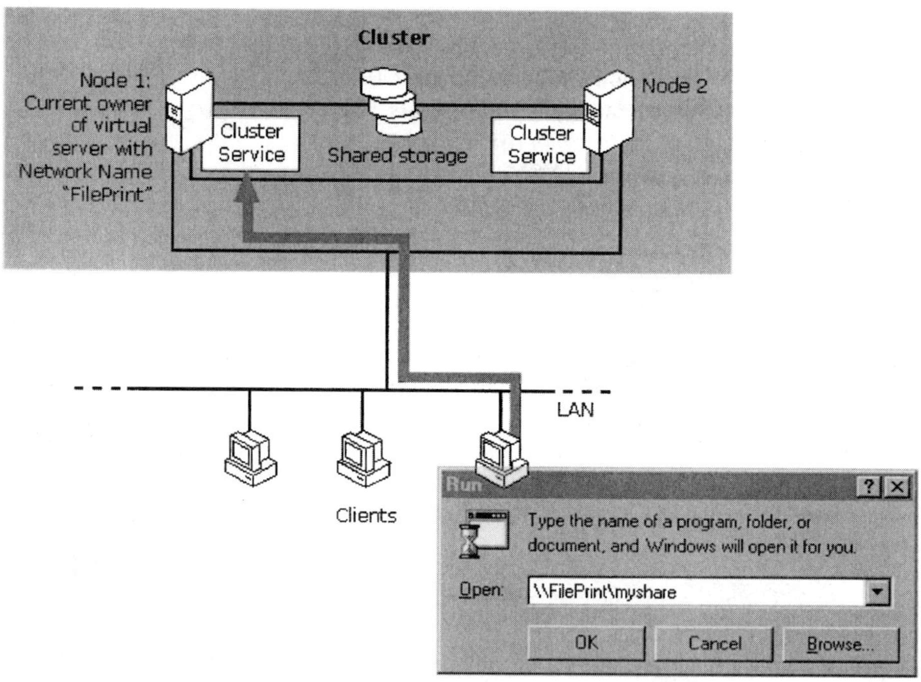

FIGURE 1 Role of Cluster Service in cluster communications. (Reprinted with permission from Microsoft.)

CLUSTER SERVICE AND RESOURCES COMMUNICATION

The Cluster Service communicates with resources through the clustering software component known as the Resource Monitor. The Resource Monitor controls and monitors cluster resources, and reports any changes in the resources to the Cluster Service. Because there is a separate Cluster

Service and one or more Resource Monitors on each node, this communication takes place in the form of interprocess communications (IPC) and has no direct effect on the network.

The Resource Monitor accepts requests from the Cluster Service and forwards those requests to the cluster resource dynamic library links (DLLs). When a resource detects a change in its state, it reports that change when polled by the Resource Monitor, which then forwards the report to the Cluster Service.

You can control how often the Resource Monitor communicates with resources by setting the "IsAlive" and "LooksAlive" polling intervals using Cluster Administrator. For more information on setting polling intervals using Cluster Administrator, see the section on setting advanced resource properties in Chapter 9.

By default, MSCS uses the Resource Monitor for all resources on a node. If a problematic resource causes a Resource Monitor to stop responding, you can run that resource in a separate Resource Monitor. Because each Resource Monitor runs as a separate process, this isolates the problematic resource.

CLUSTER SERVICE AND APPLICATIONS COMMUNICATION

Figure 2 shows the communications between the Cluster Service and applications (cluster aware and cluster unaware). Cluster management applications, such as Cluster Administrator, communicate with the Cluster Service through the standard applications programming interface (Cluster application programming interface [APIs]). Cluster management applications access the Cluster Service using RPC communication over the TCP/IP. Cluster management applications are examples of cluster-aware applications.

The Cluster Service also uses an API set to communicate with cluster resources. Cluster Service communicates with Resource Monitors. Resource Monitors use the Resource APIs to communicate with Resource DLLs. To connect to a cluster from an application, you can specify any network name in the cluster for which there is an associated IP address resource (assuming the network name and IP address resources are online).

Tip: Although clients can access cluster resources through node names instead of the cluster name, this should be avoided whenever possible. This is because the node name of a resource may become unavailable if the node becomes unavailable, or the resource moves to the other node.

Figure 2 illustrates how applications (whether MSCS aware or MSCS unaware) and the Cluster Administrator communicate with a cluster.

VIRTUAL INTERFACE ARCHITECTURE SPECIFICATION

Compaq, Intel, and Microsoft announced the Virtual Interface (VI) Architecture Specification, version 1.0, in December 1997. The VI Architecture version 1.0 specification is available at http://www.viarch.org/.

With input and participation from more than 100 companies, VI 1.0 intends to provide open, flexible, and highly scalable Clustered Server solutions. The specification hopes to take clustering to the next level of performance and enable a new class of scalable cluster products that offer high performance with broad applicability. A system area nework (SAN) is a specialized network optimized for the reliability and performance requirements of clusters.

The VI Architecture Specification aims to provide software and hardware specifications for an industry-standard high-speed cluster communication interface. The VI Architecture aims to improve the performance of distributed applications by reducing the latency associated with critical message-passing operations. The VI Architecture Specification is media, processor, and operating system

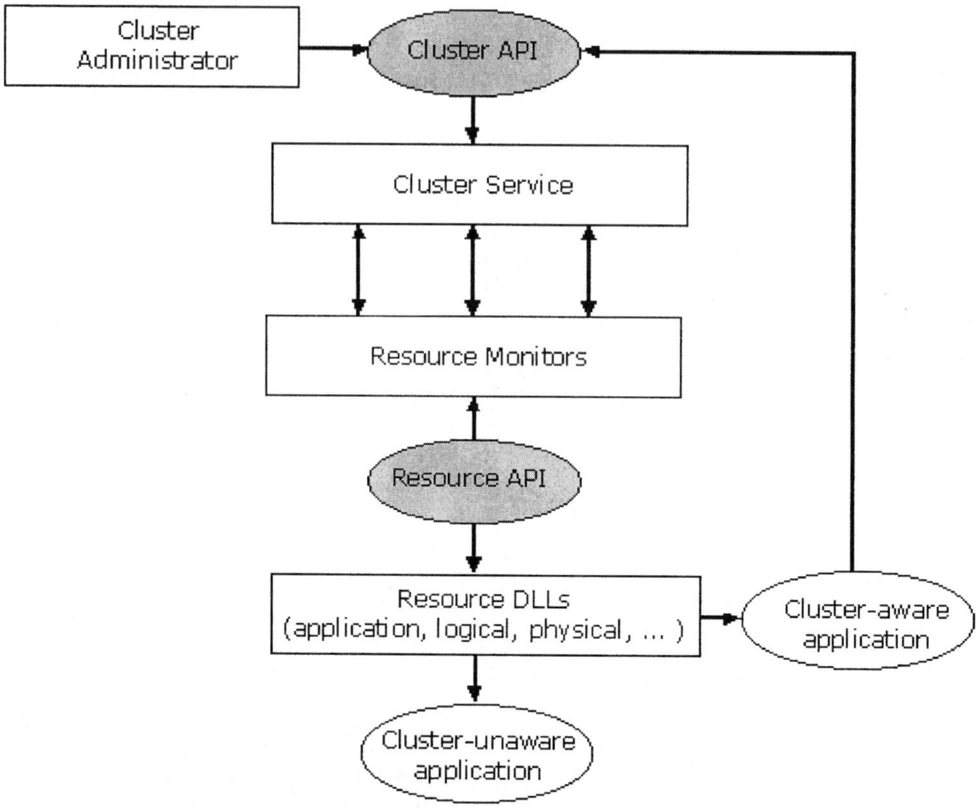

FIGURE 2 Cluster Administrator and cluster applications communication. (Reprinted with permission from Microsoft.)

independent. The specification includes software and hardware interfaces. The software interface supports a variety of programming models to simplify development while ensuring performance. The hardware interface aims to be compatible with industry-standard networking protocols such as asynchronous transfer mode (ATM), Ethernet, and Fibre Channel, as well as specialized SAN products (see SAN later) available from a variety of vendors. The VI Architecture allows for full optimization to the underlying hardware capability without trade-off in platform independence.

This specification aims to serve as the basis for the SAN, a specialized network optimized for the reliability and performance required by clusters. Expected products based on the VI Architecture Specification include high-performance SAN interface cards; high-speed, scalable switches for these SANs; and database products.

NAMING SCENARIOS

Scenario One

A cluster must be set up for the following:

- Two database shares set up for static load balancing
- Two file and print shares in node 1 (without failover ability)
- One cluster-unaware application on node 2

The network names and IP addresses required for this scenario are

1. A computer name and IP address for node 1
2. A computer name and IP address for node 2
3. A network name and IP address for the cluster
4. A network name and IP address for database group 1
5. A network name and IP address for database group 2
6. A network name and IP address for the file/print accounting group
7. A network name and IP address for the file/print engineering group

Scenario Two

A cluster must be set up for the following:

- Two file/print groups, one on node 1 and the other on node 2
- Both file/print groups that are active normally (static load balancing)
- Resources that must failover when a node fails

The network names and IP addresses required for this scenario are

1. A computer name and IP address for node 1
2. A computer name and IP address for node 2
3. A network name and IP address for the cluster
4. A network name and IP address for the file/print group 1
5. A network name and IP address for the file/print group 2

Scenario Three

A cluster must be set up for

- Running a mission-critical service on a node
- Node that should failover if the node fails
- Availability that is critical (critical availability of a mission-critical service suggesting hot standby configuration)

The network names and IP addresses required for this scenario are

1. A computer name and IP address for node 1
2. A computer name and IP address for node 2
3. A network name and IP address for the cluster
4. A network name and IP address for the group containing the mission-critical service

TROUBLESHOOTING COMMUNICATION PROBLEMS

There are a number of communication problems that can occur in the set up and operation of a cluster. Some important ones follow.

One — The resources failed over, but the nodes do not detect each other. This problem typically occurs when there is no connectivity between the nodes or with the shared SCSI device. On each node, use Services in Control Panel to confirm that the RPC service is running and to verify that the two nodes have RPC connectivity. You can verify RPC connectivity using a network analyzer, such as Network Monitor, or by using RPC Ping (which is available on the Microsoft Exchange Server CD).

Two — Second node cannot join the cluster. This situation is typically caused by improper name resolution. The problem may be due to having invalid data in the WINS cache or having the wrong binding on the WINS or DNS server for the second node. Ensure that WINS or DNS is functioning correctly on both nodes. Check the proper cluster name, node name, or IP address. Check that the cluster name resource started by using the Cluster Administrator on the first node. Check that the Cluster Service is running on the first node and that all resources within the cluster group are online before installing the second node. Ensure that TCP/IP is properly configured on both nodes, including IP connectivity to the cluster address and that the IP address is assigned to the correct adapter. If your cluster nodes use DHCP to obtain noncluster IP addresses, use **Ipconfig.exe** to verify that you have a valid primary IP address for the adapters. Your primary address is invalid if the second IP address listed is 0.0.0.0.

Three — Clients cannot connect to virtual servers. Clients may be accessing the cluster using the network name or IP address. If your clients are using network name, you can verify proper name resolution by checking the NetBT cache. You can check the NetBT cache using the Nbtstat.exe utility and determine whether or not the name had been previously resolved. If your clients are using IP addresses, follow these steps:

- Verify physical connectivity between the clients and cluster node, and between the two nodes, by pinging the group IP address from all clients and cluster nodes.
- Verify the appropriate name-resolution mechanism (WINS/DNS) by pinging the virtual server network name from each client and cluster node.
- If the virtual server has a file share resource, try to connect to the resource using **net use**.
- If you are able to connect to the file share resource, but with the wrong IP address, use **nbtstat** to display NETBIOS name registrations for the IP address you specify.
- Finally, verify the TCP/IP configuration for all adapters using **ipconfig /all**.

Four — A node has lost connectivity with the network. A node may lose connectivity due to disruptions in the physical connections. Check the hub and local cabling, both to the network and to the SCSI device. At times, the static IP addresses being used by MSCS may inadvertently be used by other resources on the network. Right-click Network Neighborhood, click **Properties**, and confirm that the configuration settings on the **Protocol** and **Services** tabs are correct.

Five — Clients cannot access a cluster resource. Ping the IP addresses of the virtual server and individual nodes to ensure that the IP address resource or network name resource for the group in which the resource is contained is online. Also ensure that the resource to be accessed is dependent on either the IP address or the network name resource. Sometimes, the client may be attempting to access the cluster from a different subnet, and DNS may not be correctly configured. Make sure that the cluster has a DNS address record in the DNS database. Finally, make sure that the cluster nodes are configured properly for name resolution using either WINS or DNS, and that clients are configured to use the same form of name resolution.

Six — A resource fails, but is not brought back online. The common causes for this problem are

- The resource is not set to restart after failure. In the resource **Policies** dialog box, make sure that **Don't restart** is not selected.
- Resource dependencies prevent the restart of the resource. If the resource needs another resource to function, the second resource may have failed. Ensure that dependent resources have been restarted.

Seven — A group cannot be moved or failed over to the other node. If a group does not failover as expected or if you are unable to manually move the group, check to ensure that

- The other node is designated as a possible owner for all resources by checking the ownership configuration in the group resource **Properties** dialog box.
- The resource property **Restart and affect the group** is selected. When a resource fails multiple times but does not failover, check the **Restart Threshold** and **Restart Period** settings.

Eight — A group failed over but did not fail back. The common causes for this problem and the appropriate solutions are

- Make sure that the group is not prevented from failing back by ensuring that the **Prevent failback** is not selected in the group Properties dialog box.
- If **Failback immediately** is selected, be sure to wait long enough for the group to failback.
- Groups failover as a whole and it is possible that when one resource in the group is prevented from failing back the entire group does not failback. Check the settings of all affected resources within a group.
- The node to which you want the group to failback must be configured as the preferred owner of the group. If it is not, MSCS leaves the groups on the node to which they failed over.

7 Cluster Programming Basics

While there are some benefits in running regular applications in Windows NT clusters, the true benefits of clusters are realized only when you develop applications that are aware of clusters and take advantage of benefits offered by clusters.

Microsoft provides a number of products and tools to assist you in the development of Windows applications including cluster applications. These products and tools include

- Cluster Server
- Cluster Server SDK
- Visual C++ and Visual Basic
- Microsoft Development Network (MSDN)

This book covers all aspects of the Cluster Server. This chapter focuses on cluster-related programming. The next chapter covers the Cluster Server SDK, how to install the SDK, and the steps involved in developing cluster-related applications using the SDK. The other chapters of the book discuss other aspects such as installation and administration. This book does not address programming using Visual C++ or Visual Basic and presumes that you are already familiar with programming Windows applications using Win32 application programming interfaces (APIs), Visual C++, MFC, SDKs, etc. If you are not familiar with programming Windows applications, I recommend my book *Advanced Windows NT Programming*, ISBN 0-07-882357-9, 1997. The MSDN is a subscription service for developers available from Microsoft.

CLUSTER PROGRAMMING CONCEPTS

There are a number of cluster-related programming concepts that you should be familiar with to develop applications and dynamic link libraries (DLLs) for clusters. These include

- APIs
- Cluster control codes
- Cluster properties
- Resource DLLs
- Cluster utility functions

Let us look at each of these concepts in more detail.

APPLICATION PROGRAMMING INTERFACES

The basis for developing Windows applications is the Win32 APIs. With the advent of Microsoft Cluster Server (MSCS), Microsoft has added a number of APIs especially for cluster programming. These include

- Cluster APIs
- Cluster Administration Extensions APIs
- Resource APIs

Let us take a look at each of these APIs.

Cluster Application Programming Interfaces

You can develop a Windows NT cluster-aware client or server application or a DLL using the Windows NT Cluster APIs. The Cluster APIs include functions to access and manage a cluster as a single entity. The Cluster APIs also include functions to manage the nodes, groups, and resources of the cluster and the cluster database. Support for Cluster APIs is implemented in the Cluster Service. Cluster APIs are also used to develop cluster management applications and resource DLLs. A complete list of the Cluster APIs and details about each API can be found in Appendix C.

Figure 1 shows the interaction of Cluster APIs, the Cluster Service, Cluster Management applications, and cluster-aware applications. As shown in Figure 1, the primary interface mechanism between cluster applications and the Cluster Service is the Cluster API DLL.

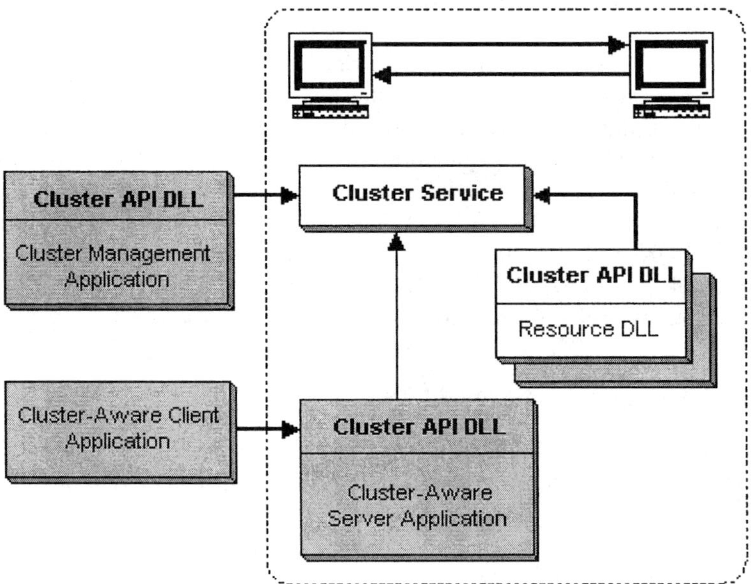

FIGURE 1 Cluster API, Cluster Service, and Cluster Application Interaction. (Reproduced with permission from Microsoft.)

Cluster APIs can be categorized into seven categories based on the function of the APIs as summarized Table 1.

Cluster APIs are also used by the Cluster Administrator and by Resource Monitors.

Cluster Administrator Extension Application Programming Interfaces

The Cluster Administrator Extension API is used for the development of Cluster Administrator Extension DLLs. Cluster Administrator Extension DLLs help administer new custom resource

TABLE 1
Cluster API Categories and Purpose

Category	Purpose
Cluster management	Provides access to event notification, cluster objects, and overall cluster state information
Group management	Provides access to each of the groups in a cluster and allows callers to change a group's membership or state and retrieve information; these functions are implemented primarily by the Cluster Service Resource and Failover Managers
Network interface management	Opens and closes the network interface, performs selected operations, and retrieves information
Cluster database management	Allows a resource DLL to access and update the cluster database; only the Cluster Service, resource DLLs, and applications controlled by resource DLLs should use the Cluster Database Management APIs
Network management	Provides access to information about networks that are monitored by the Cluster Service
Node management	Allows callers to change a node's state, perform operations, and retrieve information; the Membership Manager is the prime user of these functions
Resource management	Allows callers to perform a variety of operations on one or more resources, including retrieval of dependency information, creation and deletion of resources, and initiation of operations defined by resource control codes

types. The Cluster Administrator handles the administration functions of standard resource types and developers of new custom resource types are expected to provide the administration functions for the new resource types. The Cluster Administrator Extension APIs permit the development of Cluster Administrator Extension DLLs with an user interface that is consistent with the user interface of the Cluster Administrator for standard resource types. Implementing a Cluster Administrator Extension DLL enables all resource types to be administered with a consistent, graphic interface, and to ensure this consistency Cluster Server requires that developers implementing a resource DLL should also implement a Cluster Administrator Extension DLL.

Cluster Administrator Extension API consists of interfaces based on the Component Object Model (COM). While most of these interfaces are implemented by Cluster Administrator and called by an extension, there are a few interfaces that are implemented by the extension directly. The interfaces are defined in the CLUADMEX.IDL and the CLUADMEX.H header files. A Cluster Administrator Extension DLL is implemented as an in-process server that provides a service. An in-process server provides a service, such as a property page that displays resource properties, to clients with a specific set of COM interfaces. These interfaces are made available through objects represented by unique identifiers called class identifiers (CLSID). In-process servers include these CLSIDs in the system registry to enable them to be recognized by the clients that require their services.

Cluster Administrator Extensions can be created with or without the Resource Type AppWizard that is part of the Microsoft Developer Studio. Using the Resource Type AppWizard saves time and effort by producing a Cluster Administrator Extension that is complete and fully operational. For more information about using the Resource Type AppWizard to generate a Cluster Administrator Extension, see Using the Resource Type AppWizard.

The Cluster Administrator Extension created by the Resource Type AppWizard relies on the ActiveX Template Library (ATL) version 1.1. Developers creating Cluster Administrator Extensions without using the AppWizard can base their extensions on ATL classes or classes from an alternate class library, or implement their classes without a library. Using ATL is recommended because it is an effective way to implement a Cluster Administrator Extension.

Cluster Administration Extension Interfaces

Table 2 describes each of the extension interfaces

TABLE 2
Cluster Administrator Extension Interfaces and Descriptions

Interface	Description
IGetClusterDataInfo	Retrieves information about a cluster
IGetClusterGroupInfo	Retrieves information about a group
IGetClusterNodeInfo	Retrieves information about a node
IGetClusterObjectInfo	Retrieves information about a cluster object
IGetClusterResourceInfo	Retrieves information about a resource
IGetClusterUIInfo	Retrieves information about Cluster Administrator user interface
IWCContextMenuCallback	Adds menu items to Cluster Administrator context menu
IWCPropertySheetCallback	Adds property sheets to Cluster Administrator property pages
IWCWizardCallback	Adds a property page to Cluster Administrator Create Group or Create Resource and manages navigation
IWEExtendContextMenu	Enhances a Cluster Administrator context menu
IWEExtendPropertySheet	Enhances a Cluster Administrator property sheet
IWEExtendWizard	Enhances Cluster Administrator Create Group or Create Resource wizard
IWEInvokeCommand	Performs commands associated with items added to Cluster Administrator context menus

Cluster Administrator Extension Registration Functions

Table 3 describes the Cluster Administrator Extension registration functions.

TABLE 3
Cluster Administrator Extension Registration Functions and Descriptions

Function	Description
DllRegisterCluAdminExtension	Registers a Cluster Administrator Extension DLL with the cluster by adding information to the cluster database
DllRegisterServer	Registers a Cluster Administrator Extension DLL with COM by adding information to the Microsoft Windows NT system registry
DllUnregisterCluAdminExtension	Cancels the registration of a Cluster Administrator Extension DLL with the cluster by removing information from the cluster database
DllUnregisterServer	Cancels the registration of a Cluster Administrator Extension DLL with COM by removing information from the Windows NT system registry

Resource APIs

Resource APIs, as the name suggests, are APIs that provide the means for the Cluster Service to interface with cluster resources. The resource API defines functions, structures, and macros that allow the Cluster Service to communicate with resources.

Figure 2 shows that the interaction between the Cluster Service and resources is indirect. The Cluster Service initiates requests with a Resource Monitor, and the Resource Monitor passes them on to the resource. Status and event information is passed back from the resource DLL to the

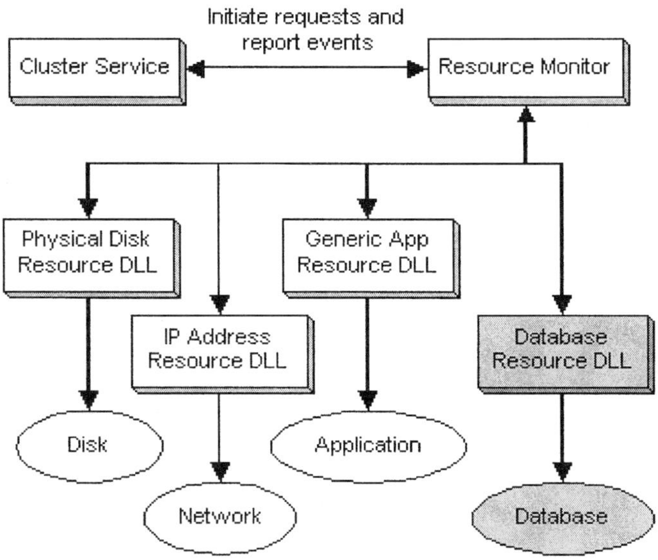

FIGURE 2 Resource API usage framework. (Reprinted with permission from Microsoft.)

Cluster Service. Note that there exists one resource DLL for each resource. The interface mechanism between the Resource monitor and the resource types are the same regardless of whether the resource type is a standard cluster resource type or a custom resource type. Figure 2 shows three standard cluster resource types (disk, network, and application) and one from a third party (database). The data flow between the Cluster Service and the resources is as follows. The Cluster Service sends requests for resources to the Resource Monitor, which in turn passes the requests on to the resource. The resource status and event information are passed back from the resource DLL to the Cluster Service.

The components of Resource APIs are

- Entry point functions
- Callback functions
- Structures and macros

Let us look at each of these components in more detail.

Entry Point Functions

Entry point functions allow a Resource Monitor to manage its resources. Table 4 lists the resource API entry point functions. As mentioned earlier, there exists a resource DLL for each resource and this DLL implements the entry point functions. Not all the entry point functions are mandatory for all resources. A resource DLL needs to implement only the entry point functions that are capable of being supported by the underlying resource.

Callback Functions

Callback functions allow a resource DLL to report status and to log events and allow the Cluster Service to request that a resource perform specific tasks. Table 5 lists the resource API callback functions.

TABLE 4
Resource API Entry Point Functions and Description

Entry point function	Description
Arbitrate	Enables a node to attempt to regain ownership of a quorum resource; this entry point function should be implemented only in resource DLLs that support the cluster quorum capable resources and should not be implemented in resource DLLs for other resources
Close	Closes a resource
IsAlive	Determines if a resource is available for use; a more rigorous check compared to LooksALive
LooksAlive	Determines if a resource appears to be available for use; a less rigorous check compared with IsALive
Offline	Marks a resource as unavailable for use after cleanup processing is completed
Online	Marks a resource as online and available for use
Open	Opens a resource; resource identifiers returned from this entry point function are used by all other entry points to identify the resource
Release	Releases a quorum resource from arbitration; this entry point function should be implemented only in resource DLLs that support the cluster quorum capable resources and should not be implemented in resource DLLs for other resources
ResourceControl	Performs a resource-related operation
ResourceTypeControl	Performs a resource-type-related operation
Startup	Loads a resource's resource DLL and returns a structure containing a function table and version number; this function table contains pointers to each of the entry point functions; all the other entry point functions are accessed through these function table pointers; startup itself is accessed through export
Terminate	Marks a resource as unavailable for use without waiting for cleanup processing to finish

TABLE 5
Resource API Callback Functions and Description

Callback function	Description
LogEvent	Logs an event for a resource; implemented by the Resource Monitor and invoked by the resource DLL to log the event in the cluster debugging log
QuorumResourceLost	Reports the loss of control of the quorum resource; implemented by the Resource Monitor in the **Arbitrate** entry point function and invoked by the resource DLL
ResourceCallback	Implemented by the resource DLL and invoked by the Cluster Service using the cluster utility function ResUtilEnumResources to enumerate resources
SetResourceStatus	Updates the status of a resource; is implemented by the Resource Monitor and invoked by the resource DLL to update resource status after the **Online** or **Offline** entry point function has returned ERROR_IO_PENDING; **SetResourceStatus** is similar to the **SetServiceStatus** function for Win32 services

*Tip: The **LogEvent** callback function does not write entries to the Windows NT event log. If you want to report events in the Windows NT event log in your resource DLL, call the Win32 function **ReportEvent**.*

Resource Application Programming Interface Structures and Macros

Resource API structures and macros are used to describe the function table that is returned by the Startup entry point function and the status of a resource. Table 6 lists the resource API structures.

TABLE 6
Resource API Structures and Descriptions

Resource API Structure	Description
CLRES_FUNCTION_TABLE	Structure that contains the version number of the resource API being used; this structure also contains pointers to all resource API entry points except **Startup**; resource DLLs that support multiple resource types must provide one function table for each resource type; the CLRES_FUNCTION_TABLE structure is defined in RESAPI.H.
CLRES_V1_FUNCTIONS	Structure that contains pointers to all resource entry points in the resource API except **Startup** for Resource API version 1.0; to create a function table for version 1.0 of the resource API, use the CLRES_V1_FUNCTION_TABLE macro (see Resource API macro in Appendix B); the CLRES_VI_FUNCTIONS structure is defined in RESAPI.H.
RESOURCE_STATUS	Structure that contains information about the status of a resource such as whether the resource is being brought online or taken offline; this parameter is passed as a parameter with the callback function **SetResourceStatus** function (see section on resource API callback functions in Appendix B); the RESOURCE_STATUS structure is defined in RESAPI.H.

CLUSTER CONTROL CODES

Cluster control codes are used to specify an operation on cluster components within many of the APIs mentioned earlier. Cluster control codes are categorized as either internal or external. Internal control codes are used by the Cluster Service only, and applications and resource DLLs cannot use them. Internal control codes are typically sent by the Cluster Service to notify a resource or resource type of an event. External codes represent operations that can be performed by applications. External cluster control codes can be grouped into the following categories:

- Resource
- Resource type
- Group
- Node

Cluster control codes are 32-b values in length. You use control to perform an operation on a cluster component by setting the appropriate values in the control code and calling the appropriate control code function defined in the Cluster API (for example, see the definition of **ClusterResourceControl** in Appendix A). The breakdown of the 32 b that make up the control code is shown in Table 7.

The different control codes and their associated descriptions are listed in Table 8.

CLUSTER PROPERTIES

Cluster properties are attributes that describe a cluster object. There are two types of cluster properties:

TABLE 7
Control Code Components

Bit Positions	Size in Bits	Description
24–31	8	This 8-b object component indicates the type of cluster object to which the control code applies; valid cluster objects include resource, resource type, group, node, etc.; third-party developers can define control codes for their own object types
23	1	This 1-b component indicates whether or not the control code represents a global operation, which must be performed on each cluster node
22	1	This 1-b component indicates whether or not the control code causes a modification to data (which in turn may generate an event notification)
21	1	This 1-b component indicates whether or not the control code is a user code defined by a third-party developer; a control code defined by an external user sets this bit; a control code defined by Cluster Server does not
20	1	This 1-b component indicates whether the control code is internal or external; internal control codes set this bit; an internal control code can be used only by the Cluster Service; applications cannot pass internal control codes as parameters to the control functions of the Cluster API; internal control codes are typically sent by the Cluster Service to notify a resource or resource type of an event; external control codes do not set this bit; applications typically use the external control codes to initiate an operation
19–2	18	This 18-b operation code describes the operation; all operation codes are defined as constants beginning with the prefix CLCTL; some of the operation codes apply only to one type of object, while other operation codes apply to multiple objects; this operation is only valid for resources
1–0	2	This 2-b access code indicates whether or not the initiator of the request requires any specific type of access (such as Read-only/Read-Write/Any) to perform the operation described by the operation code

TABLE 8
Control Code Functions and Descriptions

Control Code Function	Description
ClusterGroupControl	Performs property and other operations on a group
ClusterNetworkControl	Performs property and other operations on a network
ClusterNetInterfaceControl	Performs property and other operations on a network interface
ClusterNodeControl	Performs property and other operations on a node
ClusterResourceControl	Performs property and other operations on a resource
ClusterResourceTypeControl	Performs property and other operations on a resource type

- Common cluster properties
- Private cluster properties

A common cluster property is an attribute that exists for every instance of the type of cluster object for which it is defined. For example, the common group property FailoverThreshold exists for every group in the cluster and the common resource property RestartAction exists for every resource in the cluster and so on. Common properties are static and are not generated on demand.

A private cluster property is an attribute that exists only for specific instances of the type of object for which it is defined. Thus a given cluster object may or may not have a private cluster property. Private properties are more common for resource objects than for any other type of cluster objects. In fact, most standard resources defined by Cluster Server, with the exception of the time service resource, have at least one private property. For example, the ShareName property is a private property applicable only to file share resources. Unlike common properties, private properties can also be dynamic or computed values, which are generated on demand.

Most common and private cluster properties are stored in the cluster database, which provides easy access to the properties.

Value Lists

A value list is a collection of data values. The data values are the data portion of property values in a property list (see Property Lists next) and are returned from control code operations such as the operation to get resource dependencies or to get disk storage information.

Value lists are covered in greater detail in the next chapter. The CLUSPROP_VALUE structure is covered in detail in Appendix C.

Property Lists

A property list is very similar to a value list. Both types of lists consist of one or more entries and a unique last entry. The unique last entry is identified by CLUSPROP_SYNTAX_ENDMARK. Unlike a value list, however, the entries in a property list are more complex. While an entry in a value list consists of a CLUSPROP_VALUE structure (see Appendix C) and a data value, an entry in a property list consists of a property name (which itself is composed of subelements as shown later) and a property value. The property name is made up of:

- A CLUSPROP_VALUE structure
- A name string
- Additional padding if necessary for alignment

Property lists are covered in greater detail in the next chapter.

Common Network, Network Interface, and Resource Properties

Table 9 summarizes common network, network interface, and resource properties.

Common Resource Type, Group, and Node Properties

Table 10 summarizes common resource type, group, and node properties.

Private Resource Properties

The most common cluster component that has private properties is resources. Table 11 summarizes private resource properties.

CLUSTER STRUCTURES

Cluster structures are data structures used to specify data relating to a cluster object. For example, the data structure CLUSPROP_BINARY describes a binary data value used in a value list. The most common use for the majority of cluster structures is in a value list. Table 12 summarizes cluster structures and their associated purposes.

TABLE 9
Common Network, Network Interface, and Resource Properties

Cluster Component	Property Name	Description
Common network properties	Name property for networks	Provides the name of the network
	Address property for networks	Provides the address for the network or subnet
	AddressMask property for networks	Provides the mask that distinguishes the host and network portions of an address
	Description property for network	Provides descriptive comments about the network
	Role property for networks	Provides the role of the network in the cluster
Common network interface properties	Adapter property for network interfaces	Provides the name that is used to uniquely identify the network interface
	Address property for network interfaces	Provides the primary network address
	Description property for network interfaces	Provides descriptive comments about the network interface
	Name property for network interfaces	Provides the generated name for the network interface
	Network property for network interfaces	Provides the name of the network to which the network interface is connected
	Node property for network interfaces	Provides the name of the node where the network interface is installed
Common resource properties	DebugPrefix Property for Resources	Provides the path to the debugger to be attached to the Resource Monitor for the resource
	Description property for resources	Provides descriptive comments about the resource
	IsAlivePollInterval property for resources	Provides the recommended interval that the Cluster Service should poll the resource to determine if it is operational
	LooksAlivePollInterval property for resources	Provides the recommended interval that the Cluster Service should poll the resource to determine if it appears operational
	Name property for resources	Provides the name of the resource
	PendingTimeout property for resources	Provides the number of milliseconds that the Resource Monitor waits for a resource to change state
	PersistentState property for resources	Specifies the last known persistent state of the resource
	RestartAction property for resources	Specifies the action to perform if the resource fails
	RestartPeriod property for resources	Defines a window of time during which a specified number of restart attempts can occur
	RestartThreshold property for resources	Describes the limit of retries for the resource within the time window defined by the RestartPeriod property (see earlier)
	SeparateMonitor property for resources	Indicates whether or not the resource requires its own Resource Monitor
	Type property for resources	Specifies the display name for the resource's type

TABLE 10
Common Resource Type, Group, and Node Properties

Cluster Component	Property Name	Description
Common resource type properties	AdminExtensions property for resource types	Provides the class identifiers (CLSIDs) for the Cluster Administrator Extension DLLs associated with the specified resource type
	DebugControlFunctions property for resource types	Specifies whether or not the Cluster Service should create a separate Resource Monitor to debug the control functions of the Cluster API
	DebugPrefix property for resource types	Provides the path to the debugger to debug resources of the specified resource type running in the Resource Monitor
	Description property for resource types	Provides descriptive comments about the resource type
	DllName property for resource types	Provides the name of the DLL for the resource type
	IsAlivePollInterval property for resource types	Provides the recommended interval that the Cluster Service should poll resources of the specified resource type to determine if they are operational
	LooksAlivePollInterval property for resource types	Provides the recommended interval that the Cluster Service should poll resources of the specified resource type to determine if they appear operational
	Name property for resource type	Provides the name of the specified resource type to be used for display purposes
Common group properties	AutoFailbackType property for groups	Specifies whether or not the group should be automatically moved to its preferred owner node when that node comes back online
	Description property for groups	Provides descriptive comments about the group
	FailbackWindowStart property for groups	Provides the earliest time that the group can be moved back to its preferred node
	FailbackWindowEnd property for groups	Provides the latest time that the group can be moved back to its preferred node
	FailoverThreshold Property for Groups	Specifies the number of attempts that the Cluster Service makes to bring the group online within the time interval specified by FailoverPeriod
	FailoverPeriod property for groups	Specifies the time interval in hours within which the Cluster Service attempts to failover the group
	Name property for groups	Specifies the group name
	PersistentState property for groups	Describes the last known persistent state of the group
	Description property for nodes	Provides descriptive comments about the node
	NodeName property for nodes	Provides the node name

RESOURCE DYNAMIC LINK LIBRARIES

A Resource DLL is a dynamic link library that contains an implementation of the resource API for a specific type of resource. Each resource in a cluster has an associated DLL that acts as the interface mechanism to the resource. The resource DLL is loaded into the address space of its Resource Monitor and the Resource Monitor acts on the resource by calling the entry point functions implemented in the resource DLL. Figure 3 shows the interaction of the Cluster Service, the resource DLL, and the Resource Monitor.

TABLE 11
Private Resource Properties

Resource Type	Property Name	Description
Private properties for file share resources	MaxUsers	Specifies the number of simultaneous users that can access the file share
	Path	Specifies the path to the directory being shared
	Remark	Provides a description of the file share resource
	Security	Specifies the security access necessary to access the file share
	ShareName	Specifies the name of the file share present on the network
Private properties for generic application resources	CommandLine	Describes the command line used to invoke the application
	CurrentDirectory	Describes the directory in which the application should be run
	InteractWithDesktop	Specifies whether or not the application can provide a user interface on the desktop
	UseNetworkName	Influences the outcome of the call to GetComputerName
Private properties for generic service resources	StartupParameters	Describes the command line to pass to the service when it is started
	ServiceName	Describes the short name of the service to be run
	UseNetworkName	Influences the outcome of the call to GetComputerName
Private properties for IIS Virtual Root Resources	AccessMask	Specifies the protection required for the IIS virtual root
	Alias	Describes the subdirectory name used by clients to access the IIS virtual root
	Directory	Describes the physical location of the IIS virtual root
	ServiceName	Describes the type of Web service
Private properties for IP address resources	Address	Provides the IP address
	Network	Describes the network for which the IP address is to be created
	SubNetMask	Describes the subnet mask to be applied when routing IP address
Private properties for network name resources	Name	Provides the name of the network name resource
Private properties for physical disk resources	Drive	Specifies the drive letter of the Physical Disk
	Signature	Specifies the signature for the Physical Disk
Private properties for print spooler resources	DefaultSpoolDirectory	Provides the name of the spooler folder for the print spooler resource
	JobCompletionTimeout	Specifies the number of milliseconds before a pending job is deleted from the print spooler resource queue

While a resource DLL should be reentrant across resources of a given resource type, the DLL is non-reentrant for a given instance of a resource. With the exception of the **Terminate** function, you can assume that each of the entry points is called only once for each resource instance. The exception is. Calls to **Terminate** can occur at any time, even if other threads within the resource DLL are blocked waiting. Resource DLLs that handle multiple resources must ensure synchronization of the use of any shared global data.

TABLE 12
Cluster Structures and Purpose

Cluster Structure	Purpose
CLUSPROP_BINARY	Describes binary data
CLUSPROP_DISK_NUMBER	Describes the number of a disk
CLUSPROP_DISK_SIGNATURE	Describes the signature of a disk
CLUSPROP_DWORD	Describes numerical data
CLUSPROP_MULTI_SZ	Describes multiple strings
CLUSPROP_PARTITION_INFO	Describes information relevant to storage class resources
CLUSPROP_PROPERTY_NAME	Describes the name of a property
CLUSPROP_REQUIRED_DEPENDENCY	Describes a resource on which another resource must depend
CLUSPROP_RESOURCE_CLASS	Describes a resource class value
CLUSPROP_RESOURCE_CLASS_INFO	Describes information relevant to a resource class
CLUSPROP_SCSI_ADDRESS	Describes an address for a SCSI device
CLUSPROP_SZ	Describes a null-terminated Unicode string
CLUSPROP_ULARGE_INTEGER	Describes an unsigned large integer
CLUS_WORKER	Describes information about a worker thread
CLUSPROP_BUFFER_HELPER	Used to build or parse a property or value list
CLUSPROP_LIST	Used to access the beginning of a property list.
CLUSTERVERSIONINFO	Describes version information about the Cluster Service
RESUTIL_PROPERTY_ITEM	Contains information about a property and an offset to the property data

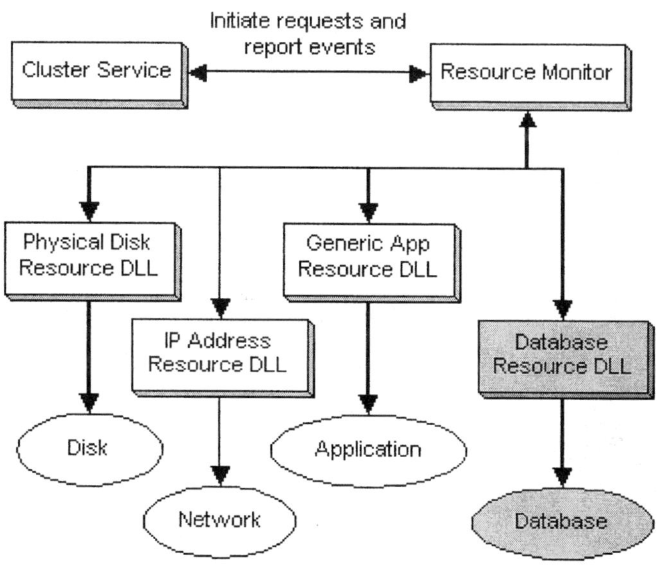

FIGURE 3 Interaction of the Cluster Service, the Resource DLL, and the Resource Monitor. (Reprinted with permissiong from Microsoft.)

CLUSTER UTILITY FUNCTIONS

Cluster utility functions are utility functions that you can include in your cluster applications and resource DLLs to perform the function provided by the utility functions. You can use these utility functions in the same manner as you use library functions. Utility functions help you in your development by saving time and programming effort.

There are a number of utility functions relating to resources, cluster database, property lists, thread management, services, etc. We will cover cluster utility functions in greater detail later in this chapter. Appendix C includes a complete list of cluster utility functions and provides more detail about each of the functions.

The cluster utility functions are implemented in RESUTILS.DLL, a DLL that is provided with Cluster Administrator. Applications and resource DLLs that use the cluster utility functions must include RESAPI.H in addition to CLUSAPI.H and link to RESUTILS.LIB.

Cluster Utility Function Types

The cluster utility functions are classified into six types:

- Resource Utility functions to access resource information
- Cluster database utility functions to access values of different types from the cluster database
- Property list utility functions
- Utility functions to handle multiple properties using an array of RESUTIL_PROPERTY_ITEM structures, commonly referred to as a property table
- Utility functions to manage threads
- Utility functions to perform a variety of tasks

Resource Utility Functions

The resource utility functions allow applications and resource DLLs perform resource-related functions such as:

- Enumerating resources and initiating operations for resources
- Retrieving information about dependencies
- Determining whether or not two handles represent the same resource
- Determining whether or not a resource type matches the resource type of a specified resource

Resource utility functions are summarized in Table 13.

TABLE 13
Resource Utility Functions and Description

Resource Utility Function	Description
ResUtilEnumResources	Enumerates all the resources in a cluster and initiates an operation for each resource
ResUtilGetResourceDependency	Returns a handle to a dependent resource of a specified type
ResUtilGetResourceNameDependency	Returns a handle to a dependent resource with a specified name and type
ResUtilResourcesEqual	Tests whether or not two resource handles represent the same resource
ResUtilResourceTypesEqual	Tests whether or not a resource type matches the resource type of a specified resource

CLUSTER DATABASE UTILITY FUNCTIONS

The cluster database utility functions handle memory allocation if required and set/retrieve data of different data types such as binary, numerical, string, etc. Cluster database utility functions are summarized in Table 14.

TABLE 14
Cluster Database Utility Functions and Description

Cluster Database Utility Function	Description
ResUtilGetBinaryValue	Returns a binary value from the cluster database
ResUtilGetDwordValue	Returns a numerical value from the cluster database
ResUtilGetMultiSzValue	Returns a multiple string value from the cluster database
ResUtilGetSzValue	Returns a string value from the cluster database
ResUtilSetBinaryValue	Sets a binary value in the cluster database
ResUtilSetDwordValue	Sets a numerical value in the cluster database
ResUtilSetExpandSzValue	Sets an expandable string value in the cluster database
ResUtilSetMultiSzValue	Sets a multiple string value in the cluster database
ResUtilSetSzValue	Sets a string value in the cluster database

PROPERTY LIST UTILITY FUNCTIONS

Property list utility functions handle the parsing and construction of property lists. Property lists are passed to and from the control code functions of the resource and Cluster APIs. The functions provided by property list utility functions include

- Enumerating private and common resource properties
- Locating a numerical or string property in a property list
- Retrieving private, default, and unknown properties of a resource
- Setting private resource properties
- Validating private resource properties

Utility functions that can be used with property lists are summarized in Table 15.

TABLE 15
Property List Utility Functions and Description

Function	Description
ResUtilAddUnknownProperties	Adds unknown properties for a given object to the end of a property list
ResUtilEnumPrivateProperties	Enumerates private properties of a resource
ResUtilEnumProperties	Enumerates the properties of a resource
ResUtilFindDwordProperty	Locates a numerical property in a property list
ResUtilFindSzProperty	Locates a string property in a property list
ResUtilGetAllProperties	Returns all the default and unknown properties for a resource
ResUtilGetPrivateProperties	Returns the private properties of a cluster object
ResUtilGetProperties	Returns specified properties for a resource
ResUtilGetPropertiesToParameterBlock	Returns properties and stores them in a parameter block
ResUtilPropertyListFromParameterBlock	Constructs a property list from a parameter block
ResUtilSetPrivatePropertyList	Sets private properties of a resource
ResUtilVerifyPrivatePropertyList	Validates private properties of a resource

Property Table Utility Functions

The property table utility functions use **RESUTIL_PROPERTY_ITEM** structures (see Appendix C for more information, including the layout of **RESUTIL_PROPERTY_ITEM**) to handle multiple properties. These utility functions use a property table, which is an array of **RESUTIL_PROPERTY_ITEM** structures. Each entry in the table includes property name, cluster database key, format, default value, minimum and maximum values, a set of flags, and offset to a parameter block containing the location of the property's data. A parameter block is a structure that includes as members either data for properties in a property table or pointers to the property data.

A list of property table utility functions and associated descriptions is contained in the following table. Some of the property table functions are also used for property lists.

TABLE 16
Property Table Functions and Description

Property Table Function	Description
ResUtilDupParameterBlock	Duplicates a parameter block
ResUtilEnumProperties	Enumerates the properties of a resource
ResUtilFreeParameterBlock	Frees a specified parameter block
ResUtilGetAllProperties	Returns all the default and unknown properties for a cluster object, such as a resource or group; this function is also used for working with a property list
ResUtilGetProperties	Returns specified properties for a resource; this function is also used for working with a property list
ResUtilGetProperty	Returns one of a resource's properties
ResUtilGetPropertySize	Returns the total number of bytes required for one or more property values
ResUtilSetPropertyParameterBlock	Sets properties for a resource from a parameter block
ResUtilSetPropertyTable	Sets properties for a resource based on a property list from a property table
ResUtilVerifyPropertyTable	Validates properties for a resource based on a property list from a property table

Service Utility Functions

The service utility functions start and stop a service and verify if a service is up and running. There are five service utility functions as shown in Table 17.

TABLE 17
Service Utility Functions and Descriptions

Function	Description
ResUtilStartResourceService	Starts a service
ResUtilStopResourceService	Stops a named service
ResUtilStopService	Stops a service identified by a handle
ResUtilVerifyResourceService	Checks if a named service is operational
ResUtilVerifyService	Checks if a service identified by a handle is operational

Miscellaneous Utility Functions

The miscellaneous utility functions take care of implementing common tasks that are useful in a variety of situations. Table 18 briefly describes these utility functions.

TABLE 18
Miscellaneous Utility Functions and Descriptions

Miscellaneous Utility Function	Description
ResUtilDupString	Duplicates a character string
ResUtilGetEnvironmentWithNetName	Creates an environment block that appends a CLUSTER_NETWORK_NAME environment variable to the current environment block
ResUtilIsPathValid	Checks whether or not a path is syntactically valid
ResUtilOpenDriver	Opens an input/output (I/O) driver
ResUtilInitializeResourceStatus	Initializes a RESOURCE_STATUS structure

Thread Management Utility Functions

The thread management utility functions create and start a worker thread and allow a pending operation to be cancelled with correct synchronization. There are four thread management utility functions as shown in the following table.

TABLE 19
Thread Management Utility Functions and Descriptions

Function	Description
ClusWorkerCheckTerminate	Determines whether or not a worker thread should exit as soon as possible
ClusWorkerCreate	Creates a worker thread
ClusWorkerTerminate	Terminates a worker thread

Cluster resources also maintain a list of nodes that can act as valid hosts. For example, a physical disk resource may be hosted only on nodes that are physically connected to the resource. Applications can retrieve this list by calling ClusterResourceEnum and passing CLUSTER_RESOURCE_ENUM_NODES as the dwType parameter.

To interact with a cluster resource, applications, and the Cluster Service call the Cluster API function ClusterResourceControl and specify as a parameter a control code. A control code is a 32-b value that describes a particular operation. Some of the operations associated with resource control codes are supported by the resource DLL; others are supported by the associated Resource Monitor.

8 Programming with the Cluster Server Software Development Kit

CLUSTER SERVER SOFTWARE DEVELOPMENT KIT

The Microsoft Cluster Server (MSCS) Software Development Kit (SDK) supports Microsoft Developer Studio for Visual C++ version 4.2 and Microsoft Visual Studio for Visual C++ version 5.0. In this chapter, we take a closer look at different topics related to Cluster Server SDK such as installing the SDK and using the SDK to develop cluster applications, and cluster dynamic link libraries (DLLs).

INSTALLING THE MICROSOFT CLUSTER SERVER SOFTWARE DEVELOPMENT KIT

The steps for installation are slightly different depending on the development environment (Visual C++ version 4.2 or Microsoft Visual Studio for Visual C++ version 5.0).

To install the Microsoft Cluster Server SDK:

1. Install Microsoft Windows NT Server network operating system version 4.0 with Service Pack 3.
2. Install Microsoft Cluster Server, selecting from one of the following:
   - Form a new cluster if your development machine is the first member of the cluster.
   - Join an existing cluster if another machine has already established the cluster.
3. Specify a disk on the shared Small Computer System Interface (SCSI) bus to use as the quorum resource.

   Tip: Although it is possible to create cluster-aware applications and DLLs on a non-clustered system, keep in mind that you need a two-machine cluster for testing. Two nodes are needed to successfully test failover. Therefore, it makes sense to do your development on a machine that is a member of an active cluster.

4. You should have either Microsoft Visual C++ version 4.2 or version 5.0 with the Unicode Microsoft Foundation Class (MFC) libraries and the Microsoft Interface Definition Language (MIDL) compiler version 3.00.44 or greater. The MIDL compiler is available with the Microsoft Platform SDK.
5. If you have Visual C++ version 4.2, download the Visual C++ 4.2b Technology Update from the Downloads and Patches area of the Visual C++ home page on the Web located at http://www.microsoft.com/visualc.
6. If you have Visual C++ version 4.2, install the Active Template Library (ATL) version 2.0 or greater. With Visual C++ version 5, ATL 2.1 is included.

7. If you are programming in Microsoft Visual Basic, verify that you have Microsoft Visual Basic version 4.0 or greater on your machine.
8. Install the Cluster Server SDK by running the SETUPSDK.EXE program from the SDK directory of the installation CD. The SETUPSDK program asks for the location of the root directory of your Microsoft Visual C++ development environment and places its files in the appropriate subdirectory.

The Cluster Server SDK contains:

- Header files
- Libraries
- Interface Definition Language (IDL) files
- Sample code
- Custom Resource Type AppWizard (This AppWizard creates skeleton versions of resource and Cluster Administrator Extension DLLs and integrates with the development environment of Microsoft Visual C++.)

Installation of Cluster Server SDK performs the following:

- Files that you need for Cluster Server programming are placed in directories under the root directory of your Visual C++ development environment.
- Files that support the Cluster Service are placed in the cluster subdirectory of your system directory.
- Cluster Administrator is now available from the Start menu.

As mentioned earlier, the installation is slightly different for Visual C++ 4.2 compared with Visual C++ 5.0. Table 1 describes the SDK files that are added to directories in your Visual C++ version 4.2 development environment and Table 2 describes the SDK files that are added to directories in your Visual C++ version 5.0 development environment.

TABLE 1
SDK Files Added to Visual C++ 4.2

Directory	Cluster Server SDK File (Visual C++ 4.2)
BIN	Cluster Administrator Extension registration program (REGCLADM.EXE)
HELP	Documentation files (MCMSDK files)
INCLUDE	CLUSAPI.H, RESAPI.H, CLUADMEX.H, CLUADMEX.IDL, and MSCLUS.IDL
LIB	CLUADMEX, CLUSAPI, and RESUTILS libraries and the MSCLUS type library
SAMPLES	SmbSmp is a resource DLL, written in C; SmbSmpEx is a Cluster Administrator Extension DLL for a File Share resource, written in C++
TEMPLATE	Resource Type AppWizard (RESTYPAW.DLL)

The following table describes the SDK files that are added to directories in your Visual C++ version 5.0 development environment.

The fast way to coding programs using the SDK is to follow the samples included. SmbSmp is a resource DLL written in C. SmbSmpEx is a Cluster Administrator Extension DLL for a file share resource, written in C++. The sample directories contain the source code and all other supporting files needed to build these DLLs. These samples manage the same resource type and are stored in a single workspace and use a single makefile. A third sample, DebugEx, is a Cluster

TABLE 2
SDK Files Added to Visual C++ 5.0

Directory	Cluster Server SDK File
BIN	Cluster Administrator Extension registration program (REGCLADM.EXE)
HELP	Documentation files (MCMSDK files)
INCLUDE	CLUSAPI.H, RESAPI.H, CLUADMEX.H, CLUADMEX.IDL, and MSCLUS.IDL
LIB	CLUADMEX, CLUSAPI, and RESUTILS libraries and the MSCLUS-type library
SAMPLE	SmbSmp, which is a resource DLL and SmbSmpEx, which is a Cluster Administrator Extension DLL
SharedIDE	Resource Type AppWizard (RESTYPAW.DLL)

Administrator Extension that you can use to debug your resource DLL. More details on DebugEx is included later in this chapter.

OVERVIEW OF USING THE CLUSTER SERVER SOFTWARE DEVELOPMENT KIT

As a programmer the Cluster Server SDK, you may perform one or more of the following tasks:

- Create a new cluster-aware application.
- Add cluster awareness to an existing application.
- Create a custom resource type by building a resource DLL to allow Cluster Server to manage your application or service as a cluster resource.
- Create a cluster management application.
- Create a Cluster Administrator Extension DLL to allow Cluster Administrator to handle your custom resource type.
- Create a setup program to install, configure, and register a resource DLL and/or a Cluster Administrator Extension DLL.

A cluster-aware application is any application that runs on a cluster node and is managed and administered as a cluster resource. A cluster-aware application is aware of its environment and is designed to take advantage of the features that clustering offers. When a cluster-aware application detects that it is running on a cluster node, it provides special functionality or performs additional tasks made available through the Cluster application programming interface (API).

Most applications can be made cluster aware. Applications that do not use Transmission Control Protocol/Internet Protocol (TCP/IP) as a network protocol, maintain data in a configurable location, or support transaction processing cannot be made cluster aware. Typical cluster aware applications include database applications, transaction processing applications, file and print server applications, and other group ware applications.

Although it is possible to use the resource DLLs provided by Cluster Server to manage your cluster-aware application, it is recommended that you create your own. By creating a resource type that fits your specific needs, you can have more control and flexibility in how Cluster Server handles your application. Creating a custom resource type enables the Resource Monitor to manage your application in ways that are specific to the application.

To create a custom resource type, you build a resource DLL using the Resource API and, as an option, a DLL to allow Cluster Administrator to include property sheets for your application. The resource DLL contains implementations of entry point functions defined in the resource API for handling the communication between the application and the Resource Monitor. The Cluster Administrator Extension DLL uses the interface methods of the Cluster Administrator Extension

API to allow the application to be administered with Cluster Administrator. Providing a Cluster Administrator Extension DLL simplifies the job of the network administrator; it enables him or her to work with your application, its dependent resources, and any other standard resources using an integrated, consistent user interface.

You can also create a cluster management application with the Cluster Server SDK. A cluster management application is an application written specifically to manage one or more clusters. Cluster management applications can typically run locally on one of the cluster nodes or remotely on a nonclustered system. Cluster Administrator is an example of a cluster management application as is the command-line tool, CLUSTER.EXE. If you need to create your own cluster management application that runs as a stand-alone application or in conjunction with Cluster Administrator, you can do so using the Cluster API.

Although Cluster Server programming applies primarily to cluster-aware and cluster management applications, Cluster Server supports a third type of application, the cluster-unaware application. A cluster-unaware application resembles a cluster-aware application in that both run on a cluster node and are managed and administered as cluster resources. The difference between applications that are cluster aware and those that are not is in their knowledge of their environment. A cluster-unaware application has no inherent knowledge of its existence in a cluster; its functionality is the same regardless of whether or not it is running in a cluster. Cluster-unaware applications are typically managed as generic application or generic service resources, but it is possible to also manage them as custom resource types.

Cluster Server programming targets two main types of development:

- Developing applications to manage clusters and cluster objects
- Developing custom resource types to allow applications and services to operate as cluster resources

Depending on the type of development that you intend to pursue, you may use one or more of the APIs included with the Cluster Server SDK. The Cluster Server SDK has a variety of different APIs, some that are sets of functions and others that are Component Object Model (COM) interfaces. Although Cluster Server supports development in C, C++, Microsoft Visual Basic, and several scripting languages, not all the APIs are meant to be used with all the languages. The following table offers a summary description of each API.

TABLE 3
Cluster Server APIs, Description, and Supported Languages

API	Description	Languages
Cluster API	Allows a resource DLL or application to communicate with the Cluster Service and cluster database	C, C++
Resource API	Allows the Cluster Service to communicate with a resource through the Resource Monitor	C, C++
Cluster Administrator Extension API	Allows property pages and context menus for a custom resource type to be integrated into Cluster Administrator	C, C++
Automation Server API	Allows an application to administer a cluster	Visual Basic, scripting languages

The Cluster API is a function-based interface used by cluster-aware applications written in C or C++. The Cluster Service implements all the functions of the Cluster API. Applications and resource DLLs make calls to these functions to access information about cluster objects.

The resource API is a function-based interface that is primarily implemented by resource DLLs written in C or C++. This API also includes a few callback functions that are used by the resource DLL to report events and status.

Cluster Automation Server is a COM-based dual interface used by cluster management applications written in Microsoft Visual Basic or one of the scripting languages. Cluster Automation Server is implemented in MSCLUS.DLL.

The Cluster Administrator Extension API is a set of COM-based interfaces that are implemented and used by Cluster Administrator Extension DLLs written in C or C++. Cluster Administrator Extension DLLs implement interfaces for enhancing Cluster Administrator objects and invoking commands. The DLLs call other interfaces in the API to retrieve information from Cluster Administrator and to add to a Cluster Administrator property sheet, wizard, or context menu.

Property Tables

A property table is an array of RESUTIL_PROPERTY_ITEM structures that is useful for working with multiple properties. Instead of using the CLUSPROP_BUFFER_HELPER structure to step through each property, applications and resource DLLs can use a property table. In combination with the utility functions written to manipulate property values, property lists, and property tables, using a property table offers developers a simpler solution to the potentially complex task of property management.

Each entry in a property table contains information about a particular property and an offset to the property data. The data, or a pointer to the data, are stored in a buffer known as a parameter block. A parameter block is typically a structure that contains one member for each data value that belongs to a property in the property table. However, because an offset is used to identify the location of data, parameter block structures can contain nonproperty members as well as property members.

The following illustration shows the relationship between a property table and a parameter block. The property table has two entries, each represented by a RESUTIL_PROPERTY_ITEM structure. The Offset member of each property table entry points to a member in the parameter block. Notice that nonproperty table data are included in the parameter block. The type of data stored in the Default, Minimum, and Maximum members as well as in the corresponding parameter block depends on the value of the Format member.

Value Lists

A value list is a collection of data values that is used as the data portion of a property value in a property list and is returned from the following control code operations:

- CLUSCTL_RESOURCE_GET_REQUIRED_DEPENDENCIES
- CLUSCTL_RESOURCE_STORAGE_GET_DISK_INFO
- CLUSCTL_RESOURCE_TYPE_GET_REQUIRED_DEPENDENCIES
- CLUSCTL_RESOURCE_TYPE_STORAGE_GET_AVAILABLE_DISKS

Because each of the data values in a value list can have a different format, type, and length, each entry in the list begins with a CLUSPROP_VALUE structure. The CLUSPROP_VALUE structure describes the data that follow it and has two members: a syntax member and a length member. The syntax member is a CLUSPROP_SYNTAX structure, a union that describes data as either a single DWORD such as CLUSPROP_SYNTAX_SCSI_ADDRESS or as a format and type such as CLUSPROP_FORMAT_DWORD and CLUSPROP_TYPE_CHARACTERISTICS.

Each entry in a value list, except the final one, is made up of a CLUSPROP_VALUE structure and data. The final entry contains only the CLUSPROP_SYNTAX_ENDMARK value.

For some types of data, one way is definitely preferred. User-defined types fall into this category and must be described with a format and type. A user-defined value type might be used with a user-defined control function. The CLUSPROP_VALUE structure's Syntax member for user-defined numerical data would be set as follows. Notice that the wType member is set to a value beginning with CLUSPROP_TYPE_USER, the beginning of the range for user-defined data types:

```
#define CLUSPROP_TYPE_MY_TYPE (CLUSPROP_TYPE_USER+1)
CLUSPROP_SYNTAX Syntax;
   Syntax.wFormat = CLUSPROP_FORMAT_DWORD;
   Syntax.wType = CLUSPROP_TYPE_MY_TYPE;
```

Other types of data can set to appropriate values either the dw member of the CLUSPROP_VALUE structure or the wFormat and wType members of the CLUSPROP_SYNTAX structure. For example, you could describe a disk number in either of the following two ways:

```
CLUSPROP_SYNTAX Syntax;
   Syntax.dw = CLUSPROP_SYNTAX_DISK_NUMBER;

CLUSPROP_SYNTAX Syntax;
   Syntax.wFormat = CLUSPROP_FORMAT_DWORD;
   Syntax.wType = CLUSPROP_TYPE_DISK_NUMBER;
```

The only difference between the two definitions is that the first example combines the format and type values at compile time while the second example combines them at run time.

The last entry in a value list is special. Because its purpose is solely to mark the end of the list, it contains only the CLUSPROP_SYNTAX portion of the CLUSPROP_VALUE structure. There are no length member and no data. The last entry appears as follows:

```
CLUSPROP_SYNTAX Syntax;
Syntax.dw = CLUSPROP_SYNTAX_ENDMARK;
```

Property Lists

A property list is similar to a value list in that both types of lists consist of one or more entries and a unique last entry, identified by CLUSPROP_SYNTAX_ENDMARK. The entries in a property list, however, are more complex than in a value list. While an entry in a value list consists of a CLUSPROP_VALUE structure and a data value, an entry in a property list consists of a property name and a property value. The property name is made up of:

- A CLUSPROP_VALUE structure
- A name string
- Additional padding if necessary for alignment

The property value is a value list plus padding if the value list is not DWORD aligned. Because each property value in a property list must always be DWORD aligned, padding is required only if the value is not yet property aligned. Typically, the value list for a property value contains two entries: one to describe the data in the property value and the other to mark the end of the list.

Any of the control codes that work with properties use a property list for input or return a property list as output. For example, ClusterResourceControl returns a property list from its handling of CLUSCTL_RESOURCE_GET_COMMON_PROPERTIES and requires a property list to handle CLUSCTL_RESOURCE_SET_COMMON_PROPERTIES.

To locate a specific property in a property list, use the utility function called ResUtilFindSzProperty. ResUtilFindSzProperty returns a pointer to the string in the property list for the specified property. ResUtilFindDwordProperty is also available. These functions are defined in the resource utility library, RESUTILS.DLL. The prototypes for these functions are located in RESAPI.H. Another option for locating information is to loop through each property until you are finished. If you do not know exactly what you are looking for, this is the only option.

The CLUSPROP_BUFFER_HELPER structure is also helpful for parsing or constructing a property list or value list. This structure is a union of pointers to the individual CLUSPROP value structures defined in CLUSAPI.H.

Enumerating Cluster Objects

One of the most common tasks of cluster-aware and cluster management applications is to enumerate objects in the cluster. Applications can enumerate specific types of objects such as resources, or choose to limit their enumeration to objects that affect a particular group or resource.

For example, to find the cluster network name resource, perform the following steps:

1. Create a resource enumerator by calling ClusterOpenEnum and specifying CLUSTER_ENUM_RESOURCE for the dwType parameter.
2. Loop through all the resources in the cluster by calling ClusterEnum repeatedly with the contents of the lpdwType parameter set to CLUSTER_ENUM_RESOURCE. For each resource:
    a. Call OpenClusterResource, setting the lpszResourceName parameter to the contents of the lpszName parameter returned from ClusterEnum.
    b. Call ClusterResourceControl with the dwControlCode parameter set to CLUSCTL_RESOURCE_GET_FLAGS.
    c. If the CLUS_FLAG_CORE flag is set, indicating that the resource is a core cluster resource, call ClusterResourceControl with the dwControlCode parameter set to CLUSCTL_RESOURCE_GET_RESOURCE_TYPE.
    d. The resource type is set to network name for the cluster Network Name resource. There is only one core resource in the cluster with the network name resource type.

Choosing Between Control Codes and Cluster Application Programming Interface Functions

There is an overlap of functionality between control codes that can perform many operations and Cluster APIs. For example, there are two ways to set the private properties of a resource in the cluster database:

1. Call ClusterResourceControl with the CLUSCTL_RESOURCE_SET_PRIVATE_PROPERTIES control code.
2. Call ClusterRegOpenKey to access the appropriate key in the database and ClusterRegSetValue to perform the update.

The rule of thumb is to always use a control code if possible, especially if the operation involves accessing the cluster database.

Control Codes and Quorum Resources

The ResourceControl entry point function for quorum resources must handle the following control codes:

- CLUSCTL_RESOURCE_GET_CLASS_INFO
- CLUSCTL_RESOURCE_STORAGE_GET_DISK_INFO

Handling CLUSCTL_RESOURCE_GET_CLASS_INFO identifies a quorum resource as a storage device. Handling CLUSCTL_RESOURCE_STORAGE_GET_DISK_INFO allows Cluster Administrator to display partition information about a quorum resource.

In your handling of CLUSCTL_RESOURCE_GET_CLASS_INFO, return a CLUS_RESOURCE_CLASS_INFO structure that is set as follows:

```
CLUS_RESOURCE_CLASS_INFO ClassInfo;

ClassInfo.rc = CLUS_RESCLASS_STORAGE;

ClassInfo.SubClass = CLUS_RESSUBCLASS_SHARED;
```

Setting these values in the CLUS_RESOURCE_CLASS_INFO structure makes a resource look like shared storage.

PROGRAMMING RESOURCE DYNAMIC LINK LIBRARIES

Although Microsoft includes a generic resource DLL in MSCS that can be used for any resource, Microsoft recommends that you implement custom resource DLLs for your applications and services to take full advantage of clustering. The reason for the recommendation is that the resource DLLs included with MSCS are very basic and provide little more than rudimentary failover/failback capability. However, you can use these DLLs to test your applications or services to determine if they benefit from a clustered environment.

The functions you implement in your resource DLL depend on the resource itself and how the resource is used in your environment. For example, the Cluster Server print spooler resource DLL checks that the group for the resource contains a single print spooler resource. The IIS virtual root resource DLL validates that the resource properties are unique and returns an error if duplicate names are found.

We cover the major steps involved in creating and using a resource DLL.

Creating a Resource Dynamic Link Library

The following are the major steps involved in creating a resource DLL:

1. The simplest way to build a resource DLL is by using the Resource Type AppWizard. The code produced by the Resource Type AppWizard uses the Microsoft Foundation Classes (MFC) and C++ language. This builds a skeletal resource DLL (and/or Cluster Administrator Extension DLL) with all the entry points defined, declared, and exported. This skeletal DLL code generated by the AppWizard provides only the most basic failover and failback capabilities. It does, however, contain comments such as TODO (to indicate where to insert additional functionality) and ADDPARAM (to indicate where to insert additional parameters or properties). These comments indicate areas where you need to add resource-specific information.

2. Use the resource API to supplement the capabilities of your resource DLL. Typically, the descriptions in the resource API help you determine if you need to implement optional entry point functions and how and when to make calls to the Resource Monitor.
3. Determine which of the many control codes for Resources your ResourceControl entry point function should support and determine how to implement that support.

Guidelines for Writing Resource DLLs

- The Resource Monitor starts invoking the Resource API entry point functions after the DLL entry point is called with the DLL_PROCESS_ATTACH flag during the initialization of the resource DLL.
- In the resource DLL, an entry point function should take no more than 300 msec to complete. If an entry point — specifically, Online, Offline, LooksAlive, or IsAlive — exceeds this limit, your DLL should spawn separate threads wherever possible to handle the lengthier operations.

  Note: The AppWizard currently generates an Online thread, and future versions generate an Offline thread as well.

- A resource DLL is non-reentrant for a given instance of a resource, although the resource DLL should be reentrant with respect to other resource identifications (IDs). The exception to non-reentrancy is the *Terminate* entry point function. Terminate can be called at any time, even when other threads within the resource DLL are blocked waiting for an Online or Offline call to complete. If a resource DLL handles more than one resource ID, it must synchronize them for any global data shared within the resource DLL.

Tools for Writing Resource DLLs

The primary programming language used to develop resource DLLs is Visual C++. You can use either the Microsoft Visual C++ development system or an equivalent. Other tools that may be useful include

- MIDL compiler version (MIDL compiler available with the Microsoft Platform SDK)
- ATL (required for the code that is generated by the Resource Type AppWizard)
- Microsoft's Platform SDK (particularly useful when setting up your build environment; also find a reference implementation of a complete resource DLL in the samples\WinBase\Cluster\SMBsmp directory in the Platform SDK root directory)

CUSTOMIZING A RESOURCE DYNAMIC LINK LIBRARY

The resource DLL that is created by the Resource Type AppWizard contains implementations of all the necessary entry point functions, but these implementations are very basic, providing only a basic failover and failback capability. There are three main reasons for customizing and enhancing the resource DLL source files that are generated by the AppWizard:

1. Create a code that allows your resources to take full advantage of the cluster environment. For example, when your resource is being taken offline, it might be advantageous to close files that are open and to delete files that are temporary.
2. Implement parameters or properties that provide information specific to your resources.

3. Support the Active/Active failover and failback capability, which enables two separate instances of your resource to run on different nodes using different data. The data reside on a disk on the shared SCSI bus.

The source files in your resource DLL project include comments that begin with TODO: to indicate where to insert additional functionality or ADDPARAM: to indicate where to insert additional parameters or properties. The following modifications are common:

1. Add library files specific to your resource type. Add lines for your resource-specific libraries after the following:

    ```
    #pragma comment(lib, "clusapi.lib")
    ```

2. Add header files specific to your resource type. Add any header files that provide definitions and declarations specific to your resource type after these lines:

    ```
    #include <clusapi.h>
    #include <resapi.h>
    #include <stdio.h>
    ```

Entry Point Functions in the Resource DLL

The resource API consists of several entry point functions that are implemented in a resource DLL and the Resource Monitor uses these entry points to manage resources supported by the DLL. Of the entry point functions, two (**Arbitrate** and **Release**) are required if (and only if) you are writing a resource DLL for a quorum resource. The remaining entry point functions are listed in the table on page 113. The complete syntax for each of the entry point functions along with descriptions of the parameters and return values is included in Appendix B.

Registering a Resource Dynamic Link Library

The registration process for your new resource DLL involves copying your project files to a file share chosen for the resource type on the cluster nodes. After the files have been copied, perform the actual registration with the following command:

```
CLUSTER -create resourcetype "Resource type name" path
```

As an alternate, call the Cluster API function CreateClusterResourceType in your setup program.

Debugging a Resource Dynamic Link Library

Debugging resource DLLs is more complicated than debugging regular Windows NT-based DLLs or applications because the Cluster Service runs as a Windows NT Service and the Resource Monitor runs as a separate process.

You can debug a resource DLL using any standard Microsoft Windows operating system-based debugger, along with the DebugEx Cluster Administrator Extension DLL (included with MSCS). The DebugEx Extension DLL allows the resource DLL to be debugged the next time the Resource Monitor is started.

Make sure you take care of the following when you want to debug resource DLLs:

- To debug a resource DLL with WinDbg, Microsoft Developer Studio, or any other Windows-based debugger, the Cluster Service must be running in the same security

Entry Point Function	Description
Startup	The Resource Monitor invokes the Startup routine once the resource DLL is loaded; Startup is the only entry point function that is exported; all other entry points that are implemented in the resource DLL are accessed through the function table returned by Startup
Open	The Resource Monitor typically calls the Open entry point function once Startup returns successfully; open is called for each resource managed by the resource DLL
Online	The Resource Monitor calls the Online entry point function once the resource is opened; online entry point function brings the resource online
LooksAlive and IsAlive	The Resource Monitor polls the resource periodically to determine its status; once the resource is online, the Resource Monitor uses the LooksAlive and IsAlive entry point functions for polling; looksAlive is a cursory check while IsAlive is a more thorough check
Offline	The Resource Monitor calls the Offline entry point function to take a resource offline and to make it unavailable to clients
Close	The Resource Monitor typically calls Close after a resource goes Offline; the Close entry point function closes a resource; close is called only once for a particular resource; use Close to deallocate any of the structures that were allocated by the Open, Offline, ResourceControl, or ResourceTypeControl entry point functions; if the resource to be closed is not yet offline, call Terminate to forcibly take it offline
Terminate	If a resource does not shut down gracefully when the Offline function is called, the Terminate entry point function is used to immediately end the process; for example, in Cluster Server file share resource DLL; Terminate uses the resource identifier as an index into a resource table that keeps track of all resources that are handled by the DLL. Terminate retrieves the address of the resource structure for the appropriate resource and uses the information in this resource structure to call the Win32 function NetShareDel to remove the share name from the server
ResourceControl and ResourceType Control	The ResourceControl and ResourceTypeControl entry point functions are optional; however, Microsoft recommends that resource DLLs implement these entry points; the Cluster Administrator and cluster-aware applications use the ClusterResourceControl and ClusterResourceTypeControl functions to communicate information to set properties (common and private), request operations, and so on; when a management or cluster-aware application calls either of these functions, the Resource Monitor invokes the ResourceControl or ResourceTypeControl functions, respectively, and the appropriate control code is passed to these entry points; Resource DLLs that implement these entry points should perform the control request specified by the control code or retrieve or set the property of the resource; control codes that are not handled by the resource DLL should return the appropriate status (by returning ERROR_INVALID_FUNCTION status) back to the Resource Monitor, and let the Resource Monitor handle it

context as the logged-on user. To ensure that you are running in the same security context as the Cluster Service, you must stop the Cluster Service, and then start the Cluster Service locally from the command line using the –debug switch.

- Before invoking the debugger, be sure to copy the symbol files from the \Symbols directory on the SDK compact disc read-only memory (CD-ROM) to your %windir%\Symbols directory, where windir is the directory where Windows is installed.
- Before invoking the debugger, be sure to copy any .pdb files for your resource DLL to the same location as your resource DLL.

Tip: You must be aware that if there are two nodes in the cluster and the other node is online, the debugger you start may be started on the other node, if that is where the resource or resource type being debugged is loaded. Also, even if you are logged on with the same account as the Cluster

Service account, it does not mean that you are running in the same security context as the Cluster Service.

When you debug a resource DLL, you can debug either the resource type or the resources that belong to the resource type, or both, as explained next.

The following are the steps to debug a resource type:

1. Set the resource type DebugControlFunctions property to TRUE.
2. Set the resource type DebugPrefix property to the path to your debugger.

When your ResourceTypeControl entry point function is called, the Cluster Service checks the settings for these properties. If DebugControlFunction is set to TRUE and DebugPrefix contains a valid path, the Cluster Service creates a new Resource Monitor process for ResourceTypeControl and attaches the specified debugger to it.

The following are the steps to debug a resource DLL:

1. Register the DebugEx Cluster Administrator DLL. DebugEx is a sample and is installed in the cluster directory of your system directory (typically C:\WINNT\CLUSTER). DebugEx is a Cluster Administrator Extension that you can use to debug your resource DLL. To set up DebugEx, specify the debugger that you wish to use. If the resource is configured to run in its own Resource Monitor, the Cluster Service attaches the specified debugger to the Resource Monitor for that resource after it has started but before any entry points in the resource DLL have been called.
2. Start the Cluster Administrator.
3. Create a new resource of the type supported by your resource DLL. Make sure that you specify that the resource should run in a separate Resource Monitor. A dedicated Resource Monitor is required during debugging to help you isolate problems and to ensure that other resources remain unaffected by those problems.
4. View the properties of the new resource by choosing Properties from the File menu after selecting the new resource.
5. Click the Debug tab.
6. In the Debug Command Prefix edit control, type the full path to your debugger. For example, if you are using MSDEV, type "c:\msdev\bin\msdev.exe." The common resource property, DebugPrefix, holds the path to the debugger that attaches to the Resource Monitor for the resource.
7. Click the OK button.
8. Stop the Cluster Service by typing "net stop clussvc."
9. Start the Cluster Service locally by typing the following command from the cluster directory:

```
start clussvc -debug
```

This command causes a command box to be displayed with the output from the Cluster Service. When the Cluster Service starts, it starts the Resource Monitor with your resource in it and attaches your debugger to it. At that point MSDEV is invoked. You can now set breakpoints in the DLL, such as SmbSampleOnlineThread. As another example, you can debug the ResourceTypeControl entry point function by attaching a debugger to the main Resource Monitor process and by setting a breakpoint at s_RmResourceTypeControl. You can also set additional breakpoints in the DLL once you step past the call to LoadLibrary.

The Platform SDK allows you to use the DebugEx Extension DLL to debug the Startup and Open entry point functions by using the DebugEx Extension and specifying the DebugPrefix value for the required resource type. Although the DebugEx Extension is optional, it allows you to use Cluster Administrator for turning debugging on and off on a resource-by-resource basis or for all resources of a particular type. Once the extension has been registered, the Debug tab appears on all resource types as well.

Special considerations apply when you want to debug while a resource is being created. To debug startup code in a resource DLL while the resource is being created, set the DebugPrefix property on the resource type ahead of time by using Cluster.exe or by bringing up properties on the resource type, clicking the Debug tab, and specifying the debugger. Then, when a resource is created, check the Use Separate Resource Monitor check box, and click the Next button to start the debugger immediately. When a resource of the specified type is created, the Resource Monitor waits until the debugger has attached and also calls DebugBreak after calling LoadLibrary. Some debuggers (such as CDB and WinDbg) also break when they attach, while others (such as MsDev) do not. In any case, the Resource Monitor displays a message in the debugger output window when the debugger attaches, after loading the resource DLL.

Tip: If you are not running the Cluster Service interactively (i.e., from the command line), trying to debug a resource DLL with the MSDEV debugger causes the appearance of error popup dialogs.

Guidelines for Writing Resource Dynamic Link Libraries

The following lists some guidelines for writing Resource DLLs:

- Sometimes you may not want your resource DLLs to be interrupted by the Cluster Service polling for resource status. You can avoid the interruption by returning an event handle to inform the service not to call the LooksAlive entry point. Then you can use the event handle to signal status information to the Cluster Service.
- Use callback functions whenever possible, because callback functions allow for asynchronous communication between the resource DLL and the Resource Monitor. The typical callback functions that regular resource DLLs use are the LogEvent and the SetResourceStatus callback functions. LogEvent is called to record resource events, and SetResourceStatus is called to communicate resource status information to the Resource Monitor.
- Initialize global data used by the resource DLL in Startup. Initialize resource-specific data in the Open entry point.
- Within a resource DLL, make use of separate threads to perform lengthy operations, such as opening resources, bringing resources online, taking them offline, and so on. Creating separate threads makes the process of communicating with the Resource Monitor (and, in turn, the Cluster Service) more efficient. If, for example, a resource takes more than 300 msec to come online, spawn a separate thread to complete the process, allowing the entry point to return immediately.
- Properties should be read in the Open function if possible. If this is not possible, they should be read in the Online function.
- If your resources need to be notified of cluster-specific events, node-specific events, group state changes, and cluster database changes or updates, create a cluster notification port (use CreateClusterNotifyPort) to handle event notifications. Note that there is a potential for a race condition if multiple threads use notification ports. For example, one thread could be calling CloseClusterNotifyPort to close the notification port while another thread, which has called GetClusterNotify, is waiting to retrieve information from the same port. You can prevent this problem by having the thread that is calling GetClusterNotify check for a CLUSTER_CHANGE_HANDLE_CLOSE event.

- Support the CLUSCTL_RESOURCE_GET_PRIVATE_PROPERTIES control function so that management tools such as Cluster.exe can set properties that have not been set yet.
- Support the CLUSCTL_RESOURCE_VALIDATE_PRIVATE_PROPERTIES and CLUSCTL_RESOURCE_SET_PRIVATE_PROPERTIES control functions so that your resource DLL can validate properties before they are saved.
- Support the CLUSCTL_RESOURCE_TYPE_GET_PRIVATE_PROPERTIES, CLUSCTL_RESOURCE_TYPE_VALIDATE_PRIVATE_PROPERTIES, and CLUSCTL_RESOURCE_TYPE_SET_PRIVATE_PROPERTIES control functions if your resource type has private properties.
- Support the CLUSCTL_RESOURCE_GET_REQUIRED_DEPENDENCIES and CLUSCTL_RESOURCE_TYPE_GET_REQUIRED_DEPENDENCIES control functions if your resources require a dependency on another resource.

PROGRAMMING CLUSTER ADMINISTRATOR EXTENSION DYNAMIC LINK LIBRARIES

Creating a Cluster Administrator Extension Dynamic Link Library

Creating a Cluster Administrator Extension DLL involves implementing some of the methods from the Cluster Administrator Extension API and making calls to others. Whereas the resource API is made up of standard functions, the Cluster Administrator Extension API is a COM-based API consisting of interfaces. Therefore, you need to be familiar with the COM programming model.

The following are the major steps involved in creating a Cluster Administrator Extension DLL:

1. The simplest way to build a Cluster Administrator Extension DLL is by using the Resource Type AppWizard. The code produced by the Resource Type AppWizard uses the MFC and C++ language. This builds a skeletal Cluster Administrator Extension DLL with all the entry points defined, declared, and exported. This skeletal DLL code generated by the AppWizard provides only the most basic failover and failback capability. It does, however, contain comments such as TODO (to indicate where to insert additional functionality) and ADDPARAM (to indicate where to insert additional parameters or properties). These comments indicate areas where you need to add resource-specific information.
2. Use the Cluster Administrator Extension API to supplement the capabilities of your Cluster Administrator Extension DLL. Typically, the descriptions in the resource API help you determine if you need to implement optional entry point functions and how and when to make calls to the Cluster Administrator.

Registering a Cluster Administrator Extension Dynamic Link Library

To register your Cluster Administrator Extension DLL, call REGCLADM.EXE followed by the complete path to the DLL as follows:

```
regcladm path
```

Next, register DebugEx so that this extension is available to aid in debugging your resource DLL. To register DebugEx, enter:

```
regcladm debugex.dll
```

If DebugEx has already been registered, the Debug tab appears as one of the tabs on the property sheet of Cluster Administrator.

There are two steps in the registration of a Cluster Administrator Extension:

- The first step is registering the extension with the cluster. The DllRegisterCluAdminExtension entry point accomplishes this registration. DllRegisterCluAdminExtension causes the AdminExtensions property to be stored in the cluster database and modified if necessary. The class identifier (CLSID) for the extension is placed in the AdminExtensions value if it is not already present.
- The second part is registering the extension with COM. The DllRegisterServer entry point accomplishes this registration. This causes a key for the ProgId (e.g., CLUADMEX.Standard) to be created below HKEY_CLASSES_ROOT and a key for the CLSID to be created below HKEY_CLASSES_ROOT\CLSID.

REGCLADM calls both DllRegisterCluAdminExtension and DllRegisterServer. Setup programs that install these extensions also need to call these two entry points. If your setup program is run on a cluster node, call both entry points. If your setup program is run on a client (e.g., a noncluster node, such as where Cluster Administrator is installed), just call DllRegisterServer.

Debugging a Cluster Administrator Extension Dynamic Link Library

The following are the steps to debug a Cluster Administrator extension DLL:

1. Run the MSDEV debugger and load the project work space that contains your Cluster Administrator extension DLL project.
2. Select the Win32 Debug version of your Cluster Administrator Extension DLL project.
3. Select Settings from the Build menu.
4. Select the entry that represents the Win32 Debug version of your Cluster Administrator Extension DLL project in the Settings For list box.
5. Select the Debug tab to switch to the Debug property page.
6. Type the full path to Cluster Administrator (typically c:\winnt\cluster\cluadmin.exe) in the Executable for debug session and press the OK button.
7. Set a breakpoint in the project, such as at the OnInitDialog method for the parameter page in the resprop.cpp source file.
8. Start Cluster Administrator in the debugger by pressing F5.
9. View the properties of a resource of the type supported by your Cluster Administrator Extension DLL.
10. Select the Parameters tab to switch to the parameters page. This should cause the debugger to halt at the breakpoint set above in step 7. The debugger should also halt when you create a new resource of the type supported by your extension DLL.

PROGRAMMING APPLICATIONS

Creating a Cluster-Aware Application

A cluster-aware application takes advantage of clustering functions provided by MSCS. The clustering functions are accessed by including calls to the Cluster Service using the Cluster API. The Cluster API, as we have seen earlier, allows an application to:

- Retrieve information about cluster objects

- Initiate operations
- Update information in the cluster database

The prerequisites necessary to create a cluster-aware application include

1. Able to fill in required data in Cluster Structures reference as well as parse the structures that hold properties and other information.
2. Make calls using the Cluster API to the Cluster Service.
3. Understand the use of cluster control codes. The cluster control codes allow you to call one of the following four Cluster API functions to perform a multitude of different operations. The specific function to be performed is controlled by setting the control code to a specific value associated with the function to be performed. The four functions controlled by cluster control codes include
   - ClusterResourceControl
   - ClusterResourceTypeControl
   - ClusterGroupControl
   - ClusterNodeControl

More details including the exact syntax and usage instructions for these functions are contained in Appendix A.

Creating a Cluster Management Application

Windows NT Cluster Server comes with its own set of administration functions. However, you can develop your own cluster management applications to supplement or supersede existing cluster administration functions. You can develop cluster management applications using Cluster APIs. If you use Microsoft Visual Basic or a scripting language, then you must use the Cluster Management Library.

You can create a cluster management application using C, C++, Microsoft Visual Basic, or a scripting language. If you are using C or C++, you are working with the Cluster API to manipulate data. If you are using Visual Basic or a scripting language, you are working with the Cluster Automation Server.

The prerequisites to create a cluster management application are

1. Familiarity with the common properties of resources, resource types, nodes, and groups (common properties covered in Chapter 7 and earlier in this chapter).
2. Familiarity with the private properties of resources associated with the Cluster Server resource types by reading Private Resource Properties (private properties are also covered in Chapter 7 and earlier in this chapter).
3. Use of Cluster Structures as mentioned earlier to be able to fill in required data in Cluster Structures reference as well as parse the structures that hold properties and other information.
4. Use of the Cluster API to the Cluster Service to make calls.

Installing a Cluster-Aware Application

After you have developed a cluster-aware application as discussed earlier, be aware that installing the application is a bit more involved than installing regular Windows applications. A cluster-aware application installation typically consists of three steps:

- Installing the application
- Configuring the cluster portion of the application
- Installing/registering the client-side administrator extensions

You should provide options for all the preceding steps to be integrated into a single setup program, or alternately perform the steps individually. Let us look at the installation steps in greater detail.

Installing the Program

This portion of the setup program is a little more involved than the setup program of a regular Windows application because this program should install a copy of the application on each node. The setup program must check to see if the application is being installed on a cluster node. You can make this check in your setup application by calling the OpenCluster function to determine if setup is running in a clustered environment. If OpenCluster indicates that the cluster is currently running, then you are running in a clustered environment. However, it is possible that you have a clustered environment, except that the cluster is not up. Thus, even if OpenCluster returns a NULL response, your setup program should check the database of installed services to determine if the Cluster Service is installed, but turned off.

If the Cluster Service is not running, it is a good idea for your setup program to give the user the option of starting the Cluster Service before proceeding with the installation. Once the application is installed on one node, the setup program could enumerate the other nodes and then use the administration shares and remote registry manipulation to install the application over the network.

Special considerations apply in case your application had been previously installed on a nonclustered machine. In this instance, the setup program should provide additional setup options for clusters. For example, your setup program should allow the application data files, not program files, to be migrated to a disk on the shared SCSI bus, register the new resource type with the cluster, and so on. Alternately, you can opt not to provide these functions and require that the application be completely reinstalled.

Tip: Do not store program files on drives connected to the cluster-shared SCSI bus. Although program files stored in shared SCSI are visible to all nodes in the cluster, storing files there causes problems when you upgrade either Microsoft Cluster Server or the application software. Such upgrades would require the cluster to be shut down completely. If you choose instead to install program files on all nodes in the cluster, you can upgrade each node individually without affecting the cluster operation. This is particularly important if the cluster is in a production environment.

Configuring the Cluster

During this phase in the installation process, the configuration portion of your setup program should create the resource type by calling the cluster management function CreateClusterResourceType, and by installing the corresponding resource DLL or DLLs that support the resource type on each node. To install a DLL, the setup program should copy it to an application installation directory on the destination drive, and register them with their full path.

Tip: The DLL should be copied to all nodes in the cluster prior to the resource type being registered. If this is not done, any instance of Cluster Administrator attached to the cluster node that does not have access to the resource DLL displays an error when it is notified that the resource type was added, and there is an attempt to read the properties of the resource type.

Finally, your program should register the Cluster Administrator extension DLL with the cluster. To register a Cluster Administrator extension with a cluster, implement the DllRegisterCluAdminExtension entry point function (in the Cluster Administrator Extension). To register a Cluster Administrator Extension in the system registry, implement the DllRegisterServer entry point function.

The network administrator may combine your custom resource type with a network name resource and its dependent resources to create a virtual server that clients can access. Your setup program should call the appropriate Cluster API functions to make sure that the network administrator places all the necessary dependencies in the same group. You should also configure the resource to use those dependencies. For example, if your newly created cluster-aware application relies on data files, determine which drive is to be used.

Installing/Registering the Client-Side Administrator Extensions

The client-side Cluster Administrator Extension is the portion of the administration extension that the Cluster Administrator tool uses. The setup program should copy it onto the machine that runs the Cluster Administrator tools and that are registered as an Inproc Server.

PROGRAMMING CUSTOM RESOURCE TYPES

Creating a Custom Resource Type

It is possible to create a new resource type that you can associate with either a cluster-aware or a cluster-unaware application. The advantages to creating your own new resource type are

- You can have the Resource Monitor manage your application in ways that are specific to your application.
- You can make administration through Cluster Administrator less complicated.

When you create a new resource type, you should expect the network administrator to combine your new type with a network name resource and its dependent resources to create a virtual server that clients can access. Make sure that the network administrator places all the necessary dependencies in the same group either by checking for this condition in your Cluster Administrator Extension or by failing to load the resource DLL if a dependency is missing.

When you create a new resource type, you should understand and keep in mind how administrators expect to interact with new types of resources. Most administrators are likely to use Cluster Administrator for interacting with new resource types. For this reason, many resource type developers typically write an extension to the Cluster Administrator to handle their new resource types. To be able to create DLLs with behavior that is consistent with the Cluster Administrator, read the Microsoft Cluster Server Administrator's Guide.

If there are required dependencies for your new resource type, support the CLUSCTL_RESOURCE_GET_REQUIRED_DEPENDENCIES control code in your resource DLL ResourceControl entry point and CLUSCTL_RESOURCE_TYPE_GET_REQUIRED_DEPENDENCIES in your ResourceTypeControl entry point. Also, check in Online that all required dependencies are available before allowing a resource to be brought online.

For example, suppose your new resource type manages a cluster-aware application that relies on data files. The network administrator might form a virtual server with this application, a network name resource, an IP address resource, and a physical disk resource holding the application data files.

It is recommended that you use the Resource Type AppWizard to create your new resource type. Because the Resource Type AppWizard creates skeletal implementations of all required entry point functions and interface methods, you can save time and effort and be assured that you are starting with working code.

When you use the Resource Type AppWizard, you have to specify parameters. The parameters are private properties that are specific to your resource type. When a network administrator runs Cluster Administrator to create a resource of the new type, your Cluster Administrator Extension prompts him or her to enter values for these properties. These values are stored in the cluster database.

The following are the steps to create a custom resource type:

1. Create a resource type project using the Resource Type AppWizard.
2. Prepare your build environment.
3. Add code to customize the source files for your resource and Cluster Administrator Extension DLLs. (See earlier section on customizing a resource DLL in this chapter.)
4. Build the resource and Cluster Administrator Extension DLLs. (See later section on building a custom resource type in this chapter.)
5. Register your new resource type. (See earlier section on registering a resource DLL in this chapter.)
6. Register your Cluster Administrator Extension DLL and the DebugEx Cluster Administrator Extension DLL.
7. Debug your resource DLL. (See earlier section on debugging a resource DLL in this chapter.)
8. Debug your Cluster Administrator Extension DLL.

Using the Resource Type AppWizard

The Microsoft Visual C++ development environment includes the Resource Type AppWizard, a wizard that guides you through the creation of a new resource type. The Resource Type AppWizard prompts for two types of information:

- Information that is common to all resources, or common properties
- Information that applies only to resources belonging to your new type, or private properties

Private properties are not shared with resources belonging to other types; they are specific to a single type. Examples of private resource properties include ShareName and Path properties for file share resources and the Signature property for physical disk resources.

The following procedure takes you through the steps necessary for creating a project to support a new resource type with the Resource Type AppWizard.

1. Start your Visual C++ development environment.
2. Select New from the File menu and then Project Workspace from the list box.
3. Select Cluster Resource Type Application from the list of project types, enter the name of the project, and press the Create button.
4. Provide a name in the Resource type name edit control.
5. If you are creating a resource type to manage a service, check the Resource that depends on a service checkbox and enter the name of the service.
6. Press the Next button.
   The Resource Parameters dialog box allows you to add parameters that are specific to your resource type, like a share name for a disk resource or a subnet mask for an IP address resource. Parameters are passed to your resource DLL to control the software associated with your new resource type. Some parameters are considered private prop-

erties of the resource and are accessible through Cluster Administrator and other management applications using the control code functions of the Cluster API.

7. For each parameter that you want to enter, press the Add button and specify the name and type of the parameter and whether or not it is required. If you specify a numerical type such as DWORD, you can enter a default value, a minimum value, and a maximum value.
8. After adding each parameter, press the OK button of the Add Parameter dialog box. Notice that the parameter and all related information is inserted into the Resource Parameters dialog box. The order in which the parameters appear dictates their order on the Parameters page in your Cluster Administrator Extension. The dialog box shows how the Resource Parameters screen appears after two parameters have been added.
9. When you have added all the parameters for the resource type, press the Finish button. A screen entitled New Project Information is displayed, providing data about the projects that you are about to create to support your new resource type. The data include the names of the projects, resource type, project files, and classes; and specify the directory in which the projects are installed.
   The New Project Information screen shows the type of data that is generated.
10. If you are satisfied with the New Project Information, press the OK button to create the projects.
11. Wait for the projects to be created and the workspace to be unloaded and reloaded. Your resource DLL and Cluster Administrator Extension DLL projects are now ready for you to use.

Building a Custom Resource Type

After you have created a project for your new resource type, attempt to build it. Use the Win32 Debug option if you would like debug versions of your DLLs and the Win32 Release option if you prefer release versions. You can build your DLLs from within Microsoft Developer Studio or from the command line with the following commands:

```
nmake /a /f project.mak CFG="ResourceType - Win32 Version"

nmake /a /f project.mak CFG="ResourceTypeEx - Win32 Version"
```

Substitute the name of your project makefile for project.mak. Substitute the name of your new resource type for ResourceType and then append an "Ex" to the resource type for ResourceTypeEx. For example, if you name your new resource TestDB, set ResourceType to TestDB and ResourceTypeEx to TestDBEx. Specify Debug or Release for the version.

If either of your build attempts fail, recheck that your environment variables are assigned correctly.

Cluster Automation Server with Visual Basic

The Microsoft Cluster Automation Server allows you to create instances of programmable objects that you can access with an application or tool that supports Automation, such as Microsoft Visual Basic. Programmable objects expose properties that can be retrieved and updated and methods that can be invoked through Visual Basic. The programmable objects provided by Cluster Server expose properties and methods that are specific to cluster management.

To prepare your environment for using the Cluster Automation Server with Visual Basic, perform the following steps:

1. Install Microsoft Visual Basic version 4.0 or later.
2. Install the Microsoft Cluster Server SDK.
3. Register MSCLUS.DLL, the DLL that contains the Cluster Automation Server. Typically, this registration is taken care of when you install the SDK. However, if you need to manually register MSCLUS.DLL, use the system registry program REGSVR32.
4. Test your environment.
   a. Launch Visual Basic and choose References from the Projects menu.
   b. If MSCLUS.DLL has been registered properly, it appears in the list of components as "MS Cluster 1.0 Type Library."
   c. Click the check box next to this item in the list to enable the Visual Basic Object Browser to include the programmable cluster objects. Then, you are able to allocate instances of these objects, call their methods, and retrieve as well as set their properties.

Using the Cluster Database

The cluster database is part of the Microsoft Windows NT registry that is resident on each cluster node. It contains information about all physical and logical elements in a cluster.

The following table lists the keys under which cluster data are stored.

TABLE 4
Cluster Database Registry Keys

Cluster Database Key	Type of Stored
DataCluster\Parameters\Groups	Information about cluster groups
Cluster\Parameters\Nodes	Information about cluster nodes
Cluster\Parameters\Quorum	Information about the quorum resource
Cluster\Parameters\Resources	Information about cluster resources
Cluster\Parameters\ResourceTypes	Information about resource types

The following data show an excerpt from the information stored in the cluster database for Cluster Server's Physical Disk resource type:

Physical Disk
  AdminExtensions : REG_MULTI_SZ : {4EC90FB0-D0BB-11CF-B5EF-00A0C90AB505}
  DllName : REG_SZ : clusres.dll
  IsAlivePollInterval : REG_DWORD : 0xea60
  LooksAlivePollInterval : REG_DWORD : 0x1388
  Name : REG_SZ : Physical Disk

Much of the information that is stored in the cluster database is property information. For the Physical Disk resource type, AdminExtensions, DllName, IsAlivePollInterval, LooksAlivePollInterval, and Name are all common properties. The entries are in order by property name, followed by type and value.

Individual resources often store both common and private property information in the cluster database. Whereas common properties apply to all resources regardless of their type, private properties apply only to resources of a specific type. For example, an IP address resource requires an address, network name, and subnet mask while a physical disk resource requires a signature.

Resources and groups store their key name as a GUID. This is the unique identifier for the resource or group. Groups store the following pieces of information in the cluster database:

- List of GUID values that identify resources that are members of the group
- Name of the group such as Cluster Group or Disk Group
- Numerical constant that indicates the group operational status

Cluster-aware applications should use the cluster database exclusively for saving state and property information; they should not use the system registry. Using the cluster database makes it easier to manage and administer the cluster and allows a resource configuration for a specific node to be modified even when the node is offline.

However, it is possible for a cluster-unaware application to use the system registry to store important information. In the event that the application is moved, it would be essential to maintain access to this information. The Cluster API includes a feature known as registry checkpointing to ensure the availability of information stored on a tree in the system registry. The application establishes a registry checkpoint by calling ClusterResourceControl with the CLUSCTL_RESOURCE_ADD_REGISTRY_CHECKPOINT control code. Whenever anything changes on the checkpointed registry tree and the application is online, the Cluster Service stores a copy of the tree in the quorum resource log file. If the application moves to another node, the Cluster Service restores the registry tree from the log file to the system registry on the new node.

To access information in the cluster database, applications should use the control code functions in the Cluster API whenever possible. The control code functions are shown in Table 5.

TABLE 5
Control Types and Functions

Control Type	Function
ClusterResourceControl	to access resource information
ClusterResourceTypeControl	to access resource type information
ClusterGroupControl	to access group information
ClusterNodeControl	to access node information

These functions provide access to state and property information through a variety of control codes. There is a different set of control codes that are valid for each function. For example, to access resource modifiable common properties, call ClusterResourceControl with the control code CLUSCTL_RESOURCE_GET_COMMON_PROPERTIES.

When an application requires information that is not exposed through a control code, usually one of the cluster database management functions included in the Cluster API can be called to retrieve the information. The database management functions are similar to the Microsoft Win32 registry functions, but there is one important difference. With the database management functions, changes made on one node are automatically distributed as they occur to all affected nodes in the cluster. Therefore, all members of a cluster have consistent access to the information. Because the Win32 registry functions lack this important replication feature, applications should never use them to access the cluster database.

Preparing a Build Environment

To prepare your environment for building and debugging resource DLLs or Cluster Administrator Extension DLLs, you must correctly set the PATH, INCLUDE, and LIB environment variables and check for the existence of required libraries. Complete the following checklist to prepare your build environment:

1. Verify that you have set your PATH, INCLUDE, and LIB environment variables to include the appropriate directories in the correct order. The Microsoft Developer Studio bin, include, and lib directories must appear first in the lists of directories for the corresponding PATH, INCLUDE, and LIB environment variables.
2. Set the PATH environment variable to a path that includes as its first directory the Developer Studio binary directory. This is typically c:\msdev\bin.
3. Set the INCLUDE environment variable to a path that includes these directories in the following order:
   a. Developer Studio directory containing header files, typically c:\msdev\include
   b. Directory containing the CLUSAPI.H header file
   c. Directory containing the ATL source files and header files, typically c:\msdev\atl
4. Set the LIB environment variable to a path that includes as its first directory the Developer Studio library directory. This is typically c:\msdev\lib.
5. Check that you have installed the Unicode version of Microsoft Foundation Classes (MFC); this library is required for building the Cluster Administrator Extension DLL.
6. Check that you have the DebugEx Cluster Administrator Extension DLL available in your cluster directory.

Tip: It is common to set your environment variables during the installation process for Microsoft Developer Studio. However, they can also be set by running VCVARS32.BAT from the BIN directory under the root of your development environment. Running VCVARS32.BAT is only necessary if you want to build from the command line rather than from within Developer Studio.

9 Microsoft Cluster Server Administration

Windows NT Cluster Server is built on top of Windows NT Server. As such, you need to be familiar with the concepts and tools for administering the Windows NT Server before you can start administering Windows NT Cluster Server.

PREREQUISITES FOR A CLUSTER SERVER ADMINISTRATOR

Microsoft recommends the following prerequisites for its course on Supporting Cluster Server:

- Working knowledge of Microsoft Windows NT Server 4.0 including sharing files, folders, and printers
- Working knowledge of Microsoft Internet Information Server 3.0 including setting up a Web site
- Completion of the "Networking Essentials" self-paced training or equivalent knowledge
- Completion of the "Administering Microsoft Windows NT 4.0" and "Supporting Microsoft Windows NT 4.0 Core Technologies" courses or equivalent knowledge
- Although not required, familiarity with Transmission Control Protocol/Internet Protocol (TCP/IP) terminology and concepts recommended, as provided in "Internetworking with Microsoft TCP/IP on Microsoft Windows NT 3.5"
- Experience supporting networks or end users

INSTALLING THE CLUSTER ADMINISTRATOR

You can install Cluster Administrator on any computer running Service Pack 3 (SP3) with version 4.0 of either Windows NT Workstation or Windows NT Server. You can also install Cluster Administrator on any computer running Windows NT Server, Enterprise Edition (which includes SP3).

When you install Cluster Administrator, Cluster.exe is also installed (in the Windows NT\System32 folder). For more information on Cluster.exe, see "Administering clusters from the command prompt" later in this chapter.

To install Cluster Administrator:

1. Run Microsoft Cluster Server (MSCS) Set up from the Microsoft Windows NT Server, Enterprise Edition 4.0 Components CD (in the MSCS\Cluster\I386 or MSCS\Cluster\Alpha folder, depending on your platform); or, if you are installing from your network, establish a network connection to the MSCS Set up files, switch to the Cluster\I386 or Cluster\Alpha folder (depending on your platform), and run Set up.exe.
2. If prompted, click Install Cluster Administrator.

3. Specify the folder you want to contain the MSCS files, and click Next. By default, MSCS installs the files in C:\Winnt\Cluster.
4. Click Finish.

ADMINISTRATION

Once a cluster is set up, as described in Chapter 4, then the Cluster Administrator has to perform ongoing administration. Administering a cluster can be viewed as an extension to the administration of a Windows NT Server where some current administration steps need to be changed and some new steps have to be added.

You can administer a Windows NT Cluster using any of the following methods:

- The Cluster Administrator Utility included with MSCS
- **Cluster.exe**, from the command line or with scripts
- Your own custom administration tools, which can be developed using the MSCS automation interfaces included in the Microsoft Platform Software Development Kit (SDK)

We cover each of these mentioned methods in this chapter. We start with the most commonly used method, the Cluster Administration Utility. We discuss the other two methods later in this chapter.

CLUSTER ADMINISTRATION UTILITY

The primary tool used by the administrator for configuration, management, and administration of a Microsoft Cluster Server is the Cluster Administrator Utility, commonly called Cluster Administrator (not to be confused with the human administrator of Clusters and/or Windows NT. To distinguish between the two, this book refers to the Cluster Administrator Utility as the Cluster Administrator and the human administrator as just Administrator).

Tip: While the clustering functions provided by MSCS work only with Windows NT Server, Enterprise Edition, it is possible to install and administer the Cluster Administrator component on any computer running SP3 with version 4.0 of either Windows NT Workstation or Windows NT Server. Thus, it is possible to administer an MSCS cluster from a Cluster Server, a nonclustered Windows NT Server, or even from a computer running Windows NT Workstation.

The introduction of MSCS introduces new cluster-related management functions that the administrator must perform. It also causes changes to current administrative tasks that the administrator performs. We start with the changes to the current administrative tasks and then look at cluster-specific administrative tasks later in this chapter.

REGULAR ADMINISTRATIVE TASKS

An administrator performs administrative tasks, on a regular basis, for a Windows NT Server. These tasks include

- Restarting a server due to a failure
- Installing backup server data
- Upgrading hardware such as adding disk or memory capacity
- Installing upgrades to software such as operating system patches
- Installing new software that requires system restart to complete installation

One of the important changes as a result of clustering to these steps is the availability of the server. These steps would have normally made the server unavailable to users. With a Cluster Server, the second node continues to make the server resources available to users. Clustering enables the administrator to perform the tasks listed earlier without warning and stopping the users from accessing the server. The administrators do not have to wait for nonpeak hours or weekends to perform many of the previously mentioned tasks.

The Cluster Administrator Utility provides the tools that help the administrator perform administrative functions. We discuss different options provided by the Cluster Administrator Utility throughout this chapter. Let us next look at a couple of these options. These are connecting to cluster and initiating a resource failure.

Connecting to a Cluster

Whenever the Cluster Administrator Utility comes up, it automatically restores the connection to the last cluster that was administered. In most cases, this is the cluster the administrator wants to work with anyway and the administrator can start using the Cluster Administrator. If the default cluster is not the cluster the administrator wants to work with, the administrator can use the **Open Connection** option on the Cluster Administrator **File** menu to access additional cluster networks and nodes.

However, the very first time the Cluster Administrator is started (after installation), there is no default cluster to connect to. In this scenario, the Cluster Administrator prompts the administrator for a cluster name to connect to. The administrator can enter either the network name of the cluster or the name of a cluster node. Network name of the cluster is the preferred choice. Node name should be used only when the cluster name does not work. One instance in which the administrator has to enter a node name is when the cluster name resource fails to come online and the administrator is unable to physically locate at a node to administer the cluster. In this case, the administrator can enter the node name and then administer the cluster from the administrator's location. Depending on whether a cluster name or node name is entered, the Cluster Administrator title bar shows Cluster Administrator — ClusterName (ClusterName) or Cluster Administrator — ClusterName (NodeName).

Initiating a Resource Failure

The administrator may want to cause a resource failure and take the resource offline. Cluster Administrator includes an option that can be used to initiate a resource failure. A failure is initiated using the **Initiate Failure** option on the pull-down menu from the **Cluster Administrator** File menu. Alternately, initiating a failure can also be accomplished by right-clicking the resource.

This option can be used for performing scheduled maintenance on a resource. This option can also be used to test the restart settings for the resource and the failover settings for the group of which the resource is a member. For example, if an administrator wants a node to attempt to restart a resource five times before the resource is failed over to the other node. The administrator can initiate failure for the resource six times and verify that the resource fails over to the other node.

Changes to Regular Administrative Tasks due to Clustering

Besides the timing and convenience aspects of administrative procedures, there are other changes required to administration procedures for Cluster Server servers installed on the network. These include

- Changes to administrative steps prior to bringing down a server
- Changes to backup procedures
- Managing servers as a single entity

Let us take a brief look at each of these changes.

Changes to Administrative Steps Prior to Bringing Down a Server

For a nonclustered server, an administrator typically issues periodic warnings to users that the server is unavailable. Warnings may not be required if one of the Cluster Servers is brought down, unless the capacity configuration of the cluster is such that there is a significant degradation in performance. In this case, a warning of degradation in service may be appropriate. As a prior step, the Cluster Administrator can move all groups from the node that is planned to be brought down to the other node of the cluster. This further reduces the time the node has to spend determining that the other node is down, and subsequently performing a failover.

Changes to Backup Procedures

Unlike the regular backup of two independent servers, backing up a cluster involves backing up the cluster servers as well as the shared storage for the cluster. The backup of the data on the shared Small Computer System Interface (SCSI) drive, or drives, should be performed via a network connection to a network name created on the cluster for backup purposes. This network name should be a member of the same cluster group as the shared SCSI drive so that if a failover occurs the network name and drive are on the same node.

For example, shared SCSI drives automatically have hidden administrative shares created for them. Therefore, in a cluster where the shared drive is drive T, it is possible to connect to \\network_name_for_backups\t$.

This connection allows backup of the data regardless of the node on which the shared SCSI drive or drives are an active resource, as long as the network name and drive are members of the same group.

Managing Servers as a Single Entity

Another important change is that Cluster Server provides the means for an administrator to manage both nodes of the cluster as a single entity. This means that the administrator can administer the servers in the cluster from a single desktop, even though the clusters may be remotely located — such as on a different floor in a building or even in another building.

Another twist to the remote administration is that the remote node in which the Cluster Administrator Utility can be installed does not have to be a cluster node. The administrator can run Cluster Server Set up, and choose to install only the Cluster Administrator Utility.

CLUSTER-SPECIFIC ADMINISTRATIVE TASKS

Cluster management applications are used for cluster-specific administrative tasks such as:

- Adding and removing resources, groups, and other cluster objects
- Establishing resource dependencies
- Configuring clusters
- Establishing failover policies
- Changing the membership of groups
- Moving a group from one node to another, etc.
- Initiating failover to perform maintenance
- Manually moving resources for load balancing
- Handling routine maintenance
- Monitoring cluster activity

Configuring Clusters

The Cluster Administrator Utility is used to configure groups and resources such as networks and disks. Specifically, the Cluster Administrator Utility is used to:

- Configure cluster group settings
    - Add, delete, and rename groups
    - Change the state of groups
    - Transfer ownership of groups from node to node
    - Group failover and failback properties

- Configure common resource settings
    - Add, delete, and rename resources
    - Change the state of resources
    - Transfer ownership of resources from one group to another
    - Resource dependencies and advanced resource settings

- Configure resource specific parameter settings
    - Resource settings for file shares
    - Resource settings for Internet Information Server (IIS) virtual root
    - Resource settings for network name
    - Resource settings for physical disk
    - Resource settings for IP address

- Configure cluster wide settings
    - Settings for quorum log
    - Settings for network priority
    - Settings for network usage
    - Settings for network adapter

Let us take a detailed look at each of these functions.

Configuring Cluster Group Settings

Adding, deleting, and renaming groups

To add a group, the administrator selects the **New** option on the Cluster Administrator **File** menu, and then clicks **Group**. This starts the new group wizard, which steps the administrator through the configuration process. The new group wizard handles most of the group settings, except failover and failback settings, which are set using the cluster group property pages. Cluster group property pages are covered later in this chapter.

The Cluster Administrator can also be used to delete and rename groups by choosing these options from the pull-down menu shown in Figure 1. Note that this menu is context sensitive and the options that are currently unavailable are automatically grayed out.

Tip: When a group is deleted, all the resources that were members of the group are also deleted.

Changing the state of groups

The state of groups can be changed from online to offline and vice versa using the pull-down menu under the File menu of the Cluster Administrator. The entries on the pull-down menu are **Bring**

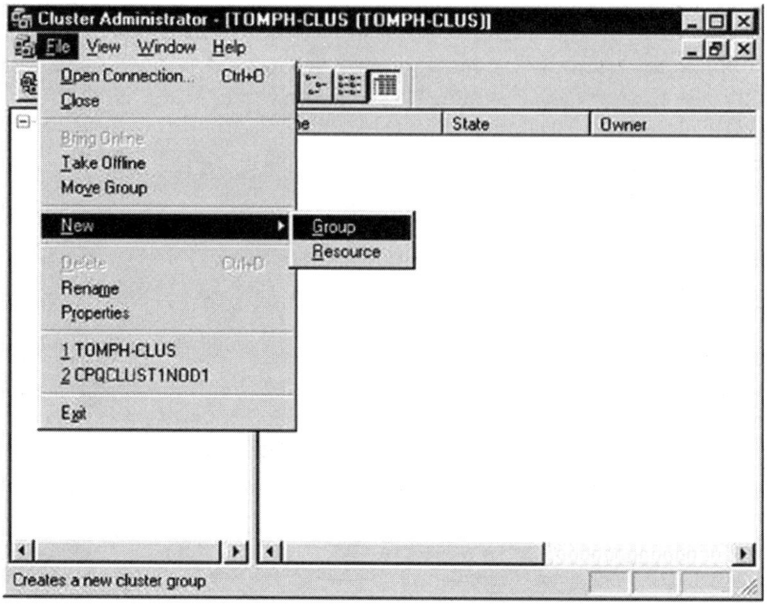

FIGURE 1 Adding a new group. (Reprinted with permission from Microsoft.)

Online and **Take Offline**. Depending on the current state of the group one of these two choices is not selectable. Alternatively, the administrator can right click on a group icon and then click **Bring Online** or **Take Offline** from the popup menu or click the **Bring Online** or **Take Offline** buttons on the toolbar.

Changing the state of a group also changes the state of all the member resources belonging to the group appropriately. The order in which the resources are changed is based on the dependencies of the resources.

Transferring ownership of groups from node to node

Cluster Administrator can be used to transfer ownership of a group. Transfer is accomplished by moving the group from one node to another.

A group can be moved by selecting the **Move Group** option on the **File** pull-down menu. Alternately, the administrator can right click a group, and then click **Move Group** or drag and drop the group between nodes in the Cluster Administrator.

A common use for transfer of ownership is to move groups from a cluster node when preparing to shut down the cluster node and then to perform a regular maintenance function mentioned earlier. When a group is moved, the resources in the group are taken offline, the group ownership is transferred to the other node, and then all the resources are brought back online.

Group failover and failback properties

Group general, failover, and failback properties are configured using group configuration property pages. The group configuration property pages are accessed by clicking a group, and then selecting **Properties** from the **File** pull-down menu. Alternately, the group configuration property pages can be accessed by right clicking a group and then clicking **Properties**, or by clicking a group and then clicking the **Properties** icon. This brings up the group configuration property dialog box shown in Figure 2. As shown in Figure 2, the dialog includes three tabs, one each for setting the group general, failover, and failback properties.

The general property page is selected by choosing the first tab in the Cluster Group Properties dialog. The general property page lets the administrator specify the name, description, and preferred

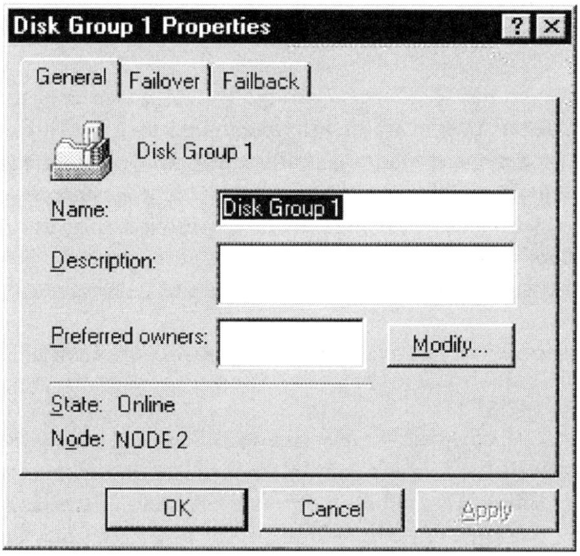

FIGURE 2 Group properties dialog.

owners of a group. The group name must be unique. Description is the group description and is optional. The preferred owner or owners are the nodes that can own the group. A group can failback only if a preferred owner is specified.

The Failover tab lets the administrator set the values for failover threshold and failover period.

Threshold is the maximum number of times that the group is allowed to failover within the failover period. If this number is exceeded within the failover period, then the Cluster Server takes the group offline. The default setting for threshold is ten.

Failover period is the maximum number of hours during which the failover threshold cannot be exceeded. If the threshold is exceeded within the failover period, then the Cluster Server takes the group offline. The default setting for the failover period is 6 h. Note that h is the default unit of measure for this field.

Failback property page is selected by choosing the third tab in the Cluster Group Properties dialog. The failback property page lets the administrator set failback for a group or even prevent failback. The failback property page settings apply to all groups.

Prevent failback is the default option and setting this option prevents the group from failing back to the node on which it was running before failover. The allow failback option permits the group to failback to the node on which it was running before failover (after the node returns to the online state). The timing can be controlled by using failback immediately (which causes failback to occur as soon as Cluster Server detects that the original node is back online) or failback between (which causes failback to occur only between the specified hours).

Configuring Common Resource Settings

The functions performed for configuring common resource settings include

- Adding, deleting, and renaming resources
- Changing the state of resources
- Transferring ownership of resources from group to group
- Configuring resource dependencies and advanced resource settings

Let us look at each of these in more detail.

Adding, deleting, and renaming resources

Adding a resource is very similar to adding a group. To add a resource, the administrator selects the **New** option on the Cluster Administrator **File** menu, and then clicks **Resource**. This starts the new resource wizard, which steps the administrator through the configuration process. The new resource wizard handles most of the resource settings, except Restart, LooksAlive, IsAlive, and Pending time-out settings, which are set using the cluster resource property pages. Cluster resource property pages are covered later in this chapter.

The Cluster Administrator can also be used to delete and rename resources.

Tip: A resource can be deleted only after all dependent resources have been deleted.

Changing the state of resources

The state of resources can be changed from online to offline and vice versa using the pull-down menu under the **File** menu of the Cluster Administrator. The entries on the pull-down menu are **Bring Online** and **Take Offline**. Depending on the current state of the resource, one of these two choices is not selectable. Alternatively, the administrator can right click on a Resource and then click **Bring Online** or **Take Offline** from the popup menu or click the **Bring Online** or **Take Offline** buttons on the toolbar.

The state of a resource may also be changed if the state of the group (of which this resource is a part) is also changed.

Transferring ownership of resources from group to group

The changing of the group to which the resource belongs transfers ownership of a resource. A resource can be transferred by clicking **Change Group** in the **File** pull-down menu. Alternately, the administrator can right click a resource, and then click **Change Group** or drag and drop the resource between groups in the Cluster Administrator.

The group to which a resource is transferred can be on the same node or a different node. If a resource is moved between groups on the same node, it stays online during the move and does not go offline. If the resource is moved to a group on a different node, it goes offline first, and then comes back online.

Resource dependencies and advanced resource settings

The resource configuration settings are set using the resource Properties dialog box. The resource Properties dialog box is accessed by clicking a resource, and then selecting **Properties** from the **File** pull-down menu. Alternately, the resource Properties dialog box can be accessed by right clicking a resource, and then clicking **Properties** in the popup menu, or by clicking a resource and then clicking the **Properties** icon. The resource configuration settings for general, dependency, and advanced properties are the same regardless of the type of the resource.

General resource properties

The general property tab lets the administrator set the resource name, description, possible owner, resource information, as well as whether or not this resource should be run in a separate Resource Monitor.

- The name of the resource is unique and cannot be changed.
- The description is an optional description of the resource.
- Possible owners are the nodes that can run the resource. If a resource is to failover from node 1 to node 2, then both nodes must be specified as possible owners. The list of possible owners is defined when the resource is created. The list of possible owners can

be changed by clicking the Modify button next to the list of possible owners in the resource Properties dialog box.

The administrator can specify that this resource must be run in a separate Resource Monitor by checking the check box. This option is useful for a resource that is being tested or is otherwise behaving incorrectly and the administrator wants to ensure that the effect of this resource is localized to one resource monitor.

In addition to the name, description, and other information about the resource listed earlier, the resource Properties dialog box also shows (such as a network name) the group to which the resource belongs, the current state of the resource (such as ONLINE), and the node on which the resource is currently running. These settings cannot be changed.

Resource dependency properties

The dependency properties of a resource can be specified using the Dependencies tab in the Resource Properties dialog box as shown in Figure 3.

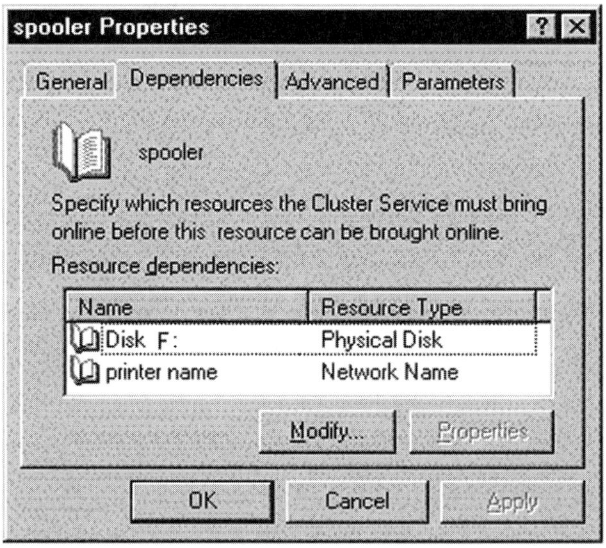

FIGURE 3 Resource Properties dialog.

The dependencies properties tab lets the administrator specify which other resources (that the current resource is dependent on) should be brought online first before the current resource can be brought online. The specification of the dependent resources includes the name and type of the resource. Dependent resource information is changed using the Modify button.

Advanced resource properties

The advanced properties of a resource can be specified using the advanced tab in the resource Properties dialog box as shown in Figure 4.

Advanced resource properties tab lets the administrator specify whether or not a resource should be automatically restarted in case the resource failed, or the group to which the resource belongs should be failed over, failover threshold, threshold period, etc.

The Restart and Do Not Restart radio buttons are mutually exclusive and determine whether the cluster server attempts to automatically restart the resource (Restart) or not (Do Not Restart) if the resource fails. Automatic restart is the default.

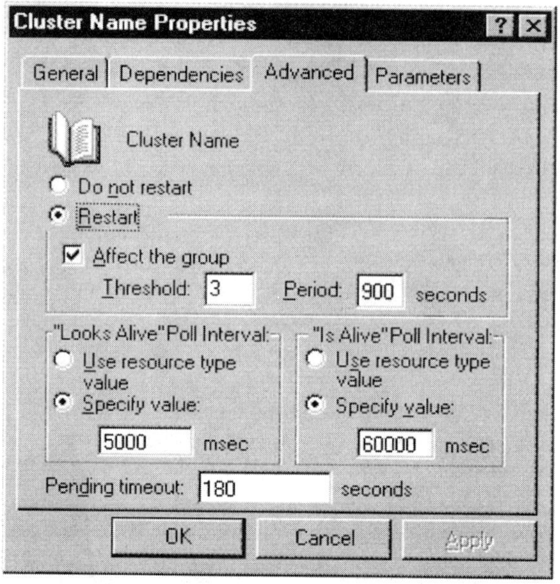

FIGURE 4 Resources advanced properties dialog.

If the resource is to be automatically restarted, the administrator can also specify whether the group to which the resource belongs should be failed over if the resource fails and is unable to be restarted. The default action is not to failover the group, which the administrator can override by selecting the check box.

Threshold is the maximum number of times that the Cluster Server attempts to restart the resource within a specified period (threshold period) before initiating failover. Threshold period is the length of time in which the threshold number of restart attempts occurs. Note that, unlike groups, which use hours as the default, the default unit of measure for this resource setting is in seconds.

The LooksAlive Poll interval lets the administrator specify the frequency (time interval) with which the Cluster Service should check the state of the resource to determine if it appears active.

The administrator can specify a value in milliseconds or let the interval be the default value. To specify a value, the administrator enters a number. To use the default value, the administrator checks the radio button with the text "Use resource type value" (under LooksAlive Poll Interval). The default value for this interval is either 5000 or 7000 msec depending on the resource type.

The IsAlive Poll interval specifies the frequency (time interval) with which the Cluster service checks the state of the resource to determine if it is online (not just appears earlier). The administrator can specify a value in milliseconds or let the interval be the default value. To specify a value, the administrator enters a number. To use the default value, the administrator checks the radio button with the text "Use resource type value" (under IsAlive Poll Interval). The default value for this interval is 60,000 msec. If you prefer the keyboard (or if the mouse is not available), note that "u" selects the "use the default value" for LooksAlive and "s" selects the "use the default value" for IsAlive.

Pending time-out specifies the length of time that a resource is in the pending state. The pending state could either be pending online or be pending offline. The Cluster Service cannot place a resource in the offline or online state until the pending time-out status is resolved. The default value for pending time-out is 900 s.

Configuring Resource-Specific Parameter Settings

In the last section, we covered configuring resource parameters that were the same for all resources. There are parameters that are unique to resources depending on the resource type, and the administrator should also configure these parameters.

The different resource types and the unique parameters of each are summarized in Table 1.

TABLE 1
Resource Unique Parameters

Resource Type	Unique Parameters
File share	Share name, path, comment/description, maximum number of users, file share permissions
IIS virtual root	Virtual directory type (FTP/WWW/Gopher), directory path, alias, user account information, access attributes
Network name	NetBIOS name for the cluster
Physical disk	Drive letters for additional shared drives
IP address	Network adapter for the IP address, the IP address itself, subnet mask

Note: Not all resource types have unique parameters, for example, the time service. Resource-specific parameters are configured using the Parameters tab in the resource Properties dialog box. Depending on the resource type, the properties tabs will have different settings required for the different resource types.

File share

The file share resource type creates share points for shared drives, for example, a share on the quorum drive.

The parameters that can be set by an administrator are

- Share name — a unique name for the share
- Path — path for the shared folder, on a shared drive
- Comment — share description (optional)
- User limit — maximum number of concurrent users
- Permissions — file share permissions

IIS virtual root settings

The IIS virtual root resource type provides failover capabilities for IIS virtual directories. See Chapter 2 for more details about IIS virtual root resource and IIS virtual directories. Figure 5 shows the parameters tab for virtual root settings.

The parameters that can be set by an administrator are

- FTP, Gopher, WWW (mutually exclusive radio button) — Specifies if this is a File Transfer Protocol (FTP), a Gopher, or a WWW virtual directory
- Directory — directory path
- Alias — alias name for the directory
- Account Information — user account information box active only if the directory path specified [in the directory setting] is in the Universal Naming Convention (UNC) format

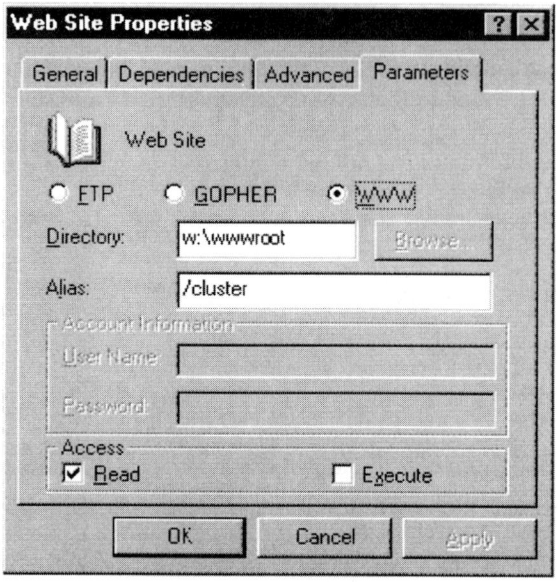

FIGURE 5 IIS virtual root settings.

and the user name and password entered here must have permission to access the UNC path over the network
- Access — The access attributes specified here such as Read, Execute, etc. being the same as the settings in Internet Service Manager and being used to control the directory attributes for the FTP and WWW virtual directories

Network name settings

The network name resource type is used to create a NetBIOS name for the cluster. .

The name must be a unique NetBIOS name. Once created, this name can be used to access any resource in the group that uses a NetBIOS name, such as a file share. There is an advantage in using a network name instead of the cluster name. Let us consider a group that contains a file share and disk resource and a network name resource used to access the file share. In this case, even if a failover occurs for the disk and file share group (and not the cluster name group), users are still able to gain access to the file share.

Physical disk settings

The physical disk resource type is used to specify drive letters for additional shared drives. Figure 6 shows the parameters tab for physical disk settings.

The shared drive must be online and visible to one node before a drive letter can be assigned to it.

IP address settings

The IP address resource type is used to add additional IP addresses to the cluster for each virtual server. Figure 7 shows the parameters tab for IP address settings.

The parameters that can be set by an administrator are

- Network to use — network adapter to be used for this IP address
- Address — the IP address in the xxx.xxx.xxx.xxx format
- Subnet mask — the subnet mask

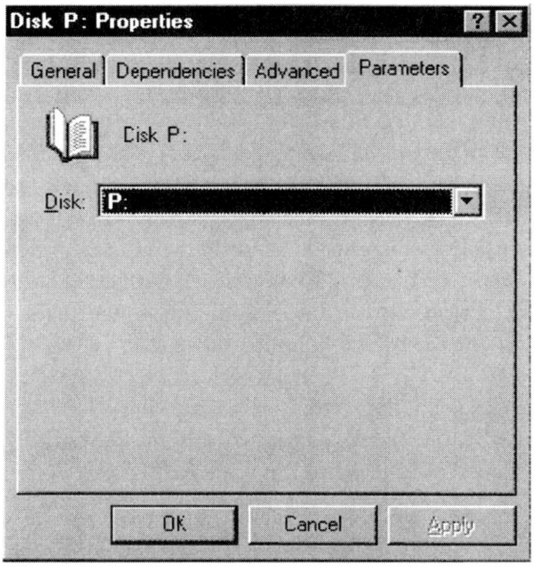

FIGURE 6 Physical disk settings.

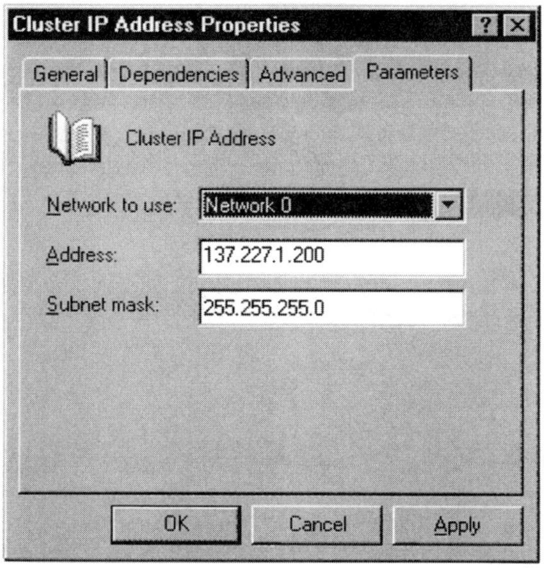

FIGURE 7 IP address settings.

Configuring Other Cluster Settings

In the earlier sections, we looked at configuring group settings and configuring common and specific settings for resources. While groups and resources are the major configuration components in a cluster, there are other cluster components that need to be configured as well. These include

- Quorum resource
- Network adapter
- Network priority
- Network usage

These components are also configured using the Cluster Administrator. Let us look at the settings for each of these cluster components in detail.

Quorum resource settings

The quorum resource may need to be configured from time to time. For example, the quorum log may need to be resized or additional storage may need to be added to the quorum resource. Settings for the quorum resource are updated using the quorum property page. Clicking the **Quorum** tab of the Cluster Properties dialog box accesses the quorum property page. The Cluster Properties dialog box is accessed by clicking the cluster name in the Cluster Administrator menu, next right clicking the cluster name, and then clicking **Properties**. Alternately, after clicking the cluster name, the administrator can select **Properties** from the **File** pull-down menu. .

The parameters that can be set by the administrator are

- Quorum resource — selects the shared drive letter used for the quorum resource
- Partition — selects the partition used to store the quorum log
- Root path — the folder used to store the quorum log (the default value for this setting being \MSCS\)
- Reset quorum log at — the log size up to which log entries are stored without erasing prior log entries (as the quorum log gets full and this limit is reached, the log starting to be overwritten in a first in/first out (FIFO) manner, the default value for this setting being 64 KB)

Network adapter settings

The description for the network adapter can be updated using the network adapter property page. This is also the only setting that can be updated on this property page. The network adapter property page is accessed by expanding **Networks**, clicking the name of the network (in the right panel, right click the node), and then clicking **Properties**. The network adapter property page is shown in Figure 8.

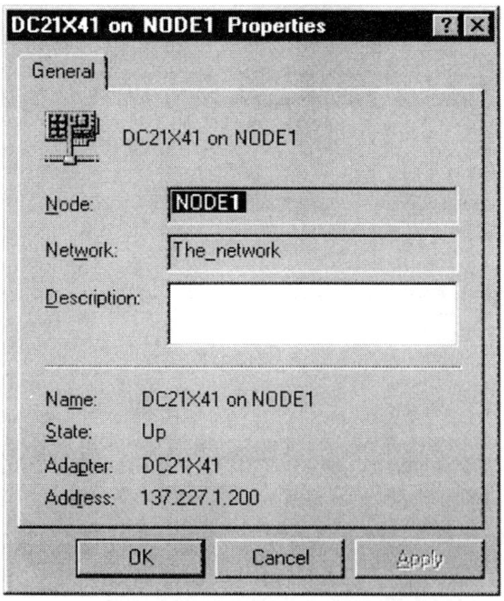

FIGURE 8 Network adapter settings.

While only the description can be updated, the network adapter property page contains useful information such as whether or not the state is UP and the IP address of the network adapter.

Network priority settings

Settings for network priority are updated using the Network Priority tab of the Cluster Properties dialog box. The Cluster Properties dialog box is accessed by clicking the cluster name in the Cluster Administrator menu, next right clicking the cluster name, and then clicking **Properties**. Alternately, after clicking the cluster name, the administrator can select **Properties** from the **File** pull-down menu. The Network Priority property page is shown in Figure 9.

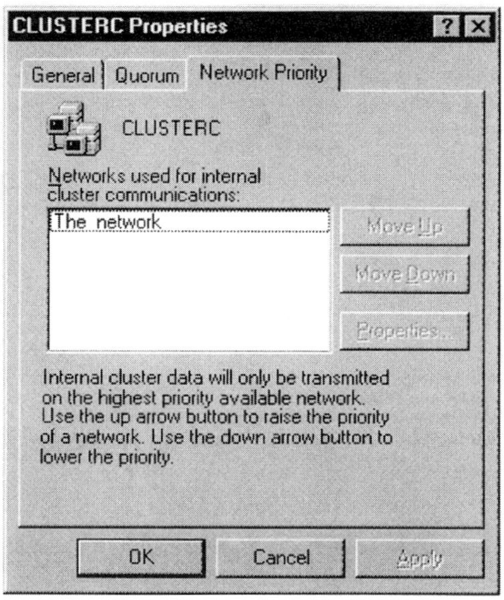

FIGURE 9 Network priority settings.

The parameters that can be set by the administrator are

- Move Up — moves the selected network priority up one level
- Move Down — moves the selected network priority down one level
- Properties — displays the selected network's Properties dialog box (alternately, the administrator clicking **network** under (Networks), right clicking to select the network, and then clicking **Properties**)

Network usage settings

The Network Usage property page is used to configure how Cluster Server uses the network for all communication, for node-to-node communication only, or for client access only. The Network Usage property page is accessed by expanding **Networks**, clicking the name of the network (in the right panel, right clicking the node), and then clicking **Properties**. The Network Usage property page is shown in Figure 10.

The parameters that can be set by the administrator are

- Name — network name (assigned at installation)
- Description — a description for the network
- Enable for cluster use — enabling the Cluster Service to use the network adapter (this check box selected by default, clearing the check box to disable use of the network adapter)

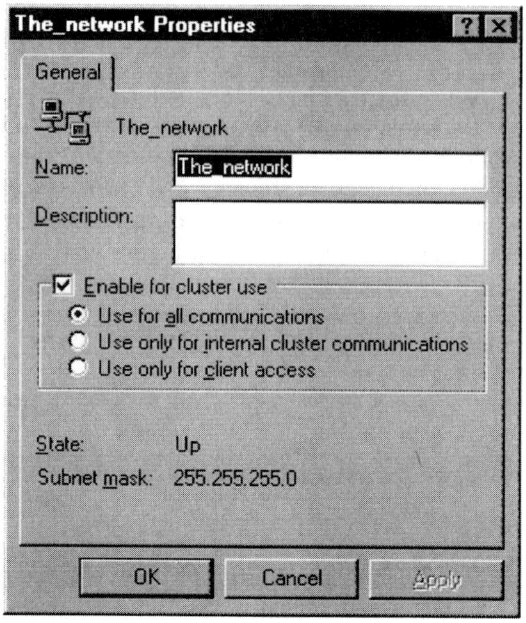

FIGURE 10 Network usage settings.

- Use for all communications — selecting this radio button causing the Cluster Service to use the network adapter for all (node-to-node and client) communications; this setting being the default and this option being also mutually exclusive with the following two use options
- Use only for internal cluster communications — selecting this radio button causing the Cluster Service to use this network adapter for node-to-node communications only
- Use only for client access — selecting this radio button causing the Cluster Service to use this network adapter only for communication with clients

OPTIMIZATION

The goal in tuning MSCS and hosted applications is to determine which hardware resource experiences the greatest demand, and then to adjust the configuration to relieve that demand and maximize total throughput. A system should be structured so that its resources are used efficiently.

For example, if the primary role of the cluster is to provide high availability of file and print services, high disk use is incurred due to the large number of files being opened and closed. File and print services also cause a heavy load on network adapters because of the large amount of data that is being transferred. It is important to make sure that your network adapter can handle the load. In this scenario, memory typically does not carry a heavy load (although memory usage can be heavy if a large amount of system memory is allocated to file system cache). Processor utilization is also typically low in this environment. In such cases, memory and processor utilization usually do not need the optimizing that other components need.

In contrast, a server-application environment (such as one running Microsoft Structured Query Language (SQL) Server, Microsoft Exchange Server, Microsoft Systems Management Server, and Microsoft System Network Architecture [SNA] Server) is much more processor- and memory-bound than a typical file-and-print-server environment because much more processing is taking place at the server. In these cases, it is best to implement high-end multiprocessor machines or processors. The disk and network loads tend to be less utilized, because the amount of data being sent over the wire and to the disk is smaller. MSCS itself uses little of the system resources either for intracluster communications or for the operation of the cluster itself.

Optimization Based on Server Role

You can optimize Windows NT Server for file-and-print-server performance or application-server performance using the Properties dialog box for the server service (which is part of the Network option in Control Panel; on the Services tab, click Server and then click Properties). You can maximize the server for file-and-print services or for application throughput (the default), or you can select a balance of the two. After you specify these settings, Windows NT Server makes other necessary registry modifications that affect performance in keeping with the balance you selected. It is recommended that you do not select Maximize Throughput for File Sharing unless the server provides only file-and-print services. Selecting this option leaves very little memory available for any other applications.

Optimizing Paging File Size and Location

The location and size of the paging files can greatly affect performance. Paging files cannot be located on the shared SCSI bus, but if multiple unshared drives are available on the individual servers, placing the paging file on a separate, fast, low-use drive can boost performance. The size setting of the paging file is also critical to performance. A paging file that must constantly expand and shrink requires additional processor and in/out (I/O) overhead. Usually, set the size of your paging file at two or two-and-a-half times the amount of installed physical memory if active applications, such as Microsoft SQL Server or Microsoft Exchange Server, are present.

Using Additional Windows NT Services on a Cluster Server

Windows Internet Name Service (WINS), Dynamic Host Configuration Protocol (DHCP), and Domain Name System (DNS) servers use additional system resources, which must be considered before implementing any of these services on a cluster server. In particular, WINS can require substantial overhead during peak logon times in large networks. In such cases, make sure that your system has the necessary capacity to perform adequately.

Although these services are not clustered, the node acts as the server of the service. If any of these services are to run on a node of an MSCS cluster, make sure to implement backup servers for each of these services to provide redundancy, just as you would normally do on your network.

TUNING

You can tune or even stop two of the Windows NT Services to further optimize performance: NetLogon and Browser. Of course, stopping these services has a limiting effect on the functionality of the server.

Tuning the NetLogon Service

The NetLogon service provides users with a single access point to a Primary Domain Controller (PDC) and all Backup Domain Controllers (BDCs). It also synchronizes the changes to the directory database stored on the PDC to all domain controllers. This service plays an important role in Windows NT networking but can negatively affect performance on cluster nodes that primarily serve applications.

On a domain controller, the Windows NT NetLogon service is responsible for:

- Synchronizing the directory-services database between the PDC and BDCs
- Validating user-account logons
- Supporting trust relationships between domains
- Providing for membership of computers in a domain

For a Cluster Server that also acts as a domain controller, it is possible to tune the NetLogon service to suit your requirements. Several registry parameters for synchronizing behavior with other domain controllers are associated with the NetLogon service. If necessary, you can even schedule the service by pausing it during busy periods and restarting it during off-peak periods. This can be accomplished with the Windows NT job scheduler with jobs that allow the starting, pausing, and restarting of services.

Tuning the Browser Service

Users often need to know which domains and computers are accessible from their local computers. Viewing all the available network resources is called browsing. The Windows NT Browser service maintains a list (called the browse list) of all available domains and servers. The browse list can be viewed using Windows NT Explorer and is provided by a browser in the domain of the local computer.

By default, every computer running Windows NT Server participates in this service. You can optimize cluster performance by preventing the cluster nodes from participating in the browser service. You can make this configuration change only by setting Windows NT registry parameters. This action does not prevent the server from browsing the network itself, and it does not prevent clients from browsing its resources.

INSTALLING WINDOWS NT SERVICE PACKS ON CLUSTER NODES

MSCS requires Windows NT Server, Enterprise Edition. You can install Windows NT Server Service Packs on MSCS nodes using the following procedure. Always install any Service Packs on both nodes.

To install a later Service Pack:

1. On one node (referred to here as node A), take all groups offline, or move them to the other node (referred to here as node B).
2. Install the Service Pack on node A and restart the computer.
3. Bring the node A groups back online, or move them back to node A from node B.
4. Take any remaining groups on node B offline, or move them to node A.
5. Install the Service Pack on node B, and then restart the computer.
6. Bring the node B groups back online, or move them back to node B from node A.

ADMINISTERING CLUSTERS FROM THE COMMAND PROMPT

You can use Cluster.exe to administer clusters from the Windows NT command prompt. You can also call Cluster.exe from command scripts to automate many cluster administration tasks. You can use Cluster.exe to administer clusters from either node of a cluster, from nodes of other MSCS clusters, or from other computers running SP3 with version 4.0 of either Windows NT Workstation or Windows NT Server. Cluster.exe is installed on all cluster nodes, and when you install only Cluster Administrator.

Cluster.exe supports the following basic commands:

- Cluster
- Cluster Node
- Cluster Group
- Cluster Resource
- Cluster ResourceType

The function of these commands and their syntax is explained in the following sections.

Command Syntax Conventions

The following syntax conventions apply to all commands. The cluster name parameter is optional. If you do not specify a cluster name, Cluster.exe attempts to connect to the cluster running on the node on which you are running Cluster.exe. When you have any names that contain spaces, you must use quotation marks around the names. When setting properties to True or False, specify 1 for true and 0 for false. You can use abbreviations wherever possible to minimize keystrokes. The following table lists the command abbreviations that Cluster.exe supports.

TABLE 2
Cluster Command Abbreviations

Option	Supported Abbreviations
AddDependency	AddDep
DllName	Dll
ListDependencies	ListDep
MoveTo	Move
Online	On
Offline	Off
PrivProperties	Priv
Properties	Prop or Props
QuorumResource	Quorum
RemoveDependency	RemoveDep
Rename	Ren
Resource	Res
ResourceType	ResType
Status	Stat
Version	Ver

Cluster Command

The basic cluster command syntax is

CLUSTER [cluster name] /option

The cluster name is optional. If you do not specify a cluster name, Cluster.exe attempts to connect to the cluster running on the node on which you are running Cluster.exe. Table 3 describes the available cluster options.

For example, to rename a cluster called Clustr1 to Clustr2, type the following at the Windows NT command prompt:

cluster Clustr1 /rename: Clustr2.

TABLE 3
Cluster Command Options

/Option	Description
/Rename:cluster name	Rename a cluster
/Version	Display the MSCS version number
/QuorumResource:resource name [/Path:path] [/Maxlogzie:size]	Change the name of the quorum resource or the location, or size of the quorum log
/List:[domain name]	Display a list of clusters in the domain to which the computer belongs, or a specified domain
/? or /Help	Display cluster syntax

Cluster Node Command

The basic Cluster Node syntax is

CLUSTER [cluster name] NODE [node name] /option

The cluster name is optional here. However, the node name is optional only for the /Status command. If no node name and no options are specified, the command defaults to /Status. Table 4 describes the available Cluster Node options.

TABLE 4
Cluster Node Command Options

Option	Description
/Status	Display the cluster node status (either Up, Down, or Paused)
/Pause	Pause a node
/Resume	Resume a paused node
/Evict	Evict a node from a cluster
/Properties [propname=propvalue]	Display the node properties; use propname=propvalue to set the value of specific node properties
/PrivProperties [propname=propvalue]	Use propname=propvalue to set the value of specific private node properties
/? Or /Help	Display Cluster Node syntax

For example, to display the status of a node named OpsNode1, type the following at the Windows NT command prompt:

cluster node opsnode1 /status

Cluster Node Common Property Names

By default, there is only one cluster node property supported by the cluster software. You can change the node description.

Cluster Node Private Property Names

There are no private properties on cluster nodes by default. However, software vendors can add private node properties to extend functionality within MSCS.

Cluster Group Command

The basic cluster group syntax is

CLUSTER [cluster name] GROUP [group name] /option

The cluster name is optional here. However, the group name is optional only for the /Status command. If you do not specify a group name when using the /Status command, Cluster.exe displays the status for all groups.

Table 5 describes the available Cluster Group options. If no group name and no options are specified, the command defaults to the /Status option.

TABLE 5
Cluster Group Command Options

Option	Description
[group name] /Status	Display the status of a group (either Online, Offline, or Partially Online)
/Status [/Node:node name]	Display all the groups that are online on a particular node
/Create	Create a new group
/Delete	Delete a group
/Rename:new group name	Rename a group
/MoveTo [:node name] [/Wait[:timeout in seconds]]	Move a group to another node
/Online [:node name] [/Wait[:timeout in seconds]]	Bring a group online
/Offline [:node name] [/Wait[:timeout in seconds]]	Take a group offline
/Properties [propname=propvalue]	Display properties of a group; use propname=propvalue to set the value of specific group properties
/PrivProperties [propname=propvalue]	Use propname=propvalue to set the value of specific private group properties
/ListOwners	Display a list of preferred owners
/SetOwners:node list	Specify preferred owner
/Rename:new group name	Rename a group
/? Or /Help	Display Cluster Group syntax

For example, to move a group called disk group 1 on the OpsClus1 cluster from OpsNode1 to OpsNode2, type the following at the Windows NT command prompt:

cluster opsclust group "disk group 1" /moveto:opsnode2

Note: With /MoveTo, /Online, and /Offline, /Wait:timeout in seconds specifies how long Cluster.exe would wait before canceling the command if the command does not complete successfully. By default, Cluster.exe waits indefinitely or until the group state changes.

Cluster Group Common Property Names

Table 6 describes the various common group property names, their uses, and valid settings.

TABLE 6
Cluster Group Common Property Names

Common Property Names	Description
Description	Describes a group
PersistentState	Describes the last known persistent state of a group (True equals online; False equals offline)
FailoverThreshold	Specifies the number of times the Cluster Service attempts to failover a group before it concludes that the group cannot be brought online anywhere in the cluster
FailoverPeriod	Specifies the interval (in hours) over which the Cluster Service attempts to failover a group
AutoFailbackType	Set to ClusterGroupPreventFailback (0) to prevent failback; set to ClusterGroupAllowFailback (1) to allow failback.
FailbackWindowStart	Specifies the start time (on a 24-h clock) for failback of a group to its preferred node; values for the FailbackWindowStart property must be between 0 (midnight) and 23 (11 P.M.) in local time for the cluster
FailbackWindowEnd	Specifies the end time (on a 24-h clock) for failback of a group to its preferred node; see FailbackWindowStart for valid values; you can set both FailbackWindowStart and FailbackWindowEnd to –1 for immediate failback

Cluster Group Private Property Names

There are no private properties on the default cluster groups, although software vendors can add private group properties to extend functionality within MSCS.

Cluster Resource Command

The basic Cluster Resource syntax is

```
CLUSTER [cluster name] RESOURCE [resource name] /option
```

The cluster name is optional here. However, the resource name is optional only for the /Status command. Table 7 describes the available Cluster Resource options.

For example, to create a print spooler resource in the Ops Print Spoolers group, type the following at the Windows NT command prompt:

```
cluster resource /create /group:"Ops Print Spoolers" /Type:"print spooler"
```

Note: With /Online and /Offline, /Wait:timeout in milliseconds specifies how long Cluster.exe would wait before canceling the command if the command does not complete successfully. By default, Cluster.exe waits indefinitely or until the resource state changes.

Cluster Resource Common Property Names

Table 8 describes the various common resource property names, their use, and valid settings.

TABLE 7
Cluster Resource Command Options

Option	Description
/Status	Display the status of a resource (either Online, Offline, or Failed)
/Create /Group:group name /Type:res-type [/Separate]	Create a new resource in a specified group; use /Separate to specify that the resource should run in a separate Resource Monitor.
/Delete	Delete a resource
/Rename:new resource name	Rename a resource
/AddOwner:node name	Add a node name to the list of possible owners
/RemoveOwner:node name	Remove a node name from the list of possible owners
/ListOwners	Display a list of possible owners
/MoveTo:group	Move the resource to a different group
/Properties [propname=propvalue]	Display the resource properties; use propname=propvalue to set the value of specific resource properties
/PrivProperties [propname=propvalue]	Use propname=propvalue to set the value of specific private resource properties
/Fail	Initiate resource failure
/Online [/Wait[:timeout in seconds]]	Bring the resource online
/Offline [/Wait[:timeout in seconds]]	Take the resource offline
/ListDependencies	List the dependencies for a resource
/AddDependency:resource	Add a dependency for a resource
/RemoveDependency:resource	Remove a dependency for a resource
/? Or /Help	Display Cluster Resource syntax

Cluster Resource Private Property Names

Some resources store private properties. For example, to see the disk signature for the disk k: resource, type the following at the Windows NT command prompt:

```
cluster resource “disk k:” /priv
```

Cluster ResourceType Command

The basic Cluster ResourceType syntax is

```
CLUSTER [cluster name] RESOURCETYPE [resource type display name] /option
```

The cluster name is optional here. However, the resource type name is optional only for the /List command. Table 9 describes the available Cluster ResourceType options. Default for ResourceType is /List if no option and no resource type are specified.

For example, to display the properties of the generic application resource type on the OpsClust1 cluster, type the following at the Windows NT command prompt:

```
cluster opsclust1 resourcetype “generic application” /properties
```

TABLE 8
Cluster Resource Common Property Names

Common Property Names	Description
Description	Change the text that describes a resource
DebugPrefix	Specify the appropriate debugger for the resource; for more information, see the Microsoft Platform SDK
SeparateMonitor	Indicates whether or not a resource shares a Resource Monitor; valid values are True and False
PersistentState	Describes the last known persistent state of a resource; because a resource cannot be online if its group is not online, it makes no sense to save the resource PersistentState property unless the resource is offline
LooksAlivePollInterval	Recommended interval in milliseconds that the Cluster Service should poll a resource to determine if it appears operational; if a resource does not have a value for the LooksAlivePollInterval property, a default value is taken from the LooksAlivePollInterval property for the resource type
IsAlivePollInterval	Interval (in milliseconds) that the Cluster Service polls a resource to determine if it is operational; if a value is not specified, a default value is taken from the IsAlivePollInterval property for the specific resource type; IsAlivePollInterval cannot be zero
RestartAction	Describes the action to perform if the resource fails; the choices are ClusterResourceDontRestart (0): Do not restart following a failure; ClusterResourceRestartNoNotify (1): If the resource exceeds its restart threshold within its restart period, MSCS does not attempt to failover the group to another node; ClusterResourceRestartNotify (2): If the resource exceeds its restart threshold within its restart period, MSCS attempts to failover the group to another node; if you do not enter a value, the default allows the resource to affect the group, which can cause the group to failover to another system.
RestartThreshold	Specifies how many times MSCS attempts to restart the resource in the RestartPeriod before failing over the group
RestartPeriod	Specifies the amount of time allowed for the restart attempts to reach the RestartThreshold before MSCS fails over the group
PendingTimeout	The amount of time that a pending online or pending offline resource has to resolve its status before MSCS puts the resource in Offline or Failed status; if the Pending time-out property is not specified, the default value is 3 minutes.

Cluster ResourceType Common Property Names

Table 10 describes the various common ResourceType property names, their use, and valid settings.

Cluster ResourceType Private Property Names

There are no private properties on the default cluster resource types, although software vendors may add private resource type properties on their resource types to extend functionality within MSCS.

DOCUMENTATION FOR THE CLUSTER ADMINISTRATOR

The following documentation is available from Microsoft to assist the Cluster Administrator in administering MSCS:

TABLE 9
Cluster ResourceType Command Options

Option	Description
/List	List the available installed resource types
/Create /DllName:dllname /Type:type name /Isalive:interval /LooksAlive:internal	Create a resource type
/Delete [/Type]	Delete a resource type; if the resource DLL cannot be accessed by the Cluster Service, specify the resource type name with the /Type option instead of specifying the resource type display name
/Properties [propname=propvalue]	Display the resource type properties; use propname=propvalue to set the value of specific resource type properties
/PrivProperties [propname=propvalue]	Use propname=propvalue to set the value of specific private resource type properties
/? Or /Help	Display Cluster ResourceType syntax

TABLE 10
Cluster ResourceType Common Property Names

Common Property Names	Use
Name	Change a resource type display name
Description	Change the text that describes a resource type
DllName	Specify the name of the dynamic link library (DLL) for a specific resource type
DebugPrefix	Specify the appropriate debugger for the resource type; for more information, see the Microsoft Platform SDK
AdminExtensions	Describe one or more class identifiers (CLSID) for Cluster Administrator Extensions
LooksAlivePoll Interval	Specify the interval (in milliseconds) that the Cluster Service polls resources of a particular resource type to determine if the resources appear operational
IsAlivePollInterval	Specify the interval (in milliseconds) that the Cluster Service polls resources of a particular resource type to determine if the resources are operational

- *"Microsoft Cluster Server Administrator's Guide"* covers the details required for an administrator to install and administer a MSCS cluster. This manual is available in soft copy form and can be accessed by clicking **Start** , -> **Programs** -> **Books Online** on all computers running Windows NT Server, Enterprise Edition. In addition, this manual is available in soft copy form on Microsoft's Technet CD.
- *"Windows NT Server, Enterprise Edition 4.0 Administrator's Guide"* covers among other topics configuring Microsoft BackOffice applications to run in a MSCS cluster.
- *"Readme"* file (Readme.doc) is available at the \MSCS folder on the Windows NT Server, Enterprise Edition 4.0 Components CD. In addition to general information about MSCS and a description of MSCS features, it contains limitations uncovered in late testing that are not documented elsewhere.

- "*Online Administrator Help*," like many other Microsoft products, is available to the MSCS Cluster Administrator to guide through administrative tasks. MSCS online Help is accessed by opening Cluster Administrator and pressing F1 or using the **Help** menu.
- Context-sensitive help is also available for all MSCS Cluster Administrator components. Context-sensitive help is accessed by first clicking the question mark button in the upper-right corner of a dialog box, and then clicking the component for which help is required.

10 Microsoft Cluster Server-Based Clustering Products and Case Studies

Many products and solutions that utilize the clustering support in Microsoft Cluster Server (MSCS) are available from Microsoft as well as from other vendors. In this chapter we take a brief look at such products and solutions. You can get additional details about a product or solution either by contacting Microsoft or the vendor.

CLUSTER SUPPORT IN MICROSOFT PRODUCTS

Microsoft has introduced new versions of some of its products to take advantage of clustering. These include Microsoft's flagship database, the Structured Query Language (SQL) Server.

STRUCTURED QUERY LANGUAGE SERVER

Microsoft SQL Server has been an early user of Windows NT clusters. Of course, the primary thrust for SQL Server to use clusters is to provide high-availability databases using failover support of the clusters. Microsoft SQL Server support for clusters started with SQL Server Enterprise Edition version 6.5, which supports two-node failover using the functionality in phase 1 of MSCS. Both machines can run different applications simultaneously. If either node fails, the surviving node picks up all applications. The next version of SQL clustering is intended to take advantage of MSCS phase 2 and currently relies on the Windows NT 2000 ship date. With MSCS phase 2, you can cluster up to 16 nodes so that they share resources and balance the workload.

Microsoft SQL Server also provides support for Object Linking and Embedding (OLE) Transactions through the Microsoft Distributed Transaction Coordinator (DTC). OLE Transactions allow Microsoft SQL Server databases to be partitioned among multiple Windows NT Server nodes, and DTC automatically manages the work of transactions that span these nodes. In addition, SQL Enterprise Manager allows an operator to monitor and manage multiple SQL Servers from a single console.

MICROSOFT EXCHANGE

Microsoft Exchange is among the first of Microsoft products to take advantage of MSCS. Clustering support was built into Exchange starting with version 5.5/E. (E is the Enterprise edition; the standard edition does not support clustering.) Exchange 5.5 uses an active/standby configuration where Exchange ordinarily runs on the active node in the cluster and automatically switches to the standby node if a problem occurs on the active node. As part of the set up, Exchange is set up to address the entire cluster, instead of addressing individual servers as it normally does. This is done using the cluster virtual server mechanism (see Chapter 3 for virtual server). You must install and configure

MSCS before installing Exchange. In fact, the Exchange set up program automatically detects if MSCS is already installed and installs the version of Exchange that is cluster enabled as shown in the next figure.

The Exchange Administrator program includes functions to let server monitors work with virtual servers.

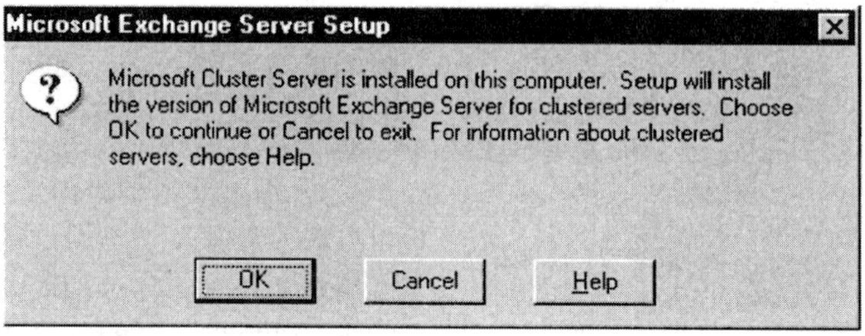

FIGURE 1 Exchange server setup detects MSCS.

CLUSTER SUPPORT FROM OTHER VENDORS

A number of vendors including Digital (now part of Compaq), Hewlett-Packard (HP), NCR, and other vendors have hardware and/or software clustering solutions based on Windows NT and/or MSCS. Let us take a brief look at each of these offerings. The Web address included with each of the following offerings provides more details about the offerings.

These vendors attempt to provide value-added services and/or provide a path for their current install base. Some vendors who offered clustering solutions based on proprietary hardware and/or software have ported or developed clustering solutions using Windows NT and MSCS. Hardware vendors have attempted to offer a tested, working solution composed of hardware, software, and network equipment for customers who prefer a complete clustering solution instead of having to get the clustering components on their own and attempt to create their own solution. Some vendors have also provided extended features not yet available in MSCS such as support for more than two cluster nodes.

CO-STANDBY*SERVER* FROM VINCA

The following is a brief summary of some of the features of Co-standby*Server* from Vinca. Additional details are available from www.vinca.com.

Co-Standby*Server* (4.1) for Windows NT is a server-clustering system that assures high availability of critical network resources including data, applications, shares, Internet Protocol (IP) addresses, and printers. Co-Standby*Server* incorporates new data mirroring technology that operates at the device driver level on individual input/output (I/O) requests, maintaining data synchronization between the cluster servers. Mirroring traffic uses a separate, dedicated interserver link, keeping your local area network (LAN) bandwidth free for client/server applications and file sharing.

Co-Standby*Server* features enhancements that deal with failover at the application level. For example, Co-Standby*Server* has Advance Application Modules for Microsoft Exchange and Microsoft SQL. This is part of Vinca's transition to providing system and core application availability in addition to mirroring technology.

LifeKeeper for Windows NT

LifeKeeper from NCR is a clustering solution that runs on NCR servers. LifeKeeper features multiple fault detection mechanisms, real-time repair, cluster administration from a single console in the cluster, and so on. Additional details can be found at www.ncr.com.

LifeKeeper supports closed cluster configurations up to 16 nodes. LifeKeeper supports the configuration and switchover or failover of an application and resources across more than two nodes. Recovery of resources during a node failover is performed in parallel as much as possible, to improve node failure recovery times. LifeKeeper configurations support the configuration of multiple network communication paths between LifeKeeper systems. As an alternative to Small Computer System Interface (SCSI), LifeKeeper NT supports data sharing using NCR's Extended Mirroring product. This functionality removes the SCSI connection distance restrictions and permits cluster configurations that may be geographically separated, but connected via a LAN such as in a campus environment. LifeKeeper NT 2.0 is certified to be compliant with the Microsoft Back Office specification requirements.

LifeKeeper provides software "Recovery Kits" that make it simple to configure LifeKeeper to fully protect critical applications. Kits are available from NCR for both UNIX (Informix, Oracle, Sybase, X.25, Transmission Control Protocol/Internet Protocol [TCP/IP], SNA, etc.) and Windows products (Informix, Oracle, Sybase, MS SQL Server, MS Exchange, MS LAN Manager, TCP /IP, Lotus Notes, SAP R/3, etc.).

Although LifeKeeper NT 2.0 supports a large subset of the Microsoft Cluster Server application programming interfaces (APIs), it does not support all Cluster APIs of MSCS. If you want to be able to easily port your application between LifeKeeper and other MSCS environments, you should ensure that you use only the MSCS APIs supported by LifeKeeper 2.0. In addition, you must choose between LifeKeeper and Microsoft Cluster Server as the cluster operating system. The cluster cannot be a heterogeneous system where some cluster members run Cluster Server and others run LifeKeeper.

Compaq Cluster Solutions

With the acquisition of Tandem and Digital, Compaq offers a number of clustering solutions.

The ProLiant 6500 Parallel Database Cluster for Oracle Parallel Server allows a cluster of Windows NT Server-based systems to simultaneously share a single Oracle database. This cluster is certified for Oracle7™ Server Release 7.3.3, Oracle8™ Server Release 8.0.4, and Oracle Parallel Server, and supports two to four nodes. This cluster also supports (Tandem) CR1000 RAID storage subsystem ServerNet interconnect technology.

The ProLiant 6500 Parallel Database Cluster lets users concurrently access the clustered database on read and write operations. Each node of the cluster can work independently of the others, allowing related applications to access the same set of data. The cluster also supports distributed operations with other Oracle servers. The cluster provides availability in the event of a failure anywhere in the cluster. In addition, Oracle Parallel Server software performs online recovery to ensure data integrity and database consistency.

Compaq also offers the Himalaya S and K series cluster offerings that used to be offered by Tandem prior to the merger.

Hewlett-Packard Cluster Support

HP has long been a major player in high-availability and clustering solutions. A book titled *Clusters for High Availability — A Primer of HP-UX Solutions* was published in 1996. HP has extended clustering solutions it has been offering in its UNIX environments to MSCS and Windows NT.

HP provides a total clustering solution including hardware, software, and services. The cluster configurations offered by HP are certified and approved by both HP and Microsoft. HP also provides required services such as those provided by certified systems engineers to perform the cluster installation. HP also provides tools to validate the operation of the cluster. HP ClusterView is intended to simplify cluster administration. To back up its clustering offerings, HP has also been offering uptime guarantees when clustering solutions are professionally installed and operated.

HP has been offering uptime guarantees for high-availability systems. HP extended its high-availability guarantee to its NT-based systems scheduled to ship beginning 1Q99. HP guarantees file system access level uptime of 99.9%. This uptime translates to less than 9 h of downtime per year. Note that the guarantee is for file system access level uptime only (and does not include database, network, or application availability). To qualify for the guarantee, customers should buy a preconfigured cluster of two HP LXr 8000 NetServers running NT Enterprise Server and HP OpenView/Manage X. A two-node cluster is required. Customers should also buy the HP highest level of service and support. HP is expected to provide more extensive uptime guarantees, beyond the file system access level, during the next 12 to 24 months. The guarantee covers unplanned downtime only.

CASE STUDIES

The following case studies show Windows NT Clustering Solutions at work in seven real-life examples.*

BlueCross/BlueShield of Oregon

As part of a large, nationwide insurance provider, BlueCross/BlueShield of Oregon combines Citrix WinFrame software with Cubix RemoteServ/IS hardware to create a clustering solution that supports its remote users. BlueCross/BlueShield supports its health care facilities, employees, and partners through this connection so users can access centralized billing and patient information. In this configuration, WinFrame provides remote access and Cubix adds availability and load balancing.

Cubix provides clustering within one cabinet, which reduces the need for computer room floor space. BlueCross/BlueShield configured each of two Cubix cabinets with two dual-processor Pentium Pro systems and one single-processor Pentium Pro system. The Cubix hardware is currently configured to let as many as 15 users dial in simultaneously. However, BlueCross/BlueShield can expand the Cubix system well beyond this configuration. BlueCross/BlueShield plans to replicate this solution as the need arises. The Cubix hardware keeps the cluster load-balanced, and in the event of a failure, the system redirects a user to an available node. "The management software is really slick. You can instantly see errors reported to the administrator's desktop," said systems administrator David Blackledge. "The Cubix hardware is really easy to maintain, and administrators can support the system from their desk."

Although Blackledge recommends this solution to anyone looking for solid remote access, he would like to see a more flexible licensing model. In a WinFrame environment, the licenses are tied to the processors. If one central processing unit (CPU) dies, your licenses might not transfer to the surviving node. Certain licenses can float between processors; however, you must have a minimum of five licenses per motherboard.

---

* The case studies are an extract from Mark Smith's article in June 1998 issue of *Windows NT Magazine* titled "NT Clustering Solutions Are Here?" (copyright 1998 *Windows NT Magazine*. Reprinted with permission).

BOOKS.COM

Books.com claims to be the first Web-based bookstore to offer online purchasing of books, videos, and music. The company went live in 1992, and Books.com now serves more than 60,000 user sessions per day from its clustered Web site.

To update information for its online store, Books.com developers make changes to an NT file server at one location. The company uses a T1 connection and Octopus DataStar software to replicate changes to three separate nodes in another location. To cluster and load-balance the three nodes, Books.com uses Convoy Cluster Software on HP NetServers.

This configuration lets each node handle one-third of the user load. When a user visits the Web site, the system combines files from the NT file server with data in Sybase and Oracle databases to dynamically generate the information the user's Web browser displays.

"The most common problem is blue screens on NT Server," said administrator Dennis Anderson. When a Convoy node fails, the other nodes pick up the load, and end users are unaware of any disruption in service. Fortunately, Anderson can Telnet into the Sentry Ambassador remote power-up box and restart the system if a node fails during the night. After the system reboots, the recovered node can rejoin the cluster. Octopus DataStar then uses its journal of changes to synchronize the node. Most of the objects the system replicates to the nodes are small Hypertext Markup Language (HTML) files, so the recovered node usually resynchronizes within 30 s after rebooting. The Convoy node then rejoins the cluster about 10 s later.

Books.com required load balancing and failover in its clustering solution, so it had to eliminate all but a few solutions from consideration. The company downloaded a demonstration of Convoy Cluster Software from the Valence Research Web site. The demonstration helped seal the Books.com decision. "Convoy Cluster Software performs really well," said Anderson. "You don't really notice it, but it works."

Despite the success of this solution the company has discovered one annoying problem: Convoy cannot detect when Internet Information Server (IIS) fails. As a result, when IIS fails, the entire cluster fails. Anderson uses Ipswitch WhatsUp to work around this problem. Now if IIS fails, WhatsUp stops that node, and Convoy removes it from the cluster and alerts Anderson via pager. Anderson hopes Convoy will detect this type of problem in future versions.

"NT is not a very robust Web-serving platform," said Anderson. "NT has a lot of maturing to do." Specifically, Anderson would like Microsoft to focus on reliability.

CELANESE

Celanese runs a continuous flow (24 × 7) process to manufacture 1000- to 1200-lb (4 × 4 × 4) bales of acetate cellulose tow for producing cigarette filters and suit liners. If the process stops for 1 min, the bale harden and require a massive cleanup and restart process that can take days.

In the past, Celanese employees had to continually measure the manufacturing equipment (e.g., programmable logic controllers, scales, presses, extrusion devices, sensors, and dryers) to determine whether or not individual bales met the strict quality standards of the company. Now, the company has automated the process using Gensym G2, an NT-based software solution. G2 continually receives measurements from the manufacturing equipment and uses its built-in expert system software to determine the quality of the bales. G2 records quality measurements into its Structured Query Language (SQL) Server database and adjusts equipment as necessary. At specified intervals, the SAP AG production planning system queries the database for acceptable bales and records them into an Oracle NT database.

So why did Celanese decide to use an NT cluster solution? "We felt like that's where everything was headed. Doing the same thing with UNIX would cost $500,000," said administrator Jim Fraser. "The advantages of having a common platform for our business and manufacturing users are too numerous for the accountants to ignore. I'm not afraid to use NT. I supported HPUX for 7 years, and NT is just as stable as HP."

When Celanese automated its manufacturing process, the company had only one requirement: absolutely no downtime. This requirement let Celanese narrow its search for a clustering solution to one vendor — Marathon Technologies. Marathon Endurance 4000 software and hardware solution is truly fault tolerant. Both the data and compute nodes are completely redundant. As a result, client machines do not need to restart following a system failure, and the G2 software cannot fail. Future versions of the product will support symmetric multiprocessing (SMP) nodes. Endurance 4000 ties four systems (Celanese uses four 200M=Hz servers) together to create one cluster.

Celanese selected Marathon Endurance 4000 because it is the only solution available with subsecond failover time. In fact, it does not really failover, it just disconnects the redundant node. Celanese has experienced two hardware failures, and the Marathon cluster worked both times without a hitch. In less than 5 msec the surviving node took over the load. "Marathon Endurance 4000 is a wonderful solution," said administrator Jim Fraser. "Marathon works hard for its customers."

First Union Capital Markets Group

Corporate e-mail is the mission-critical application of the 1990s. Take your mail server offline for a few minutes, and watch your Help desk light up like a Christmas tree. First Union Capital Markets Group in North Carolina uses MSCS to keep its Exchange and file-and-print servers running 24 × 7. Previously, the company had to use twice as many clusters to do the same amount of work they do today. "In the old days, I had Compaq standby clusters. Now I use active/active clusters, and both nodes are working," said Sid Vyas, First Union CIO. "I'm saving a huge amount of money on the hardware."

Vyas recommends a single-vendor clustering solution. During the testing phase, First Union unsuccessfully tried to mix and match hardware. Vyas also recommends a fiber channel connection over a SCSI-switching solution for increased throughput on the disk, and a 50% faster failover time, and an increased length of cable between nodes (500 m vs. 25 ft).

Vyas chose Compaq ProLiant servers to run MSCS because Compaq was the only company to certify a fiber channel connection. This configuration lets First Union place its servers and storage in separate buildings and keep nodes in separate data centers on different floors of the building. Distributing the computing resources increases the fault tolerance in case of a disaster.

Vyas admits MSCS has a problem with duplicate shared names. Two shares cannot have the same name after failover. If you have the same share names on each node, the failing node share disappears. In addition, print queues must have unique names on each node, even though they might point to the same printer. First Union has notified Microsoft of this shortcoming, but was still waiting for a solution at press time.

Vyas said that future plans include clustering SQL Server. The First Union database of choice is Sybase on UNIX; however, the company is developing many new applications on SQL Server.

IBM World Registry Division

Imagine developing applications that are so top secret that you cannot back them up on tape. This scenario became reality for Mark Shoger of Keane Federal Systems. IBM World Registry Division (WRD) hired Keane to help with the company's development efforts. Keane said WRD needed a real-time backup system to handle open files and systems policies. WRD could not have any removable media, because it would void the company's top-secret classification requirements. Finally, WRD needed 99.99% availability and no data loss. To meet these requirements, the company turned to the Computer Associates' ARCserve Replication real-time backup and recovery system.

WRD has 500 users attached to four large NT servers that handle development, and the company runs Lotus Notes Domino for group communications. Each of the four primary servers connects to a backup server that mirrors the data on the other four servers.

ARCserve Replication runs on each server and monitors threshold levels such as hard disk space and network performance. The primary servers are dual Pentium II systems with 512 MB of RAM and 4 GB of storage (16 GB total), and a backup server with 20 GB of storage.

The payoff for using this NT-based solution is simple. If a problem occurs, such as a hard disk crash, ARCserve Replication detects the problem and switches users to the backup server within a few seconds. The users are unaware that any change has taken place. Shoger can replace the failed hard disk at his leisure. He then initiates the failback procedure, which synchronizes the new disk and reroutes the users to the primary server. "I've been doing network administration for a long time and this failure and recovery process impresses me. "One time, a NIC failed and the system ran the whole weekend on the backup server before I noticed it," said Shoger. He also points out that the ARCserve Replication software was easy to install and maintain.

Shoger recommends this system for large networks. It requires an extra system for backup and recovery, which may be prohibitive for small networks. If you need this kind of protection, Shoger recommends using a backup system that has 25% more power than any of the systems it is protecting.

Looking ahead, WRD might implement an additional backup server at a remote site for disaster recovery. Such a configuration would help keep the company up and running, even if the primary data center blew up.

John C. Lincoln Hospital

Downtime is not an option for the John C. Lincoln Hospital level 1 trauma center in Arizona. To maintain its level 1 status, the hospital must be able to respond to a life-threatening emergency at all times. Vinca StandbyServer for NT software keeps the trauma center 7000-user NT environment continuously running.

So how does this solution work? Imagine that the primary server fails and displays a blue screen. Within 30 s, the first set of users are working on the standby server. However, because not all applications failover gracefully to the standby server, some users experience a general program failure (GPF) and have to reboot. After they reboot they automatically connect to the standby server and are up and running. To restore the primary server, you simply break the mirror, reboot the primary server, reestablish the mirror, and reboot the primary server again.

The hospital chose Vinca because of its low overhead on the primary server. "Vinca runs clean and light, and you hardly know it's there," said Mark Jablonski, former network administrator for the hospital. "Overall, Vinca is a sleep saver. If users are working at night, you can keep sleeping," said Jablonski. "Anything that keeps my beeper from going off is a friend of mine."

Jablonski recommends researching the resource overhead before you buy. "If the Primary Domain Controller goes over 50% CPU utilization, it's hard to log on to the PDC," he said. He recommends checking the cluster solution to ensure the CPU utilization does not go through the roof. You may also want to check your clustering solution against your night load when you run backups, virus scanners, and other administrative applications. "It's at night when you get beeped," said Jablonski.

Besides researching the resource overhead, you need to check the reliability of the clustering solution: Does it failover five out of five times? "Vinca is successful 90% of the time. Sometimes you must restart services manually on failover," said Jablonski. Also, look for quality support. Vinca support is helpful and knowledgeable. For 24 × 7 support, you can purchase Vinca's 24 × 7 premium support.

The hospital plans to implement an active/active cluster. With the current active/standby configuration, nine of the nodes are not active. Jablonski said that the hospital is investigating active/active solutions.

Surplus Direct

Do you want a great deal on hardware and software? That is the promise of Surplus Direct, which acts as a clearinghouse for publishers, distributors, and retailers of overstocked, factory refurbished, or distressed inventories. Surplus Direct sells or auctions these items over the Web. To provide its customers with the best service, the company needed a solution that could run 24 × 7 and scale easily. In addition, the company dynamically generates about 90 to 95% of its Web pages from a SQL Server database. These requirements led Surplus Direct to use a combination of NT products for its clustering solution.

Surplus Direct uses Resonate Dispatch Manager software, which is part of the Resonate Central Dispatch product, to monitor incoming Web traffic by open connections, CPU load, and network latency. The software balances the incoming Web traffic with its clustered schedulers. The schedulers assign the workload to one of six front-end IIS-based Web servers. These schedulers get a workout right before auction closing at 11 A.M. each day when Web traffic spikes considerably. The Web servers request data from SQL Server systems running on Tandem CS150 clustered hardware. Surplus Direct uses MSCS to provide the clustering software.

Surplus Direct likes using Dispatch Manager to produce bar charts and tables to graphically monitor the pool of schedulers and Web servers. In addition, the company uses LANWARE's NTManage to graphically monitor the network traffic running through its routers, hubs, and switches.

Surplus Direct also takes advantage of the system scalability. The company can easily add front-end servers, which increase the throughput of the Web sites. Surplus Direct uses Visual SourceSafe to handle source-code version control and replicate pages and changes among all Web server nodes. The company uses Westwind Technology Webconnect to access SQL Server from the Web servers. "I've been able to sleep better at night because there's no single point of failure," said administrator Mark Daley.

Surplus Direct looked for hardware solutions during evaluation, but could not find anything that supported virtual IP addresses. The company needed each user session to stay in the assigned pool. Surplus Direct also needed a software solution that let it use the fastest machines available and add as many Web servers as necessary. "Be patient in finding the right solution — stay very objective," advised Daley.

Tulip Computers

Is NT ready for the enterprise? Tulip Computers thinks so. The company produces and develops personal computers (PCs) for the European and Asian business-to-business market. In addition, Tulip recently purchased Commodore, which makes computers for the European consumer market. Tulip currently has 700 employees and a revenue of $300 million.

Tulip uses a two-node LifeKeeper active/standby cluster to run an Oracle 7 on NT database on NCR 4300 4 × 200 hardware with 1.5 GB of RAM and 80 GB of hard disk space. Five different application servers running SAP materials management, production planning, sales and distribution, warehouse, and financial controlling modules access the Oracle on NT database. Each application server runs on an NCR four-way SMP server.

Although Tulip has not clustered these applications, the company plans to put the SAP application servers into LifeKeeper clusters to maximize availability.

John Hoogendoorn, Tulip's Information Systems (IS) manager, recommends running a database application on an active/standby cluster configuration instead of an active/ active configuration. He believes you can more easily recover and manage this environment. Hoogendoorn also recommends finding a cluster-aware backup solution. The Tulip current backup solution is not cluster aware, so Hoogendoorn bought a separate backup system for the standby node of the cluster.

"The NCR hardware has worked so well that we haven't seen it failover in production," said Hoogendoorn. He adds, "But we've tried to manually failover and that worked." Hoogendoorn said that the system completely failed over in 5 min. LifeKeeper has developed various recovery kits (or scripts) to handle specific recovery needs for applications such as SAP and Oracle. For a complete list of recovery kits, visit LifeKeeper's Web site.

Appendix A
Cluster API Reference

INTRODUCTION

This appendix supplements the information in Chapter 7 on cluster programming and also provides the detailed information about the Cluster application programming interfaces (APIs) you can use for cluster programming. For each API, a brief description, the actual API syntax including all the parameters, a description of the parameters, the results of the API call, and programming notes are included.

CONVENTIONS USED

Function names are in bold and must be used as shown. Parameter values are in italics and the programmer can choose any variable name. Parameter keywords and keywords that are part of the function call are in capitals. Valid parameter and return values are shown with a reduced font (e.g., TRUE).

The call syntax of each function is provided and this is followed by:

- Input parameters to the function
- Input and output parameters to the function
- Output parameters
- Return values
- Programming notes

Note: These five items may not be described for all the functions. These APIs are listed here in a format suitable for quick reference to supplement the cluster programming chapter. More detailed information about these APIs is available in Microsoft product documentation and Microsoft Development Network (MSDN).

FUNCTION CATEGORIES

The following major categories of functions are covered in this appendix:

- Network Interface Management Functions
- Cluster Management Functions
- Node Management Functions
- Group Management Functions
- Resource Management Functions
- Cluster Database Management Functions

CloseClusterNetwork

The **CloseClusterNetwork** function invalidates the network handle and closes the network connection.

BOOL WINAPI **CloseClusterNetwork** (
HNETWORK *hNetwrk*
);

Input Parameters

HNetwrk — Handle to the network to close

Return Values

TRUE — The operation was successful.
FALSE — The operation was unsuccessful.

Programming Notes

If the return value is FALSE and you need additional information about the error, call the Win32 function **GetLastError**.

ClusterNetworkCloseEnum

The **ClusterNetworkCloseEnum** function closes an enumerator used for iterating through objects on a network.

DWORD WINAPI **ClusterNetworkCloseEnum**(
HNETWORKENUM *hNetwrkEnum*
);

Input Parameters

hNetwrkEnum — Handle to the network enumerator object to be closed

Return Values

ERROR_SUCCESS — The operation was successful.

If the operation was unsuccessful, **ClusterNetworkCloseEnum** returns a Win32 error value.

Programming Notes

The handle to the closed network enumerator object is invalidated. The handle is initially validated and returned by the **ClusterNetworkOpenEnum** function.

ClusterNetworkEnum

The **ClusterNetworkEnum** function enumerates network objects and returns an object name for each invocation.

DWORD WINAPI **ClusterNetworkEnum**(
HNETWORKENUM *hNetwrkEnum*,
DWORD *dwIndx*,
LPDWORD *lpdwType*,
LPWSTR *lpszName*,
LPDWORD *lpcbName*
);

Input Parameters

HNetwrkEnum — Handle to an existing enumeration object originally returned by the **ClusterNetworkOpenEnum** function.

dwIndx — Index used to identify the next entry to be enumerated. This parameter should be zero for the first call to **ClusterNetworkEnum** and then incremented for subsequent calls.

Parameters that are both Input and Output

lpcbName — On input, this parameter is a buffer pointer. On output, this parameter points to the count of characters in the name pointed to by the *lpszName* parameter (minus the terminating NULL character).

Output Parameters

lpdwType — Pointer to the type of object returned. The following object type is returned with each call:

CLUSTER_NETWORK_ENUM_NETINTERFACES — Network interface object

lpszName — Pointer to returned object name

Return Values

ERROR_SUCCESS — The operation was successful.

ERROR_NO_MORE_ITEMS — There are no more objects of the requested type.

ERROR_MORE_DATA — The buffer pointed to by *lpszName* is not big enough to hold the retrieved data. The *lpcbName* parameter is set to the minimum buffer length that can contain all the retrieved data.

Programming Notes

If you want to write an application to iterate through a collection of network objects and enumerate all the network interface objects of different types, use the following steps:

- Set the *dwType* parameter of **ClusterNetworkOpenEnum** to CLUSTER_NETWORK_ENUM_NETINTERFACES (to specify network interfaces as the object type to be enumerated).
- Call **ClusterNetworkOpenEnum** to open a network enumerator that can process network interface objects.
- With the handle that **ClusterNetworkOpenEnum** returns, call **ClusterNetworkEnum** iteratively to retrieve each of the objects.
- With the same handle that **ClusterNetworkOpenEnum** returned, call **ClusterNetworkCloseEnum** to release the enumerator after retrieving all objects.

ClusterNetworkOpenEnum

The **ClusterNetworkOpenEnum** function opens an enumerator to iterate through network objects.

```
HNETWORKENUM WINAPI   ClusterNetworkOpenEnum(
                      HNETWORK hNetwrk,
                      DWORD dwType
                      );
```

Input Parameters

hNetwrk — Network Handle.

dwType — Bitmask containing the object types to be enumerated. Valid values are

CLUSTER_NETWORK_ENUM_NETINTERFACES — Enumerate the network interface objects on the network.

CLUSTER_NETWORK_ENUM_ALL — Enumerate all objects on the network.

Return Values
If the operation was successful, **ClusterNetworkOpenEnum** returns a handle to a network enumerator.
NULL — The operation was unsuccessful.

Programming Notes
If the return value is null and you need additional information, call the Win32 function **GetLastError**.
ClusterNetworkOpenEnum can create enumerators for iterating through all the objects on a network or only the network interface objects and you can decide by setting the bitmask appropriately in your application.
Also see the programming notes for **ClusterNetworkEnum**.

ClusterNetworkControl
The **ClusterNetworkControl** function initiates an operation specified by the control code.

DWORD WINAPI **ClusterNetworkControl**(
HNETWORK *hNetwrk*,
HNODE *hHostNode*,
DWORD *dwCtrlCode*,
LPVOID *lpInBuf*,
DWORD *cbInBufSz*,
LPVOID *lpOutBuf*,
DWORD *cbOutBufSz*,
LPDWORD *lpcbBytesRet*
);

Input Parameters
hNetwrk — Handle to the network where the operation is to be initiated.
hHostNode — Handle to the node hosting the affected network. This parameter is optional.
dwCtrlCode — Control code for the operation to be performed. For a list of the valid control code values see the programming notes for this function.
lpInBuf — Pointer to the input buffer that contains the information needed for the operation to be performed. Set this parameter to null if no information is needed.
cbInBufSz — Number of bytes in the buffer pointed to by *lpInBuf*.
cbOutBufSz — Number of bytes in the output buffer pointed to by *lpOutBuf*. You can set this parameter to zero if you do not know how much data are to be returned

Parameters that are both Input and Output
lpcbBytesRet — Pointer to the number of bytes in the buffer pointed to by *lpOutBuf* that were actually filled in as a result of the operation. You can pass NULL for *lpcbBytesRet* if you do not want **ClusterNetworkControl** to pass back the actual number of bytes in the output buffer.

Output Parameters
lpOutBuf — Pointer to the output buffer. This parameter is null if nothing is returned.

Return Values

ERROR_SUCCESS — The operation was successful.

ERROR_MORE_DATA — The output buffer pointed to by *lpOutBuf* is not large enough to hold the retrieved data. The *lpcbBytesRet* parameter points to the required size for the output buffer.

If the operation was unsuccessful, **ClusterNetworkControl** returns a Win32 error value.

Programming Notes

ClusterNetworkControl is a general-purpose function that can be used to initiate a number of operations on the network (as long as they are allowed operations). The operations are specified using control codes. The typical operations you can perform include

- Retrieving properties and other data
- Updating properties and other data
- Data enumeration
- Data validation

Table 1 summarizes the control codes you can use to initiate network operations and their descriptions.

TABLE 1
Control Codes for Networks and Associated Descriptions

Control Code	Description
CLUSCTL_NETWORK_ENUM_COMMON_PROPERTIES	This control code is used to retrieve a list of the common network properties
CLUSCTL_NETWORK_ENUM_PRIVATE_PROPERTIES	This control code is used to retrieve a list of private network properties
CLUSCTL_NETWORK_GET_CHARACTERISTICS	This control code is used to request the intrinsic characteristics of a network
CLUSCTL_NETWORK_ENUM_COMMON_PROPERTIES	This control code is used to request the read/write common properties for a network
CLUSCTL_NETWORK_GET_FLAGS	This control code is used to request the flags that are set for a network
CLUSCTL_NETWORK_GET_NAME	This control code is used to retrieve the name of a network
CLUSCTL_NETWORK_GET_PRIVATE_PROPERTIES	This control code is used to request the read/write private properties for a network
CLUSCTL_NETWORK_GET_RO_COMMON_PROPERTIES	This control code is used to request the read-only common properties for a network
CLUSCTL_NETWORK_GET_RO_PRIVATE_PROPERTIES	This control code is used to request the read-only private properties for a network
CLUSCTL_NETWORK_SET_COMMON_PROPERTIES	This control code is used to update the common properties for a network
CLUSCTL_NETWORK_SET_PRIVATE_PROPERTIES	This control code is used to update the private properties for a network
CLUSCTL_NETWORK_UNKNOWN	This control code indicates a request for an unknown operation
CLUSCTL_NETWORK_VALIDATE_COMMON_PROPERTIES	This control code is used to check whether or not specific properties and property values are valid as common network properties
CLUSCTL_NETWORK_VALIDATE_PRIVATE_PROPERTIES	This control code is used to check whether or not specific properties and property values are valid as private properties for a network

If **ClusterNetworkControl** returns ERROR_MORE_DATA, set *cbOutBufSz* to the number of bytes pointed to by *lpcbBytesRet* and call the function again.

ClusterNetworkControl always returns ERROR_SUCCESS when the *dwControlCode* parameter is set to the clusctl_network_unknown control code.

GetClusterNetworkState

The **GetClusterNetworkState** function returns the current state of a network.

```
CLUSTER_NETWORK_STATE WINAPI GetClusterNetworkState(
                                      HNETWORK hNetwrk
                                      );
```

Input Parameters

hNetwrk — Handle to the network for which the current state information is obtained

Return Values

If the operation was successful, **GetClusterNetworkState** returns the current state of the network. The current state of the network is one of four possible values as shown in Table 2.

TABLE 2
Network States and Associated Descriptions

State	Description
ClusterNetworkStateUp	The network is operational and all communication paths are open
ClusterNetworkStatePartitioned	The network is operational, but two or more nodes on the network are unable to communicate
ClusterNetworkStateDown	The network is not operational; none of the nodes on the network can communicate
ClusterNetworkStateUnavailable	State information for the network is unavailable

If the operation was unsuccessful, GetClusterNetworkState returns ClusterNetworkStateUnknown.

Programming Notes

The ClusterNetworkStatePartitioned state is commonly caused by a path problem involving the nodes that are unable to communicate.

The ClusterNetworkStateUnavailable state is caused by the network Role property being set to ClusterNetworkRoleNone.

If you get ClusterNetworkStateUnknown and you need additional information about the cause of the problem, call the Win32 function **GetLastError**.

GetClusterNetworkId

The **GetClusterNetworkId** function returns the identifier of a network.

```
DWORD WINAPIGetClusterNetworkId(
            HNETWORK hNetwrk,
            LPWSTR lpszNetwrkId,
```

```
LPDWORD lpcchNetwrkId
);
```

Input Parameters
hNetwrk — Handle to a network

Parameters that are both Input and Output
lpcchNetwrkId — On input, this parameter points to a buffer. On output, this parameter points to a count of characters in the network identifier pointed to by *lpszNetwrkId*.

Output Parameters
lpszNetwrkId — Pointer to the identifier of the network associated with *hNetwrk*, including the terminating NULL character.

Return Values
ERROR_SUCCESS — The operation was successful.
ERROR_MORE_DATA — The buffer pointed to by *lpszNetwrkId* is not long enough. The *lpcchNetwrkId* parameter is set to the required buffer length.

If the operation was unsuccessful for a reason other than insufficient size in the buffer pointed to by *lpszNetwrkId*, **GetClusterNetworkId** returns a Win32 error value.

Programming Notes
When **GetClusterNetworkId** returns, the variable pointed to by *lpcchNetwrkId* contains the number of characters stored in the buffer. The count returned does not include the terminating null character.

OpenClusterNetwork
The **OpenClusterNetwork** function opens a network connection and returns a handle to it.

```
HNETWORK WINAPI OpenClusterNetwork(
                HCLUSTER hCluster,
                LPCWSTR lpszNetwrkNam
                );
```

Input Parameters
hCluster — Handle to a network.
lpszNetwrkNam — Pointer to an existing network name.

Return Values
NULL — The operation was unsuccessful.
Network handle — If the operation was successful, **OpenClusterNetwork** returns a network handle.

Programming Notes
If the operation was not successful and you need additional information, call the Win32 function **GetLastError**.

SetClusterNetworkName
The **SetClusterNetworkName** function sets the name for a network.

```
DWORD WINAPI SetClusterNetworkName(
                HNETWORK hNetwrk,
                LPCWSTR lpszName
                );
```

Input Parameters
hNetwrk — Handle to a network whose name is to be set
lpszName — Pointer to the new network name

Return Values
ERROR_SUCCESS — The operation was successful.

If the operation was unsuccessful, **SetClusterNetworkName** returns a Win32 error value.

SetClusterNetworkPriorityOrder
The **SetClusterNetworkPriorityOrder** function sets the priority order for the set of networks used for internal communication between cluster nodes.

```
DWORD WINAPI SetClusterNetworkPriorityOrder(
                HCLUSTER hCluster,
                DWORD NetwrkCnt,
                HNETWORK NetwrkLst[]
                );
```

Input Parameters
hCluster — Handle to the cluster where the network priority order is to be set
NetwrkCnt — Number of items in the list specified by the *NetwrkLst* parameter
NetwrkLst — Prioritized array of handles to network objects

Return Values
ERROR_SUCCESS — The operation was successful.
ERROR_NOT_ENOUGH_MEMORY — Operation unsuccessful due to insufficient memory.
ERROR_INVALID_PARAMETER — Duplicate network in *NetwrkLst*.

If the operation was unsuccessful, **SetClusterNetworkPriorityOrder** returns a Win32 error value.

Programming Notes
- The first handle in the array has the highest priority.
  - All networks used for node-to-node communication must appear in the list.
  - The list must contain only those networks that are used for internal cluster communications.
  - Duplicates are not allowed in the list.
  - Internal communication is always carried on the highest priority network that is available between two nodes.

NETWORK INTERFACE MANAGEMENT FUNCTIONS

The functions in the Cluster API for managing a network interface in a cluster open and close the network interface, perform selected operations, and retrieve information. The following functions are included in the Cluster API for managing network interfaces:

Function	Description
CloseClusterNetInterface	Closes a network interface handle
ClusterNetInterfaceControl	Initiates an operation affecting a network interface
GetClusterNetInterface	Returns the name of a node interface to a network in a cluster
GetClusterNetInterfaceState	Returns the current state of a network interface
OpenClusterNetInterface	Opens a handle to a network interface

CloseClusterNetInterface

The **CloseClusterNetInterface** function closes a network interface handle.

```
BOOL WINAPI   CloseClusterNetInterface(
              HNETINTERFACE hNetIntFace
              );
```

Input Parameters
hNetIntFace — Handle to the network interface to be closed

Return Values
TRUE — The operation was successful.
FALSE — The operation was unsuccessful.

Programming Notes
If the operation was not successful and you need additional information, call the Win32 function **GetLastError**. The network interface handle used in *hNetIntFace* is the handle obtained from a prior call to **OpenClusterNetInterface**.

ClusterNetInterfaceControl

The **ClusterNetInterfaceControl** function initiates an operation affecting a network interface.

```
DWORD WINAPI ClusterNetInterfaceControl(
              HNETINTERFACE hNetIntFace,
              HNODE hHostNode,
              DWORD dwCtrlCode,
              LPVOID lpInBuf,
              DWORD cbInBufSz,
              LPVOID lpOutBuf,
              DWORD cbOutBufSz,
              LPDWORD lpcbBytesRet
              );
```

Input Parameters

hNetIntFace — Handle to the network interface to be affected by the operation.

hHostNode — Handle to the node hosting the affected network interface. This parameter is optional.

dwCtrlCode — Control code that specifies the operation to be performed.

lpInBuf — Pointer to the input buffer with information required for the operation. This parameter can be NULL if no information is required for the operation.

cbInBufSz — Number of bytes in the buffer pointed to by *lpInBuf*.

cbOutBufSz — Number of bytes in the output buffer pointed to by *lpOutBuf*. This parameter can be set to zero if you do not know how much data are to be returned.

Parameters that are both Input and Output

lpcbBytesRet — Pointer to the number of bytes in the buffer pointed to by *lpOutBuf* that were actually filled in as a result of the operation. You can set the value of this parameter to null if you do not want **ClusterNetInterfaceControl** to pass back the number of bytes in the output buffer.

Output Parameters

lpOutBuf — Pointer to the output buffer. Set this parameter value to null if nothing needs to be returned.

Return Values

ERROR_SUCCESS — The operation was successful.

ERROR_MORE_DATA — The output buffer pointed to by *lpOutBuf* is not large enough to hold the retrieved data. The *lpcbBytesRet* parameter points to the actual size required for the output buffer.

If the operation was unsuccessful, **ClusterNetInterfaceControl** returns a Win32 error value.

Programming Notes

When **ClusterNetInterfaceControl** returns error_more_data, set *cbOutBufSz* to the number of bytes pointed to by *lpcbBytesRet* and call the function again.

ClusterNetInterfaceControl is a general-purpose function for initiating an operation that affects a network interface. The scope of allowable operations is defined by the set of control codes specified for network interfaces.

GetClusterNetinterface

The **GetClusterNetInterface** function returns the name of a node interface to a network in a cluster.

```
DWORD WINAPI GetClusterNetInterface(
        HCLUSTER hCluster,
        LPCWSTR lpszNodeNam,
        LPCWSTR lpszNetwrkNam,
        LPWSTR lpszIntfaceNam,
        LPDWORD lpcbIntfaceNam
        );
```

Input Parameters

hCluster — Handle to a cluster

lpszNodeNam — Pointer to the name of the node in the cluster

lpszNetwrkNam — Pointer to the name of the network

Parameters that are both Input and Output

lpcbIntfaceNam — On input, this parameter points to a variable that specifies the size (in characters) of the buffer pointed to by *lpszIntfaceNam*, including the terminating null character. On output, this parameter points to a variable that contains the number of characters stored in the output buffer not including the terminating NULL character.

Output Parameters

lpszIntfaceNam — Pointer to an output buffer holding the name of the network interface

Return Values

ERROR_SUCCESS — The network interface name was returned successfully.

ERROR_MORE_DATA — The name to be returned is longer than can fit in the buffer pointed to by *lpszIntfaceNam*.

If the operation was unsuccessful, **GetClusterNetInterface** can also return a Win32 error.

GetClusterNetInterfaceState

The **GetClusterNetInterfaceState** function returns the current state of a network interface.

CLUSTER_NETINTERFACE_STATE WINAPI **GetClusterNetInterfaceState**(
HNETINTFACE *hNetIntFace*
);

Input Parameters

hNetIntFace — Handle to the network interface for which the current state information is being obtained.

Return Values

If the operation was successful, **GetClusterNetInterfaceState** returns the current state of the network, which is represented by one of the following values:

State	Description
ClusterNetworkUp	The network interface is operational
ClusterNetInterfaceFailed	The network interface is not operational; the common cause for this state is a hardware failure
ClusterNetInterfaceUnreachable	None of the active nodes in the cluster can access the network interface
ClusterNetworkUnavailable	State information is unavailable

If the operation was unsuccessful, **GetClusterNetInterfaceState** returns ClusterNetInterfaceState-Unknown.

Programming Notes

If the operation was not successful and you need additional information, call the Win32 function **GetLastError**.

OpenClusterNetInterface
The **OpenClusterNetInterface** function opens a handle to a network interface.

```
HNETINTFACE WINAPI  OpenClusterNetInterface(
                        HCLUSTER hCluster,
                        LPCWSTR lpszIntfaceNam
                        );
```

Input Parameters
hCluster — Handle to a cluster
lpszIntfaceNam — Pointer to the name of the network interface to be opened

Return Values
If the operation was successful, **OpenClusterNetInterface** returns an open handle to the specified network interface.
NULL— The operation was unsuccessful.

Programming Notes
If the operation was not successful and you need additional information, call the Win32 function **GetLastError**.

CLUSTER MANAGEMENT FUNCTIONS

The cluster management functions in the Cluster API provide the following functions:

- Access to event notifications
- Access to cluster objects
- Cluster state information

Table 3 shows the functions included in the Cluster API for cluster management.

CloseCluster
The **CloseCluster** function invalidates a cluster handle and closes a connection to the cluster.

```
BOOL WINAPI    CloseCluster(
                   HCLUSTER hCluster
                   );
```

Input Parameters
hCluster — Handle to the cluster to be closed

Return Values
TRUE — The operation was successful.
FALSE — The operation was unsuccessful.

Programming Notes
If the operation was not successful and you need additional information, call the Win32 function **GetLastError**.

TABLE 3
Cluster Management Functions and Descriptions

Function	Description
CloseCluster	Closes a connection to a cluster by invalidating its handle
CloseClusterNotifyPort	Closes a notification port established through **CreateClusterNotifyPort** by invalidating its handle
ClusterCloseEnum	Closes a cluster enumerator object by invalidating its handle, a handle returned from **ClusterOpenEnum**
ClusterEnum	Enumerates objects in a cluster, returning the name of one object with each call
ClusterOpenEnum	Opens an enumerator for iterating through objects in a cluster
ClusterResourceTypeControl	Initiates an operation affecting a resource type
CreateClusterNotifyPort	Creates a notification port to handle cluster event notification
CreateClusterResourceType	Creates a new resource type in a cluster
DeleteClusterResourceType	Removes a resource type from a cluster
GetClusterInformation	Returns a cluster's name and version
GetClusterNotify	Returns the next notification event from a notification port
GetClusterQuorumResource	Returns the name of a cluster's quorum resource
OpenCluster	Opens a connection to a cluster and returns a handle to it
RegisterClusterNotify	Adds an event type to the list of events stored for a notification port
SetClusterName	Sets the name for a cluster
SetClusterQuorumResource	Sets the quorum resource for a cluster

CloseClusterNotifyPort
The **CloseClusterNotifyPort** function invalidates a notification port handle and closes the notification port.

```
BOOL WINAPI   CloseClusterNotifyPort(
              HCHANGE hChg
              );
```

Input Parameters
hChg — Handle to the notification port to be closed

Return Values
TRUE — The operation was successful.
FALSE — The operation was unsuccessful.

Programming Notes
If the operation was not successful and you need additional information, call the Win32 function **GetLastError**.

ClusterCloseEnum
The **ClusterCloseEnum** function invalidates the handle to a cluster enumerator object and closes the cluster enumerator object.

```
DWORD WINAPI ClusterCloseEnum(
              HCLUSENUM hEnum
              );
```

Input Parameters
hEnum — Handle to the cluster enumerator object to be closed

Return Values
ERROR_SUCCESS — The operation was successful.

If the operation was unsuccessful, **ClusterCloseEnum** returns a Win32 error value.

ClusterEnum
The **ClusterEnum** function enumerates objects in a cluster. Each **ClusterEnum** call returns the name of one cluster object.

```
DWORD WINAPI ClusterEnum(
        HCLUSENUM hEnum,
        DWORD dwIndx,
        LPDWORD lpdwType,
        LPWSTR lpszName,
        LPDWORD lpcbName
        );
```

Input Parameters
hEnum — Handle to an existing enumeration object.
dwIndx — Index used to identify the next entry to be enumerated. Set this parameter to zero for the first call to **ClusterEnum**. It is incremented for each subsequent calls to **Cluster-Enum**.

Output Parameters
lpdwType — Pointer to the type of object returned. Valid types returned are
CLUSTER_ENUM_NODE — The object is a node in the cluster.
CLUSTER_ENUM_RESTYPE — The object is a resource type in the cluster.
CLUSTER_ENUM_RESOURCE — The object is a resource in the cluster.
CLUSTER_ENUM_GROUP — The object is a group in the cluster.
lpszName — Pointer to the name of the returned object.

Parameters that are both Input and Output
lpcbName — On input, this parameter points to a buffer. On output, this parameter points to the count of characters in the name pointed to by the *lpszName* parameter minus the terminating NULL character.

Return Values
ERROR_SUCCESS — The operation was successful.
ERROR_NO_MORE_ITEMS — There are no more objects of the requested type to be returned.
ERROR_MORE_DATA — The buffer pointed to by *lpszName* is not long enough to hold the required number of characters. The *lpcbName* parameter has been set to the required buffer length.

Programming Notes
The **ClusterEnum** function is used to iterate through a collection of cluster objects. The handle used in this function is the handle returned by a call to **ClusterOpenEnum**. The cluster objects can be of different types. If you want to enumerate all the nodes in a cluster, call **ClusterOpenEnum** to open a cluster enumerator that can process nodes. Set the *dwType* parameter to

CLUSTER_ENUM_NODE to specify nodes as the object type to be enumerated. You can also enumerate more than one object type at the same time. If you want to enumerate nodes and groups, set *dwType* to CLUSTER_ENUM_NODE | CLUSTER_ENUM_GROUP. The *lpdwType* parameter points to the type of object that is retrieved.

ClusterOpenEnum

The **ClusterOpenEnum** function opens an enumerator for iterating through objects in a cluster.

HCLUSENUM WINAPI **ClusterOpenEnum**(
    HCLUSTER *hCluster*,
    DWORD *dwType*
    );

Input Parameters

hCluster — Handle to a cluster.

dwType — Bitmask that specifies the object types to be enumerated. The following are valid values:

CLUSTER_ENUM_GROUP — Enumerate the groups in the cluster.
CLUSTER_ENUM_NODE — Enumerate the nodes in the cluster.
CLUSTER_ENUM_RESTYPE — Enumerate the resource types in the cluster.
CLUSTER_ENUM_RESOURCE — Enumerate the resources in the cluster.

Return Values

If the operation was successful, **ClusterOpenEnum** returns a handle to a cluster enumerator.

NULL — The operation was unsuccessful.

Programming Notes

If the operation was not successful and you need additional information, call the Win32 function **GetLastError**.

ClusterOpenEnum can create enumerators for iterating different cluster objects:

- Groups
- Nodes
- Resource types
- Resources

The typical sequence of calls you would make to enumerate a set of cluster objects is as follows:

- Call the **ClusterOpenEnum** function for the type of cluster object you need by setting the *dwType* parameter. You can also enumerate more than one object type at the same time. **ClusterOpenEnum** returns a handle.
- Call **ClusterEnum** iteratively to access all the cluster object or objects of the required type or types using the handle obtained with ClusterOpenEnum.
- Process the cluster objects.
- When you have finished processing, call **ClusterCloseEnum**.

For more information, see the programming notes for **ClusterEnum**.

ClusterResourceTypeControl

The **ClusterResourceTypeControl** is a general-purpose function to initiate an operation on a resource type.

DWORD WINAPI **ClusterResourceTypeControl**(
HCLUSTER *hCluster*,
LPCWSTR *ResTypName*,
HNODE *hHostNode*,
DWORD *dwCtrlCode*,
LPVOID *lpInBuf*,
DWORD *cbInBufSz*,
LPVOID *lpOutBuf*,
DWORD *cbOutBufSz*,
LPDWORD *lpcbBytesRet*
);

Input Parameters

hCluster — Handle to the cluster that contains the resource type.

ResTypName — Pointer to the name of the resource type.

hHostNode — Handle to the node hosting the affected resource type. This parameter is optional.

dwCtrlCode — Control code that specifies the operation to be performed. For a list of valid Control Codes, see the programming notes for this function.

lpInBuf — Pointer to the input buffer containing information needed for the operation. This parameter can be NULL if no information is needed.

cbInBufSz — Number of bytes in the buffer pointed to by *lpInBuf*.

cbOutBufSz — Number of bytes in the output buffer pointed to by *lpOutBuf*. You can set this parameter to zero if you do not know how much data are to be returned.

Parameters that are both Input and Output

lpcbBytesRet — Pointer to the number of bytes in the buffer pointed to by *lpOutBuf* that were actually filled in as a result of the operation. You can pass NULL for this parameter if you do not want **ClusterResourceTypeControl** to pass back the number of bytes in the output buffer.

Output Parameters

lpOutBuf — Pointer to the output buffer with information resulting from the operation, or null if nothing need be returned.

Return Values

ERROR_SUCCESS — The operation was successful.

ERROR_MORE_DATA — The output buffer pointed to by *lpOutBuf* is not large enough to hold the retrieved data. The *lpcbBytesRet* parameter points to the required size of the output buffer to hold all the data.

If the operation was unsuccessful, **ClusterResourceTypeControl** returns a Win32 error value.

Programming Notes

Table 4 summarizes the control codes you can use to initiate operations and their descriptions. The typical operations you can perform include retrieving and updating properties and other data, data enumeration and validation, etc.

The control codes just listed are external control codes — control codes that you can pass in your application to initiate operations. Besides these external control codes, there are also internal control codes — control codes that only the Cluster Service can pass to a control function. The Cluster Service uses these codes to notify a resource DLL of an event. Resource DLLs should add

TABLE 4
External Control Codes for Resource Types

Control Code	Description
CLUSCTL_RESOURCE_TYPE_ENUM_COMMON_PROPERTIES	This control code is used to retrieve a list of the common resource type properties
CLUSCTL_RESOURCE_TYPE_ENUM_PRIVATE_PROPERTIES	This control code is used to retrieve a list of private resource type properties
CLUSCTL_RESOURCE_TYPE_GET_CHARACTERISTICS	This control code is used to request the intrinsic characteristics of a resource type
CLUSCTL_RESOURCE_TYPE_GET_CLASS_INFO	This control code is used to request the class and subclass of a resource type
CLUSCTL_RESOURCE_TYPE_ENUM_COMMON_PROPERTIES	This control code is used to request the read/write common properties of a resource type
CLUSCTL_RESOURCE_TYPE_GET_FLAGS	This control code is used to request the flags that are set for a resource type
CLUSCTL_RESOURCE_TYPE_GET_PRIVATE_PROPERTIES	This control code is used to request the read/write private properties for a resource type
CLUSCTL_RESOURCE_TYPE_GET_REGISTRY_CHECKPOINTS	This control code is used to request a list of all the checkpoints that the resource type requires or sets
CLUSCTL_RESOURCE_TYPE_GET_REQUIRED_DEPENDENCIES	This control code is used to request a list of all required dependencies for a resource type
CLUSCTL_RESOURCE_TYPE_GET_RO_COMMON_PROPERTIES	This control code is used to request the read-only common properties for a resource type
CLUSCTL_RESOURCE_TYPE_GET_RO_PRIVATE_PROPERTIES	This control code is used to request the read-only private properties for a resource type
CLUSCTL_RESOURCE_TYPE_SET_COMMON_PROPERTIES	This control code is used to update the common properties for a resource type
CLUSCTL_RESOURCE_TYPE_SET_PRIVATE_PROPERTIES	This control code is used to update the private properties for a resource type
CLUSCTL_RESOURCE_TYPE_STORAGE_GET_AVAILABLE_DISKS	This control code is used to request information about available disk resources
CLUSCTL_RESOURCE_TYPE_UNKNOWN	This control code is used to test whether or not a resource dynamic link library (DLL) supports control code processing for resource types
CLUSCTL_RESOURCE_TYPE_VALIDATE_COMMON_PROPERTIES	This control code is used to check whether or not specific properties are valid common properties for a resource type
CLUSCTL_RESOURCE_TYPE_VALIDATE_PRIVATE_PROPERTIES	This control code is used to check whether or not specific properties are valid private properties for a resource type

codes to their **ResourceTypeControl** entry point functions to handle these codes and respond to the associated event. Table 5 lists the internal control codes for resource types and associated description.

TABLE 5
Internal Control Codes for Resource Types

Control Code	Description
CLUSCTL_RESOURCE_TYPE_INSTALL_NODE	This control code is used by the Cluster Service to notify a resource DLL that a node is being added to the cluster
CLUSCTL_RESOURCE_TYPE_EVICT_NODE	This control code is used by the Cluster Service to notify a resource DLL that a node is being permanently removed from the cluster

When **ClusterResourceTypeControl** returns ERROR_MORE_DATA, set *cbOutBufSz* to the number of bytes pointed to by *lpcbBytesRet* and call the function again.

CreateClusterNotifyPort

The **CreateClusterNotifyPort** function creates a notification port to handle cluster event notification.

```
HCHANGE WINAPI CreateClusterNotifyPort(
                    HCHANGE hChg,
                    HCLUSTER hCluster,
                    DWORD dwFilter,
                    DWORD dwNotfyKey
                    );
```

Input Parameters

hChg — Handle to a notification port or INVALID_HANDLE_VALUE. An existing handle, the events specified in *dwFilter* are added to the notification port. If *hChg* is INVALID_HANDLE_VALUE, it indicates that a new handle should be created.

hCluster — Handle to the cluster or INVALID_HANDLE_VALUE. The cluster handle is the handle to the cluster to be associated with the notification port identified by *hChg*. INVALID_HANDLE_VALUE, indicates that the notification port should not be associated with a cluster. If *hChg* is not set to INVALID_HANDLE_VALUE, then *hCluster* cannot be set to INVALID_HANDLE_VALUE.

dwFilter — Bitmask of flags. The flags describe the events to cause notifications to be stored in the queue.

CLUSTER_CHANGE_CLUSTER_PROPERTY — Indicates that a notification should be issued when the prioritized list of internal networks has changed.

CLUSTER_CHANGE_CLUSTER_STATE — Reserved for future use.

CLUSTER_CHANGE_GROUP_ADDED — Indicates that a notification should be issued when a new group is created in the cluster.

CLUSTER_CHANGE_GROUP_DELETED — Indicates that a notification should be issued when an existing group is deleted.

CLUSTER_CHANGE_GROUP_PROPERTY — Indicates that a notification should be issued when the properties of an existing group change, such as changing the group name or adding/removing a resource from the group.

CLUSTER_CHANGE_GROUP_STATE — Indicates that a notification should be issued when a group changes state. Valid cluster group state values are listed under the function **GetClusterGroupState** later in this appendix.

CLUSTER_CHANGE_HANDLE_CLOSE — Indicates that a notification should be issued when a handle associated with a cluster object has closed.

CLUSTER_CHANGE_NETINTERFACE_ADDED — Indicates that a notification should be issued when a new network interface is added to a cluster node.

CLUSTER_CHANGE_NETINTERFACE_DELETED — Indicates that a notification should be issued when a network interface is permanently removed from a cluster node.

CLUSTER_CHANGE_NETINTERFACE_PROPERTY — Indicates that a notification should be issued when the properties of an existing network interface change.

CLUSTER_CHANGE_NETINTERFACE_STATE — Indicates that a notification should be issued when a network interface changes state. Valid network interface state values are listed under the function **GetClusterNetInterfaceState** later in this appendix.

CLUSTER_CHANGE_NETWORK_ADDED — Indicates that a notification should be issued when a new network is added to the cluster environment.

CLUSTER_CHANGE_NETWORK_DELETED — Indicates that a notification should be issued when a network is permanently removed from the cluster environment.

CLUSTER_CHANGE_NETWORK_PROPERTY — Indicates that a notification should be issued when the properties of an existing network change.

CLUSTER_CHANGE_NETWORK_STATE — Indicates that a notification should be issued when a network changes state. Valid network state values are listed under the function **GetClusterNetworkState** later in this appendix.

CLUSTER_CHANGE_NODE_ADDED — Indicates that a notification should be issued when a new node is added to the cluster. A node can only be added when Cluster Server is initially installed on the node.

CLUSTER_CHANGE_NODE_DELETED — Indicates that a notification should be issued when a node is permanently removed from a cluster.

CLUSTER_CHANGE_NODE_PROPERTY — Reserved for future use.

CLUSTER_CHANGE_NODE_STATE — Indicates that a notification should be issued when a node changes state. Valid node state values are listed under the function **GetClusterNodeState** later in this appendix.

CLUSTER_CHANGE_QUORUM_STATE — Reserved for future use.

CLUSTER_CHANGE_REGISTRY_ATTRIBUTES — Indicates that a notification should be issued when a cluster database key attributes are changed.

CLUSTER_CHANGE_REGISTRY_NAME — Indicates that a notification should be issued when the name of a cluster database key has changed. See descriptions of the **ClusterRegCreateKey** function (which creates a new database key) and the **ClusterRegDeleteKey** function (which deletes a key).

CLUSTER_CHANGE_REGISTRY_SUBTREE — Indicates that the other CLUSTER_CHANGE_REGISTRY events apply to the entire cluster database. If this flag is not included, the events apply only to the specified key.

CLUSTER_CHANGE_REGISTRY_VALUE — Indicates that a notification should be issued when a value of the specified cluster database key is changed or deleted. See the descriptions of **ClusterRegSetValue** (which changes database key values) and **ClusterRegDeleteValue** (which deletes database key values).

CLUSTER_CHANGE_RESOURCE_ADDED — Indicates that a notification should be issued when a new resource is created in the cluster. See the description of **CreateClusterResource** function.

CLUSTER_CHANGE_RESOURCE_DELETED — Indicates that a notification should be issued when a resource is deleted. See the description of **DeleteClusterResource** function.

CLUSTER_CHANGE_RESOURCE_PROPERTY — Indicates that a notification should be issued when the properties of a resource change. The events that can trigger this notification and the associated functions are summarized in Table 6.

TABLE 6
Resource Change Events and Associated Functions

Resource Change Event	Functions that Cause the Event
Change the name of a resource	**SetClusterResourceName**
Change a resource list of possible owner nodes	**AddClusterResourceNode**
	RemoveClusterResourceNode
Change a resource dependencies	**AddClusterResourceDependency**
	RemoveClusterResourceDependency

CLUSTER_CHANGE_RESOURCE_STATE — Indicates that a notification should be issued when a resource changes state or when a resource is moved from one group to another with **ChangeClusterResourceGroup**. Valid resource state values are listed under the function **GetClusterResourceState** later in this appendix.

CLUSTER_CHANGE_RESOURCE_TYPE_ADDED — Indicates that a notification should be issued when a new resource type is created in the cluster. See the description of **CreateClusterResourceType** function.

CLUSTER_CHANGE_RESOURCE_TYPE_DELETED — Indicates that a notification should be issued when an existing resource type is deleted. See the description of **DeleteClusterResourceType** function.

dwNotfyKey — Any value that is associated with retrieving notifications from the created notification port. The *dwNotfyKey* is returned from **GetClusterNotify** when an event of one of the types specified in *dwFilter* occurs.

Return Values

If the operation was successful, return the handle to a notification port.

If the operation was unsuccessful, **CreateClusterNotifyPort** returns NULL.

Programming Notes

If the operation was unsuccessful and you need additional information about the error, call the Win32 function **GetLastError**.

CreateClusterResourceType

The **CreateClusterResourceType** function creates a new resource type in a cluster.

```
DWORD WINAPI CreateClusterResourceType(
                HCLUSTER hCluster,
                LPCWSTR lpszResTypName,
                LPCWSTR lpszDispName,
                LPCWSTR lpszResTypDll,
                DWORD dwLooksAlivePollInt,
                DWORD dwIsAlivePollInt
                );
```

Input Parameters

hCluster — Handle to the cluster to receive the new resource type.

lpsz*ResTypName* — Pointer to the name of the new resource type. The specified name must be unique within the cluster.

lpszDispName — Pointer to the display name for the new resource type. The display name is what is seen by administrators.

lpszResTypDll — Pointer to the fully qualified name of the resource DLL for the new resource type.

dwLooksAlivePollInt — Default value to be used as the poll interval needed by the new resource type **LooksAlive** function. The *dwLooksAlivePollInt* parameter is used to set the resource type's LooksAlivePollInterval property. The unit for this value is milliseconds.

dwIsAlivePollInt — Default value to be used as the poll interval needed by the new resource type **IsAlive** function. The *dwIsAlivePollInt* parameter is used to set the resource type's IsAlivePollInterval property. The unit for this value is milliseconds.

Return Values

ERROR_SUCCESS — The operation was successful.

If the operation was unsuccessful, **CreateClusterResourceType** returns a Win32 error value.

Programming Notes
If you are developing a new resource type, you must follow the following steps:

- Define the resource type in the cluster database.
- Register the resource type with the Cluster Service.
- Install the resource DLLs for the new type on each node in the cluster.
- Install the Cluster Administrator Extension DLLs for the new type on each node in the cluster.

You can use the **CreateClusterResourceType** function for the first two steps previously listed. In addition, if Cluster Administrator is used on systems that are not member nodes, the extension DLLs must also be installed on those systems.

DeleteClusterResourceType
The **DeleteClusterResourceType** function removes a resource type from a cluster.

```
DWORD WINAPI DeleteClusterResourceType(
                HCLUSTER hCluster,
                LPCWSTR lpszResTypName
                );
```

Input Parameters
hCluster — Handle to the cluster containing the resource type to be removed
lpsz*ResTypName* — Pointer to the name of the resource type to be removed

Return Values
ERROR_SUCCESS — The operation was successful.

If the operation was unsuccessful, **DeleteClusterResourceType** returns a Win32 error value.

Programming Notes
Before calling this function make sure that all resources of this type have been deleted. Otherwise, the call fails.
The **DeleteClusterResourceType** function removes the resource type from the cluster database and unregisters it with the Cluster Service. You must take care of deleting the resource DLL for the resource type from each node in the cluster.

GetClusterInformation
The **GetClusterInformation** function retrieves a cluster's name and version.

```
DWORD WINAPI GetClusterInformation(
                HCLUSTER hCluster,
                LPWSTR lpszClustrNam,
                LPDWORD lpcchClustrNam,
                LPCLUSTERVERSIONINFO lpClustrInf
                );
```

Input Parameters
hCluster — Handle to a cluster

Output Parameters

lpszClustrNam — Pointer to the name of the cluster identified by *hCluster*, including the terminating NULL character

lpClustrInf —NULL or a pointer to a CLUSTERVERSIONINFO structure describing the version of the Cluster API for the cluster

Parameters that are both Input and Output

lpcchClustrNam — On input, this parameter points to a buffer. On output, this parameter points to a count of characters in the cluster name pointed to by *lpszClustrNam*, including the terminating NULL character.

Return Values

ERROR_SUCCESS — The operation was successful.

ERROR_MORE_DATA — The buffer pointed to by *lpszClustrNam* is not long enough to hold all the characters. The *lpcchClustrNam* parameter is set to the required buffer length.

If the operation was unsuccessful for a reason other than insufficient buffer size, **GetClusterInformation** returns a Win32 error value.

Programming Notes

When **GetClusterInformation** returns, the variable pointed to by *lpcchClustrNam* contains the number of characters stored in the buffer. The count returned does not include the terminating NULL character.

When *lpClustrInf* is not NULL, the dwVersionInfoSize member of this structure is set as follows:

```
lpClustrInf->dwVersionInfoSize = sizeof(CLUSTERVERSIONINFO);
```

GetClusterNotify

The **GetClusterNotify** function returns information relating to the next notification event stored for a notification port.

```
DWORD WINAPI GetClusterNotify(
        HCHANGE hChg,
        LPDWORD lpdwNotfyKey,
        LPDWORD lpdwFiltrTyp,
        LPWSTR lpszName,
        LPDWORD lpcchNam,
        DWORD dwMillisecs
        );
```

Input Parameters

hChg — Handle to a notification port created with the **CreateClusterNotifyPort** function

dwMillisecs — Time-out value that specifies notification wait duration

Output Parameters

lpdwNotfyKey — Pointer to the notification key for the port identified by *hChg*.

lpdwFiltrTyp — Pointer to the type of returned event. See the description of **CreateClusterNotifyPort** for a list of valid event types.

lpszName — Pointer to the name of the object that triggered the event. Table 7 describes the contents of *lpszName* by event type.

TABLE 7
Event Types and Object Names

Value of lpszName	Value of lpdwFiltrTyp
New group name	CLUSTER_CHANGE_GROUP_ADDED
Deleted group name	CLUSTER_CHANGE_GROUP_DELETED
Name of changed group	CLUSTER_CHANGE_GROUP_PROPERTY
Name of changed group	CLUSTER_CHANGE_GROUP_STATE
Name of object being closed	CLUSTER_CHANGE_HANDLE_CLOSE
Name of new node	CLUSTER_CHANGE_NODE_ADDED
Name of deleted node	CLUSTER_CHANGE_NODE_DELETED
Name of changed node	CLUSTER_CHANGE_NODE_PROPERTY
Name of changed node	CLUSTER_CHANGE_NODE_STATE
Relative name of changed cluster database key	CLUSTER_CHANGE_REGISTRY_ATTRIBUTES
Relative name of changed cluster database key	CLUSTER_CHANGE_REGISTRY_NAME
Relative name of changed cluster database key	CLUSTER_CHANGE_REGISTRY_VALUE
New resource name	CLUSTER_CHANGE_RESOURCE_ADDED
Deleted resource name	CLUSTER_CHANGE_RESOURCE_DELETED
Name of changed resource	CLUSTER_CHANGE_RESOURCE_PROPERTY
Name of changed resource	CLUSTER_CHANGE_RESOURCE_STATE
Name of new resource type	CLUSTER_CHANGE_RESOURCE_TYPE_ADDED
Name of deleted resource type	CLUSTER_CHANGE_RESOURCE_TYPE_DELETED

Parameters that are both Input and Output

lpcchNam — On input, this parameter points to the count of characters in the buffer pointed to by *lpszName*. On output, this parameter points to the count of characters stored in the buffer pointed to by *lpszName*, excluding the trailing NULL.

Return values

ERROR_SUCCESS — The notification was successfully returned.

ERROR_INVALID_HANDLE — The handle represented in the *hChg* parameter is invalid. It may have been closed by another thread.

WAIT_TIMEOUT — The call timed out before the notification could be successfully returned.

If the notification was not successfully returned, **GetClusterNotify** returns a Win32 error value.

Programming Notes

If the notification was not successfully returned and you need additional information about the error, call the Win32 function **GetLastError**.

GetClusterQuorumResource

The **GetClusterQuorumResource** function returns the cluster quorum resource name.

```
DWORD WINAPI GetClusterQuorumResource(
        HCLUSTER hCluster,
        LPWSTR lpszResNam,
        LPDWORD lpcbResNam,
        LPWSTR lpszDevNam,
        LPDWORD lpcbDevNam,
        LPDWORD lpdwMaxQuorumLogSz
        );
```

Input Parameters

hCluster — Handle to an existing cluster

Output Parameters

lpszResNam — Pointer to a string containing the name of the cluster quorum resource

lpszDevNam — Pointer to a NULL-terminated string containing the name of the device where the quorum resource resides

lpdwMaxQuorumLogSz — Pointer to the maximum size of the quorum resource.log

Parameters that are both Input and Output

lpcbResNam — On input, this parameter points to the count of characters in the buffer pointed to by the *lpszResNam* parameter including the terminating NULL character. On output, this parameter points to the count of characters in the buffer, excluding the terminating NULL character.

lpcbDevNam — On input, this parameter points to the count of characters in the buffer pointed to by the *lpszDevNam* parameter including the terminating NULL character. On output, this parameter points to the count of characters stored in the buffer, excluding the terminating NULL character.

Return Values

ERROR_SUCCESS — The operation was successful.

ERROR_MORE_DATA — The buffer pointed to by *lpszResNam* is not big enough to hold the required number of characters. The *lpcbResNam* parameter has been set to the required buffer length.

If the operation was unsuccessful, GetClusterQuorumResource returns a Win32 error value.

OpenCluster

The **OpenCluster** function opens a connection to a cluster and returns the handle to the connection.

```
HCLUSTER WINAPI   OpenCluster(
                  LPCWSTR lpszClustrNam
                  );
```

Input Parameters

lpszClustrNam — Pointer to the name of an existing cluster or NULL. Passing the NULL value causes the handle to the cluster to which the local computer belongs to be returned.

Return Values

If the operation was successful, **OpenCluster** returns a cluster handle.

If the operation was unsuccessful, **OpenCluster** returns NULL.

Programing Notes

If the operation was unsuccessful and you need additional information about the reason for failure, you can call the Win32 function **GetLastError**.

RegisterClusterNotify

The **RegisterClusterNotify** function adds an event type to the list of events stored for a notification port.

```
DWORD WINAPI RegisterClusterNotify(
        HCHANGE hChg,
        DWORD dwFilter,
        HANDLE hObj,
        DWORD dwNotfyKey
        );
```

Input Parameters

hChg — Handle to a notification port. Notification ports are created with the **CreateClusterNotifyPort** function. Please see the description of **CreateClusterNotifyPort** in this appendix.

dwFilter — Bitmask of flags that specify an event. The specified event is added to the set of events that are currently being monitored by the notification port. For additional information about these event types, see the description of **CreateClusterNotifyPort** in this appendix. The valid flag values that the *dwFilter* parameter can be set to are

CLUSTER_CHANGE_GROUP_DELETED — Indicates that a notification should be issued when an existing resource group is deleted.

CLUSTER_CHANGE_GROUP_PROPERTY — Indicates that a notification should be issued when the properties of an existing resource group are changed.

CLUSTER_CHANGE_GROUP_STATE — Indicates that a notification should be issued when a resource group changes state.

CLUSTER_CHANGE_HANDLE_CLOSE — Indicates that a notification should be issued when a handle to a cluster object is closed.

CLUSTER_CHANGE_NODE_DELETED — Indicates that a notification should be issued when a node is permanently removed from a cluster.

CLUSTER_CHANGE_NODE_PROPERTY — Reserved for future use.

cluster_change_node_state — Indicates that a notification should be issued when a node changes state.

CLUSTER_CHANGE_REGISTRY_ATTRIBUTES — Indicates that a notification should be issued when a cluster database key's attributes are changed.

CLUSTER_CHANGE_REGISTRY_NAME — Indicates that a notification should be issued when a change to a name is made in the cluster database.

CLUSTER_CHANGE_REGISTRY_SUBTREE — Indicates that the other CLUSTER_CHANGE_REGISTRY events apply to the root of the cluster database and to all the subkeys. If CLUSTER_CHANGE_REGISTRY_SUBTREE is not specified, the notifications apply only to the root.

CLUSTER_CHANGE_REGISTRY_VALUE — Indicates that a notification should be issued when a value of the specified cluster database key is changed or deleted.

CLUSTER_CHANGE_RESOURCE_DELETED — Indicates that a notification should be issued when a resource is deleted.

CLUSTER_CHANGE_RESOURCE_PROPERTY — Indicates that a notification should be issued when the properties of a resource change.

CLUSTER_CHANGE_RESOURCE_STATE — Indicates that a notification should be issued when a resource changes state.

hObj — Handle to the object affected by the event specified in the *dwFilter* parameter. The type of handle depends on the value of *dwFilter* as is described in Table 8.

The cluster database functions return a valid cluster database key that can be used to set *hObj* when *dwFilter* is set to an event type affecting the cluster database.

dwNotfyKey — This notification key is returned from GetClusterNotify when the requested event occurs.

TABLE 8
Object Types and Filters

Value of *dwFilter*	Value of *hObject*
CLUSTER_CHANGE_GROUP_DELETED	HGROUP
CLUSTER_CHANGE_GROUP_PROPERTY	HGROUP
CLUSTER_CHANGE_GROUP_STATE	HGROUP
CLUSTER_CHANGE_NODE_DELETED	HNODE
CLUSTER_CHANGE_NODE_PROPERTY	HNODE
CLUSTER_CHANGE_NODE_STATE	HNODE
CLUSTER_CHANGE_REGISTRY_ATTRIBUTES	HKEY
CLUSTER_CHANGE_REGISTRY_NAME	HKEY
CLUSTER_CHANGE_REGISTRY_SUBTREE	HKEY
CLUSTER_CHANGE_REGISTRY_VALUE	HKEY
CLUSTER_CHANGE_RESOURCE_DELETED	HRESOURCE
CLUSTER_CHANGE_RESOURCE_PROPERTY	HRESOURCE
CLUSTER_CHANGE_RESOURCE_STATE	HRESOURCE

Return Values
ERROR_SUCCESS — The operation was successful.

If the operation was unsuccessful, **RegisterClusterNotify** returns a Win32 error value.

Programming Notes
The **RegisterClusterNotify** function enables you to register an additional event that affects a node, a resource, or a group. To receive notifications of events relating to cluster database changes, one or more of the flags applicable to the database (flags that start with the prefix CLUSTER_CHANGE_REGISTRY) must be set in the *dwFilter* parameter. Notifications of events relating to cluster database changes can be obtained only using this function. You cannot manually edit the registry cluster entries to start notifications for database changes. Prior to calling this function, your application should have already created a notification port using **CreateClusterNotifyPort**.

SetClusterName
The **SetClusterName** function sets the name for a cluster.

```
DWORD WINAPI SetClusterName(
        HCLUSTER hCluster,
        LPCWSTR lpszNewClustrNam
        );
```

Input Parameters
hCluster — Handle to the cluster to be renamed
lpszNewClustrNam — Pointer to the new cluster name

Return Values
ERROR_RESOURCE_PROPERTIES_STORED — The operation was successful.

If the operation was unsuccessful, **SetClusterName** returns a Win32 error value.

Programming Notes
Due to dependency considerations, changes to cluster name do not become effective until the network name resource is brought back online.

SetClusterQuorumResource
The **SetClusterQuorumResource** function sets the quorum resource for a cluster.

DWORD WINAPI **SetClusterQuorumResource**(
    HRESOURCE *hRes*,
    LPCWSTR *lpszDevNam*,
    DWORD *dwMaxQuorumResLogSize*
    );

Input Parameters
hRes — Handle to the new quorum resource
lpszDevNam — Pointer to the name of the device where the quorum resource resides
dwMaxQuorumResLogSize — Maximum size for the log file to be maintained by the quorum resource

Return Values
ERROR_SUCCESS — The operation was successful.
ERROR_RESOURCE_NOT_ONLINE — The quorum resource is not online.

If the operation was unsuccessful, **SetClusterQuorumResource** can also return a Win32 error value.

NODE MANAGEMENT FUNCTIONS

The node management functions in the Cluster API let you perform node-related operations, change the state of a node, and retrieve information. The node management functions are implemented primarily by the Cluster Service Membership Manager. The node management functions are summarized in Table 9.

TABLE 9
Node Management Functions

Function	Description
CloseClusterNode	Closes a node by invalidating its handle
ClusterNodeControl	Initiates an operation affecting a node
EvictClusterNode	Deletes a node from the cluster database
GetClusterNodeId	Returns the identifier of a cluster node

These functions are described in more detail later.

CloseClusterNode
The **CloseClusterNode** function closes a node by invalidating its handle.

BOOL WINAPI **CloseClusterNode**(
    HNODE *hNode*
    );

Input Parameters
hNode — Handle to an existing node

Return Values
TRUE — The operation was successful.
FALSE — The operation was unsuccessful.

Programming Notes
If the operation was unsuccessful and you need additional information about the reason for failure, you can call the Win32 function **GetLastError**.

ClusterNodeControl
The **ClusterNodeControl** is a general-purpose function used to initiate a number of node-related operations.

```
DWORD WINAPI ClusterNodeControl(
        HNODE hNode,
        HNODE hHostNode,
        DWORD dwCtrlCode,
        LPVOID lpInBuf,
        DWORD cbInBufSz,
        LPVOID lpOutBuf,
        DWORD cbOutBufSz,
        LPDWORD lpcbBytesRet
        );
```

Input Parameters
hNode — Handle to the node that handles the operation.
hHostNode — This parameter contains a handle or NULL. If NULL, the node represented by *hNode* performs the operation. If not NULL, the node whose handle is contained in this parameter performs the specified operation instead of the node specified in *hNode*.
dwCtrlCode — Control code that defines the operation to be performed. For a list of the valid control code values, see the programming notes for this function.
lpInBuf — Pointer to the input buffer that contains information needed for the operation. This parameter can be null if no information is needed.
cblnBufSz — Number of bytes in the buffer pointed to by *lpInBuf*.
cbOutBufSz — Number of bytes in the output buffer pointed to by *lpOutBuf*.

Output Parameters
lpOutBuf — Pointer to the output buffer with information resulting from the operation. This parameter can be NULL if nothing needs to be returned.

Parameters that are both Input and Output
lpcbBytesRet — Pointer to the number of bytes in the buffer pointed to by *lpOutBuf* that were actually filled as a result of the operation. You can set this parameter to NULL, if you do not want **ClusterNodeControl** to pass back the number of bytes in the output buffer.

Return Values

ERROR_SUCCESS — The operation was successful.

ERROR_MORE_DATA — The output buffer pointed to by *lpOutBuf* is not large enough to hold the data being returned. The *lpcbBytesRet* parameter points to the size required for the output buffer.

If the operation was unsuccessful, **ClusterNodeControl** returns a Win32 error value.

Programming Notes

The operations that can be performed using **ClusterNodeControl** are defined by the set of control codes for nodes. All control codes for node operations are external control codes. There are no internal control codes for node operations. The list of valid control codes for node operations is specified in Table 10.

TABLE 10
Node Control Codes and their Descriptions

Control Code	Description
CLUSCTL_NODE_ENUM_COMMON_PROPERTIES	This control code is used to retrieve a list of the common node properties
CLUSCTL_NODE_ENUM_PRIVATE_PROPERTIES	This control code is used to retrieve a list of the private node properties
CLUSCTL_NODE_GET_CHARACTERISTICS	This control code is a request for a mask that describes the intrinsic characteristics of a node
CLUSCTL_NODE_GET_COMMON_PROPERTIES	This control code is a request for the read/write common properties of a node

When **ClusterNodeControl** returns ERROR_MORE_DATA, you can set *cbOutBufSz* to the number of bytes pointed to by *lpcbBytesRet* and call the function again.

EvictClusterNode

The **EvictClusterNode** function deletes a node from the cluster database.

DWORD WINAPI**EvictClusterNode**(
HNODE *hNode*
);

Input Parameters

hNode — Handle to the node to be deleted

Return Values

ERROR_SUCCESS — The operation was successful

If the operation was unsuccessful, **EvictClusterNode** returns a Win32 error value.

Programming Notes

To reinstate an evicted node, remove Cluster Server from the evicted node and then reinstall Cluster Server. During Cluster Server installation, choose the option to join an existing cluster.

GetClusterNodeId

The **GetClusterNodeId** function returns the unique identifier of a cluster node.

```
DWORD WINAPIGetClusterNodeId(
        HNODE hNode,
        LPWSTR lpszNodeId,
        LPDWORD lpcchNodeId
        );
```

Input Parameters

hNode — This parameter contains either the handle to the node with the identifier to be returned or NULL. If this parameter is set to NULL, the node identifier that is returned is that of the node on which the application is running. The node identifier is returned in *lpszNodeId*

Output Parameters

lpszNodeId — Pointer to the unique identifier of the node represented by *hNode*

Parameters that are both Input and Output

lpcchNodeId — On input, this parameter points to the count of characters in the buffer that is pointed to by the *lpszNodeId* parameter (including the NULLl terminator). On output, this parameter points to the count of characters stored in the buffer (excluding the NULL terminator).

Return Values

ERROR_SUCCESS — The operation was successful.

ERROR_MORE_DATA — The buffer pointed to by *lpszNodeId* is not long enough to hold the required number of characters. In this case the actual buffer size required is returned in *lpcchNodeId* by **GetClusterNodeId**.

If the operation was unsuccessful, **GetClusterNodeId** returns a Win32 error value.

Programming Notes

If *hNode* is set to NULL and your application is running on an active cluster node, **GetClusterNodeId** returns the identifier of the node on which your application is running.

You may have a requirement if you are writing a resource DLL to determine the node identifier of the node on which the DLL is executing. **GetClusterNodeId** provides this function for you.

A cluster node identifier is a unique identifier that does not change if the node name is changed.

GetClusterNodeState

The **GetClusterNodeState** function returns the current state of a node.

```
CLUSTER_NODE_STATE WINAPIGetClusterNodeState(
        HNODE hNode
        );
```

Input Parameters

hNode — Handle to the node for which state information should be returned

Return Values

If the operation was successful, **GetClusterNodeState** returns the current state of the node. The state values that a node can have are listed in the Table 11.

TABLE 11
Node States and Descriptions

State	Description
ClusterNodeUp	The node is operational
ClusterNodeDown	The node is not operational
ClusterNodeJoining	The node is in the process of joining a cluster
ClusterNodePaused	The node has temporarily suspended activity

If the operation was unsuccessful, **GetClusterNodeState** returns ClusterNodeStateUnknown. For more detailed information about the error, call the Win32 function GetLastError.

Programming Notes

When a node is operating as an active member of a cluster, it is in the ClusterNodeUp state. A node that is up responds to updates to the cluster database, can host and manage groups, and can maintain communication with other nodes in the cluster.

When a node is trying to form or rejoin a cluster or is down, it is in the ClusterNodeDown state. A node that is down is not an active cluster member and it may or may not be running. The Cluster Service may have started and then failed, or may have failed to start completely.

When a node is operating as an active member of a cluster but cannot host any resources or resource groups, it is in the ClusterNodePaused state. Nodes that are undergoing maintenance are typically placed in this state.

OpenClusterNode

The **OpenClusterNode** function opens a node and returns its handle.

HNODE WINAPI **OpenClusterNode**(
HCLUSTER *hCluster*,
LPCWSTR *lpszNodeNam*
);

Input Parameters

hCluster — Handle to a cluster
lpszNodeNam — Pointer to the name of an existing node

Return Values

If the operation was successful, **OpenClusterNode** returns a node handle.
If the operation was unsuccessful, **OpenClusterNode** returns NULL.

Programming Notes
The cluster used in this function is the handle returned by the **OpenCluster** function. If the operation was unsuccessful and you need additional information about the error, call the Win32 function **GetLastError**.

PauseClusterNode
The **PauseClusterNode** function causes a node to be placed in ClusterNodePaused state.

DWORD WINAPI **PauseClusterNode**(
HNODE *hNode*
);

Input Parameters
hNode — Handle to the node to be placed in ClusterNodePaused state.

Return Values
ERROR_SUCCESS — The operation was successful.

If the operation was unsuccessful, **PauseClusterNode** returns a Win32 error value.

Programming Notes
A node in the ClusterNodePaused state is an active member of a cluster but the node cannot host any resources or resource groups. This means that administrators cannot move groups to the node in the ClusterNodePaused state. This also means that groups that would normally failover to the node cannot do so when it is in the paused state. However, groups that are currently owned by the paused node continue to be owned by the node. Paused node groups and resources can be taken offline, but they cannot be brought online. The paused state is persistent — a paused node that is rebooted continues to be paused when it comes back up.

ResumeClusterNode
The **ResumeClusterNode** function causes a paused node to change its state to ClusterNodeUp and resume full cluster activity.

DWORD WINAPI **ResumeClusterNode**(
HNODE *hNode*
);

Input Parameters
hNode — Handle to the node to change from the paused state

Return Values
ERROR_SUCCESS — The operation was successful.

If the operation was unsuccessful, **ResumeClusterNode** returns a Win32 error value.

GROUP MANAGEMENT FUNCTIONS

The group management functions in the Cluster API provide the following:

- Change a group membership
- Change a group state
- Retrieve information about the group

The group management functions are implemented primarily by the Cluster Service Resource and Failover Managers. Table 12 summarizes the group management functions.

TABLE 12
Group Management Functions and Descriptions

Function	Description
CloseClusterGroup	Invalidates a group handle and closes the group
ClusterGroupCloseEnum	Invalidates a group enumerator object's handle and closes the group enumerator object
ClusterGroupControl	Initiates a group-related operation
ClusterGroupEnum	Enumerates the resources in a group; each call to this function returns the name one resource in the group; this function also enumerates nodes that are possible owners of a group; in this case, each call to this function returns the name of a node
ClusterGroupOpenEnum	Opens an enumerator for iterating through group resources and/or the nodes that are possible owners of the group
CreateClusterGroup	Adds a group to a cluster and returns a handle to the newly added group
DeleteClusterGroup	Removes a group from a cluster
GetClusterGroupState	Returns the current state of a group
MoveClusterGroup	Moves a group and all the resources that belong to the group from one node to another
OfflineClusterGroup	Takes an online group offline
OnlineClusterGroup	Takes a group that is offline and brings it online
OpenClusterGroup	Opens a group and returns the group's handle
SetClusterGroupName	Sets the name for a group
SetClusterGroupNodeList	Sets the preferred node list for a group

CloseClusterGroup

The **CloseClusterGroup** function invalidates a group handle and closes the group.

BOOL WINAPI **CloseClusterGroup**(
HGROUP *hGrp*
);

Input Parameters
hGrp — Handle to the group to be closed

Return Values
TRUE — The operation was successful.
FALSE — The operation was unsuccessful.

Programming Notes
If the operation was unsuccessful and you need additional information about the error, call the Win32 function **GetLastError**.

ClusterGroupCloseEnum

The **ClusterGroupCloseEnum** function invalidates a group enumerator object handle and closes the group enumerator object.

```
DWORD WINAPI ClusterGroupCloseEnum(
        HGROUPENUM hGrpEnum
        );
```

Input Parameters

hGrpEnum — Handle to the group enumerator object to be closed

Return Values

ERROR_SUCCESS — The operation was successful.

If the operation was unsuccessful, **ClusterGroupCloseEnum** returns a Win32 error value.

ClusterGroupControl

The **ClusterGroupControl** is a general-purpose function used to initiate a group-related operation.

```
DWORD WINAPI ClusterGroupControl(
        HGROUP hGrp,
        HNODE hHostNode,
        DWORD dwCtrlCode,
        LPVOID lpInBuf,
        DWORD cbInBufSz,
        LPVOID lpOutBuf,
        DWORD cbOutBufSz,
        LPDWORD lpcbBytesRet
        );
```

Input Parameters

hGrp — Handle to the group on which the group operation is to be performed.

hHostNode — This parameter can contain a handle, NULL, or the parameter can be omitted (optional). If non-NULL, this parameter contains the handle to the node to perform the operation. The operation is specified by the control code (*dwCtrlCode* parameter). If NULL, the node that owns the group performs the operation.

dwCtrlCode — Control code that defines the operation to be performed. For a list of valid control code values, see the programming notes for this function.

lpInBuf — Pointer to the input buffer that contains information needed for the operation. This parameter can be NULL if no information is needed.

cbInBufSz — Number of bytes in the buffer pointed to by *lpInBuf*.

Output Parameters

lpOutBuf — Pointer to the output buffer with information resulting from the operation, or NULL if nothing needs to be returned.

cbOutBufSz — Number of bytes in the output buffer pointed to by *lpOutBuf*.

Parameters that are both Input and Output

lpcbBytesRet — Pointer to the number of bytes in the buffer pointed to by *lpOutBuf* that were actually filled as a result of the operation. You can set this parameter to NULL if you do not want **ClusterGroupControl** to pass back the number of bytes in the output buffer.

Return Values

ERROR_SUCCESS — The operation was successful.

ERROR_MORE_DATA — The output buffer pointed to by *lpOutBuf* is not large enough to hold the retrieved data. The *lpcbBytesRet* parameter points to the actual size required for the output buffer.

If the operation was unsuccessful, **ClusterGroupControl** returns a Win32 error value.

Programming Notes

The set of valid operations that can be performed using **ClusterGroupControl** is defined by the set of control codes for groups. All control codes for groups are external control codes. There are no internal control codes for groups. The list of valid control codes for groups is specified in Table 13.

TABLE 13
Control Codes for Groups

Control Code	Description
CLUSCTL_GROUP_ENUM_COMMON_PROPERTIES	This control code is used to retrieve a list of the common group properties
CLUSCTL_GROUP_ENUM_PRIVATE_PROPERTIES	This control code is used to retrieve a list of the private group properties
CLUSCTL_GROUP_GET_CHARACTERISTICS	This control code is used to request a mask that describes the intrinsic characteristics of a group
CLUSCTL_GROUP_GET_COMMON_PROPERTIES	This control code is used to request the read/write common properties for a group
CLUSCTL_GROUP_GET_FLAGS	This control code is used to request a bitmask describing the flags that are currently set for a group
CLUSCTL_GROUP_GET_NAME	This control code is used to request the name of a group
CLUSCTL_GROUP_GET_PRIVATE_PROPERTIES	This control code is used to request the read/write private properties for a group
CLUSCTL_GROUP_GET_RO_COMMON_PROPERTIES	This control code is used to request the read-only common properties for a group
CLUSCTL_GROUP_GET_RO_PRIVATE_PROPERTIES	This control code is used to request the read-only private properties for a group
CLUSCTL_GROUP_SET_COMMON_PROPERTIES	This control code is used to update the common properties for a group
CLUSCTL_GROUP_SET_PRIVATE_PROPERTIES	This control code is used to update the private properties for a group
CLUSCTL_GROUP_UNKNOWN	This control code indicates a request for an unknown operation
CLUSCTL_GROUP_VALIDATE_COMMON_PROPERTIES	This control code is used to check whether or not specific properties are valid common properties for a group
CLUSCTL_GROUP_VALIDATE_PRIVATE_PROPERTIES	This control code is used to check whether or not specific properties are valid private properties for a group

ClusterGroupControl always returns ERROR_SUCCESS when the *dwControlCode* parameter is set to CLUSCTL_GROUP_UNKNOWN.

When **ClusterGroupControl** returns ERROR_MORE_DATA, set *cbOutBufSz* to the number of bytes pointed to by *lpcbBytesRet* and call the function again.

ClusterGroupEnum

The **ClusterGroupEnum** function enumerates the resources in a group. Each call to this function returns the name of one resource in the group. This function also enumerates nodes that are possible owners of a group. In this case, each call to this function returns the name of a node.

DWORD WINAPI **ClusterGroupEnum**(
HGROUPENUM *hGrpEnum*,
DWORD *dwIndx*,
LPDWORD *lpdwType*,
LPWSTR *lpszResNam*,
LPDWORD *lpcbName*
);

Input Parameters
hGrpEnum — Handle to a group enumerator object returned
dwIndx — Index of the resource or node to be returned

Output Parameters
lpdwType — Pointer to the type of object returned by **ClusterGroupEnum**. Valid values are
CLUSTER_GROUP_ENUM_CONTAINS — The object is one of the resources in the group.
CLUSTER_GROUP_ENUM_NODES — The object is one of the nodes that is a possible owner of the group.
lpszResNam — Pointer to the name of the returned resource or node, including the terminating NULL character.

Parameters that are both Input and Output
lpcbName — On input, this parameter points to the count of characters in the buffer pointed to by the *lpszResNam* parameter. This size should include the terminating NULL character. On output, this parameter points to the count of characters stored in the buffer, excluding the terminating NULL character.

Return Values
ERROR_SUCCESS — The operation was successful.
ERROR_NO_MORE_ITEMS — There are no more resources or nodes to be returned.
ERROR_MORE_DATA — The buffer pointed to by *lpszResNam* is not long enough to hold the required number of characters. In this case, the contents of the *lpcbName* parameter are set to the required buffer length to hold all the data.

If the operation was unsuccessful due to a problem other than those described with the ERROR_NO_MORE_ITEMS or ERROR_MORE_DATA values, **ClusterGroupEnum** returns a Win32 error value.

Programming Notes
The handle to the group enumerator object is the handle generated by calling the **ClusterGroupOpenEnum** function.
The *dwIndx* parameter is initialized to zero when this function is called the first time. The index is incremented for each subsequent call.

ClusterGroupOpenEnum
The **ClusterGroupOpenEnum** function opens an enumerator. This enumerator is used to iterate through group resources. This enumerator is also used to iterate through the nodes that are possible owners of the group.
HGROUPENUM WINAPI **ClusterGroupOpenEnum**(
HGROUP *hGrp*,
DWORD *dwType*
);

Input Parameters

hGrp — Handle to the group to be enumerated.

dwType — Bitmask that describes the objects to be enumerated. Valid values are

CLUSTER_GROUP_ENUM_CONTAINS — Enumerate all the resources in the group identified by *hGrp*.

CLUSTER_GROUP_ENUM_NODES — Enumerate all the nodes that are possible owners of the group identified by *hGrp*.

Return Values

If the operation was successful, **ClusterGroupOpenEnum** returns a handle to an enumerator.

NULL — The operation was unsuccessful

Programming Notes

If the operation was successful and you need additional details about the reasons for failure, call the Win32 function **GetLastError**.

The handle returned by **ClusterGroupOpenEnum** is passed to the **ClusterGroupEnum** function.

CreateClusterGroup

The **CreateClusterGroup** function adds a group to a cluster and returns a handle to the newly added group.

```
HGROUP WINAPI  CreateClusterGroup(
               HCLUSTER hCluster,
               LPCWSTR lpszGrpName
               );
```

Input Parameters

hCluster — Handle to the cluster to which the group should be added.

lpszGrpName — Pointer to the name of the group to be added to the cluster specified by *hCluster*. The group specified by the group name may or may not exist. If it exists, **CreateClusterGroup** adds the group to the cluster specified by *hCluster*. If there is no group by the name specified by the *lpszGrpName* parameter, **CreateClusterGroup** creates it.

Return Values

If the operation was successful, **CreateClusterGroup** returns a group handle.

NULL — The operation was unsuccessful.

Programming Notes

If the operation was unsuccessful and you want more details about the error, call the Win32 function **GetLastError**.

DeleteClusterGroup

The **DeleteClusterGroup** function removes a group from a cluster.

```
DWORD WINAPI DeleteClusterGroup(
             HGROUP hGrp
             );
```

Input Parameters
hGrp — Handle to the group to be removed

Return Values
ERROR_SUCCESS — The operation was successful.

If the operation was unsuccessful, **DeleteClusterGroup** returns a Win32 error value.

Programming Notes
The **DeleteClusterGroup** function only removes groups that are empty. The function call fails if the group is not empty (and contains some resources, e.g.). You must ensure that a group is empty before it can successfully be deleted.

GetClusterGroupState
The **GetClusterGroupState** function returns the current state of a group.

```
CLUSTER_GROUP_STATE WINAPI  GetClusterGroupState(
                            HGROUP hGrp,
                            LPWSTR lpszNodeNam,
                            LPDWORD lpcbNodeNam
                            );
```

Input Parameters
hGrp — Handle to the group for which state information is to be returned.

Output Parameters
lpszNodeNam — Pointer to the name of the node in the cluster where the group identified by *hGrp* is currently online or NULL. This parameter is optional.

Parameters that are both Input and Output
lpcbNodeNam — On input, this parameter points to a count of characters in the buffer pointed to by *lpszNodeNam*, including the terminating NULL character. On output, this parameter points to a count of characters in the name contained in the buffer pointed to by *lpszN-odeNam*, excluding the terminating null character.

Return Values
If the operation was successful, **GetClusterGroupState** returns the current state of the group, which is represented by one of values in Table 14 that follows.
If the operation was unsuccessful, this function returns ClusterGroupStateUnknown.

Programming Notes
The current state of a group is returned by **GetClusterGroupState**. The valid group state values and associated descriptions are listed in Table 14.
If the operation was unsuccessful and you need additional information about the reasons for error, you can call the Win32 function **GetLastError**.

MoveClusterGroup
The **MoveClusterGroup** function moves a group including all the group resources from one node to another.

TABLE 14
Group State Values and Descriptions

Group State	**Description**
ClusterGroupFailed	The group is not operational but has not yet been taken offline
ClusterGroupOnline	The group is operational
ClusterGroupOffline	The group is not operational
ClusterGroupPartialOnline	One or more of the resources in the group has been brought online

DWORD WINAPI **MoveClusterGroup**(
HGROUP *hGrp*,
HNODE *hDestNode*
);

Input Parameters
hGrp — Handle to the group to be moved from one node to another.
hDestNode — Handle to the node where the moved group should be brought back online or NULL. This parameter is optional.

Return Values
ERROR_SUCCESS — The reassignment of ownership of the group has been completed.
ERROR_IO_PENDING — The reassignment of ownership of the group is in progress.

If the operation was unsuccessful, **MoveClusterGroup** returns a Win32 error value.

Programming Notes
The return value from **MoveClusterGroup** indicates whether or not the group has successfully changed ownership. However, it does not imply anything about the state of the group or the state of any of its resources. That is, if the group was in the online state prior to the move, it may or may not be online on its new node when **MoveClusterGroup** returns, regardless of the return value.

After the ownership of the group has been successfully reassigned, **MoveClusterGroup** returns and the Cluster Service attempts to restore the group and its resources to its previous state on the new node. For example, if before the move the group was partially online with an offline generic service resource and an online physical disk resource, then after the move the Cluster Service attempts to bring the physical disk resource online on the new node. The generic service resource remains offline.

Because the ERROR_SUCCESS return value indicates only that the ownership of the group has changed, callers of MoveClusterGroup must assume that ERROR_SUCCESS implies ERROR_IO_PENDING and wait for completion. The caller may wait by either:

- Polling the state of each resource in the group
- Creating a notification port and waiting for the appropriate CLUSTER_CHANGE_RESOURCE_STATE events to arrive

When all the resources in the group have been brought online, you can assume that the move operation has completed and that the resources have been restored to their original state.

When *hDestNode* is set to null, **MoveClusterGroup** attempts to move the group to the best possible node. If there is no node available that can accept the group, the function fails. **MoveClusterGroup** also fails if **MoveClusterGroup** determines that the group cannot be brought online on the node identified by the *hDestNode* parameter.

OfflineClusterGroup

The **OfflineClusterGroup** function takes an online group offline.

DWORD WINAPI **OfflineClusterGroup**(
    HGROUP *hGrp*
    );

Input Parameters

hGrp — Handle to the group to be taken offline

Return Values

ERROR_SUCCESS — The operation was successful.
ERROR_IO_PENDING — The operation is in progress.
If the operation was unsuccessful, **OfflineClusterGroup** returns a Win32 error value.

OnlineClusterGroup

The **OnlineClusterGroup** function brings a group currently offline back online.

DWORD WINAPI **OnlineClusterGroup**(
    HGROUP *hGrp*,
    HNODE *hDestNode*
    );

Input Parameters

hGrp — Handle to the group to be brought online.
hDestNode — Handle to the node where the group identified by *hGrp* should be brought online or NULL. This parameter is optional.

Return Values

ERROR_SUCCESS — The operation was successful.
ERROR_HOST_NODE_NOT_AVAILABLE — A suitable host node was not available.
ERROR_IO_PENDING — The operation is in progress.

If the operation was unsuccessful, **OnlineClusterGroup** can also return a Win32 error value.

Programming Notes

If the group cannot be brought online on the node specified by the *hDestNode* parameter, **OnlineClusterGroup** fails.
If the *hDestNode* parameter is set to NULL, **OnlineClusterGroup** brings the group online on the current node.

OpenClusterGroup

The **OpenClusterGroup** function opens a group and returns the group handle.

HGROUP WINAPI **OpenClusterGroup**(
    HCLUSTER *hCluster*,
    LPCWSTR *lpszGrpName*
    );

Input Parameters

hCluster — Handle to a cluster that includes the group to be opened
lpszGrpName — Name of the group to be opened

Return Values

If the operation was successful, **OpenClusterGroup** returns a group handle.
NULL — The operation was unsuccessful.

Programming Notes

If the operation was unsuccessful and you need additional information about the reasons for error, call the Win32 function **GetLastError**.

SetClusterGroupName

The **SetClusterGroupName** function sets the name of a group.

```
DWORD WINAPI SetClusterGroupName(
                HGROUP hGrp,
                LPCWSTR lpszGrpName
                );
```

Input Parameters

hGrp — Handle to the group to be named
lpszGrpName — Pointer to the new name for the group identified by *hGrp*

Return Values

ERROR_SUCCESS — The operation was successful.

If the operation was unsuccessful, **SetClusterGroupName** returns a Win32 error value.

SetClusterGroupNodeList

The **SetClusterGroupNodeList** function sets the preferred node list for a group.

```
DWORD WINAPI SetClusterGroupNodeList(
                HGROUP hGrp,
                DWORD cNodeCnt,
                HNODE phNodeLst[]
                );
```

Input Parameters

hGrp — Handle to the group to be assigned the list of nodes
cNodeCnt — Count of nodes in the list identified by *phNodeLst*
phNodeLst — Array of handles to nodes

Return Values

ERROR_SUCCESS — The operation was successful.

If the operation was unsuccessful, **SetClusterGroupNodeList** returns a Win32 error value.

Programming Notes

The order of nodes within the *phNodeLst* array is by preference. The first node in the array is the most preferred to be assigned and the last node the least preferred.

The number of nodes in the *phNodeLst* array is specified by the *cNodeCnt* parameter.

RESOURCE MANAGEMENT FUNCTIONS

The resource management functions in the Cluster API allows you to perform a number of operations on one or more resources such as

- Create resources.
- Delete resources.
- Initiate an operation using a resource control code.
- Retrieve information about dependencies.

Resource Management Functions are summarized in Table 15.

TABLE 15
Resource Management Functions and Descriptions

Function	Description
AddClusterResourceDependency	Creates a dependency relationship between two resources
AddClusterResourceNode	Adds a node to the list of potential nodes that are capable of running a resource
CanResourceBeDependent	Determines if one resource can be dependent on another resource
ChangeClusterResourceGroup	Moves a resource from one group to another
CloseClusterResource	Invalidates a resource handle and closes the resource
ClusterResourceCloseEnum	Invalidates a resource enumerator object handle and closes the resource enumerator object
ClusterResourceControl	Initiates an operation on a resource
ClusterResourceEnum	Enumerates a resource's dependent resources and/or nodes; returns the name of one resource/node with each call
ClusterResourceOpenEnum	Opens an enumerator for iterating through a resource's dependencies and nodes
CreateClusterResource	Creates a resource in a cluster
DeleteClusterResource	Removes an offline resource from a cluster
FailClusterResource	Initiates a resource failure
GetClusterResourceState	Returns the current state of a resource
OfflineClusterResource	Takes an online resource offline
OnlineClusterResource	Brings an offline resource back online
OpenClusterResource	Opens a resource and returns a handle to it
RemoveClusterResourceDependency	Removes a node from the list of potential nodes that can host a resource
RemoveClusterResourceNode	Removes a dependency relationship between two resources
SetClusterResourceName	Sets the name for a resource

AddClusterResourceDependency

The **AddClusterResourceDependency** function creates a dependency relationship between two resources.

DWORD WINAPI **AddClusterResourceDependency**(
HRES *hRes*,
HRES *hDepOn*
);

Input Parameters
hRes — Handle to the dependent resource
hDepOn — Handle to the dependent resource on which the resource identified by *hRes* depends.

Return Values
ERROR_SUCCESS — The operation was successful.

If the operation was unsuccessful, **AddClusterResourceDependency** returns a Win32 error value.

Programming Notes
Resources in a dependency relationship must be moved together. The dependent resource must be brought online after the resource on which it depends.
The two resources identified by *hRes* and *hDepOn* must be in the same group. If *hRes* is currently online, *hDepOn* must also be currently online.

AddClusterResourceNode
The **AddClusterResourceNode** function adds a node to the list of potential nodes that are capable of running the resource.

DWORD WINAPI **AddClusterResourceNode**(
HRES *hRes*,
HNODE *hNode*
);

Input Parameters
hRes — Handle to a resource that adds a node to the list of potential owners
hNode — Handle to the node to be added to the list of potential owners of the resource identified by *hRes*

Return Values
ERROR_SUCCESS — The operation was successful.

If the operation was unsuccessful, **AddClusterResourceNode** returns a Win32 error value.

CanResourceBeDependent
The **CanResourceBeDependent** function determines if one resource can be dependent on another resource.

BOOL WINAPI CanResourceBeDependent(
HRES *hRes*,
HRES *hResDep*
);

Input Parameters

hRes — Handle to first resource.

hResDep — Handle to the second resource on which the first resource may or may not depend, based on the **CanResourceBeDependent** function call

Return Values

TRUE — The first resource (identified by *hRes*) can depend on the second resource (identified by *hResDep*).

FALSE — The first resource (identified by *hRes*) cannot depend on the second resource (identified by *hResDep*).

Programming Notes

The rules for resource dependencies must be satisfied for this function call to work correctly. These rules include

- Both resources must be members of the same group.
- Resources cannot be recursively dependent on each other. The resource identified by *hResDep* cannot depend on the resource identified by *hRes*, either directly or indirectly.

ChangeClusterResourceGroup

The **ChangeClusterResourceGroup** function moves a resource from one group to another.

```
DWORD WINAPI ChangeClusterResourceGroup(
                HRES hRes,
                HGROUP hGrp
                );
```

Input Parameters

hRes — Handle to the resource to be moved

hGrp — Handle to the group that should receive the resource identified by *hRes*

Return Values

ERROR_SUCCESS — The operation was successful.

If the operation was unsuccessful, **ChangeClusterResourceGroup** returns a Win32 error value.

Programming Notes

The same node, regardless of the resource state, must own both the group to which the resource currently belongs and to which the new group the resource is moving.

If the resource identified by *hRes* has dependencies, all the resources in its dependency tree are to be moved to the group identified by *hGrp*. That is, if resource A depends on resource B and resource B depends on resource C, a call to **ChangeClusterResourceGroup** with *hRes* representing resource A, resource B, or resource C results in all three resources being moved.

CloseClusterResource

The **CloseClusterResource** function invalidates a resource handle and closes the resource.

```
BOOL WINAPI  CloseClusterResource(
               HRES hRes
               );
```

Input Parameters
hRes — Handle to the resource to be closed

Return Values
TRUE — The operation was successful.
FALSE — The operation was unsuccessful.

Programming Notes
The handle to the resource to be closed by **CloseClusterResource** is the handle returned from either **OpenClusterResource** or **CreateClusterResource**.
If the operation was unsuccessful and you need additional information about the error, you can call the Win32 function **GetLastError**.

ClusterResourceCloseEnum
The **ClusterResourceCloseEnum** function invalidates a resource enumerator object handle and closes the resource enumerator object.

```
DWORD WINAPI ClusterResourceCloseEnum(
        HRESENUM hResEnum
        );
```

Input Parameters
hResEnum — Handle to the resource enumerator to be closed

Return Values
ERROR_SUCCESS — The operation was successful.

If the operation was unsuccessful, **ClusterResourceCloseEnum** returns a Win32 error value.

Programming Notes
The Handle to the resource enumerator object to be closed is the handle returned from **ClusterResourceOpenEnum**.

While most of the time you can guess the function name based on what the function does, this is one instance the guess may not work. While closing a cluster resource is **CloseClusterResource**, you may expect closing a cluster resource enumerator is **CloseClusterResourceEnum**. The guess is incorrect because the actual name is ClusterResourceCloseEnum.

ClusterResourceControl
The **ClusterResourceControl** function initiates a resource-related operation.

```
DWORD WINAPI ClusterResourceControl(
        HRES hRes,
        HNODE hHostNode,
        DWORD dwCtrlCode,
        LPVOID lpInBuf,
        DWORD cbInBufSz,
        LPVOID lpOutBuf,
        DWORD cbOutBufSz,
        LPDWORD lpcbBytesRet
        );
```

Input Parameters

hRes — Handle to the resource to be controlled.

hHostNode — Handle to the node in which the resource operation is to be performed or NULL. If NULL, the node that owns the resource identified by *hRes* performs the operation.

dwCtrlCode — Resource control code that defines the operation to be performed. For a list of the valid values for the *dwCtrlCode* parameter, see the programming notes for this function.

lpInBuf — Pointer to a buffer that contains the information needed for the operation. This parameter can be NULL if no information is needed.

cbInBufSz — Number of bytes in the buffer pointed to by *lpInBuf*.

Output Parameters

lpOutBuf — Pointer to the buffer that contains the data retrieved from the operation. This parameter may be NULL if nothing is returned.

cbOutBufSz — Number of bytes in the buffer pointed to by *lpOutBuf*.

Parameters that are both Input and Output

lpcbBytesRet — Pointer to the actual number of bytes of *lpOutBuf* filled in the buffer as a result of the operation. You can pass null for *lpcbBytesRet* if you do not want **ClusterResourceControl** to pass back the number of bytes in the output buffer.

Return Values

ERROR_SUCCESS — The operation was successful.

ERROR_MORE_DATA — The output buffer pointed to by *lpOutBuf* is not large enough to hold the retrieved data. The *lpcbBytesRet* parameter points to the actual size required for the output buffer.

If the operation was unsuccessful, **ClusterResourceControl** returns a Win32 error value.

Programming Notes

The set of valid operations that can be performed using **ClusterResourceControl** is defined by the set of control codes for resources.

When **ClusterResourceControl** returns ERROR_MORE_DATA, set *cbOutBufSz* to the number of bytes pointed to by *lpcbBytesRet* and call the function again.

ClusterResourceEnum

The **ClusterResourceEnum** function enumerates a resource's dependent resources and/or nodes. This function returns the name of one resource/node with each call.

```
DWORD WINAPI ClusterResourceEnum(
                    HRESENUM hResEnum,
                    DWORD dwIndx,
                    LPDWORD lpdwType,
                    LPWSTR lpszName,
                    LPDWORD lpcchNam
                    );
```

Input Parameters

hResEnum — Handle to a resource enumerator object

dwIndx — Index of the resource or node object to return

Output Parameters

lpdwType — Type of object returned by **ClusterResourceEnum**. Valid types are

CLUSTER_RESOURCE_ENUM_DEPENDS — The object is a resource on which the resource identified by *hRes* directly depends.

CLUSTER_RESOURCE_ENUM_PROVIDES — The object is a resource that depends on the resource identified by *hRes*.

CLUSTER_RESOURCE_ENUM_NODES — The object is a node that can host the resource identified by *hRes*.

lpszName — Pointer to the name of the returned object, including the terminating NULL character.

Parameters that are both Input and Output

lpcchNam — On input, this parameter points to the count of characters in the buffer pointed to by the *lpszName* parameter, including the terminating NULL character. On output, this parameter points to the count of characters stored in the buffer, excluding the terminating NULL character.

Return Values

ERROR_SUCCESS — The operation was successful.

ERROR_NO_MORE_ITEMS — There are no more objects to be returned.

If the operation was unsuccessful due to a problem other than not having more objects to return, **ClusterResourceEnum** returns a Win32 error value.

Programming Notes

The handle to a resource enumerator object used in **ClusterResourceEnum** is the handle returned from a call to **ClusterResourceOpenEnum**.

You should set the *dwIndx* parameter to zero for the first call to **ClusterResourceEnum**. You should increment the *dwIndx* parameter for subsequent calls.

ClusterResourceOpenEnum

The **ClusterResourceOpenEnum** function opens an enumerator for iterating through a resource's dependencies and nodes.

```
HRESENUM WINAPI  ClusterResourceOpenEnum(
                 HRES hRes,
                 DWORD dwType
                 );
```

Input Parameters

hRes — Handle to a resource.

dwType — Bitmask that specifies the type of cluster objects to be enumerated. Valid bitmask values are the following:

CLUSTER_RESOURCE_ENUM_DEPENDS — Enumerate resources on which the resource identified by *hRes* directly depends.

CLUSTER_RESOURCE_ENUM_PROVIDES — Enumerate resources that directly depend on the resource identified by *hRes*.

CLUSTER_RESOURCE_ENUM_NODES — Enumerate nodes that can host the resource identified by *hRes*.

Return Values
NULL — The operation was unsuccessful.

If the operation was successful, **ClusterResourceOpenEnum** returns an enumeration handle.

Programming Notes
If the operation was unsuccessful and you need more detailed information about the error, call the Win32 function **GetLastError**.

CreateClusterResource
The **CreateClusterResource** function creates a resource in a cluster.

```
HRES WINAPI  CreateClusterResource(
             HGROUP hGrp,
             LPCWSTR lpszResNam,
             LPCWSTR lpszResType,
             DWORD dwFlags
             );
```

Input Parameters
hGrp — Handle to the group in which the resource is being created.
lpszResNam — Pointer to the name of the new resource.
lpszResType — Pointer to the type of the new resource.
dwFlags — Bitmask describing how the resource should be added to the cluster. The *dwFlags* parameter is optional. If set, the following value is valid:
CLUSTER_RESOURCE_SEPARATE_MONITOR — This resource should be created using a separate resource monitor. This resource does not use a shared resource monitor.

Return Values
If the operation was successful, **CreateClusterResource** returns a resource handle.
NULL — The operation was not successful.

Programming Notes
You must follow some common rules about creating new resources when you call **Create-ClusterResource**:
- The specified resource name must be unique within the cluster.
- The resource type must have already been defined in the cluster

If the operation was unsuccessful, and you need additional information about the error, call the Win32 function **GetLastError**.

DeleteClusterResource
The **DeleteClusterResource** function removes an offline resource from a cluster.

```
DWORD WINAPI DeleteClusterResource(
             HRES hRes
             );
```

Input Parameters
hRes — Handle to an offline resource

Return Values

ERROR_SUCCESS — The operation was successful.

ERROR_RESOURCE_NOT_OFFLINE — The resource identified by *hRes* is not currently offline.

If the operation was unsuccessful, **DeleteClusterResource** returns a Win32 error value.

Programming Notes
The resource you want to remove must be offline. If the resource you want to remove is not already offline, you get an error.

FailClusterResource
The **FailClusterResource** function initiates a resource failure.

DWORD WINAPI **FailClusterResource**(
    HRES *hRes*
    );

Input Parameters

hRes — Handle to the resource that is to be failed

Return Values

ERROR_SUCCESS — The operation was successful.

If the operation was unsuccessful, **FailClusterResource** returns a Win32 error value.

Programming Notes
The resource identified by *hRes* is treated as inoperable, causing the cluster to initiate the same failover process that would result if the resource had actually failed. Applications call **FailClusterResource** to test their policies for restarting resources and groups.

GetClusterResourceNetworkName
The **GetClusterResourceNetworkName** function retrieves the network name from the Network Name resource on which a resource is dependent.

BOOL WINAPI **GetClusterResourceNetworkName**(
    HRES *hRes*,
    LPWSTR *lpBuf*,
    LPDWORD *nSize*
    );

Input Parameters

hRes — Handle to the dependent resource

Output Parameters

lpBuf — This parameter points to a buffer that contains a NULL-terminated character string containing the network name of the Network Name resource.

Parameters that are Input and Output

nSize — On input, this parameter points to a count of characters in the buffer pointed to by *lpBuf*. On output, this parameter points to a count of characters in the network name of the network name resource contained in the buffer pointed to by *lpBuf*, excluding the terminating NULL character.

Return Values

TRUE — The operation was successful.
FALSE — The operation was unsuccessful.

Programming Notes

You can call **GetClusterResourceNetworkName** to enumerate the dependencies of the resource identified by *hRes* in an attempt to find a Network Name resource on which the resource depends.

GetClusterResourceState

The **GetClusterResourceState** function returns the current state of a resource.

```
CLUSTER_RESOURCE_STATE WINAPIGetClusterResourceState(
                                        HRES hRes,
                                        LPWSTR lpszNodeNam,
                                        LPDWORD lpcchNodeNam,
                                        LPWSTR lpszGrpName,
                                        LPDWORD lpcchGrpName
                                        );
```

Input Parameters

hRes — Handle to the resource for which state information is being returned

Output Parameters

lpszNodeNam — Pointer to the node name in the cluster where the group of the resource identified by *hRes* is currently online. You can specify NULL, if the node name is not required.

lpszGrpName — Pointer to the name of the group that has as a member the resource identified by *hRes*. This parameter can be NULL if the group name is not required.

Parameters that are both Input and Output

lpcchNodeNam — On input, this parameter points to a count of characters in the buffer pointed to by *lpszNodeNam*. On output, this parameter points to a count of characters in the name contained in the buffer pointed to by *lpszNodeNam*, excluding the terminating NULL character.

lpcchGrpName — On input, this parameter points to a count of characters in the buffer pointed to by *lpszGrpName*, including the terminating NULL character. On output, this parameter points to a count of characters stored in the buffer pointed to by *lpszGrpName*, excluding the terminating null character.

Return Values

If the operation was successful, **GetClusterResourceState** returns the current state of the resource. See Programming Notes for a list of valid states and descriptions.

If the operation was unsuccessful, this function returns ClusterResourceStateUnknown. ClusterResourceStateUnknown indicates that an error has occurred and the exact state of the resource could not be determined. For more detailed information about the error, call the Win32 function **GetLastError**.

Programming Notes

If *lpszGrpName* is NULL, the *lpcchGrpName* parameter is ignored.

The states of a resource and associated descriptions are summarized in Table 16.

TABLE 16
Resource States and Descriptions

Resource State	Description
ClusterResourceInitializing	The resource is initializing
ClusterResourceOnline	The resource is operational and functioning normally
ClusterResourceOffline	The resource is offline
ClusterResourceFailed	The resource has failed
ClusterResourcePending	The resource is in the process of coming online or going offline
ClusterResourceOnlinePending	The resource is in the process of coming online
ClusterResourceOfflinePending	The resource is in the process of going offline

Resource state changes can occur when the failover process takes place or when the administrator manually makes a state transition. When a group is failed over, the states of each resource are altered according to their dependencies on the other resources in the group. The Resource Monitor is responsible for managing these state transitions in response to Cluster Service commands and a resource DLL response when calls are made to its IsAlive and LooksAlive entry points.

The initial state for any resource is the ClusterResourceOffline state. When a resource is offline, it is unavailable for use by a client or another resource. The Cluster Service may request that the Resource Monitor brings an offline resource online. To place a resource in the ClusterResourceOffline state, the Resource Monitor calls the resource Offline entry point function and unloads the resource DLL. The resource is removed from the Resource Monitor list and any Resource Monitor state related to that resource is discarded.

When a resource is in the ClusterResourceOnline state, it is available for use.

When a resource is in one of the pending states, either ClusterResourceOfflinePending or ClusterResourceOnlinePending, it is in the process of either being brought online or taken offline. The pending states are transitional. If after a predetermined amount of time the resource cannot be brought online or taken offline, the resource is set to the ClusterResourceFailed state. The pending states are entered whenever the Online or Offline entry points return ERROR_IO_PENDING. The pending states are expected to last less than a few seconds. If the resource DLL does not complete the transition from a pending state to a more stable state within a fixed period of time (typically 3 min), the Cluster Service Resource Manager terminates the resource by calling its Terminate entry point function and tries again according to the policies defined for the resource.

A resource enters the ClusterResourceFailed state if either its IsAlive or LooksAlive entry point fails. The Cluster Service is subsequently notified by the Resource Monitor that continues to poll the resource to detect transient faults. When the resource recovers, the Resource Monitor brings the resource back online unless the Cluster Service explicitly asks the Resource Monitor to take it offline.

OfflineClusterResource

The **OfflineClusterResource** function takes an online resource offline.

```
DWORD WINAPI OfflineClusterResource(
                    HRES hRes
                    );
```

Input Parameters

hRes — Handle to the resource to be taken offline

Return Values

ERROR_SUCCESS — The operation was successful.

ERROR_IO_PENDING — The resource or one of the resources on which it depends has returned ERROR_IO_PENDING from its offline entry point function.

If the operation was unsuccessful, **OfflineClusterResource** returns a Win32 error value.

OnlineClusterResource

The **OnlineClusterResource** function brings an offline or failed resource back online.

DWORD WINAPI **OnlineClusterResource**(
HRES *hRes*
);

Input Parameters

hRes — Handle to the resource to be brought back online

Return Values

ERROR_SUCCESS — The operation was successful.

ERROR_IO_PENDING — The resource or one of the resources on which it depends has returned ERROR_IO_PENDING from its online entry point function.

If the operation was unsuccessful, **OnlineClusterResource** returns a Win32 error value.

OpenClusterResource

The **OpenClusterResource** function opens a resource and returns a handle to the resource.

HRES WINAPI **OpenClusterResource**(
HCLUSTER *hCluster*,
LPCWSTR *lpszResNam*
);

Input Parameters

hCluster — Handle to a cluster in which the resource is to be opened

lpszResNam — Pointer to the name of the resource to be opened

Return Values

If the operation was successful, **OpenClusterResource** returns a handle to the opened resource.

NULL — The operation was unsuccessful.

Programming Notes

If the operation was unsuccessful and you need additional information about the error, call the Win32 function **GetLastError**.

RemoveClusterResourceNode

The **RemoveClusterResourceNode** function removes a node from the list of nodes that can host a resource.

```
DWORD WINAPI RemoveClusterResourceNode(
                    HRES hRes,
                    HNODE hNode
                    );
```

Input Parameters:

hRes — Handle to the target resource

hNode — Handle to the node which should be removed from the list of potential host nodes for the resource identified by *hRes*

Return Values

ERROR_SUCCESS — The operation was successful.

If the operation was unsuccessful, **RemoveClusterResourceNode** returns a Win32 error value.

RemoveClusterResourceDependency

The **RemoveClusterResourceDependency** function removes a dependency relationship between two resources.

```
DWORD WINAPI RemoveClusterResourceDependency(
                    HRES hRes,
                    HRES hDepOn
                    );
```

Input Parameters

hRes — Handle to the dependent resource

hDepOn — Handle to the resource on which the resource identified by *hRes* is dependent

Return Values

ERROR_SUCCESS — The operation was successful.

If the operation was unsuccessful, **RemoveClusterResourceDependency** returns a Win32 error value.

SetClusterResourceName

The **SetClusterResourceName** function sets the name for a resource.

```
DWORD WINAPI SetClusterResourceName(
                    HRES hRes,
                    LPCWSTR lpszResNam
                    );
```

Input Parameters

hRes — Handle to a resource whose name is to be set

lpszResNam — Pointer to the new name for the resource identified by *hRes*

Return Values

ERROR_SUCCESS — The operation was successful.

If the operation was unsuccessful, **SetClusterResourceName** returns a Win32 error value.

CLUSTER DATABASE MANAGEMENT FUNCTIONS

The cluster database management functions allow a cluster-aware application or resource DLL to access and update the cluster database. The cluster database management functions provide one way to access the cluster database. The other way is through the control code functions of the Cluster API. Of the two methods, use of the control code functions is better than use of the cluster database management functions to access the cluster database. The cluster database management functions should only be used when the control code functions are inadequate. Microsoft recommends against the use of the Win32 registry functions in place of the cluster database management functions. Although the registry functions are similar to the Cluster Database Management Functions, they are unsupported in the cluster environment because they do not support data replication or logging.

The Cluster Database Management Functions are broadly classified as follows:

- **ClusterResourceControl**
- **ClusterResourceTypeControl**
- **ClusterGroupControl**
- **ClusterNodeControl**

The functions available to manage the cluster database are summarized in Table 17.

TABLE 17
Cluster Database Management Functions

Function	Description
ClusterRegCloseKey	Releases the handle to a cluster database key
ClusterRegCreateKey	Creates a specified cluster database key; if the key already exists in the database, **ClusterRegCreateKey** opens it without making changes
ClusterRegDeleteKey	Deletes a cluster database key
ClusterRegDeleteValue	Removes a named value from a cluster database key
ClusterRegEnumKey	Enumerates the subkeys of an open cluster database key
ClusterRegEnumValue	Enumerates the values of an open cluster database key
ClusterRegGetKeySecurity	Returns a copy of the security descriptor protecting the specified cluster database key
ClusterRegOpenKey	Opens a cluster database key
ClusterRegQueryInfoKey	Returns information about a cluster database key
ClusterRegQueryValue	Returns the name, type, and data components associated with a value for an open cluster database key
ClusterRegSetKeySecurity	Sets the security attributes for a cluster database key
ClusterRegSetValue	Sets a value for a cluster database key
GetClusterGroupKey	Opens the root of the cluster database subtree for a group
GetClusterKey	Opens the root of the cluster database subtree for a cluster
GetClusterNetInterfaceKey	Opens the root of the cluster database subtree for a network interface object
GetClusterNetworkKey	Opens the root of the cluster database subtree for a network
GetClusterNodeKey	Opens the root of the cluster database subtree for a node
GetClusterResourceTypeKey	Opens the root of the cluster database subtree for a resource type.

ClusterRegCloseKey

The **ClusterRegCloseKey** function releases the handle to a cluster database key.

```
LONG WINAPI ClusterRegCloseKey(
                HKEY hKey
                );
```

Input Parameters

hKey — Handle to the cluster database key to be closed

Return Values

ERROR_SUCCESS — The operation was successful.

If the operation was unsuccessful, **ClusterRegCloseKey** returns a Win32 error value.

ClusterRegCreateKey

The **ClusterRegCreateKey** function creates a specified cluster database key.

```
LONG WINAPI ClusterRegCreateKey(
                HKEY hKey,
                LPCWSTR lpszSubKey,
                DWORD dwOptns,
                REGSAM samReqd,
                LPSECURITY_ATTRIBUTES lpSecAttr,
                PHKEY phKey,
                LPDWORD lpdwDisp
                );
```

Input Parameters

hKey — Handle to an open cluster database key. This parameter cannot be NULL.

lpszSubKey — Pointer to a NULL-terminated string that specifies the name of the subkey to be created or opened. If the *lpszSubKey* parameter points to an empty string, **ClusterRegCreateKey** returns a handle to the database key represented by *hKey*.

dwOptns — Specifies special options for this key. The options supported by *dwOptns* are

- REG_OPTION_VOLATILE — The opened or created key is volatile and not persistent (i.e., the information is stored in memory and is not preserved when the system is restarted).

samReqd — Mask that specifies the desired security access for the new key. Valid values for this parameter are

- KEY_ALL_ACCESS — Combination of the following values — KEY_QUERY_VALUE, KEY_ENUMERATE_SUB_KEYS, KEY_NOTIFY, KEY_CREATE_SUB_KEY, KEY_CREATE_LINK, and KEY_SET_VALUE access
- KEY_CREATE_LINK — Permission to create a symbolic link
- KEY_ENUMERATE_SUB_KEYS — Permission to enumerate subkeys
- KEY_EXECUTE — Permission for read access
- KEY_NOTIFY — Permission for change notification
- KEY_QUERY_VALUE — Permission to query subkey data
- KEY_READ — Combination of KEY_QUERY_VALUE, KEY_ENUMERATE_SUB_KEYS, and KEY_NOTIFY ACCESS
- KEY_SET_VALUE — Permission to change subkey data
- KEY_WRITE — Combination of KEY_SET_VALUE and KEY_CREATE_SUB_KEY access

lpSecAttr – This parameter points to a SECURITY_ATTRIBUTES structure that contains the security descriptor for the new key in the contents of the *lpSecurityDescriptor* member or NULL. If *lpSecAttr* is NULL, the key gets a default security descriptor.

Output Parameters

phKey — Pointer to the handle to the opened or created key.

lpdwDisp — Pointer to a value that describes whether the key pointed to by *lpszSubKey* was opened or created. Valid values are

REG_CREATED_NEW_KEY — The key did not exist and was created.

REG_OPENED_EXISTING_KEY — The key existed and was opened.

Return Values

ERROR_SUCCESS — The operation was successful.

If the operation was unsuccessful, **ClusterRegCreateKey** returns a Win32 error value.

Programming Notes

If the key you are trying to create already exists in the database, **ClusterRegCreateKey** opens it without making changes. You can check if a key was created or opened by checking the value of the *lpdwDisp* parameter.

The subkey specified by the *lpszSubKey* parameter must follow the rules for subkeys:

- Must be a child key of the key identified by *hKey*
- Must not begin with the backslash character (\ )
- Must not be NULL

You should set the *bInheritHandle* member of the SECURITY_ATTRIBUTES structure to FALSE, because cluster database handles are not inheritable.

You should call **ClusterRegCloseKey** to close the key handle created by **ClusterRegCreateKey** when you finished processing.

ClusterRegDeleteKey

The **ClusterRegDeleteKey** function deletes a cluster database key.

```
LONG WINAPI   ClusterRegDeleteKey(
              HKEY hKey,
              LPCWSTR lpszSubKey
              );
```

Input Parameters

hKey — Handle to a key that is currently open.

lpszSubKey – This parameter points to a null-terminated string that contains the name of the key to be deleted. This parameter cannot be NULL.

Return Values

ERROR_SUCCESS — The operation was successful.

If the operation was unsuccessful, **ClusterRegDeleteKey** returns a Win32 error value.

Programming Notes

The key pointed to by *lpszSubKey* cannot have subkeys. If you attempt to delete keys that have subkeys using **ClusterRegDeleteKey**, the function returns an error. This behavior is different from that of the **RegDeleteKey** function that deletes a key from the system registry on Windows 95, although this behavior is consistent with the behavior of **RegDeleteKey** on the Windows NT Server.

ClusterRegDeleteValue
The **ClusterRegDeleteValue** function removes a named value from a cluster database key.

```
DWORD WINAPI ClusterRegDeleteValue(
        HKEY hKey,
        LPCWSTR lpszValNam
        );
```

Input Parameters
hKey — Handle to a key that is currently open, in which the named value should be removed
lpszValNam — Pointer to the name of the key value to be removed

Return Values
ERROR_SUCCESS — The operation was successful.

If the operation was unsuccessful, **ClusterRegDeleteValue** returns a Win32 error value.

Programming Notes
The behavior of this function is very similar to that of the Win32 function **RegDeleteValue**.

ClusterRegEnumKey
The **ClusterRegEnumKey** function enumerates the subkeys of an open cluster database key. **ClusterRegEnumKey** retrieves information about one subkey each time it is called.

```
LONG WINAPI    ClusterRegEnumKey(
        HKEY hKey,
        DWORD dwIndx,
        LPWSTR lpszName,
        LPDWORD lpcchNam,
        PFILETIME lpftLastWriteTime
        );
```

Input Parameters
hKey — Handle to a currently open key, or NULL. If you specify NULL, **ClusterRegEnumKey** enumerates keys from the root of the cluster database on the node on which the application is running.
dwIndx — Index used to identify the next subkey to be enumerated. You should set this parameter to zero the first time you call **ClusterRegEnumKey** and increment it for each subsequent call.

Output Parameters
lpszName — This parameter points to a buffer that receives the name of the subkey, including the terminating NULL character.
lpftLastWriteTime — Pointer to the last update time of the enumerated subkey.

Parameters that are both Input and Output
lpcchNam — On input, this parameter points to a count of characters in the buffer pointed to by the *lpszName* parameter including the terminating NULL character. On output, this parameter points to a count of characters stored in the buffer, excluding the terminating NULL character.

Return Values

ERROR_SUCCESS — The operation was successful.

ERROR_NO_MORE_ITEMS — There are no more subkeys to be returned.

If the operation was unsuccessful due to a problem other than not having any more subkeys to return, **ClusterRegEnumKey** returns a Win32 error value.

Programming Notes

Do not depend on the order in which **ClusterRegEnumKey** returns subkeys. The subkeys can be returned in any order. This is because subkeys are not ordered and any new subkey can have an arbitrary index.

Because **ClusterRegEnumKey** enumerates keys from the root of the database on the node on which the application is running when *hKey* is set to NULL, **ClusterRegEnumKey** fails if the node is not part of a cluster.

ClusterRegEnumKey copies only the name of the subkey to the buffer, not the full key hierarchy.

ClusterRegEnumValue

The **ClusterRegEnumValue** function enumerates the values of an open cluster database key.

```
DWORD WINAPI ClusterRegEnumValue(
        HKEY hKey,
        DWORD dwIndx,
        LPWSTR lpszValNam,
        LPDWORD lpcchValName,
        LPDWORD lpdwType,
        LPBYTE lpbData,
        LPDWORD lpcbData
        );
```

Input Parameters

hKey — Handle to the cluster database key to enumerate.

dwIndx — Index that identifies the next value to be enumerated. Set this parameter to zero the first time you call **ClusterRegEnumValue** and increment it for each subsequent call.

Output Parameters

lpszValNam — Pointer to the name of the returned value, including the terminating NULL character.

lpdwType — Pointer to the type code for the value entry or NULL. NULL is used when the type code is not required. The type code can be one of the following values listed in Table 18.

lpbData — Pointer to the data for the value entry. This parameter can be NULL if the data is not required.

Parameters that are both Input and Output

lpcchValName — On input, this parameter points to a count of characters in the buffer pointed to by the *lpszValNam* parameter including the terminating NULL character. On output, this parameter points to a count of characters stored in the buffer, excluding the terminating NULL character.

lpcbData — On input, this parameter points to a count of bytes in the buffer pointed to by the *lpbData* parameter. On output, this parameter points to a count of bytes stored in the buffer, excluding the terminating null character.

TABLE 18
Type Codes and Descriptions

Type Code	Description
REG_BINARY	Binary data in any form
REG_DWORD	A 32-b number
REG_EXPAND_SZ	A NULL-terminated Unicode string that contains unexpanded references to environment variables (e.g., "%PATH%")
REG_MULTI_SZ	An array of NULL-terminated Unicode strings, terminated by two NULL characters
REG_NONE	No defined value type
REG_SZ	A NULL-terminated Unicode string

Return Values
ERROR_SUCCESS — The operation was successful.
ERROR_NO_MORE_ITEMS — There are no more values to be returned.

If the operation was unsuccessful due to a problem other than not having any more values to return, **ClusterRegEnumValue** returns a Win32 error value.

Programming Notes
Subkeys of a key are not ordered and any new subkey has an arbitrary index. This means that **ClusterRegEnumValue** may return values in any order. Also see the programming notes for **ClusterRegEnumKey**.
The *lpcbData* parameter can be null only if the *lpbData* parameter is also NULL.
The behavior of this function is very similar to that of the Win32 function **RegEnumKey**.

ClusterRegGetKeySecurity
The **ClusterRegGetKeySecurity** function returns a copy of the security descriptor for the specified cluster database key.

```
LONG WINAPI ClusterGetKeySecurity(
                HKEY hKey,
                SECURITY_INFORMATION SecInfo,
                PSECURITY_DESCRIPTOR pSecDescriptor,
                LPDWORD lpcbSecDescriptor
                );
```

Input Parameters
hKey — Handle to a cluster database key
SecInfo — A SECURITY_INFORMATION structure that indicates the requested security descriptor

Output Parameters
pSecDescriptor — Pointer to a SECURITY_DESCRIPTOR structure containing a copy of the requested security descriptor

Parameters that are both Input and Output
lpcbSecDescriptor — On input, this parameter points to a count of the number of bytes in the buffer pointed to by *pSecDescriptor*. On output, this parameter points to a count of the number of bytes written to the buffer.

Return Values
ERROR_SUCCESS — The operation was successful.

If the operation was unsuccessful, **ClusterRegGetKeySecurity** returns a Win32 error value.

ClusterRegOpenKey
The **ClusterRegOpenKey** function opens a cluster database key.

LONG WINAPI **ClusterRegOpenKey**(
HKEY *hKey*,
LPCWSTR *lpszSubKey*,
REGSAM *samReqd*,
PHKEY *phKey*
);

Input Parameters
hKey — Handle to a cluster database key that is currently open. This parameter cannot be NULL.
lpszSubKey — Pointer to a NULL-terminated string specifying the name of a subkey that **ClusterRegOpenKey** opens or creates. See the programming notes for the rules of subkeys.
samReqd — Mask that specifies the desired security access for the new key.

Output Parameters
phKey — Pointer to a handle to the opened/created key

Return Values
ERROR_SUCCESS — The operation was successful.

If the operation was unsuccessful, **ClusterRegOpenKey** returns a Win32 error value.

Programming Notes
The subkey specified by the *lpszSubKey* parameter must follow the rules for subkeys:
- Must be a child key of the key identified by *hKey*
- Must not begin with the backslash character (\ )
- Must not be NULL

You should call **ClusterRegCloseKey** to close the key handle opened by **ClusterRegOpenKey** when you have finished processing.
The behavior of **ClusterRegOpenKey** is very similar to that of the Win32 functions **RegOpenKey** and **RegOpenKeyEx**.

ClusterRegQueryInfoKey
The **ClusterRegQueryInfoKey** function returns information about a cluster database key.

LONG WINAPI **ClusterRegQueryInfoKey**(
HKEY *hKey*,
LPDWORD *lpcSubKeys*,
LPDWORD *lpcbMaxSubKeylen*,
LPDWORD *lpcVal*,

```
LPDWORD lpcbMaxValNamLen,
LPDWORD lpcbMaxValLen,
LPDWORD lpcbSecDescriptor,
PFILETIME lpftLastWriteTime
);
```

Input Parameters

hKey — Handle to a cluster database key

lpcSubKeys — Pointer to a count of the number of subkeys contained by the cluster database key represented by *hKey*

lpcbMaxSubKeylen — NULL or pointer to a count of the number of characters in the subkey with the longest name, excluding the terminating NULL character

lpcVal — Pointer to a count of the number of values associated with the cluster database key or NULL

lpcbMaxValNamLen — NULL or pointer to a count of the number of characters in the longest value name of the cluster database key, excluding the terminating NULL character

lpcbMaxValLen — Pointer to a count of the number of bytes of the longest data component among the cluster database key values or NULL

lpcbSecDescriptor — Pointer to a count of the number of bytes in the cluster database key security descriptor or NULL

lpftLastWriteTime — Pointer to the time that the cluster database key or any of its value entries was last modified or NULL

Return Values

ERROR_SUCCESS — The operation was successful.

If the operation was unsuccessful, **ClusterRegQueryInfoKey** returns a Win32 error value.

ClusterRegQueryValue

The **ClusterRegQueryValue** function returns the name, type, and data components associated with a value for an open cluster database key.

```
LONG WINAPI ClusterRegQueryValue(
    HKEY hKey,
    LPCWSTR lpszValNam,
    LPDWORD lpdwValType,
    LPBYTE lpbData,
    LPDWORD lpcbData
    );
```

Input Parameters

hKey — Handle to the cluster database key to query

lpszValNam — Pointer to the name of the value to be queried

Output Parameters

lpdwValType — Pointer to the key value type. The value returned through this parameter is one of the values specified in Table 19:

TABLE 19
Key Value Types and Descriptions

Value Type	Description
REG_BINARY	Binary data
REG_DWORD	A 32-b number
REG_EXPAND_SZ	A NULL-terminated Unicode string that contains unexpanded references to environment variables (e.g., "%PATH%")
REG_MULTI_SZ	An array of NULL-terminated Unicode strings, terminated by two NULL characters
REG_NONE	No defined value type
REG_SZ	A NULL-terminated Unicode string

The *lpdwValType* parameter can be NULL if the type is not required.
lpbData — Pointer to the value data. This parameter can be NULL if the data are not required.

Parameters that are both Input and Output
lpcbData — On input, this parameter points to the count of bytes in the buffer pointed to by the *lpbData* parameter. On output, this parameter points to the count of bytes in the value data, which are placed in the contents of *lpbData.*

Return Values

ERROR_SUCCESS — The operation was successful.
ERROR_MORE_DATA — The buffer pointed to by *lpbData* is not large enough to hold the data for the value. The required buffer size is returned by **ClusterRegQueryValue** in the contents of *lpcbData.*
ERROR_NO_MORE_ITEMS — There are no more values.

Programming Notes
The *lpcbData* parameter can be NULL only if the *lpbData* parameter is also NULL.
If you want to know the exact buffer size required, set *lpbData* to NULL and call **ClusterRegQueryValue**. **ClusterRegQueryValue** returns ERROR_SUCCESS and stores the size of the value data in the contents of *lpcbData.*
If *lpdwValType* is set to REG_SZ, REG_MULTI_SZ, or REG_EXPAND_SZ, then *lpbData* also includes a NULL terminator.
The behavior of **ClusterRegQueryValue** is similar to that of the related Win32 function **RegQueryValue**.

ClusterRegSetKeySecurity
The **ClusterRegSetKeySecurity** function sets the security attributes of a cluster database key.

```
LONG WINAPI ClusterRegSetKeySecurity(
            HKEY hKey,
            SECURITY_INFORMATION SecInfo,
            PSECURITY_DESCRIPTOR pSecDescriptor
            );
```

Input Parameters
hKey — Handle to a cluster database key

SecInfo — A SECURITY_INFORMATION structure that specifies the contents of the security descriptor pointed to by *pSecDescriptor*

pSecDescriptor — Pointer to a SECURITY_DESCRIPTOR structure that describes the security attributes to set for the key corresponding to *hKey*

Return Values

ERROR_SUCCESS — The operation was successful.

If the operation was unsuccessful, **ClusterRegSetKeySecurity** returns a Win32 error value.

Programming Notes

ClusterRegSetKeySecurity will generate a CLUSTER_CHANGE_REGISTRY_ATTRIBUTES event for all registered notification ports.

The behavior of **ClusterRegSetKeySecurity** is similar to that of the related Win32 function **RegSetKeySecurity**.

ClusterRegSetValue

The **ClusterRegSetValue** function sets a value for a cluster database key.

DWORD WINAPI **ClusterRegSetValue**(
HKEY *hKey*,
LPCWSTR *lpszValNam*,
DWORD *dwType*,
CONST BYTE * *lpbData*,
DWORD *cbData*
);

Input Parameters

hKey — Handle to a cluster database key.

lpszValNam — Pointer to the name of the value to set. If a value with this name is not already present in the resource, **ClusterRegSetValue** adds it to the resource.

dwType — Type of information to be stored as the value data. This parameter can be one of the following values specified in Table 20.

TABLE 20
Value Types and Descriptions

Value Type	Description
REG_BINARY	Binary data
REG_DWORD	A 32-b number
REG_EXPAND_SZ	A NULL-terminated Unicode string that contains unexpanded references to environment variables (e.g., "%PATH%")
REG_MULTI_SZ	An array of NULL-terminated Unicode strings, terminated by two NULL characters
REG_NONE	No defined value type
REG_SZ	A NULL-terminated Unicode string

lpbData — Pointer to the data to be stored with the name pointed to by *lpszValNam*.
cbData — Count of bytes in the data pointed to by the *lpbData* parameter. If the data are of type REG_SZ, REG_EXPAND_SZ, or REG_MULTI_SZ, *cbData* must include the size of the terminating NULL character.

Return Values
ERROR_SUCCESS — The operation was successful.

If the operation was unsuccessful, **ClusterRegSetValue** returns a Win32 error value.

Programming Notes
If the operation was unsuccessful and you need additional information about the error, call the Win32 function **GetLastError**.
The behavior of **ClusterRegSetValue** is similar to the related Win32 function **RegSetValue**.

GetClusterGroupKey
The **GetClusterGroupKey** function returns a handle to a cluster database key representing the subtree root for a group.

HKEY WINAPI **GetClusterGroupKey**(
HGROUP *hGrp*,
REGSAM *samReqd*
);

Input Parameters
hGrp — Handle to a group
samReqd — Access mask that describes the desired security access for the new key

Return Values
If the operation was successful, **GetClusterGroupKey** returns a database key handle for the group.
NULL — The operation was unsuccessful.

Programming Notes
You should call **ClusterRegCloseKey** to close the key handle retrieved by **GetClusterGroupKey** when you have finished processing.
If the operation was unsuccessful and you need more detailed information about the error, call the Win32 function **GetLastError**.

GetClusterKey
The **GetClusterKey** function returns a handle to a cluster database key representing the cluster database subtree root for a cluster.

HKEY WINAPI **GetClusterKey**(
HCLUSTER *hCluster*,
REGSAM *samReqd*
);

Input Parameters

hCluster — Handle to a cluster

samReqd — Access mask that specifies the desired security access for the new key

Return Values

If the operation was successful, **GetClusterKey** returns a database key handle for the cluster.

NULL — The operation was unsuccessful.

Programming Notes

You should call **ClusterRegCloseKey** to close the key handle retrieved by **GetClusterKey** when you have finished processing.

If the operation was unsuccessful and you need more detailed information about the error, call the Win32 function **GetLastError**.

GetClusterNetInterfaceKey

The **GetClusterNetInterfaceKey** function returns a handle to a cluster database key representing the subtree root for a network interface.

```
HKEY WINAPI  GetClusterNetInterfaceKey(
             HNETINTFACE hNetIntFace,
             REGSAM samReqd
             );
```

Input Parameters

hNetIntFace — Handle to a network interface

samReqd — Access mask that specifies the desired security access for the new key

Return Values

If the operation was successful, **GetClusterNetInterfaceKey** returns a registry key handle for the network interface.

NULL — The operation was unsuccessful.

Programming Notes

You should call **ClusterRegCloseKey** to close the key handle retrieved by **GetClusterKey** when you have finished processing.

If the operation was unsuccessful and you need more detailed information about the error, call the Win32 function **GetLastError**.

GetClusterNetworkKey

The **GetClusterNetworkKey** function returns a handle to a cluster database key representing the subtree root for a network.

```
HKEY WINAPI  GetClusterNetworkKey(
             HNETWORK hNetwrk,
             REGSAM samReqd
             );
```

Input Parameters

hNetwrk — Handle to a network

samReqd — Access mask that specifies the desired security access for the new key

Return Values

If the operation was successful, GetClusterNetworkKey returns a registry key handle for the network.

NULL — The operation was unsuccessful.

Programming Notes

You should call **ClusterRegCloseKey** to close the key handle retrieved by **GetClusterNetworkKey** when you have finished processing.

If the operation was unsuccessful and you need more detailed information about the error, call the Win32 function **GetLastError**.

GetClusterNodeKey

The **GetClusterNodeKey** function returns a handle to a cluster database key representing the subtree root for a node.

```
HKEY WINAPI GetClusterNodeKey(
                HNODE hNode,
                REGSAM samReqd
                );
```

Input Parameters

hNode — Handle to a node

samReqd — Access mask that specifies the desired security access for the new key

Return Values

If the operation was successful, **GetClusterNodeKey** returns a registry key handle for the node.

NULL — The operation was unsuccessful.

Programming Notes

You should call ClusterRegCloseKey to close the key handle retrieved by **GetClusterNodeKey** when you have finished processing.

If the operation was unsuccessful and you need more detailed information about the error, call the Win32 function **GetLastError**.

GetClusterResourceKey

The **GetClusterResourceKey** function returns a handle to a cluster database key representing the subtree root a resource.

```
HKEY WINAPI GetClusterResourceKey(
                HRES hRes,
                REGSAM samReqd
                );
```

Input Parameters

hRes — Handle to a resource

samReqd — Access mask that describes the desired security access for the opened key

Return Values
If the operation was successful, **GetClusterResourceKey** returns a registry key handle for the resource.
NULL — The operation was unsuccessful.

Programming Notes
You should call **ClusterRegCloseKey** to close the key handle retrieved by **GetClusterResourceKey** when you have finished processing.
If the operation was unsuccessful and you need more detailed information about the error, call the Win32 function **GetLastError**.

GetClusterResourceTypeKey
The **GetClusterResourceTypeKey** function returns a handle to a cluster database key representing the subtree root for a resource type.

HKEY WINAPI **GetClusterResourceTypeKey**(
HCLUSTER *hCluster*,
LPCWSTR *lpszTypeNam*,
REGSAM *samReqd*
);

Input Parameters
hCluster — Handle to a cluster
lpszTypeNam — Pointer to the name of a resource type
samReqd — Access mask that specifies the desired security access for the opened key

Return Values
If the operation was successful, **GetClusterResourceTypeKey** returns a registry key handle for the resource type.
NULL — The operation was unsuccessful.

Programming Notes
You should call ClusterRegCloseKey to close the key handle retrieved by **GetClusterResourceTypeKey** when you have finished processing.
If the operation was unsuccessful and you need more detailed information about the error, call the Win32 function **GetLastError**.

Appendix B
Resource API Reference

This appendix supplements the information in Chapter 7 on cluster programming and also provides the detailed information about the Resource application programming interface (APIs) you can use for cluster programming. For each API, a brief description, the actual API syntax including all the parameters, a description of the parameters, the results of the API call, and programming notes are included.

CONVENTIONS USED

The conventions used are the same conventions used for Cluster APIs in Appendix A. If you are already familiar with the conventions, you can skip ahead to the APIs.

Function names are in bold and must be used as shown. Parameter values are in italics and the programmer can choose any variable name. Parameter keywords and keywords that are part of the function call are in capitals. Valid parameter and return values are shown with a reduced font (e.g., TRUE)

The call syntax of each function is provided and this is followed by:

- Input parameters to the function
- Input and Output parameters to the function
- Output parameters
- Return values
- Programming Notes

Note: The five items listed may not be described for all functions. APIs are listed here in a format suitable for quick reference to supplement the cluster programming chapter. More detailed information about these APIs is available in Microsoft product documentation and Microsoft Development Network (MSDN).

RESOURCE API OVERVIEW

The resource API defines functions, structures, and macros that allow the Cluster Service to communicate with resources. The communication between the Cluster Service and the resources is indirect. The Cluster Service initiates requests with a Resource Monitor and the Resource Monitor passes them to the resource. Status and event information is passed back from the resource direct link library (DLL) to the Cluster Service.

The following diagram shows how control flows from the Cluster Service through the Resource Monitor and a resource DLL to resources. The diagram shows four resource DLLs, three for Cluster Service resource types and one for a resource type defined by a third-party developer.

The resource API consists of:

- Entry point functions
- Callback functions
- Structures and macros

The rest of this appendix covers these in more detail.

RESOURCE API ENTRY POINT FUNCTIONS

The resource API entry point functions are implemented in a resource DLL to allow a Resource Monitor to manage its resources. Most of the entry point functions are required, but some are optional depending on the functionality provided by the resource. For example, the **Arbitrate** and **Release** entry point functions must be implemented for resources that can act as the cluster quorum resource and must not be implemented for non-quorum capable resources.

The following table briefly describes the entry point functions in the Resource API.

Entry Point Function	Description
Arbitrate	Allows a node to attempt to regain ownership of a quorum resource
Close	Closes a resource
IsAlive	Determines if a resource is available for use
LooksAlive	Determines if a resource appears to be available for use
Offline	Marks a resource as unavailable for use after cleanup processing is completed
Online	Marks a resource as available for use
Open	Opens a resource
Release	Releases a quorum resource from arbitration
ResourceControl	Performs an operation that applies to a resource
ResourceTypeControl	Performs an operation that applies to a resource type
Startup	Loads a resource's resource DLL and returns a structure containing a function table and version number
Terminate	Marks a resource as unavailable for use without waiting for cleanup processing to finish

The function table returned by Startup contains pointers to each of the entry point functions. Startup is the only entry point function that is exported. The other entry point functions are accessed through the function table.

A resource DLL is non-reentrant for a given instance of a resource. That is, with one exception, resource DLL developers should expect each of their entry points to be called only once for each resource instance. The exception is Terminate. Calls to Terminate can occur at any time, even if other threads within the resource DLL are blocked waiting for an Online or Offline call to complete.

A resource DLL is reentrant with respect to resource identifiers, represented by the RESID data type. Resource identifiers are returned from the Open entry point function and supplied to all other entry points to identify a resource. Resource DLLs that handle multiple resource identifiers must be prepared to synchronize the use of any shared global data.

Arbitrate

The **Arbitrate** entry point function allows a node to attempt to regain ownership of a quorum resource. This entry point function is optional and is implemented only for quorum-capable resources.

```
DWORD WINAPI Arbitrate(
        RESID ResId,
        PQUORUM_RESOURCE_LOST LostQuorumRes
        );
```

Input Parameters

ResId — Resource identifier of the quorum resource to be owned

LostQuorumRes — Pointer to a callback function, which is to be called if the arbitration fails and control of the quorum resource is lost, after being successfully gained

Return Values

ERROR_SUCCESS — The arbitration was successful.

If the arbitration was not successful, **Arbitrate** returns a Win32 error code.

Programming Notes

Arbitrate should take less than 300 msec to complete.

Arbitrate is called only after both Startup and Open have been called.

If **Arbitrate** is successful, make sure that only the current node can successfully arbitrate for the quorum resource by continually replacing the reservation made on it once per second.

Close

The **Close** entry point function closes a resource.

```
VOID WINAPI Close(
        RESID ResId
        );
```

Input Parameters

ResId — Resource identifier of the resource to be closed

Return Values

None

Programming Notes

You should be sure to dedicate all the structures that were allocated by any of the following functions:

- **Open**
- **Online**
- **ResourceControl**
- **ResourceTypeControl**

Close should be called only once for a particular resource.

If the resource to be closed is not yet offline, call **Terminate** to force the resource offline.

Your implementation of **Close** takes less than 300 msec to complete. If this time limit is exceeded, the Cluster Service handles the situation properly.

Call the Win32 function **SetLastError** just before returning.

IsAlive

The **IsAlive** entry point function determines if a resource is actually available for use (online and functioning properly).

```
BOOL WINAPIIsAlive(
        RESID ResId
        );
```

Input Parameters

ResId — Resource identifier for the resource to be polled

Return Values

TRUE — The resource is online and functioning properly.

FALSE — The resource is not functioning properly.

Programming Notes

The set of procedures that you need to implement **IsAlive** depends on your resource. Some of the procedures typically performed for **IsAlive** are

- Determine if the application is running. (This simple procedure is implemented by the Cluster Server in its resource DLL for the generic application resource.)
- Determine if data can be read from the resource.
- Determine if data can be written to the resource.
- Check for a particular state of the resource.

Unlike **LooksAlive**, which determines whether or not a resource appears to be available, **IsAlive** should determine if the resource is actually available.

Make your implementation of **IsAlive** take about 50 msec or less to complete. At the very most, you should ensure that **IsAlive** does not block processing for more than 300 msec. If your implementation must take longer than 300 msec, you can have a separate thread dedicated to performing the polling operation and/or return the result of the last poll performed by the separate thread.

Call the Win32 function **SetLastError** just before returning.

LooksAlive

The **LooksAlive** entry point function determines if a resource appears to be available for use.

```
BOOL WINAPILooksAlive(
        RESID ResId
        );
```

Input Parameters

ResId — Resource identifier for the resource to poll

Return Values:

TRUE — The resource appears to be available (online and functioning properly).

FALSE — The resource is not functioning properly.

Programming Notes

If **LooksAlive** fails, the Resource Monitor calls your **IsAlive** entry point function to determine if the resource is actually not functioning.

Unlike **IsAlive**, which determines whether or not a resource is actually available for use, **LooksAlive** determines whether the resource appears to be available. The preferred target time for **LooksAlive** to complete is 150 msec. As an upper bound, you should ensure that **LooksAlive** does not block processing for more than 300 msec. One way of ensuring that your implementation of **LooksAlive** does not take longer than 300 msec is to have a separate thread dedicated to performing the polling operation and/or return the result of the last poll performed by the separate thread.

Call the Win32 function **SetLastError** just before returning.

Offline

The **Offline** entry point function takes a resource offline (the resource goes to ClusterResourceOffline state) and is unavailable once cleanup processing is completed.

```
DWORD WINAPI Offline(
        RESID ResId
        );
```

Input Parameters

ResId — Resource identifier for the resource to be taken offline

Return Values

ERROR_SUCCESS — The request is completed successfully and the resource is offline.

ERROR_IO_PENDING — The request is still pending and a separate thread has been activated to process the offline request.

If the operation was unsuccessful for other reasons, **Offline** should return a Win32 error value. If **Offline** returns a Win32 error value, the Resource Monitor logs an event and calls the Terminate entry point.

Programming Notes

You should ensure that **Offline** takes less than 300 msec to complete. However, if it takes more than 300 msec, you should perform the following:

- Start a separate thread to complete the request.
- Return ERROR_IO_PENDING immediately.
- Make the thread that is processing the request periodically report status information to the Resource Monitor by calling the **SetResourceStatus** callback function.
- Keep calling **SetResourceStatus** until one of the following two situations occurs:
  - The resource is placed in the *ClusterResourceOffline* state.
  - A time-out occurs (the request exceeds the time limit). The time limit is stored in the *PendingTimeout* common property and is 3 min by default.

A time-out causes the Resource Monitor to call **Terminate** to abort the offline request. You must ensure that all necessary cleanup operations are completed before you return from **Offline**.

Online

The **Online** entry point function brings a resource online (marks a resource as available for use).

```
DWORD WINAPI Online(
        RESID ResId,
        PHANDLE EvntHnd
        );
```

Input Parameters:

ResId — Resource identifier for the resource to be made available

Parameters that are both Input and Output

EvntHnd — On input, *EvntHnd* is NULL. On output, *EvntHnd* contains a handle that is signaled when the resource detects a failure. Usually, this is a handle to a system object, such as a process. For example, if *EvntHnd* represents a process and the process is terminated, the *EvntHnd* is signaled and the Resource Monitor is notified.

EvntHnd can also be set to NULL on output, indicating that the resource does not support asynchronous event notification.

Return Values

ERROR_SUCCESS — The operation was successful, and the resource is now online and available for use.

ERROR_RESOURCE_NOT_AVAILABLE – The resource is not available. A common cause for this is that the resource was arbitrated with some other systems, and one of the other systems won the arbitration.

ERROR_IO_PENDING — The request to bring the resource online is pending. A thread has been activated to process the online request.

Programming Notes

You should ensure that **Online** takes less than 300 msec to complete. However, if it takes more than 300 msec, you should perform the following:

- Start a separate thread to complete the request.
- Return ERROR_IO_PENDING immediately.
- Make the thread that is processing the request periodically report status information to the Resource Monitor by calling the **SetResourceStatus** callback function.
- Keep calling **SetResourceStatus** until one of the following two situations occurs:
  - The resource is placed in the *ClusterResourceOnline* state.
  - A time-out occurs (the request exceeds the time limit). The time limit is stored in the *PendingTimeout* common property and is 3 min by default.

A time-out causes the Resource Monitor to call **Terminate** to abort the **Online** request.

Even though you got a copy of the Resource properties from your **Open** entry point function, it is a good idea to refresh the private properties of the resource in the event that changes have occurred since that time. You can refresh the private properties of the resource to be brought online in your **Online** entry point function. To refresh the private properties, call **ClusterResourceControl** (see Appendix A for more information) twice, passing CLUSCTL_RESOURCE_GET_PRIVATE_PROPERTIES in the *dwCtrlCode* parameter for the first call and CLUSCTL_RESOURCE_GET_RO_PRIVATE_PROPERTIES for the second call. Whenever possible, do not handle node-specific properties. If you must maintain node-specific properties, record them in the cluster database under a local machine key based on the node identifier. You can retrieve the node identifier by calling **GetClusterNodeId**.

Return a valid handle in *EvntHnd* to use event notification to inform the Resource Monitor of a resource state. When a resource DLL supports event notification, the Resource Monitor still calls its **IsAlive** function to thoroughly check for status but does not call **LooksAlive**.

Open

The **Open** entry point function opens a resource using the name of the resource and returns its resource identifier.

```
RESID WINAPI  Open(
              LPCWSTR ResNam,
              HKEY ResKey,
              RESOURCE_HANDLE ResHnd
              );
```

Input Parameters

ResNam — Name of the resource to be opened

ResKey — Cluster database key of the cluster that contains the resource represented by *ResNam*

ResHnd — Handle to be passed to the **SetResourceStatus** callback function in the **Startup** entry point function

Return Values

If the operation was successful, **Open** returns a resource identifier (RESID).

If the operation was unsuccessful, **Open** returns null.

Programming Notes

Open should allocate all the structures necessary to bring the new resource online as well as retrieve the resource private properties. To retrieve the private properties of a resource, call **ClusterResourceControl** (see Appendix A for more information) twice, passing CLUSCTL_RESOURCE_GET_PRIVATE_PROPERTIES in the *dwControlCode* parameter for the first call and CLUSCTL_RESOURCE_GET_RO_PRIVATE_PROPERTIES for the second call. To ensure that the latest changes are picked up, resource DLLs should also retrieve their private properties in their **Online** function (see the programming notes for **Online** earlier).

The resource identifier returned by **Open** is used in future calls to other resource API entry points to identify the resource. The resource is identified using the *ResHnd* handle. Do not close the handle represented by the *ResHnd* parameter. Do not use the handle for any purpose other than passing it to the Resource Monitor through either the **LogEvent** or **SetResourceStatus** callback functions.

To make sure that the resource is in the *Offline* state when **Open** returns, read the resource **PersistentState property**. This is important if a resource cannot be online on more than one node simultaneously, such as when two nodes cannot simultaneously use the same IP address. If there is no chance that the resource could be online prior to the start of the Cluster Service, then taking the resource offline in your implementation of Open is not necessary.

Whenever possible, do not handle node-specific properties. If you must maintain node-specific properties, record them in the cluster database under a local machine key based on the node identifier. You can retrieve the node identifier by calling **GetClusterNodeId**.

For example, your resource DLL for managing a disk resource may need to maintain different drive names for each node if the nodes maintain different numbers of disks. That is, the physical drive may assume one name on one node and a different name on another node. Handle this situation by having cluster database keys for each of the node computer names, and parse for additional parameters under the node-specific cluster database keys, which are based on the node identifier.

Make your implementation of **Open** complete as quickly as possible, preferably within 300 msec. However, even if you take a longer time, the Cluster Service handles this situation properly.

Call the Win32 function **SetLastError** just before returning.

Release

The **Release** entry point function releases the quorum resource from arbitration.

```
DWORD WINAPI Release(
                RESID ResId
                );
```

Input Parameters

ResId — Resource identifier for the quorum resource that is to be released

Return Values

ERROR_SUCCESS — The operation was successful and the quorum resource was successfully released. The quorum resource is not being defended.

ERROR_HOST_NODE_NOT_OWNER – The operation was requested without the quorum resource having been previously arbitrated.

If the quorum resource is not successfully released, **Release** returns a Win32 error code.

Programming Notes

You should aim for **Release** to finish in less than 300 msec. Common scenarios when **Release** is implemented are when the Cluster Service is shut down or when the quorum resource has to be physically moved to another node in the cluster.

Release is implemented for quorum resources only.

ResourceControl

The **ResourceControl** entry point function performs a resource-related operation as identified by the control code parameter.

DWORD WINAPI **ResourceControl**(
RESID *ResId*,
DWORD *CtrlCode*,
LPVOID *InBuf*,
DWORD *InBufSz*,
LPVOID *OutBuf*,
DWORD *OutBufSz*,
LPDWORD *BytesRet*
);

Input Parameters

ResId — Resource identifier of the resource related to the operation that is to be performed.

CtrlCode — Control code that specifies the operation to be performed. For a list of the valid values for the *CtrlCode* parameter, see the programming notes later.

InBuf — Pointer to a buffer containing data to be used in the operation. *InBuf* can be NULL if no data are required.

InBufSz — Size, in bytes, of the buffer pointed to by *InBuf*.

OutBufSz — Size, in bytes, of the available space pointed to by *OutBuf*.

Output Parameters

OutBuf — Pointer to a buffer containing data resulting from the operation. *OutBuf* can be NULL if the operation does not need to return data.

BytesRet — Number of bytes in the buffer pointed to by *OutBuf* that actually contain data.

Return Values

ERROR_SUCCESS — The specified operation was completed successfully.

ERROR_INVALID_FUNCTION — Specified operation is invalid. This is commonly due to the fact that the resource DLL may not support the operation represented by *CtrlCode*. In some cases this is an indication to the Resource Monitor to process the request.

If the operation was unsuccessful, **ResourceControl** returns a Win32 error value.

Programming Notes

The control codes for resources are summarized in the following table. Control codes are of two types — external and internal. External control codes are control codes that applications can pass to the control functions of the Cluster API to initiate operations. Internal control codes are control codes that only the Cluster Service can pass to a control function. For more details about control codes, see Chapter 7.

It is preferable not to provide support for some of the codes because they depend on the standard processing that the Resource Monitor supplies. For example, see CLUSCTL_RESOURCE_GET_CHARACTERISTICS earlier.

To request that the Resource Monitor process a control code, return ERROR_INVALID_FUNCTION. You can return this value for a control code regardless of whether or not you include support for the code in **ResourceControl**. Some resource DLLs support a control code to augment the functionality that the Resource Monitor supplies.

The preferred target time limit for **ResourceControl** to finish is less than 300 msec.

ResourceTypeControl

The **ResourceTypeControl** entry point function performs a resource type-related operation as identified by the control code parameter.

```
DWORD WINAPI ResourceTypeControl(
                LPCWSTR ResTypNam,
                DWORD CtrlCode,
                LPVOID InBuf,
                DWORD InBufSz,
                LPVOID OutBuf,
                DWORD OutBufSz,
                LPDWORD BytesRet
                );
```

Input Parameters

ResTypNam — Type of resource on which the operation is to be performed.

CtrlCode — Control code that represents the operation to be performed. For a list of all valid values for the *CtrlCode* parameter, see the programming notes for **ResourceControl** earlier.

InBuf — Pointer to a buffer that contains the data to be used in the operation. *InBuf* can be NULL if the operation does not require data.

InBufSz — Size of the input buffer pointed to by *InBuf*, in bytes.

OutBufSz – Size of the output buffer pointed to by *OutBuf*, in bytes.

Output Parameters

OutBuf — Pointer to a buffer containing data resulting from the operation. *OutBuf* can be NULL if the operation returns no data.

BytesRet — Number of bytes in the buffer pointed to by *OutBuf* that contain actual data.

Return Values

ERROR_SUCCESS — The specified operation was completed successfully.

ERROR_INVALID_FUNCTION — Specified operation is invalid. This is commonly due to the fact that the resource DLL may not support the operation represented by *CtrlCode*. In some cases this is an indication to the Resource Monitor to process the request.

TABLE 1
Control Codes for Resources

Control Code	Implementation Support	Type
CLUSCTL_RESOURCE_ADD_REGISTRY_CHECKPOINT	Optional	External
CLUSCTL_RESOURCE_DELETE_REGISTRY_CHECKPOINT	Optional	External
CLUSCTL_RESOURCE_ENUM_COMMON_PROPERTIES	Optional	External
CLUSCTL_RESOURCE_ENUM_PRIVATE_PROPERTIES	Support is mandatory	External
CLUSCTL_RESOURCE_GET_CHARACTERISTICS	Do not include support for this control code because it may override important processing provided by the Resource Monitor	External
CLUSCTL_RESOURCE_GET_CLASS_INFO	Optional	External
CLUSCTL_RESOURCE_GET_COMMON_PROPERTIES	Optional	External
CLUSCTL_RESOURCE_GET_FLAGS	Optional	External
CLUSCTL_RESOURCE_GET_NAME	Optional	External
CLUSCTL_RESOURCE_GET_PRIVATE_PROPERTIES	Support is mandatory; permits the setting of nonstring private properties on a newly created resource using the command-line tool CLUSTER.EXE	External
CLUSCTL_RESOURCE_GET_REGISTRY_CHECKPOINTS	Support is mandatory if your resource DLL needs to replicate a portion of the system registry	External
CLUSCTL_RESOURCE_GET_REQUIRED_DEPENDENCIES	Support is mandatory if resources handled by your resource DLL have required dependencies	External
CLUSCTL_RESOURCE_GET_RESOURCE_TYPE	Optional	External
CLUSCTL_RESOURCE_GET_RO_COMMON_PROPERTIES	Optional	External
CLUSCTL_RESOURCE_GET_RO_PRIVATE_PROPERTIES	Support is mandatory.	External
CLUSCTL_RESOURCE_SET_COMMON_PROPERTIES	Optional	External
CLUSCTL_RESOURCE_SET_PRIVATE_PROPERTIES	Support is mandatory.	External
CLUSCTL_RESOURCE_STORAGE_GET_DISK_INFO	Optional	External
CLUSCTL_RESOURCE_STORAGE_IS_PATH_VALID	Optional	External
CLUSCTL_RESOURCE_UNKNOWN	Optional	External
CLUSCTL_RESOURCE_VALIDATE_COMMON_PROPERTIES	Optional	External
CLUSCTL_RESOURCE_VALIDATE_PRIVATE_PROPERTIES	Support is mandatory; used in conjunction with validating private properties before setting them	External
CLUSCTL_RESOURCE_ADD_DEPENDENCY	Optional	Internal
CLUSCTL_RESOURCE_ADD_OWNER	Optional	Internal
CLUSCTL_RESOURCE_CLUSTER_NAME_CHANGED	Optional	Internal
CLUSCTL_RESOURCE_DELETE	Optional	Internal
CLUSCTL_RESOURCE_EVICT_NODE	Optional	Internal

TABLE 1 (CONTINUED)
Control Codes for Resources

Control Code	Implementation Support	Type
CLUSCTL_RESOURCE_INSTALL_NODE	Optional	Internal
CLUSCTL_RESOURCE_REMOVE_ DEPENDENCY	Optional	Internal
CLUSCTL_RESOURCE_REMOVE_OWNER	Optional	Internal
CLUSCTL_RESOURCE_SET_NAME	Optional	Internal

If the operation was unsuccessful, **ResourceTypeControl** should return a Win32 error value.

Programming Notes

While **ResourceTypeControl** should be implemented by all resource DLLs, it is not necessary to provide code to handle all the control codes that are defined for resource types listed in Table 1 earlier. You must provide support for the control codes listed as mandatory.

To request that the Resource Monitor process a control code, return ERROR_INVALID_FUNCTION. You can return this value for a control code regardless of whether or not you include support for the code in **ResourceTypeControl**. Some resource DLLs support a control code to augment the functionality that the Resource Monitor supplies.

The preferred target time limit for **ResourceTypeControl** to finish is less than 300 msec.

Startup

The **Startup** entry point function loads a resource DLL and returns a structure containing a function table. The information returned by **Startup** includes the Resource API version number and the specific names for the entry points.

```
DWORD WINAPI Startup(
        LPCWSTR ResType,
        DWORD MinVerSupp,
        DWORD MaxVerSupp,
        SET_RESOURCE_STATUS_ROUTINE SetResStat,
        PLOG_EVENT_ROUTINE LogEvnt,
        PCLRES_FUNCTION_TABLE * FuncTbl
        );
```

Input Parameters

ResType — Type of resource being loaded and started.

MinVerSupp — Minimum version of the resource API supported by Cluster Server.

MaxVerSupp — Maximum version of the resource API supported by Cluster Server. At present, only Resource API version 1.0 is supported.

SetResStat — Pointer to a callback function. The resource DLL calls the callback function pointed by *SetResStat* to update its status after returning ERROR_IO_PENDING from Online or Offline.

LogEvnt — Pointer to a callback function. The resource DLL calls the callback function pointed by *LogEvnt* to report events for the resource.

Output Parameters

FuncTbl — Pointer to a CLRES_FUNCTION_TABLE structure that describes the Resource API version and the specific names of the entry points. Details of the CLRES_FUNCTION_TABLE structure are listed at the end of this appendix.

Return Values

ERROR_SUCCESS — The request was successful.

ERROR_REVISION_MISMATCH — The resource does not support a version that is within the range identified by the *MinVerSupp* and *MaxVerSupp* parameters.

If the operation was unsuccessful, **Startup** should return a Win32 error value.

Programming Notes

If your resource supports more than one version of the resource API, you should return a function table for the latest version that is less than or equal to the *MaxVerSupp* parameter (at present, only Resource API version 1.0 is supported).

The **Startup** entry point function returns a function table that includes the following:

- The supported interface version of the resource API
- Entry points for all other functions required by the supported version of the Resource API

If the version of the function table pointed to by the *FuncTbl* parameter is not within range, your resource cannot be loaded successfully.

The preferred target time limit for **Startup** to finish is less than 300 msec.

Terminate

The **Terminate** entry point function immediately marks a resource as unavailable for use without waiting for threads that may have pending Online or Offline requests for the resource to complete.

```
VOID WINAPI Terminate(
        RESID ResId
        );
```

Input Parameters

ResId — Resource identifier of the resource to be terminated

Return Values

None

Programming Notes

The Terminate entry point function instantly marks a resource as unavailable for use without waiting for any cleanup processing to complete. For example, if there are any threads processing Online or Offline requests for the resource, these requests are canceled and the resource is taken offline immediately.

The preferred target time limit for **Terminate** to finish is less than 300 msec. However, the Cluster Service handles the situation properly if this time limit is exceeded.

RESOURCE API CALLBACK FUNCTIONS

Resource API Callback Functions record an event for a resource, report that control of the quorum resource has been lost, perform resource-specific tasks, and update the status of a resource as shown in the following table.

TABLE 2
Resource API Callback Functions and Descriptions

Resource API Callback Function	Function Description
LogEvent	Logs an event associated with a resource
QuorumResourceLost	Reports that control of the quorum resource is lost
ResourceCallback	Performs resource-specific tasks; this callback function is called by the cluster utility function **ResUtilEnumResources** for each resource that is enumerated by **ResUtilEnumResources**
SetResourceStatus	Updates the status of a resource

Thus, of the four resource API callback functions, three are implemented by the Resource Monitor and called by a resource DLL while one is implemented by a resource DLL and called by the Cluster Service. A resource DLL invokes a Resource Monitor callback function to report status and to log events. A resource DLL implements the **ResourceCallback** function to perform tasks in response to the cluster utility function **ResUtilEnumResources** enumerating resources.

LogEvent

The **LogEvent** callback function logs an event associated with a resource to the cluster debugging log.

VOID WINAPI **LogEvent**(
RESOURCE_HANDLE *ResHnd*,
LOG_LEVEL *LogLvl*,
LPCWSTR *FrmtStr*
);

Input Parameters

ResHnd — Handle of the resource whose associated event is to be logged.

LogLvl — Constant that represents the logging level of the event and is for information only. Valid values are shown in the following table and are in the order from least to most severe.

Logging Level	Description
LOG_INFORMATION	The event is informational
LOG_WARNING	The event is reporting a failure that may have happened; it is uncertain whether or not a failure really did occur
LOG_ERROR	The event affects a single component; other components are not affected and the integrity of the rest of the node is not compromised
LOG_SEVERE	The event is reporting a severe failure that affects multiple components or the integrity of the entire system is compromised or expected to be compromised

FrmtStr — Pointer to a formatted Unicode string that includes the information to be recorded. This string must be in the same format as is passed to the Win32 function FormatMessage.

Return Values

None

Programming Notes

The value for *ResHnd* is the handle passed in during the **Open** call for this resource. The **LogEvent** function logs events and errors to the cluster debugging log, not the Windows NT event log. If you want to report events in the Windows NT event log, your resource DLL must call the Win32 function **ReportEvent**. The **LogEvent** function is implemented by the Resource Monitor and is called by a resource DLL. Resource DLLs receive a pointer to the **LogEvent** function as an input parameter to their **Startup** entry point function.

The format of the logged message looks like:

ResTypNam <specific resource name>: message.

ResTypNam is the resource type (e.g., generic application). The specific resource name is the user-friendly name for the specific resource of the resource type and message is the message delivered by the resource DLL to the Resource Monitor.

The **LogEvent** callback function logs to the cluster debugging log, which must be enabled. To enable the cluster debugging log:

- Set the CLUSTERLOG environment variable to a complete path identifying the location of the log file. The default name for the log file is cluster.log and the default location is the cluster directory.
- Set the size of the log file in the ClusterLogSize entry in the cluster database under HKEY_LOCAL_MACHINE\Cluster. The size is a DWORD value that indicates the number of megabytes that the log file can hold. If this value is set to zero, logging is disabled.

QuorumResourceLost

The **QuorumResourceLost** function is called by a resource DLL to notify the Resource Monitor that control of the quorum resource is lost.

```
VOID WINAPI QuorumResourceLost(
        RESOURCE_HANDLE ResHnd
        );
```

Input Parameters

ResHnd — Handle of the resource to which this callback applies

Return Values

None

Programming Notes

The value for *ResHnd* is the handle passed in during the **Open** call for this resource. The **QuorumResourceLost** function is called by a resource DLL to notify the Resource Monitor that control of the quorum resource has been lost in the **Arbitrate** entry point function. A pointer to the Resource Monitor **QuorumResourceLost** function is passed to a quorum resource DLL in the call to **Arbitrate**.

ResourceCallback

The **ResourceCallback** function performs resource-specific tasks. **ResourceCallback** is called by the cluster utility function **ResUtilEnumResources** for each resource that **ResUtilEnumResources** enumerates.

DWORD WINAPI **ResourceCallback**(
 RESOURCE_HANDLE *hOrig*,
 RESOURCE_HANDLE *hRes*,
 PVOID *lpParm*
 );

Input Parameters

hOrig — Handle of the original resource (the resource identified by *hSelf* in **ResUtilEnumResources**)

hRes — Handle to a resource of the same type as the original resource

lpParm — Pointer to the parameter passed to **ResUtilEnumResources**

Return Values

ERROR_STATUS — The operation associated with the **ResourceCallback** function was successful

If the operation was unsuccessful, **ResourceCallback** returns one or more Win32 appropriate error values; for example, the IIS virtual root resource DLL implementation of **ResourceCallback** returns ERROR_DUP_NAME for a duplicate resource error and ERROR_INVALID_PARAMETER for a parameter error.

Programming Notes

If *hSelf* is specified in the call to **ResUtilEnumResources** as NULL, *hOrig* also is NULL. If *hSelf* is specified in the call to **ResUtilEnumResources** as non-NULL, your **ResourceCallback** function is invoked for each resource except the *hSelf* resource. Also, if *lpszResType* is specified in the call to **ResUtilEnumResources**, it is only called for resources of that type.

SetResourceStatus

The **SetResourceStatus** function is called to update the status of a resource after its **Online** or **Offline** entry point function has returned ERROR_IO_PENDING.

VOID WINAPI **SetResourceStatus**(
 RESOURCE_HANDLE *ResHnd*,
 PRESOURCE_STATUS *ResStat*
 );

Input Parameters

ResHnd — Handle of the resource whose status is to be updated.

ResStat — Pointer to a RESOURCE_STATUS structure that contains information about the resource state. The RESOURCE_STATUS structure is described in detail at the end of this appendix.

Return Values

None

Programming Notes

SetResourceStatus is implemented by the Resource Monitor and is similar to the Win32 function **SetServiceStatus**.

The *ResHnd* parameter should contain the same handle from the **Open** entry point for this resource. A pointer to the function is passed to the resource implementation of **Startup**. Resource DLLs should call **SetResourceStatus** after their **Online** or **Offline** entry point function has returned ERROR_IO_PENDING and not at any other time. Call SetResourceStatus until the resource is placed in either the ClusterResourceOnline/ClusterResourceOffline state or the time limit stored in the resource PendingTimeout property has been exceeded.

Update the current state of a resource whenever necessary after you have returned ERROR_IO_PENDING. If the resource is in one of the pending states, increment the values for the CheckPoint and WaitHint members of the RESOURCE_STATUS structure and set the ResourceState member to ClusterResourceOnlinePending or ClusterResourceOfflinePending before you begin calling **SetResourceStatus**.

There is no need to call **SetResourceStatus** to set the state of a resource to a pending state because the Resource Monitor automatically sets it to the appropriate pending state whenever **Online** or **Offline** returns ERROR_IO_PENDING.

RESOURCE API STRUCTURES AND MACROS

The resource API contains structures and macros that are used to describe the function table that is returned by the **Startup** entry point function and describes the status of a resource. The function table contains the version number of the resource API being used by a resource DLL. The function table also holds pointers to each of the resource DLL entry point functions. Resource DLLs that support multiple resource types must provide one function table for each resource type.

The structure that is used to describe status information for a resource, RESOURCE_STATUS, is passed as a parameter with the **SetResourceStatus** function.

Cluster Server defines the following macros and structures:

Structure or Macro	Description
CLRES_FUNCTION_TABLE	Structure that contains the version of the Resource API and pointers to all resource API entry points (except **Startup**)
CLRES_V1_FUNCTION_TABLE	Macro that creates a function table for Resource API version 1.0
CLRES_V1_FUNCTIONS	Structure that contains pointers to all resource entry points in the resource API except **Startup** for Resource API 1.0
RESOURCE_STATUS	Structure that contains information about a resource that is being brought online or taken offline

CLRES_FUNCTION_TABLE

The **CLRES_FUNCTION_TABLE** structure describes a function table for any version of the resource API. The CLRES_FUNCTION_TABLE structure is defined in RESAPI.H.

```
typedef struct CLRES_FUNCTION_TABLE {
        DWORD TableSize;
        DWORD Version;
        union {
        CLRES_V1_FUNCTIONS V1Functions;
        }
        } CLRES_FUNCTION_TABLE; *PCLRES_FUNCTION_TABLE;
```

where

TableSize is the Count of bytes in the structure, taken from the constant CLRES_V1_FUNCTION_SIZE.
Version is the Number of the supported version of the Resource API, taken from the constant CLRES_VERSION_V1_00.
V1Functions is the Table of entry points included in the Resource API version 1.0.

Programming Notes
The CLRES_FUNCTION_TABLE structure contains the version of the resource API that the DLL is using and a structure that has pointers to all resource API entry points except **Startup**.

Except for the following entry points, there must be valid pointers (non-NULL) for all resource API entry point functions:

- **Arbitrate**
- **Release**
- **ResourceControl**
- **ResourceTypeControl**

Of these, only the first two members are guaranteed to be at the same offset within the CLRES_FUNCTION_TABLE structure. All other entries within this structure are dependent on the version of the Resource API.

To create a function table for version 1.0 of the Resource API, use the CLRES_V1_FUNCTION_TABLE macro.

CLRES_V1_FUNCTION_TABLE
The **CLRES_V1_FUNCTION_TABLE** macro initializes a function table for version 1 of the Resource API. The **CLRES_V1_FUNCTION_TABLE** macro is defined in RESAPI.H.

typedef struct **CLRES_V1_FUNCTION_TABLE**(
_Name, *_Version*, *_Prefix*, *_Arbitrate*,
_Release, *_ResControl*, *_ResTypeControl*)

where

Name is the Label for the function table.
Version is the exact version, such as CLRES_VERSION_V1_00.
Prefix is the prefix to be appended to the front of each of the names of the entry points in the function table.
Arbitrate is the name of the **Arbitrate** entry point.
Release is the name of the **Release** entry point.
ResControl is the name of the **ResourceControl** entry point.
ResTypeControl is the name of the **ResourceTypeControl** entry point.

Programming Notes
The CLRES_V1_FUNCTION_TABLE macro creates a function table for version 1.0 of the Resource API using the version specified by the Version parameter and the label specified by the Name parameter. The actual names of the entry points are generated by combining the prefix specified in the Prefix parameter with the generic names as defined in the Resource API. For example, if Prefix is set to the string "Test," then the name of the Open function would be "TestOpen." The optional entry point functions may be null.

The resulting function table includes the following members.

TABLE 3
Function Table Member Names and Descriptions

Member Name	Description
PrefixOpen	The name of the Open entry point
PrefixClose	The name of the Close entry point
PrefixOnline	The name of the Online entry point
PrefixOffline	The name of the Offline entry point
PrefixTerminate	The name of the Terminate entry point
PrefixLooksAlive	The name of the LooksAlive entry point
PrefixRelease	The name of the Release entry point or NULL
PrefixArbitrate	The name of the Arbitrate entry point or NULL
PrefixIsAlive	The name of the IsAlive entry point
PrefixResControl	The name of the ResourceControl entry point or NULL
PrefixResTypeControl	The name of the ResourceTypeControl entry point or NULL

CLRES_V1_FUNCTIONS

The **CLRES_V1_FUNCTIONS** structure contains pointers to all Resource API version 1.0 entry points except **Startup**. The **CLRES_VI_FUNCTIONS** structure is defined in RESAPI.H.

```
typedef struct _CLRES_V1_FUNCTIONS
        POPEN_ROUTINE Open;
        PCLOSE_ROUTINE Close;
        PONLINE_ROUTINE Online;
        POFFLINE_ROUTINE Offline;
        PTERMINATE_ROUTINE Terminate;
        PLOOKS_ALIVE_ROUTINE LooksAlive;
        PIS_ALIVE_ROUTINE IsAlive;
        PARBITRATE_ROUTINE Arbitrate;
        PRELEASE_ROUTINE Release;
        PRESOURCE_CONTROL_ROUTINE ResourceControl;
        PRESOURCE_TYPE_CONTROL_ROUTINE ResourceTypeControl
        } CLRES_V1_FUNCTIONS, *PCLRES_V1_FUNCTIONS;
```

where

Open is the pointer to the Open entry point.
Close is the pointer to the Close entry point.
Online is the pointer to the Online entry point.
Offline is the pointer to the Offline entry point.
Terminate is the pointer to the Terminate entry point.
LooksAlive is the pointer to the LooksAlive entry point.
IsAlive is the pointer to the IsAlive entry point.
Arbitrate is the pointer to the Arbitrate entry point.
Release is the pointer to the Release entry point.
ResourceControl is the pointer to the ResourceControl entry point.
ResourceTypeControl is the pointer to the ResourceTypeControl entry point.

Programming Notes
The CLRES_V1_FUNCTIONS structure is the function table that is returned by the **Startup** function in Resource API 1.0.

Except for the following entry points, there must be valid pointers (non-NULL) for all other Resource API entry point functions:

- **Arbitrate**
- **Release**
- **ResourceControl**
- **ResourceTypeControl**

Of these, only the first two members are guaranteed to be at the same offset within the CLRES_FUNCTION_TABLE structure. All other entries within this structure are dependent on the version of the Resource API.

RESOURCE_STATUS
The **RESOURCE_STATUS** structure contains information about a resource that is being brought online or taken offline. This structure is used as a parameter to the callback function **SetResource-Status**. The **RESOURCE_STATUS** structure is defined in RESAPI.H.

```
typedef struct_RESOURCE_STATUS {
        CLUSTER_RESOURCE_STATE ResourceState;
        DWORD CheckPoint;
        DWORD WaitHint;
        HANDLE EvntHnd;
        } RESOURCE_STATUS, *PRESOURCE_STATUS;
```

where
ResourceState is the value describing the state of a resource. Valid values follow:

Resource State Value	Description
ClusterResourceUnavailable	An error occurred trying to retrieve the state, typically because the server is no longer available; call the Win32 function GetLastError for more information
ClusterResourceOnline	The resource is online and available
ClusterResourceOffline	The resource is offline and unavailable
ClusterResourceFailed	The resource has failed
ClusterResourceOnlinePending	The resource is in the process of being placed online; the CheckPoint member should be greater than the previous value of this member
ClusterResourceOfflinePending	The resource is in the process of being put offline

CheckPoint is the value that increases sequentially by one whenever a new status is reported for the resource. The starting value for *CheckPoint* should be zero.
WaitHint is the number of msec expected until the next time that status is reported.
EvntHnd is the handle to an event that indicates when the resource has failed.

Programming Notes
Resource DLLs typically set the *ResourceState* member to ClusterResourceOnline or ClusterResourceOffline. However, if *ResourceState* is set to ClusterResourceOnlinePending or ClusterResourceOfflinePending, then the *CheckPoint* member should be greater than the previous value reported for *CheckPoint*.

Before returning the ClusterResourceUnavailable state in the *ResourceState* member, a resource DLL should call the Win32 function **SetLastError**.

Resource DLLs set the *EvntHnd* member to a handle that is signaled when a resource fails.

Appendix C
Cluster Utility Functions

INTRODUCTION

This appendix, along with Appendix A and Appendix B, supplements the information in Chapter 7 on cluster programming. This appendix deals with cluster utility functions. The cluster utility functions save programming time by providing shortcuts for implementing common programming tasks such as application or resource dynamic link library (DLL) tasks. Before you start serious cluster programming, it would be worth your while to check the available cluster utility functions.

The cluster utility functions are implemented in RESUTILS.DLL. The RESUTILS.DLL is the DLL that is provided with the Cluster Administrator. Your application and resource DLLs that want to use the cluster utility functions must include RESAPI.H in addition to the regular CLUSAPI.H. In addition, you should also link to RESUTILS.LIB.

For each function, a brief description, the actual function call syntax including all the parameters, a description of the parameters, the results of the function call, and programming notes are included.

CONVENTIONS USED

Function names are in bold and must be used as shown. Parameter values are in italics and the programmer can choose any variable name. Parameter keywords and keywords that are part of the function call are in capitals. Valid parameter and return values are shown with a reduced font (e.g., TRUE).

The call syntax of each function is provided and this is followed by:

- Input parameters to the function
- Input and Output parameters to the function
- Output parameters
- Return values
- Programming notes

Note: All five listed items may not be described for all the functions. These Application programming interfaces (APIs) are listed here in a format suitable for quick reference to supplement the cluster programming chapter. More detailed information about these APIs is available in Microsoft product documentation and Microsoft Development Network (MSDN).

Let us look at each of the cluster utility functions in detail.

ClusWorkerCreate

The **ClusWorkerCreate** utility function creates a worker thread. A worker thread is a thread that is created to offload work from a main thread so that the main thread is not blocked.

DWORD WINAPI**ClusWorkerCreate**(
    PCLUS_WORKER *Worker*,
    PWORKER_START_ROUTINE *lpStartAddr*,
    PVOID *lpParm*
    );

Input Parameters

lpStartAddr — Pointer to the address of a function that should be processed by the worker thread.

lpParm — Parameter to pass to the function whose address is pointed to by *lpStartAddr.*

Output Parameters

Worker — Pointer to a CLUS_WORKER structure that is filled in with a handle to the created thread and a flag that indicates whether or not the handle should be terminated. For more details about the CLUS_WORKER structure, see programming notes later.

Return Values

ERROR_SUCCESS — The operation was successful and the thread was created successfully.

If the operation was unsuccessful, **ClusWorkerCreate** returns a Win32 error value.

Programming Notes

You normally should never have to refer to or change the members of the CLUS_WORKER structure. The CLUS_WORKER structure contains information about a worker thread. The CLUS_WORKER structure is shown next.

```
typedef struct_CLUS_WORKER {
        HANDLE hThread;
        BOOL Terminate;
        } CLUS_WORKER;
```

where

hThread is the handle to the worker thread and *Terminate* is a flag that indicates whether or not the thread is to be terminated.

The CLUS_WORKER structure is defined in RESAPI.H.

ClusWorkerCheckTerminate

The **ClusWorkerCheckTerminate** function determines whether or not a worker thread should exit as soon as possible.

```
BOOL WINAPI ClusWorkerCheckTerminate(
        PCLUS_WORKER Worker
        );
```

Input Parameters

Worker — Pointer to a CLUS_WORKER structure that describes the thread to be checked. For more details about the CLUS_WORKER structure, see previous programming notes for **ClusWorkerCreate**.

Return Values

TRUE — The thread should terminate.

FALSE — The thread should not terminate.

Programming Notes
ClusWorkerCheckTerminate determines whether or not the thread pointed to by *Worker* should exit by checking the Terminate member of the CLUS_WORKER structure. The Terminate member is used to perform an orderly and efficient termination when multiple threads call **ClusWorkerCheckTerminate** on the same worker thread. The first call sets Terminate to TRUE. The second and subsequent calls check that Terminate is set and return immediately without waiting for the worker thread to exit.

ClusWorkerTerminate
The **ClusWorkerTerminate** utility function terminates a worker thread.

VOID WINAPI **ClusWorkerTerminate**(
PCLUS_WORKER *Worker*
);

Input Parameters
Worker — Pointer to a CLUS_WORKER structure that describes the thread to be checked. For more details about the CLUS_WORKER structure, see earlier programming notes for **ClusWorkerCreate**.

Return Values
This function has no return values.

Programming Notes
ClusWorkerTerminate checks the hThread and Terminate members of the CLUS_WORKER structure pointed to by *Worker*. If hThread is non-NULL and Terminate is set to FALSE, then this is the first call to **ClusWorkerTerminate**. In this case, the function waits for the thread to exit before returning. Otherwise, **ClusWorkerTerminate** has been called previously and the Terminate member would have been set to TRUE. In this case, the function may return before the thread has terminated.

ResUtilAddUnknownProperties
The **ResUtilAddUnknownProperties** utility function adds unknown properties for a given object to the end of a property list. Unknown properties are properties that are specific to a resource, but foreign to the resource DLL.

DWORD WINAPI **ResUtilAddUnknownProperties**(
PVOID *ClustKey*,
Const PRESUTIL_PROPERTY_ITEM *PropTabl*,
PVOID *OutBuf*,
DWORD *OutBufSz*,
LPDWORD *BytesRet*,
LPDWORD *Reqd*
);

Input Parameters
ClustKey — Pointer to the cluster database key that identifies the location where the unknown properties are to be added.
PropTabl — Pointer to an array of RESUTIL_PROPERTY_ITEM structures describing known properties. A property table is defined as an array of RESUTIL_PROPERTY_ITEM

structures. Many of the Cluster Resource Utility functions use property tables as input or output parameters. For more details about the RESUTIL_PROPERTY_ITEM structure, see programming notes later.

OutBufSz — Size of the property list pointed to by *OutBuf.*

Parameters that are both Input and Output

OutBuf — Pointer to a property list to which the unknown properties are appended.

BytesRet — On input, this parameter points to the number of bytes in use in the property list pointed to by *OutBuf.* On output, this parameter points to the total number of bytes in the property list pointed to by *OutBuf.*

Reqd — Pointer to the required number of bytes if the property list is too small to hold the unknown properties.

Return Values

ERROR_SUCCESS — The operation was successful and the unknown properties were added successfully.

ERROR_NOT_ENOUGH_MEMORY — The operation was unable to allocate enough memory.

If the operation was unsuccessful, **ResUtilAddUnknownProperties** returns a Win32 error value.

Programming Notes

ResUtilAddUnknownProperties reads unknown properties directly from the cluster database without involving the resource DLL. Bypassing the resource DLL permits a resource to be extended by another resource or an application. Unknown properties are private properties. Unknown common properties are not allowed.

The RESUTIL_PROPERTY_ITEM structure contains information about a property and is used in the following ways:

- Building or parsing a property list
- Reading or updating properties
- Serving an entry in a property table

The RESUTIL_PROPERTY_ITEM structure is shown next.

```
typedef struct_RESUTIL_PROPERTY_ITEM {
        LPWSTR Name;
        LPWSTR KeyName;
        DWORD Format;
        DWORD Default;
        DWORD Minimum;
        DWORD Maximum;
        DWORD Flags;
        DWORD Offset;
        } RESUTIL_PROPERTY_ITEM;
```

where

Name is the name of the property described in the structure.

KeyName is the name of the cluster database subkey for the property.

Format is the format of the property such as CLUSPROP_FORMAT_BINARY or CLUSPROP_FORMAT_DWORD (see CLUSPROP_SYNTAX for a list of valid format values).
Default is the default data value for the property.
Minimum is the minimum data value for the property. For data values with the CLUSPROP_FORMAT_BINARY and CLUSPROP_FORMAT_MULTI_SZ formats, the Minimum member contains the size in bytes of the default data value specified by Default.
Maximum is the maximum data value for the property.
Flags contain the bitmask that describes the property. Valid values are RESUTIL_PROPITEM_READ_ONLY and RESUTIL_PROPITEM_REQUIRED.
Offset is the byte offset to the property data in a buffer known as a parameter block.

The type of data in the parameter block differs depending on its format, as indicated by the Format member. For example, if the Format member is set to CLUSPROP_FORMAT_DWORD, the data in the parameter block referenced by Offset is a DWORD value.

The RESUTIL_PROPERTY_ITEM structure is defined in RESAPI.H.

ResUtilDupParameterBlock

The **ResUtilDupParameterBlock** utility function duplicates a parameter block. A parameter block is a buffer or structure that contains the data or pointers to data for the properties described in a property table.

DWORD WINAPI **ResUtilDupParameterBlock**(
        LPBYTE *OutParms*,
    Const LPBYTE *InParms*,
    Const PRESUTIL_PROPERTY_ITEM *PropTabl*
        );

Input Parameters

InParms — Pointer to the original parameter block.
PropTabl — Pointer to an array of RESUTIL_PROPERTY_ITEM structures describing properties in the original parameter block. For more details about the RESUTIL_PROPERTY_ITEM structure, see the earlier programming notes for **ResUtilAddUnknownProperties**.

Output Parameters

OutParms — Pointer to the duplicated parameter block

Return Values

ERROR_SUCCESS — The operation was successful and the parameter block was duplicated successfully.

If the operation was unsuccessful, **ResUtilDupParameterBlock** returns a Win32 error value.

Programming Notes

ResUtilDupParameterBlock copies the data found in the input parameter block pointed to by *InParms* to the output parameter block pointed to by *OutParms*. For simple variables, this is just a simple copy. If, however, a variable in the parameter block is a pointer, memory for the data is allocated using the Win32 function **LocalAlloc**. The responsibility for freeing this allocated memory is yours and you can do it in one of two ways. You can deallocate this memory by calling either **LocalFree** for each pointer variable in the output parameter block or by calling **ResUtilFreePa-**

rameterBlock. You must make sure that you deallocate memory whether **ResUtilDupParameterBlock** succeeds or fails.

ResUtilDupString

The **ResUtilDupString** utility function duplicates a character string.

```
PWSTR WINAPI ResUtilDupString(
                LPCWSTR Val
                );
```

Input Parameters

Val — Pointer to the string to be duplicated

Return Values

If the operation was successful, **ResUtilDupString** returns a pointer to a buffer containing the duplicate string.

If the operation was unsuccessful, **ResUtilDupString** returns null.

Programming Notes

If the operation was unsuccessful and you need additional information about the error, call the Win32 function **GetLastError**.

ResUtilEnumPrivateProperties

The **ResUtilEnumPrivateProperties** utility function enumerates the private properties of a resource.

```
DWORD WINAPI ResUtilEnumPrivateProperties(
                PVOID ClustKey,
                PVOID OutBuf,
                DWORD OutBufSz,
                LPDWORD BytesRet,
                LPDWORD Reqd
                );
```

Input Parameters

ClustKey — Key that identifies the location of the private properties in the cluster database

OutBufSz — Size of the output buffer pointed to by *OutBuf*

Output Parameters

OutBuf — Pointer to an output buffer containing the names of the enumerated properties

BytesRet — Pointer to the total number of bytes returned in the output buffer

Reqd — Pointer to the required number of bytes if the output buffer is too small to hold all of the enumerated properties

Return Values

ERROR_SUCCESS — The enumeration was successful.

ERROR_BAD_ARGUMENTS — One or more of the input parameters were invalid.

ResUtilEnumProperties

The **ResUtilEnumProperties** utility function enumerates the properties of a resource.

```
DWORD WINAPI ResUtilEnumProperties(
```

```
Const   PRESUTIL_PROPERTY_ITEM PropTabl,
        PVOID OutBuf,
        DWORD OutBufSz,
        LPDWORD BytesRet,
        LPDWORD Reqd
        );
```

Input Parameters

PropTabl — Pointer to an array of RESUTIL_PROPERTY_ITEM structures describing the properties to be enumerated. For more details about the RESUTIL_PROPERTY_ITEM structure, see the earlier programming notes for **ResUtilAddUnknownProperties**.

OutBufSz — Size in bytes of the output buffer pointed to by *OutBuf.*

Output Parameters

OutBuf — Pointer to the output buffer in which to return the names of all the properties. The properties are returned in multiple string format. Each property name is stored as a null-terminated string and the last property name is followed by a final terminating null character.

BytesRet — Pointer to the total number of bytes in the property list pointed to by *OutBuf.*

Reqd — Number of bytes required if the output buffer is too small.

Return Values

ERROR_SUCCESS — The enumeration was successful.

ERROR_BAD_ARGUMENTS — One or more of the input parameters were invalid.

ResUtilEnumResources

The **ResUtilEnumResources** utility function enumerates all the resources in a cluster. It also initiates an operation on each resource.

```
DWORD WINAPI ResUtilEnumResources(
        HRESOURCE hSelf,
        LPCWSTR lpszResTypName,
        LPRESOURCE_CALLBACK pResCallBck,
        PVOID pParm
        );
```

Input Parameters

hSelf — Handle to a resource. **ResUtilEnumResources** enumerates all the resources in the cluster to which the resource with the handle *hSelf* belongs. This parameter is optional.

lpszResTypName — Pointer to a name of a resource type. This parameter is used to narrow the scope of resources to be enumerated. If *lpszResTypName* is specified, only resources of the specified type are enumerated. This parameter is optional.

pResCallBck — Pointer to the **ResourceCallback** function to call for each resource, or for each resource that matches the filter specified by *lpszResTypName.*

pParm — Parameter to be passed to the **ResourceCallback** function.

Return Values

ERROR_SUCCESS — The enumeration was successful and subsequent calls to the resource callback functions were successful.

error_no_more_items — All the resources have been enumerated and there are no more resources left.

If the operation was unsuccessful, **ResUtilEnunResources** also returns a Win32 error.

Programming Notes

ResUtilEnumResources opens the current cluster by calling **OpenCluster** and returns a resource enumeration handle by calling **ClusterOpenEnum** with the *dwType* parameter set to CLUSTER_ENUM_RESOURCE.

ResUtilEnumResources invokes the **ResourceCallback** function for a resource only when the *hSelf* parameter is NULL. When *hSelf* is set to a valid resource handle, **ResourceCallback** is not invoked for the resource identified by *hSelf.* Another instance when **ResourceCallback** is not invoked is when *lpszResTypName* is specified. In this case, **ResourceCallback** is called only for resources of the specified type.

The type of tasks performed by **ResourceCallback** depends on the resource type. For example, Cluster Server print spooler resource DLL may check to ensure that the group for the resource contains only a single print spooler resource.

ResUtilFindDwordProperty

The **ResUtilFindDwordProperty** utility function locates a numerical property in a property list.

```
DWORD WINAPI ResUtilFindDwordProperty(
        Const   PVOID Buf,
                DWORD BufSz,
                LPCWSTR PropNam,
                LPDWORD FndDword
                );
```

Input Parameters

Buf — Pointer to the value list in which to locate the numerical value
BufSz — Size, in bytes, of the data in the buffer
PropNam — Pointer to the name of the value to be located
FndDword — Pointer to the located numerical value

Return Values

ERROR_SUCCESS — The attempt to locate the value was successful.
ERROR_INVALID_DATA — The data format is incorrect.
ERROR_FILE_NOT_FOUND — The numerical property could not be located in the property list.

ResUtilFindSzProperty

The **ResUtilFindSzProperty** utility function locates a string property in a property list.

```
DWORD WINAPI ResUtilFindSzProperty(
        Const   PVOID Buf,
                DWORD BufSz,
                LPCWSTR PropNam,
                LPWSTR *FndStrng
                );
```

Input Parameters

Buf — Pointer to the property list in which to locate the string property
BufSz — Size, in bytes, of the data in the Buffer
PropNam — Pointer to the name of the string property to be located
FndStrng — Pointer to the value from the property list containing the string property pointed to by *PropNam*

Return Values

ERROR_SUCCESS — The attempt to locate the string was successful.
ERROR_NOT_ENOUGH_MEMORY — Insufficient memory to complete the operation.
ERROR_INVALID_DATA — The data format is incorrect.
ERROR_FILE_NOT_FOUND — The string property could not be located in the value list.

ResUtilFreeParameterBlock

The **ResUtilFreeParameterBlock** utility function deallocates memory that has been allocated for a parameter block.

```
void WINAPI ResUtilFreeParameterBlock(
                LPBYTE OutParms,
        Const   LPBYTE InParms,
        Const   PRESUTIL_PROPERTY_ITEM PropTabl
                );
```

Input Parameters

InParms — Pointer to the parameter block to use as a reference.
PropTabl — Pointer to an array of RESUTIL_PROPERTY_ITEM structures describing the properties in the input parameter block. For more details about the RESUTIL_PROPERTY_ITEM structure, see the earlier programming notes for **ResUtilAddUnknownProperties**.

Parameters that are both Input and Output

OutParms — Pointer to the parameter block to deallocate

Return Values

None

Programming Notes

ResUtilFreeParameterBlock deallocates any memory allocated for a variable that is a member of the output parameter block. However, the member to be deallocated must not also be pointed to by the input parameter block.

ResUtilGetAllProperties

The **ResUtilGetAllProperties** utility function returns a property list for a cluster object. The property list includes all the default and unknown properties for the cluster object.

```
DWORD WINAPI ResUtilGetAllProperties(
                PVOID ClustKey,
        Const   PRESUTIL_PROPERTY_ITEM PropTabl,
                PVOID OutBuf,
                DWORD OutBufSz,
                LPDWORD BytesRet,
                LPDWORD Reqd
                );
```

Input Parameters

ClustKey — Pointer to the cluster key that contains the location of the properties to retrieve.

PropTabl — Pointer to an array of RESUTIL_PROPERTY_ITEM structures that describe the properties to be retrieved. For more details about the RESUTIL_PROPERTY_ITEM structure, see the earlier programming notes for **ResUtilAddUnknownProperties**.
OutBufSz — Size of the output buffer pointed to by *OutBuf*, in bytes.

Output Parameters
OutBuf — Pointer to an output buffer in which to return the property list
BytesRet — Pointer to the total number of bytes returned in the property list pointed to by *OutBuf*
Reqd — Pointer to the actual number of bytes required, if *OutBuf* is too small

Return Values
ERROR_SUCCESS — The requested properties were returned successfully.
ERROR_BAD_ARGUMENTS — One or more of the input parameters were invalid.
ERROR_NOT_ENOUGH_MEMORY — Enough memory was not allocated.

If the operation was unsuccessful, **ResUtilGetAllProperties** also returns a Win32 error value.

Programming Notes
ResUtilGetAllProperties makes an entry in the property list for each property that is either included in the property table or included in the cluster database below the key identified by the *ClustKey* parameter (regardless of whether or not the property is included in the property table).

ResUtilGetBinaryValue
The **ResUtilGetBinaryValue** utility function returns a binary value from the cluster database. It combines the tasks of allocating memory and calling the appropriate Cluster API.

```
DWORD WINAPI ResUtilGetBinaryValue(
                HKEY ClustKey,
                LPCWSTR ValNam,
                LPBYTE * OutVal,
                DWORD * OutValSz
                );
```

Input Parameters
ClustKey — Cluster database Key that identifies the location of the value to be retrieved.
ValNam — Pointer to the name of the value to be retrieved

Output Parameters
OutVal — Address of the pointer to the retrieved value
OutValSz — Pointer to a DWORD in which the size (in bytes) of the buffer pointed to by *OutVal* is returned

Return Values
ERROR_SUCCESS — The database value was returned successfully.
ERROR_NOT_ENOUGH_MEMORY — Enough memory was not allocated.

If the operation was not successful, **ResUtilGetBinaryValue** can return the Win32 error codes that are returned by **ClusterRegQueryValue**.

Programming Notes
ResUtilGetBinaryValue performs the following:

- Allocates the necessary memory for the value
- Calls the Cluster API function ClusterRegQueryValue

However, the memory that has been allocated is not freed and must be freed by you when you are finished using the allocated memory. You can call the Win32 function **LocalFree** to release the memory.

ResUtilGetDwordValue
The **ResUtilGetDwordValue** utility function returns a numeric value from the cluster database. **ResUtilGetDwordValue** calls the Cluster API function ClusterRegQueryValue to retrieve the numerical value.

```
DWORD WINAPI ResUtilGetDwordValue(
        HKEY ClustKey,
        LPCWSTR ValNam,
        LPDWORD OutVal,
        DWORD DefVal
        );
```

Input Parameters
ClustKey — Key identifying the location of the numerical value in the cluster database
ValNam — Pointer to the name of the value to be retrieved
DefVal – Default value to be returned if the value pointed to by *ValNam* is not found

Output Parameters
OutVal — Pointer to the retrieved value

Return Values
ERROR_SUCCESS — The operation was successful.
ERROR_INVALID_PARAMETER — The value pointed to by *ValNam* is not a numerical value.

If the operation was not successful, **ResUtilGetDwordValue** can return the Win32 error codes that are returned by **ClusterRegQueryValue**.

ResUtilGetEnvironmentWithNetName
The **ResUtilGetEnvironmentWithNetName** utility function creates an environment block that appends a CLUSTER_NETWORK_NAME environment variable to the current environment block.

```
LPVOID WINAPI ResUtilGetEnvironmentWithNetName(
        HRESOURCE hRes
        );
```

Input Parameters
hRes — Handle to the resource used to set the CLUSTER_NETWORK_NAME environment variable

Return Values

If the operation was successful, **ResUtilGetEnvironmentWithNetName** returns a pointer to the new environment block.

If the operation was unsuccessful, **ResUtilGetEnvironmentWithNetName** returns NULL.

Programming Notes

Handle to the resource pointed by *hRes* is dependent on the network name resource and the environment variable that is appended to the current environment block is set to the name property of the network name resource for the resource identified by *hRes*. You can then pass this environment block to the Win32 function **CreateProcess** to create an environment for Cluster Server operations.

If the operation was unsuccessful and you need additional information about the error, call the Win32 function **GetLastError**.

ResUtilGetMultiSzValue

The **ResUtilGetMultiSzValue** utility function returns a multiple string value from the cluster database.

```
DWORD WINAPI ResUtilGetMultiSzValue(
                    HKEY ClustKey,
                    LPCWSTR ValNam,
                    LPBYTE * OutVal,
                    LPDWORD OutValSz
                    );
```

Input Parameters

ClustKey — Key identifying the location of the multiple string value in the cluster database

ValNam — Pointer to the name of the value to be retrieved

Output Parameters

OutVal — Address of the pointer to the retrieved value.

OutValSz — Pointer to a DWORD that contains the size of the buffer pointed to by *OutVal* is returned. The buffer size is in bytes.

Return Values

ERROR_SUCCESS — The operation was successful.

ERROR_NOT_ENOUGH_MEMORY — Enough memory was not allocated.

If the operation was not successful, **ResUtilGetMultiSzValue** may return Win32 error codes returned by **ClusterRegQueryValue**.

Programming Notes

As with some of the earlier functions, it is your responsibility to release the memory allocated for the value, by calling the Win32 function **LocalFree**.

ResUtilGetPrivateProperties

The **ResUtilGetPrivateProperties** utility function returns the private properties of a resource.

```
DWORD WINAPI ResUtilGetPrivateProperties(
                    PVOID ClustKey,
                    PVOID OutBuf,
                    DWORD OutBufSz,
                    LPDWORD BytesRet,
```

```
                    LPDWORD Reqd
                    );
```

Input Parameters

ClustKey — Pointer to the cluster database key that identifies the location of the private properties to be retrieved

OutBufSz — Size of the output buffer pointed to by *OutBuf*

Output Parameters

OutBuf — Pointer to an output buffer in which a property list with the names and values of the private properties is returned

BytesRet — Pointer to the total number of bytes in the property list pointed to by *OutBuf*

Reqd — Pointer to the actual number of bytes required if the OutBuffer is too small to hold all the private properties

Return Values

ERROR_SUCCESS — The operation was successful and the private properties were returned.

ERROR_BAD_ARGUMENTS — One or more of the input parameters were invalid.

ERROR_NOT_ENOUGH_MEMORY — Enough memory was not allocated.

If the operation was unsuccessful, **ResUtilGetPrivateProperties** returns a Win32 error value.

ResUtilGetProperties

The **ResUtilGetProperties** utility function returns a property list containing specified properties for a cluster object.

```
DWORD WINAPI ResUtilGetProperties(
                    PVOID ClustKey,
          Const     PRESUTIL_PROPERTY_ITEM PropTabl,
                    PVOID OutBuf,
                    DWORD OutBufSz,
                    LPDWORD BytesRet,
                    LPDWORD Reqd
                    );
```

Input Parameters

ClustKey — Pointer to the cluster database key that identifies the location of the properties to be retrieved.

PropTabl — Pointer to an array of RESUTIL_PROPERTY_ITEM structures that describe the properties to be retrieved. For more details about the RESUTIL_PROPERTY_ITEM structure, see the earlier programming notes for **ResUtilAddUnknownProperties**.

OutBufSz — Size in bytes of the output buffer pointed to by *OutBuf*.

Output Parameters

OutBuf — Pointer to an output buffer that returns the property list

BytesRet — Pointer to the total number of bytes in the property list pointed to by *OutBuf*

Reqd — Pointer to the actual number of bytes required, if OutBuffer is too small to contain the returned properties

Return Values

ERROR_SUCCESS — The operation was successful and the requested properties were returned.
ERROR_BAD_ARGUMENTS — One or more of the input parameters were invalid.
ERROR_NOT_ENOUGH_MEMORY — Enough memory was not allocated.

If the operation was unsuccessful, **ResUtilGetProperties** returns a Win32 error value.

ResUtilGetPropertiesToParameterBlock

The **ResUtilGetPropertiesToParameterBlock** utility function returns properties and stores them in a parameter block.

```
DWORD WINAPI ResUtilGetPropertiesToParameterBlock(
              PVOID ClustKey,
        Const PRESUTIL_PROPERTY_ITEM PropTabl,
              LPBYTES OutParms,
              BOOL ChkReqdProp,
              LPWSTR *ErrProp
              );
```

Input Parameters

ClustKey — Pointer to the cluster database key that identifies the location of the properties to be retrieved.

PropTabl — Pointer to an array of RESUTIL_PROPERTY_ITEM structures that describe the properties to be processed. For more details about the RESUTIL_PROPERTY_ITEM structure, see the earlier programming notes for **ResUtilAddUnknownProperties.**

ChkReqdProp — Specifies whether or not an error should be generated if required properties are missing.

Output Parameters

OutParms — Pointer to the output parameter block to be filled with returned properties

ErrProp — Address of the string pointer in which to return the name of the error generated by a missing required property

Return Values

ERROR_SUCCESS — The operation was successful and properties were successfully stored in the parameter block.
ERROR_BAD_ARGUMENTS — One or more of the input parameters were invalid.
ERROR_NOT_ENOUGH_MEMORY — Enough memory was not allocated.

If the operation was unsuccessful, **ResUtilGetPropertiesToParameterBlock** returns a Win32 error value.

Programming Notes

The *ErrProp* parameter is optional and needs to be specified only if you are checking for required properties. The property table pointed to by *PropTabl* can include default values.

ResUtilGetProperty

The **ResUtilGetProperty** utility function returns a specified property.

```
DWORD WINAPI ResUtilGetProperty(
              PVOID ClustKey,
        Const PRESUTIL_PROPERTY_ITEM Prop,
              PVOID *OutBuf,
```

```
                LPDWORD OutBufSz
                );
```

Input Parameters
ClustKey — Pointer to the cluster database key identifying the location of the property to be retrieved.
Prop — Pointer to a RESUTIL_PROPERTY_ITEM structure that describes the property to be retrieved. For more details about the RESUTIL_PROPERTY_ITEM structure, see the earlier programming notes for **ResUtilAddUnknownProperties**.

Parameters that are both Input and Output
OutBufSz — Pointer to the size in bytes of the output buffer pointed to by *OutBuf*

Output Parameters
OutBuf — Pointer to an output buffer in which to return the requested property

Return Values
ERROR_SUCCESS — The operation was successful and the specified property was successfully retrieved.
ERROR_BAD_ARGUMENTS — One or more of the input parameters were invalid.

ResUtilGetPropertySize
The **ResUtilGetPropertySize** utility function returns the size (in bytes) required for a specified property.

```
DWORD WINAPI ResUtilGetPropertySize(
                PVOID ClustKey,
        Const   PRESUTIL_PROPERTY_ITEM Prop,
                LPDWORD BufSz,
                LPDWORD ItemCnt
                );
```

Input Parameters
ClustKey — Cluster database key identifying the location of the property whose size is required
Prop — Pointer to a RESUTIL_PROPERTY_ITEM structure describing the property whose size is required

For more details about the RESUTIL_PROPERTY_ITEM structure, see the earlier programming notes for **ResUtilAddUnknownProperties**.

Parameters that are both Input and Output
BufSz — Pointer to the total number of bytes required for the property value. The number of bytes returned includes the CLUSPROP_VALUE structure and the data. For more details about the CLUSPROP_VALUE structure, see later programming notes.
ItemCnt — Pointer to the total number of properties. This value is incremented to include this property if **ResUtilGetPropertySize** is successful.

Return Values
ERROR_SUCCESS —The operation was successful and the size of the property was successfully retrieved.
ERROR_BAD_ARGUMENTS — One or more of the input parameters were invalid.

Programming Notes
The CLUSPROP_VALUE structure is used to describe the format, type, and length of a data value used in a value list. The CLUSPROP_VALUE structure is used as a generic header in all the structures that describe data of a particular type, such as CLUSPROP_BINARY and CLUSPROP_SZ.

```
typedef struct_CLUSPROP_VALUE {
        CLUSPROP_SYNTAX Syntax;
        DWORD cbLength;
        } CLUSPROP_VALUE;
```

where

Syntax is the CLUSPROP_SYNTAX union that describes a value.
cbLength is the count of bytes in the data that follow this CLUSPROP_VALUE structure. This count does not include the value header. It is an actual byte count. If there is padding to fulfill the DWORD boundary requirement, the padding characters are not included in *cbLength*. To move past the data in a single entry in the property list, use the ALIGN_CLUSPROP macro that rounds up to the next DWORD value in the list.

The CLUSPROP_VALUE structure is defined in CLUSAPI.H.

ResUtilGetResourceDependency
The **ResUtilGetResourceDependency** utility function returns a handle to a dependent resource of a specified type. This utility function loops through all available dependent resources of a given resource and selects the dependent resource of the specified type.

```
HRESOURCE WINAPI ResUtilGetResourceDependency(
                 HANDLE hSelf,
                 LPCWSTR lpszResType
                 );
```

Input Parameters
hSelf — Handle to the resource on which the dependent resource depends
lpszResType — Pointer to the type of the dependent resource

Return Values
If the operation was successful, **ResUtilGetResourceDependency** returns a handle to the dependent resource.
If the operation was unsuccessful, **ResUtilGetResourceDependency** returns NULL.

Programming Notes
You are responsible for closing the handle to the dependent resource returned by **ResUtilGetResourceDependency** by calling **CloseClusterResource**.

If the operation was unsuccessful and you need additional information about the error, call the Win32 function **GetLastError**.

ResUtilGetResourceDependency uses a number of Cluster APIs and loops through available resources. This function sets up an enumerator for the resource identified by *hSelf* by calling **ClusterResourceOpenEnum**. The dwType parameter of **ClusterResourceOpenEnum** is set to

CLUSTER_RESOURCE_ENUM_DEPENDS. It then calls **ClusterResourceEnum** to enumerate a dependent resource and **OpenClusterResource** to open the enumerated resource. It then calls **ResUtilResourceTypesEqual** to compare the type of the enumerated resource with the type pointed to by *lpszResType*. If the types match, the handle to the dependent resource is returned. If the types do not match, this function continues its search with the remaining dependent resources.

ResUtilGetResourceNameDependency

The **ResUtilGetResourceNameDependency** utility function returns a handle to a dependent resource with a specified name and type. This function performs the same function as the previous function **ResUtilGetResourceDependency**, with the exception that you pass the name instead of a handle for the resource whose dependents you are searching for.

```
HRESOURCE WINAPI ResUtilGetResourceNameDependency(
                        LPCWSTR lpszResNam,
                        LPCWSTR lpszResType
                        );
```

Input Parameters

lpszResNam — Pointer to the name of the resource whose dependents are to be retrieved
lpszResType — Pointer to the type of the dependent resource to be retrieved

Return Values

If the operation was successful, **ResUtilGetResourceNameDependency** returns a handle to the dependent resource.

If the operation was unsuccessful, **ResUtilGetResourceNameDependency** returns null.

Programming Notes

You are responsible for closing the handle to the dependent resource returned by **ResUtilGetResourceNameDependency** by calling **CloseClusterResource**.

If the operation was unsuccessful and you need additional information about the error, call the Win32 function **GetLastError**.

This function works exactly in the same way as **ResUtilGetResourceDependency** (see earlier), with the exception that the resource name (instead of a resource handle) is used to locate the resource whose dependents you are searching for.

ResUtilGetSzValue

The **ResUtilGetSzValue** utility function allocates memory and retrieves a string value from the cluster database.

```
LPWSTR WINAPI ResUtilGetSzValue(
                    HKEY ClustKey,
                    LPCWSTR ValNam
                    );
```

Input Parameters

ClustKey — Key identifying the location of the value in the cluster database that is to be retrieved
ValNam — Name of the value to be retrieved

Return Values

If the operation was successful, **ResUtilGetSzValue** returns a pointer to a buffer containing the string value.

If the operation was unsuccessful, **ResUtilGetSzValue** returns NULL.

Programming Notes

If the operation was unsuccessful and you need additional information about the error, call the Win32 function **GetLastError**.

After allocating the necessary memory for the string parameter value, **ResUtilGetSzValue** calls the Cluster API function **ClusterRegQueryValue** to access the cluster database. Although **ResUtilGetSzValue** allocates memory to hold the value retrieved from the database, the responsibility for freeing this allocated memory is yours. You can call the Win32 function **LocalFree** to release the allocated memory.

ResUtilInitializeResourceStatus

The **ResUtilInitializeResourceStatus** utility function initializes a RESOURCE_STATUS structure.

VOID WINAPI **ResUtilInitializeResourceStatus**(
PRESOURCE_STATUS *ResStat*
);

Input Parameters

ResStat — Pointer to the RESOURCE_STATUS structure to be initialized. For more details about the RESOURCE_STATUS structure, please refer to the programming notes.

Return Values

None

Programming Notes

The RESOURCE_STATUS structure contains information about a resource that is being brought online or taken offline. This structure is used as a parameter to the callback function **Set ResourceStatus**.

typedef struct _RESOURCE_STATUS {
CLUSTER_RESOURCE_STATE *ResourceState*;
DWORD *CheckPoint*;
DWORD *WaitHint*;
HANDLE *EventHandle*;
} RESOURCE_STATUS;

where

ResourceState is a value describing the state of a resource. Valid values are listed in the following table.

CheckPoint is a value that increases sequentially by one whenever a new status is reported for the resource. The starting value for CheckPoint should be zero.

WaitHint is the number of milliseconds expected until the next time that status is reported.

EventHandle is the handle to an event that indicates when the resource has failed.

The RESOURCE_STATUS structure is defined in RESAPI.H.

Resource State Value	Description
ClusterResourceUnavailable	An error occurred trying to retrieve the state, typically because the server is no longer available; the caller should call the Win32 function **GetLastError** for more information
ClusterResourceOnline	The resource is online and available
ClusterResourceOffline	The resource is offline and unavailable
ClusterResourceFailed	The resource has failed
ClusterResourceOnlinePending	The resource is in the process of being placed online; the CheckPoint member should be greater than the previous value of this member
ClusterResourceOfflinePending	The resource is in the process of being put offline

ResUtilIsPathValid
The **ResUtilIsPathValid** utility function is used to check whether or not the syntax of a path is valid.

BOOL WINAPI**ResUtilIsPathValid**(
LPCWSTR *Path*
);

Input Parameters
Path — Pointer to the path to be syntax checked

Return Values
TRUE — The path pointed to by *Path* is valid.
FALSE — The path pointed to by *Path* is not valid.

Programming Notes
ResUtilIsPathValid does not check for the validity of paths that span networks.

ResUtilOpenDriver
The **ResUtilOpenDriver** utility function opens an Input/Output (I/O) driver.

DWORD WINAPI **ResUtilOpenDriver**(
HANDLE **Hnd*,
LPWSTR *DrvrNam*
);

Input Parameters
DrvrNam — Pointer to the name of the I/O driver to be opened

Output Parameters
Hnd — Pointer of a handle to the opened driver

Return Values
ERROR_SUCCESS — The operation completed successfully and the handle to the opened I/O driver has been returned.

If the operation was unsuccessful, **ResUtilOpenDriver** returns a Win32 error value.

ResUtilPropertyListFromParameterBlock

The **ResUtilPropertyListFromParameterBlock** utility function constructs a property list from a parameter block.

DWORD WINAPI **ResUtilPropertyListFromParamcterBlock**(
    Const PRESUTIL_PROPERTY_ITEM *PropTabl*,
        PVOID *OutBuf*,
        DWORD *OutBufSz*,
    Const LPBYTE *InParms*,
        LPDWORD *BytesRet*,
        LPDWORD *Reqd*
        );

Input Parameters

PropTabl — Pointer to an array of RESUTIL_PROPERTY_ITEM structures that describes the parameter block to be processed. For more details about the RESUTIL_PROPERTY_ITEM structure, see the earlier programming notes for **ResUtilAddUnknownProperties**.

OutBufSz — Size of the output buffer.

InParms — Parameter block containing the properties to be used in the construction of the property list.

Output Parameters

OutBuf — Pointer to an output buffer. The output buffer contains the constructed property list with the names and values of the properties in the parameter block.

BytesRet — Pointer to the total number of bytes in the property list pointed to by *OutBuf*.

Reqd — Pointer to the number of bytes that is required if the Output Buffer is too small to hold the properties from the parameter block.

Return Values

ERROR SUCCESS — The operation was successful and the properties list was constructed successfully.

ERROR_BAD_ARGUMENTS — One or more of the input parameters were invalid.

ERROR_NOT_ENOUGH_MEMORY — Not enough memory was allocated.

If the operation was unsuccessful, **ResUtilPropertyListFromParameterBlock** returns a Win32 error value.

ResUtilResourcesEqual

The **ResUtilResourcesEqual** utility function tests whether or not two resource handles represent the same resource by retrieving and comparing the resource names.

BOOL WINAPI**ResUtilResourcesEqual**(
        HRESOURCE *hSelf*,
        HRESOURCE *hRes*
        );

Input Parameters

hSelf, hRes — Handles to the resources to be compared

Return Values
TRUE — The resources are the same.
FALSE — The resources are not the same.

Programming Notes
ResUtilResourcesEqual performs the following:

- **ResUtilResourcesEqual** retrieves the resource names by passing the CLUSCTL_RESOURCE_GET_NAME control code to the **ClusterResourceControl** function.
- It compares the retrieved resource names.
- If the names are the same, the resources are equal.

ResUtilResourceTypesEqual
The **ResUtilResourceTypesEqual** utility function checks to see if a given resource type matches the resource type name of a specified resource.

BOOL WINAPI**ResUtilResourcesTypesEqual**(
LPCWSTR *lpszResTypNam*,
HRESOURCE *hRes*
);

Input Parameters
lpszResTypNam — Pointer to the name of the resource type name to be checked
hRes — Handle of the resource whose type is to be checked against

Return Values
TRUE— The resource types are the same.
FALSE— The resources types are not the same.

Programming Notes
ResUtilResourceTypesEqual performs the following:

- **ResUtilResourceTypesEqual** retrieves the resource type by passing the CLUSCTL_RESOURCE_GET_RESOURCE_TYPE control code to the **ClusterResourceControl** function.
- **ResUtilResourceTypesEqual** compares the resource type name pointed to by *lpszResTypNam* with the resource type name of the resource identified by *hRes*.
- If the two resource type names are the same, **ResUtilResourceTypesEqual** returns true.

ResUtilResourceTypesEqual compares the resource type name and not the resource type display name.

ResUtilSetBinaryValue
The **ResUtilSetBinaryValue** utility function sets a binary value in the cluster database.

DWORD WINAPI **ResUtilSetBinaryValue**(
HKEY *ClustKey*,
LPCWSTR *ValNam*,

```
Const   LPBYTE NewVal,
        DWORD NewValSz,
        LPBYTE * OutVal,
        LPDWORD OutValSz
        );
```

Input Parameters

ClustKey — Key that identifies the location of the binary value in the cluster database
ValNam — Name of the value to be updated
NewVal — Pointer to the new binary value
NewValSz — Size of the new binary value

Parameters that are both Input and Output

OutVal — Address of a pointer to the new binary value
OutValSz — Pointer to a DWORD in which the size in bytes of the value pointed to by *OutVal* is returned

Return Values

ERROR_SUCCESS — The operation completed successfully and the database was updated.
ERROR_NOT_ENOUGH_MEMORY – Not enough memory was allocated.

ResUtilSetBinaryValue also returns Win32 error codes returned by **ClusterRegSetValue**.

Programming Notes

ResUtilSetBinaryValue performs the following:

- Allocates memory for the *OutVal* pointer using the Win32 function LocalAlloc
- Calls the Cluster API function **ClusterRegSetValue**
- Copies the new value returned to the buffer

When you call **ResUtilSetBinaryValue**, you must ensure that buffers are deallocated from the buffer using the Win32 function **LocalFree**.

ResUtilSetDwordValue

The **ResUtilSetDwordValue** utility function sets a numerical value in the cluster database.

```
DWORD WINAPI ResUtilSetDwordValue(
        HKEY ClustKey,
        LPCWSTR ValNam,
        DWORD NewVal,
        LPDWORD OutVal
        );
```

Input Parameters

ClustKey — Key to the location of the numerical value in the cluster database
ValNam — Name of the value to be updated
NewVal — New value (DWORD)

Parameters that are both Input and Output
OutVal — Pointer to the location where the updated value should be copied

Return Values
ERROR_SUCCESS — The operation completed successfully and the numerical value was set in the cluster database.

If the operation was unsuccessful, **ResUtilSetDwordValue** returns a Win32 error value.

Programming Notes
ResUtilSetDwordValue calls the Cluster API function **ClusterRegSetValue** to update the cluster database.

ResUtilSetExpandSzValue
The **ResUtilSetExpandSzValue** utility function allocates memory and sets an expandable string value in the cluster database. An expandable string value contains data that represent a null-terminated Unicode string that contains unexpanded references to environment variables such as "%PATH%."

DWORD WINAPI **ResUtilSetExpandSzValue**(
HKEY *ClustKey*,
LPCWSTR *ValNam*,
LPCWSTR *NewVal*,
LPWSTR * *OutVal*
);

Input Parameters
ClustKey — Key to the location of the expandable string value in the cluster database
ValNam — Name of the value to be updated
NewVal — Pointer to the new expandable string value

Parameters that are both Input and Output
OutVal — Pointer to a string containing the updated value

Return Values
ERROR_SUCCESS — The operation completed successfully and the expandable string value was set in the cluster database.
ERROR_NOT_ENOUGH_MEMORY — Not enough memory was allocated.

ResUtilSetExpandSzValue returns Win32 error codes returned by **ClusterRegSetValue**.

Programming Notes
ResUtilSetExpandSzValue allocates memory for the new value and calls the Cluster API function **ClusterRegSetValue**.

ResUtilSetMultiSzValue
The **ResUtilSetMultiSzValue** utility function sets a multiple string value in the cluster database. A multiple string value contains data that represent an array of null-terminated strings, terminated by two null characters.

```
DWORD WINAPI ResUtilSetMultiSzValue(
                 HKEY ClustKey,
                 LPCWSTR ValNam,
                 LPCWSTR NewVal,
                 DWORD NewValSz,
                 LPWSTR * OutVal,
                 LPDWORD OutValSz
                 );
```

Input Parameters
ClustKey — Key to the location of the multiple string value in the cluster database
ValNam — Name of the value to be updated
NewVal — Pointer to the new multiple string value
NewValSz — Size of the new value

Parameters that are both Input and Output
OutVal — Address of the pointer to the new value
OutValSz — Pointer to the size of the new value

Return Values
ERROR_SUCCESS — The operation completed successfully and the multiple string value was successfully set in the cluster database.
ERROR_NOT_ENOUGH_MEMORY — Enough memory was not allocated.

ResUtilSetMultiSzValue returns Win32 error codes returned by **ClusterRegSetValue**.

Programming Notes
Res**UtilSetMultiSzValue** allocates memory for the new value and calls the Cluster API function **ClusterRegSetValue**.

ResUtilSetPrivatePropertyList
The **ResUtilSetPrivatePropertyList** utility function sets the private properties of a resource.

```
DWORD WINAPI ResUtilSetPrivatePropertyList(
                 PVOID ClustKey,
Const            PVOID InBuf,
                 DWORD InBufSz
                 );
```

Input Parameters
ClustKey — Cluster database key to the location of the private properties to be set
InBuf — Pointer to an input buffer containing a property list with the names and values of the properties to be set
InBufSz — Pointer to the size of the input buffer pointed to by *InBuf*, in bytes

Return Values
ERROR_SUCCESS — The operation was successful and the properties were updated successfully.
ERROR_BAD_ARGUMENTS — One or more of the input parameters were invalid.
ERROR_INVALID_DATA — Length of property data was invalid.

ERROR_INSUFFICIENT_BUFFER — The input buffer pointed to by *InBuf* was NULL.
ERROR_INVALID_PARAMETER — The syntax of a property name was invalid.

Programming Notes
The properties that are set in **ResUtilSetPrivatePropertyList** are placed in the portion of the cluster database below the specified key for the object. The value placed in the database is exactly as specified by the names in the property list. For example, if the name of a property contains backslash characters (\), each string preceding a backslash character is to be interpreted as a subkey name, and the last string following the last backslash character is to be interpreted as the value name.

ResUtilSetPropertyParameterBlock
The **ResUtilSetPropertyParameterBlock** utility function is used to set properties in the cluster database from a parameter block. A parameter block is a buffer or structure that contains the data or pointers to data for the properties described in a property table.

```
DWORD WINAPI ResUtilSetPropertyParameterBlock(
                PVOID ClustKey,
        Const   PRESUTIL_PROPERTY_ITEM PropTabl,
                PVOID Reserved,
        Const   LPBYTE InParms,
        Const   LPVOID InBuf,
                DWORD InBufSz,
                LPBYTE OutParms
                );
```

Input Parameters
ClustKey — Cluster database key to the location for the properties to be set.
PropTabl — Pointer to an array of RESUTIL_PROPERTY_ITEM structures describing the properties to be set. For more details about the RESUTIL_PROPERTY_ITEM structure, see the earlier programming notes for **ResUtilAddUnknownProperties**.
Reserved — Not used. Reserved for future use.
InParms — Pointer to an input parameter block containing the data for the properties described in the property table pointed to by *PropTabl.*
InBuf — Pointer to the input buffer containing a property list or null. If *InBuf* is not null, any properties listed in the property list that are not listed in the property table are also to be set in the cluster database.
InBufSz — Size in bytes of the input buffer pointed to by *InBuf.*

Output Parameters
OutParms — Optional pointer to a parameter block to receive data copied from the *InParms* parameter.

Return Values
ERROR_SUCCESS – The operation was successful and the properties were successfully set.
ERROR_INVALID_PARAMETER — The syntax, format, or type of property in the property table pointed to by *PropTabl* is incorrect or a property is read-only and cannot be updated.
ERROR_BAD_ARGUMENTS — One or more of the input parameters were invalid.

ResUtilSetPropertyTable

The **ResUtilSetPropertyTable** utility function is used to set properties, including unknown properties, in the cluster database. The properties are set based on a property list from a property table. The properties to be set are described using the RESUTIL_PROPERTY_ITEM structures.

```
DWORD WINAPI ResUtilSetPropertyTable(
              PVOID ClustKey,
        Const PRESUTIL_PROPERTY_ITEM PropTabl,
              PVOID Reserved,
              BOOL AllowUnknownProp,
        Const PVOID InBuf,
              DWORD InBufSz,
              OPTIONAL LPBYTE OutParms
              );
```

Input Parameters

ClustKey — Cluster database key to the location of the properties to be set.

PropTabl — Pointer to an array of RESUTIL_PROPERTY_ITEM structures describing the properties to be set. For more details about the RESUTIL_PROPERTY_ITEM structure, see the earlier programming notes for **ResUtilAddUnknownProperties**.

Reserved — Not used. Reserved for future use.

AllowUnknownProp — Flag to indicate whether or not unknown properties should be accepted. This parameter is set to TRUE if they should be accepted and FALSE if they should not be accepted.

InBuf — Pointer to the input buffer containing a property list.

InBufSz — Size of the input buffer pointed to by *InBuf*, in bytes.

Output Parameters

OutParms — Pointer to a parameter block to hold returned data. This parameter is optional. If specified, parameters are only written if they differ from those in the input buffer.

Return Values

ERROR_SUCCESS — The operation was successful and the properties were successfully set.

ERROR_BAD_ARGUMENTS — One or more of the input parameters were invalid.

ERROR_INSUFFICIENT_BUFFER — The size of the input buffer specified in *InBufSz* is too small to hold the returned data.

ERROR_INVALID_DATA — The input buffer pointed to by *InBuf* is NULL, a property name is not valid, or a property value is too small.

ERROR_INVALID_PARAMETER — The syntax, format, or type of property in the property table pointed to by *PropTabl* is incorrect or a property is read-only and cannot be set.

ResUtilSetSzValue

The **ResUtilSetSzValue** utility function allocates memory and calls the Cluster API function **ClusterRegSetValue** to set a string value in the cluster database.

```
DWORD WINAPI ResUtilSetSzValue(
              HKEY ClustKey,
              LPCWSTR ValNam,
              LPCWSTR NewVal,
              LPWSTR * OutVal
              );
```

Input Parameters
ClustKey — Key to the location of the string value in the cluster database
ValNam — Name of the value to be updated
NewVal — Pointer to the new string value

Parameters that are both Input and Output
OutVal — Address of a pointer to the new string value

Return Values
ERROR_SUCCESS — The operation completed successfully and the string value was set.
ERROR_NOT_ENOUGH_MEMORY — Enough memory was not allocated.

ResUtilSetSzValue returns Win32 error codes are returned by **ClusterRegSetValue**.

Programming Notes
ResUtilSetSzValue deallocates the previous value, if necessary.

ResUtilStartResourceService
The **ResUtilStartResourceService** utility function starts a service.

DWORD WINAPI **ResUtilStartResourceService**(
LPCTSTR *ServNam*,
LPHANDLE *ServHnd*
);

Input Parameters
ServNam — Name of the service to be started.
ServHnd — Optional pointer to a handle in which the handle to the started service is returned.

Return Values
ERROR_SUCCESS — The operation completed successfully and the service was successfully started.
ERROR_SERVICE_NEVER_STARTED — The service was not started.

If the operation was unsuccessful, **ResUtilStartResourceService** returns a Win32 error value.

Programming Notes
You must close the handle returned by **ResUtilStartResourceService** by calling the cluster utility function **ResUtilStopService** or the Win32 function **CloseServiceHandle**.

ResUtilStopResourceService
The **ResUtilStopResourceService** utility function stops a service.

DWORD WINAPI **ResUtilStopResourceService**(
LPCTSTR *ServNam*
);

Input Parameters
ServNam — Name of the service to be stopped.

Return Values

ERROR_SUCCESS — The operation completed successfully and the service was stopped.
ERROR_TIMEOUT — Service did not stop after a reasonable number of retries.

If the operation was unsuccessful, **ResUtilStopResourceService** returns a Win32 error value.

ResUtilStopService

The **ResUtilStopService** utility function stops a service.

DWORD WINAPI **ResUtilStopService**(
HANDLE *ServHnd*
);

Input Parameters

ServHnd — Handle of the service to be stopped.

Return Values

ERROR_SUCCESS — The operation completed successfully and the service was stopped.
ERROR_TIMEOUT — Service did not stop after a reasonable number of retries.

If the operation was unsuccessful, **ResUtilStopService** returns a Win32 error value.

Programming Notes

ResUtilStopService closes the handle specified in *ServHnd* when it stops the service.

ResUtilVerifyPrivatePropertyList

The **ResUtilVerifyPrivatePropertyList** utility function verifies that a private property list is correctly formatted.

DWORD WINAPI **ResUtilVerifyPrivatePropertyList**(
Const PVOID *InBuf*,
DWORD *InBufSz*
);

Input Parameters

InBuf — Pointer to an input buffer containing the property list to be verified
InBufSz — Size of the input buffer pointed to by *InBuf*

Return Values

ERROR_SUCCESS — The operation completed successfully and the property list was successfully verified.

If the operation was unsuccessful, **ResUtilVerifyPrivatePropertyList** returns a Win32 error value.

ResUtilVerifyPropertyTable

The **ResUtilVerifyPropertyTable** utility function verifies that a property table is correctly formatted. Optionally the property table can include unknown properties.

DWORD WINAPI **ResUtilVerifyPropertyTable**(
Const PRESUTIL_PROPERTY_ITEM *PropTabl*,
PVOID *Reserved*,
BOOL *AllowUnknownProp*,

```
Const   PVOID InBuf,
        DWORD InBufSz,
        LPBYTE OutParms
        );
```

Input Parameters

PropTabl — Pointer to the array of RESUTIL_PROPERTY_ITEM structures to be verified. For more details about the RESUTIL_PROPERTY_ITEM structure, see the earlier programming notes for **ResUtilAddUnknownProperties.**

Reserved – Not used. Reserved for future use.

AllowUnknownProp — Indicates whether or not unknown properties should be allowed in the property table. Unknown properties are allowed when this parameter is set to TRUE and not allowed when this parameter is set to FALSE.

InBuf — Pointer to the input buffer containing the property list to be processed.

InBufSz — Size in bytes of the input buffer pointed to by *InBuf.*

Output Parameters

OutParms — Pointer to the parameter block to hold returned data. This parameter is optional.

Return Values

ERROR_SUCCESS — The operation completed successfully and the property list was successfully verified.

If the operation was unsuccessful, **ResUtilVerifyPropertyTable** returns a Win32 error value.

ResUtilVerifyResourceService

The **ResUtilVerifyResourceService** utility function is used to check if a service is either starting or running.

```
DWORD WINAPI ResUtilVerifyResourceService(
        LPCTSTR ServNam
        );
```

Input Parameters

ServNam — Name of the service to be checked

Return Values

ERROR_SUCCESS — The operation completed successfully. The service is operational and is either starting or running.

ERROR_SERVICE_NOT_ACTIVE — The service is neither starting nor running.

If **ResUtilVerifyResourceService** is unable to determine whether or not the service is starting or running, it returns a Win32 error value.

ResUtilVerifyService

The ResUtilVerifyService utility function is used to check if a service is either starting or running. Unlike the utility function **ResUtilVerifyResourceService** that checks for a service by its name, **ResUtilVerifyService** checks for a service by its handle.

```
DWORD WINAPI ResUtilVerifyService(
        HANDLE ServHnd
        );
```

Input Parameters

ServHnd — Handle of the service to be checked

Return Values

ERROR_SUCCESS — The operation completed successfully. The service is operational and is either starting or running.

ERROR_SERVICE_NOT_ACTIVE — The service is neither starting nor running.

If **ResUtilVerifyService** cannot determine whether or not the service is starting or running, it returns a Win32 error value.

Glossary

adapter. An integrated circuit expansion board that communicates with and controls a device or system.

arbitration. Process of granting ownership of the quorum resource. A quorum resource implements the Arbitrate and Release entry point functions in its resource DLL to support arbitration.

Asynchronous Transfer Mode (ATM). A high-speed cell-switching network technology for LANs and WANs that handles data and real-time voice and video.

availability. The ability of a system to be up and providing service. The aim of the Cluster Server is to make continuous operation possible regardless of failures. Cluster Server makes applications highly available.

Backup Domain Controller (BDC). Microsoft Windows NT Server network operating system that contains copies of the user account information and is available to authenticate users when they log on to the domain. BDCs also provide authentication fault tolerance. If the Primary Domain Controller (PDC) is down for any reason, BDCs are available to authenticate users and guarantee their access to network resources.

bandwidth. Amount of data per second that can be transferred from one device to another. Bandwidth is limited by (1) the speed of transfer, (2) the "width" of the pipe, (3) the number of pipes, and (4) the overhead of sending data through the pipe.

bus. A collection of wires in a cable, or copper traces on a circuit board, used to transmit data, status, and control signals. EISA, PCI, and SCSI are examples of buses.

Checkpoint Manager. Software component in the Cluster Service that is responsible for saving data in the log file maintained by the quorum resource.

client application. Application software that is running on a network client system and does not necessarily perform name translation or establish connections.

client/server model. Architecture that splits an application into a front-end client component and a back-end server component. The client component running on a workstation gathers data from the user, prepares it for the server, and issues a request to the server. On the back end, the server waits for requests from its clients. When it receives a request, the server processes it and returns the requested information to the client. The client then presents the data to the user through its own user interface.

cluster. A computing environment created by connecting two or more computers with shared storage devices (such as a shared SCSI disk or RAID subsystem) for the purpose of improving system availability in the event of the failure of some of the computers within the cluster. Computers within the cluster back each other to ensure that the cluster as a whole is available. Clusters provide benefits other than improved availability. Storage devices are assigned to one of the computers in a cluster for normal operation, but may be accessed by another computer in the cluster in the event of a failure. To users, a cluster is accessed and managed as a single system regardless of the number of computer systems that make up the cluster.

Cluster Administrator. Cluster Server application that is used to manage and administer a cluster. Cluster Administrator can run on a client or server machine regardless of whether or not the machine is an active member of a cluster.

Cluster Administrator extension. Software component that implements the Cluster Administrator Extension API for allowing Cluster Administrator to administer a new resource type.

Cluster Administrator Extension API. Cluster Administrator Extension API consists of interfaces based on the Component Object Model (COM). Cluster Administrator Extension APIs provide for the development of custom resource types and associated extension DLLs.

Cluster API. Collection of functions that are implemented by the Cluster Service and used by a cluster-aware client or server application, a cluster management application, or a resource DLL. The Cluster APIs include functions to access and manage a cluster as a single entity. The Cluster API includes functions to manage cluster components including nodes, groups, resources, and the cluster database.

Cluster Automation Server. The library of COM-based interfaces that developers writing in Visual Basic and various scripting languages use to create cluster management applications.

cluster-aware application. Server application that can run on a cluster node and can be managed as a cluster resource.

cluster control codes. Cluster control codes describe an operation on cluster components such as resource, resource type, group, and node. Cluster control codes are 32-b values in length.

cluster member. A node that is an active participant of a cluster. A cluster member is in constant communication with the other members of the cluster and maintains a current version of the cluster database.

cluster node. *See* **node**.

cluster properties. Cluster properties are attributes that describe a cluster object. There are two types of cluster properties — common cluster properties and private cluster properties. A common cluster property is an attribute that exists for every instance of the type of cluster object for which it is defined. A private Cluster property is an attribute that exists only for specific instances of the type of object for which it is defined. Most cluster properties are stored in the cluster database to provide easy access. See **property lists and property table** later in this glossary.

cluster resource. – *See* **resource**.

Cluster Service. Cluster Server software component implemented as a Microsoft Windows NT service that controls all aspects of cluster operation and manages the configuration database. Every node in a cluster runs one instance of the Cluster Service.

cluster structures. Cluster structures are data structures used to specify data relating to a cluster object. For example, the data structure CLUSPROP_BINARY describes a binary data value used in a value list. The most common use for the majority of cluster structures is in a value list. *See* **value lists** and **property lists**.

cluster-unaware application. Client application that can run on a cluster node and can be managed as a cluster resource, but has no inherent knowledge of its cluster environment. Client applications function the same regardless of whether they are running on a node in a cluster or on a nonclustered system.

cluster utility functions. Utility functions that can be included in your cluster applications and resource DLLs to perform the function provided by the utility functions. Utility functions are used in the same manner as library functions. Utility functions help in the development of cluster applications and resource DLLs by saving time and programming effort.

communications line. Physical connection by which information flows from the network into the computer. Examples are twisted-pair, coaxial, and fiber-optic cable.

Communications Manager. Software component in the Cluster Service that maintains communication between cluster members and blocks communication when a node fails.

Configuration Failover Manager Database (CFMD). A database of registry updates for cluster information that keeps both servers in the cluster synchronized by using transactional semantics.

continuous availability. When a system is not expected to have any planned or unplanned downtime. Typically required in financial transaction and real-time processing applications, continuously available systems are designed to be serviced when the system is up.

core network name resource. The network name resource for the cluster.

Database Manager. Software component in the Cluster Service that manages the cluster database.

dependency. The relationship between two resources. Examples of dependencies are an application resource that is dependent on a disk resource for its data, or a file share resource that is dependent on a disk resource for a shared folder. The relationship between the resources dictates that the resources belong to the same group and run in the same node. The relationship also dictates the order in which the resources are taken offline and brought back online.

device driver. A software module that provides an interface for communication between the operating system and system hardware (e.g., a SCSI controller).

disk mirroring. Fault-tolerant technique that writes data simultaneously to two disks using the same disk controller. The disks operate in tandem, constantly storing and updating the same files. Mirroring alone does not ensure data protection. If both disks fail at the same time, you still lose data.

disk striping. Spreading data over multiple disk drives. Data are interleaved by bytes or sectors/blocks across the drives.

Domain Name System (DNS). Service that maps friendly names to IP addresses. DNS is used on the Internet for resolving names to Internet addresses.

downtime. The time duration when a system is unavailable for service.

Ethernet. Widely used LAN developed by Xerox, Digital, and Intel. Ethernet networks connect up to 1024 nodes at 10 Mbps per second over twisted pair, coax, and optical fiber.

Event Log Manager. Replicates the Windows NT event log records across the nodes of a cluster. The Windows NT Event Viewer attached to any one of the nodes can be used to view cluster events.

failback. The process of automatic migration of one or more resource groups back to a primary node when the primary node returns to operational status after a failure. In the prior example, IIS will failback to Node 1.

failed. State that applies to a cluster resource that is unavailable. A resource is placed in the failed state after an unsuccessful attempt has been made by the Cluster Service to bring it online.

failover. The process of relocating services and a resource/group of resources from one node that fails to another node that is operational. For example, a cluster may have two nodes, node 1 and node 2. The Internet Information Server (IIS) may be running on node 1 and providing Internet services. When node 1 fails, IIS failover to node 2 occurs and Internet services are continued. The offline and online transitions between resources occur in a predefined order. Resources that have other resources dependent on them are taken offline after the dependent resources are taken offline. Similarly, dependent resources are brought online first before resources on which they are dependent are brought online.

Failover Manager. Software component in the Cluster Service that works with the Resource Manager to manage resources and groups and initiate failover operations.

failover object. Any cluster service or resource for which you want to ensure availability in the event of a system failure. Failover objects can be disks, database applications on the servers, or file shares.

failover policy. Parameters that an administrator can set using Cluster Administrator to affect failover operations of a group. These parameters include the FailoverThreshold and FailoverPeriod properties.

failover time. Amount of time it takes a group to complete the failover process. *See* **failover.**

failure. A malfunction of a component such as hardware or software that renders the failed component unable to perform its intended function.

fault tolerance. A method of ensuring continuous or nonstop availability. While components can fail, systems are designed to be available even with such failures. Fault-tolerant systems are implemented by configuring a mirror of the primary system that remains in hot standby mode — idle and unused until a failure occurs. Fault tolerance is a relatively costly method of ensuring availability, because the backup system computing capacity is not used until the failure of the primary system.

file share resource. A file or print share that applications can access using a network path. Cluster Server provides a resource DLL to manage file share resources.

generic application resource. A cluster-aware or cluster-unaware application that is running on a cluster node and being managed as a cluster resource. Cluster Server provides a resource DLL to manage Generic Application resources.

generic service resource. A Microsoft Windows NT service that is running on a cluster node and is being managed as a cluster resource. Cluster Server provides a resource DLL to manage generic service resources.

Global Update Manager. Software component in the Cluster Service that provides a global update service that is used by other components in the Cluster Service.

group. A collection of resources to be configured/managed as a single unit. For example, if a group is set up to provide a virtual server function, then the group contains all the resources needed for a virtual server such as a network name resource and an IP address resource. Resources dependent on each other must be part of the same group. In addition, all resources within a group must also be online on the same node in the cluster.

hardware mirroring. The setting up of disk arrays in a mirrored configuration. Mirroring is performed using hardware, unlike software mirroring where the mirroring is implemented in software.

heartbeat. Message that is sent regularly by the Cluster Service on one node to the Cluster Service on an alternate node to maintain communication and detect failure.

highly available. System that provides an acceptable level of service for an extended period of time. Highly available systems are designed and operated to have minimal planned or unplanned downtime. If a highly available system is down, it is expected to be brought back up relatively quickly.

host adapter. Circuitry that translates between a processor internal bus and a different bus, such as a SCSI. On the SCSI bus, a host acts as an initiator and the peripheral acts as the target.

hot plug capability. The ability of a component (such as a disk array) in a system to support the insertion of hardware such as disks or cards while the component is up and operational.

hot swap capability. The ability of a system to support the replacement of hardware components such as disks or cards while the system is up and operational.

hub. Central connecting device in a network that joins communications lines together in a star configuration.

idle standby. A backup system that is a mirror of the primary system in "hot standby" to the primary system in a cluster. In the standby mode, the backup system is not used and is idle.

IIS virtual root resource. A virtual root to be used with Internet Information Server (IIS) that supports the WWW, FTP, and Gopher services. IIS virtual root resources may have dependencies on IP address resources, network name resources, and/or physical disk resources. Virtual roots containing access information are not supported. Cluster Server provides a resource DLL for managing IIS virtual root resources.

interconnect. Private network that connects nodes in a cluster.

IP address resource. A 32-b number in dotted decimal format that represents an Internet Protocol (IP) address. Cluster Server provides a resource DLL for managing IP address resources. When a group contains an IP address resource and a network name resource, it can be accessed by clients as a virtual server.

LAN. Local Area Network. The servers and clients in a cluster are connected by LANs.

latency. Time between two events.

load balancing. The ability to partition the workload by assigning resources (such as disks and databases) to servers in the cluster and defining failover/failback policies. This provides an efficient and effective use of server resources.

logical unit. Physical or virtual device addressable through a SCSI target device. A physical device can have more than one logical unit.

Mean time between failure (MTBF). Metric typically used by hardware manufacturers to indicate the average time between failures of components.

Mean time to repair (MTTR). Metric used to provide an indication of the time to diagnose and repair a failure.

Membership Manager. Software component in the Cluster Service that maintains information about the current membership of the cluster.

name resolution. The process of translating computer names to IP addresses. Cluster clients use name resolution services to find cluster resources. MSCS also uses name resolution when a node joins another node to form a cluster. Techniques used to perform name resolution include the Windows Internet Name Service (WINS), the Domain Name System (DNS), and IP broadcast name resolution.

name server. Software installed on the cluster servers that works with the client software to create the illusion of a single system through aliases. By using aliases, the client is unaware of the name of each server or how the cluster workload is distributed.

network name resource. A friendly name of an entity that exists on a network. Cluster Server provides a resource DLL for managing network name resources. When a group contains a network name resource and an IP address resource, it can be accessed by clients as a virtual server.

network partition. Situation that occurs when there is a network failure and one node in a cluster cannot receive heartbeat signals from the other node; also known as split brain syndrome.

No Remote Memory Access (NORMA). Clustering architecture where all memory is local to each system and all communication between systems consists of message passing. Shared-disk architectures are sometimes included in this classification.

node. Each computer that is a member of a cluster. In a Windows NT Cluster, each computer runs the Microsoft Windows NT Server operating system. A cluster node can be either an active or an inactive member of a cluster.

NTFS. NT File System. The standard file system for the Windows NT operating system.

offline. State that applies to a cluster resource, group, or node, marking that object as unavailable. The Cluster Service of an offline node may or may not be running.

online. State that applies to a cluster resource, group, or node, marking that object as available. When a node is online, it is an active member of the cluster and can own and run groups as well as honor cluster database updates, contribute votes to the quorum algorithm, and maintain heartbeats.

packet switching. Transmission technique that maximizes the use of digital transmission facilities by simultaneously transmitting packets of digital data from many sources on a single communications channel. This networking technology breaks up a message into smaller pieces for transmission. It is the most common form of data transmission technology used in LANs and WANs.

parameter block. A parameter block is a buffer or structure that contains the data (or pointers to the data) for one or more properties described in a property table. Entries in a property table contain an offset to a property block.

partitioned. A state in which one or more of the nodes in a cluster cannot communicate with the other cluster members.

paused. State that applies to a node that is a fully active member in the cluster, but cannot own or run groups. The paused state is provided to allow an administrator to perform maintenance.

pending. State that refers to a resource that is in the process of being brought online or taken offline.

Peripheral Component Interconnect (PCI). Local bus for personal computers that provides a high-speed data path between the processor and peripheral devices.

physical disk resource. Disk on a SCSI bus connected to two or more nodes that contains shared folders or storage. Cluster Server provides a resource DLL for managing physical disk resources.

planned downtime. A known system outage that is anticipated and scheduled to occur.

preservation of transaction state. System design for preventing the loss of data in a transitional state.

Primary Domain Controller (PDC). Microsoft Windows NT Server network operating system that manages all the domain-user account information.

print spooler resource. A network printer that applications access using a network IP address instead of an individual name. Cluster Server provides a resource DLL for managing print spooler resources.

property list. A collection of information used to describe multiple properties in control code operations. Each entry except the final one in a property list contains a property name and property value. The property name contains a CLUSPROP_VALUE structure, a name string, and padding if necessary to align the name on a DWORD boundary. The property value contains a CLUSPROP_VALUE structure, data, and padding if necessary. The final entry contains only the CLUSPROP_SYNTAX_ENDMARK value.

property table. An array of RESUTIL_PROPERTY_ITEM structures used as an input parameter to or output parameter from a cluster resource utility function. Each entry in a property table contains information about a property and an offset to the property data in a buffer known as a parameter block.

pulling a group. Process of transferring control of all groups in a cluster to one or more alternate nodes when the current node fails. The remaining nodes negotiate for ownership of each group and when negotiation is complete, the nodes update their cluster databases.

pushing a group. Process of restarting a group on a different node when one of its resources fails. This process can be initiated manually by an administrator, causing each of the affected resources to gracefully shut down prior to the failover, or by the Resource Manager.

quorum. Voting mechanism used to guarantee that specific data necessary for recovery can be maintained consistently between all cluster members. This mechanism involves a special resource called the quorum resource. The recovery data are stored by the quorum resource, typically a SCSI disk or fault-tolerant disk set that can be owned by one cluster node at any point in time. When the node that owns the quorum resource fails, the surviving nodes arbitrate to take over its ownership. Each quorum resource receives one vote and that vote is transitively passed to the node that currently owns the resource. By default there is only one quorum resource per cluster. The Cluster Service Membership Manager maintains the quorum mechanism.

quorum-capable resource. A cluster resource that can act as a cluster quorum resource. A quorum-capable resource must provide a means for persistent storage of configuration information necessary for recovery and a means for arbitration. Arbitration is the process by which cluster nodes effectively negotiate for ownership of the quorum resource. The SCSI reserve and release functions are examples of this type of arbitration support. In Cluster Server version 1.0, only physical disk resources and fault=tolerant disk set resources are quorum capable.

quorum log. A file that maintains a history of all the transactions affecting the cluster database on any of the cluster nodes. The log is stored on the cluster quorum resource and is also referred to as the recovery log.

quorum resource. The quorum-capable resource selected to maintain the configuration data necessary for recovery of the cluster. These data contain details of all changes that have been applied to the cluster database. The quorum resource is generally accessible to other cluster resources so that any cluster node has access to the most recent database changes.

RAID (redundant array of independent disks). A group of storage devices configured to provide higher data transfer rates and data recovery/fault tolerance. RAID can be configured in different ways called levels. The RAID levels vary from level 0 through level 5. A RAID device uses two or more magnetic or optical disks set up to duplicate the data written to disks. RAID can be implemented through software, or in the disk controller hardware.

recovery log. *See* **quorum log**.

redundancy. A method of protecting against component failures by building in additional backup components of a system.

reliability. A probability that indicates the degree to which data in a transfer is guaranteed to arrive at its destination in its intended form. Reliability refers to three distinct attributes: (1) the degree to which a system or component achieves a transfer, (2) the degree to which a system or component can fail and the transfer can still occur, and (3) the degree to which the integrity of the data is preserved.

resource. A physical or logical entity that is owned by a cluster node. Applications, disks, and file shares are examples of resources. Resources provide a service to clients. A resource is the basic unit managed by the Cluster Service of the node. Resources can be brought online and taken offline. A resource can only be hosted on a single cluster node at any given time.

resource API. Set of functions that allow a resource DLL to communicate with the Resource Monitor. Some of the functions are implemented by a resource DLL and others are implemented by the Resource Monitor.

resource class. Numerical value that is used to identify resources of similar capability, such as resources that can act as storage devices.

resource DLL. A dynamic link library that contains an implementation of the resource API for a specific type of resource. Each resource in a cluster has an associated DLL that acts as the interface mechanism to the resource. The resource DLL is loaded into the address space of its Resource Monitor and the Resource Monitor acts on the resource by calling the entry point functions implemented in the resource DLL.

Resource Manager. Software component in the Cluster Service that works with the Cluster Service Failover Manager to manage resources and groups and to initiate failover operations.

Resource Monitor. Cluster software component that manages communication between the Cluster Service of a node and one or more of its resources.

router. An intelligent hub that routes traffic to a designated channel.

scalability. Ability to incrementally add one or more systems, as needed, to an existing cluster when the overall load of the cluster exceeds its capabilities.

server application. Application software running on a cluster node, regardless of whether or not it does service registration.

service. Data or operation made available to network clients through a virtual server, a resource group that contains a network name resource as well as an IP address resource; not necessarily a Microsoft Windows NT Service.

service level agreement (SLA). A contract that specifies the operational times for a system along with acceptable intervals or percentages of planned and/or unplanned downtimes. In addition, SLAs can also specify cost and penalty information.

shared device model. *See* **shared disk model**.

shared disk model. Clustering architecture where all systems share devices.

shared memory model. Clustering architecture where all systems share a single main memory through which all traffic between devices must flow.

shared nothing model. Clustering architecture where systems share neither memory nor devices. Each processor has its own memory and a copy of the operating system. Connections between processors are optimized because messages are passed across a high-speed, dedicated bus. Cluster Server uses shared nothing clusters.

shared resource. Cluster organization in which some resources are accessible to all systems in the cluster.

SCSI-2. The second generation of SCSI, which includes many improvements to SCSI-1, including fast, wide SCSI.

SCSI-3. The third generation of SCSI, which introduces improvements to the parallel bus and high-speed bus architectures.

Small Computer System Interface (SCSI). A smart protocol that permits high data transfer rates when connecting several classes of peripheral devices to a host system without requiring modifications to hardware and software.

SMB share resource. *See* **file share resource**.

software mirroring. The creation of extra copies of data written to a disk using software (contrast this with hardware mirroring where the extra copies are created using hardware — *see* **hardware mirroring** earlier).

storage shim driver. Cluster software that works with the operating system and the drivers in the I/O stack. It acts as a switch that mediates access to disks and ensures that user data are not corrupted.

symmetric multiprocessing (SMP). A computer architecture in which computing capacity is increased by adding CPUs. Multiple CPUs share global memory and a single copy of the operating system. Application processes run as if they were on a single processor system.

System. *See* **node**.

10Base-T. Twisted-pair Ethernet connection, commonly used for wiring desktops to Ethernet hubs and switches to reduce costs.

100Base-T. Proposed standard for a 100 Mbps LAN. 100Base-T would be completely compatible with the 10 Mbps 10Base-T, but would be 10 times as fast.

TCP/IP. Transmission Control Protocol/Internet Protocol is an industry-standard suite of protocols providing communications in a heterogeneous environment. While TCP/IP is best known for its access to the Internet and Internet resources, TCP/IP is also well suited as an enterprise networking protocol because it provides interoperability between different types of computer systems.

time service. Cluster Server resource that maintains consistent time across nodes in a cluster.

UNC. Universal naming convention for LANMAN protocol. This is the traditional \\server\share syntax.

Uniform Memory Access (UMA). Model where multiple processors share a common memory bus. All accesses to memory take the same length of time.

Universal Datagram Protocol (UDP). Connectionless, unreliable transport service that is used by Microsoft for logon, browsing, and name resolution.

unplanned downtime. An unexpected system outage.

value list. A collection of data values. The data values are the data portion of property values in a property list and are typically returned from control code operations. Each entry except the final one in a value list is made up of a CLUSPROP_VALUE structure and data. The final entry contains only the CLUSPROP_SYNTAX_ENDMARK value.

virtual circuit. Form of communicating where, when a transmission is complete, the transmitted information is guaranteed to be received by the intended recipient or an error is returned. Also, messages are delivered in order and are never duplicated.

virtual server. Collection of services that gives the appearance of an actual Microsoft Windows NT Server network operating system to clients. A virtual server is typically a group containing all the resources to run a particular application, such as a network name resource and an IP address resource.

Windows Internet Name Service (WINS). An enhanced NetBIOS Name Server (NBNS) designed by Microsoft to register NetBIOS computer names and resolve them to IP addresses for both local and remote hosts.

Windows Sockets 2. Network programming interface at the Transport Layer in the ISO reference model. Windows Sockets 2 is included with Microsoft Windows NT version 4.0.

Bibliography

The following is a listing of books and papers for additional reading related to clustering technology and MSCS.

BOOKS

1. Pfister, G. F., *In Search of Clusters*, Prentice-Hall, Englewood Cliffs, NJ, 1995. (*In Search of Clusters* offers an excellent introduction to clustering technology including a description of the common programming models.)
2. Rajagopal, R., Ed., *Handbook of Heterogeneous Networking*, Auerbach Publications, Boca Raton, FL, 1999.
3. Rajagopal, R., *Windows NT, UNIX, NetWare Migration and Coexistence: A Professional's Guide*, CRC Press, Boca Raton, FL, 1998.
4. Rajagopal, R. and Monica, S., *Advanced Windows NT Programming*, Osborne/McGraw-Hill, New York, 1997.
5. Weygant, P. S., *Clusters for High Availability: A Primer of HP-UX Solutions*, Prentice-Hall, Englewood Cliffs, NJ, 1996.

PAPERS

1. Kronenberg, N., Levey, H., and Strecker, W., VAXclusters: A closely coupled distributed system, *ACM Trans. Comput. Syst.*, 4(2), 1986.

URLS

1. Microsoft's web page http://www.microsoft.com/ntserver/ contains the latest information about MSCS including upgrade information.
2. Tandem Servernet information is available at http://www.tandem.com/MENU_PGS/SNET_PGS/TECHINFO.HTM.
3. The VI Architecture version 1.0 specification, mentioned in Chapter 6, is available at http://www.viarch.org/.

MICROSOFT DOCUMENTATION

1. *Microsoft Cluster Server Administrator's Guide*, covers the details required for an administrator to install and administer a MSCS cluster. This manual is available in soft copy form and can be accessed by clicking **Start** , -> **Programs** -> **Books Online** on all

computers running Windows NT Server, Enterprise Edition. In addition, this manual is available in soft copy form on the Microsoft's Technet CD.

2. *Windows NT Server, Enterprise Edition 4.0 Administrator's Guide* covers among other topics configuring Microsoft BackOffice applications to run in a MSCS cluster.
3. *Readme* file. The Readme.doc file is available at the \MSCS folder on the Windows NT Server, Enterprise Edition 4.0 Components CD. In addition to general information about MSCS and a description of MSCS features, it contains limitations uncovered in late testing which are not documented elsewhere.
4. *Online Administrator Help* — Like many other Microsoft products, online help is available to the MSCS Cluster Administrator to guide through administrative tasks. MSCS online Help is accessed by opening Cluster Administrator and pressing F1 or using the **Help** menu. Context-sensitive help is also available for all MSCS Cluster Administrator components. Context-sensitive help is accessed by first clicking the question mark button in the upper right corner of a dialog box, and then clicking the component for which help is required.
5. For more information on the Windows NT TCP/IP protocol suite, see Part 1 of the *Windows NT Server Version 4.0 Networking Supplement.* To access this book online on a computer running Windows NT Server, click **Start**, point to **Programs**, and click **Books Online**.

HARDWARE COMPATIBILITY LIST

As mentioned in Chapter 4, Microsoft maintains a list of hardware that has been tested and certified for compatibility. This list is available at http://www.microsoft.com/hwtest/hcl.

While it is a good idea to check this list even for stand alone server and workstation hardware selection, it is even more important to check this list for clusters, because Microsoft only supports specific configurations in the compatibility list. Microsoft does not provide best effort support for clustered systems as it does for NT Server or NT Workstation.

A snapshot of the list is shown next. The category option lets you pick six cluster-related categories — Cluster, Cluster/fibrechannel adapter, Cluster/Raid, Cluster/Raid Controller, Cluster/Raid System, and Cluster/SCSI Adapter.

Choosing Cluster results in a list of systems from different hardware vendors. The next figure shows some Compaq servers.

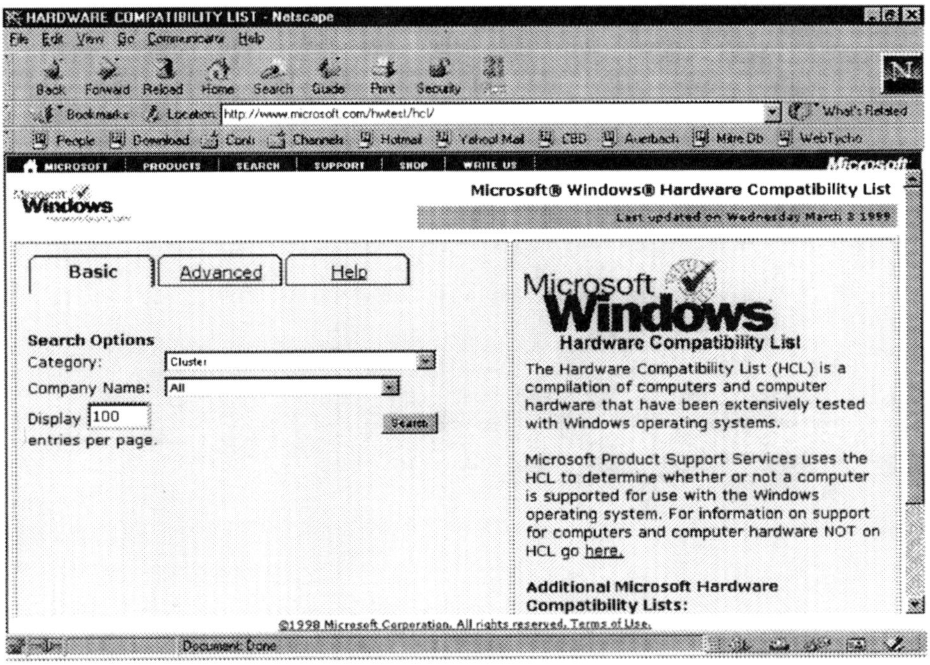
HARDWARE COMPATIBILITY LIST - Netscape
File Edit View Go Communicator Help
Back Forward Reload Home Search Guide Print Security
Bookmarks Location: http://www.microsoft.com/hwtest/hcl/
What's Related
People Download Conf Channels Hotmail Yahoo! Mail CBD Auerbach Mare Db WebTycho
MICROSOFT PRODUCTS SEARCH SUPPORT SHOP WRITE US
Microsoft
Windows
Microsoft® Windows® Hardware Compatibility List
Basic
Advanced
Help
Search Options
Category:
Cluster
Company Name:
All
Display
100
entries per page.
Search
Microsoft Windows
Hardware Compatibility List
The Hardware Compatibility List (HCL) is a compilation of computers and computer hardware that have been extensively tested with Windows operating systems.
Microsoft Product Support Services uses the HCL to determine whether or not a computer is supported for use with the Windows operating system. For information on support for computers and computer hardware NOT on HCL go here.
Additional Microsoft Hardware Compatibility Lists:
©1998 Microsoft Corporation. All rights reserved. Terms of Use.
Document: Done

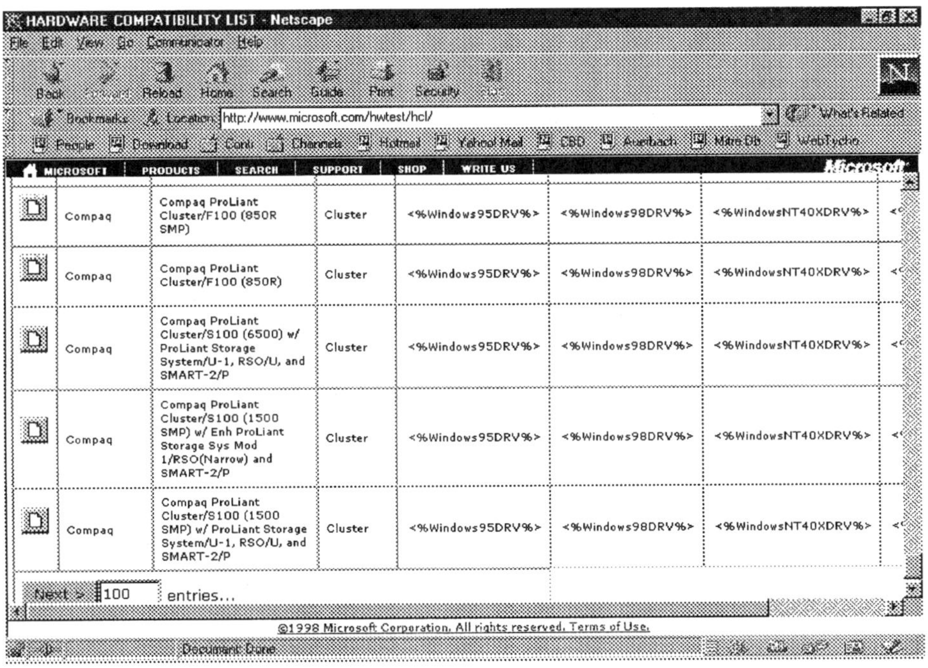
HARDWARE COMPATIBILITY LIST - Netscape
File Edit View Go Communicator Help
Back Forward Reload Home Search Guide Print Security
Bookmarks Location: http://www.microsoft.com/hwtest/hcl/
What's Related
People Download Conf Channels Hotmail Yahoo! Mail CBD Auerbach Mare Db WebTycho
MICROSOFT PRODUCTS SEARCH SUPPORT SHOP WRITE US
Microsoft
Compaq
Compaq ProLiant Cluster/F100 (850R SMP)
Cluster
<%Windows95DRV%>
<%Windows98DRV%>
<%WindowsNT40XDRV%>
Compaq
Compaq ProLiant Cluster/F100 (850R)
Cluster
<%Windows95DRV%>
<%Windows98DRV%>
<%WindowsNT40XDRV%>
Compaq
Compaq ProLiant Cluster/S100 (6500) w/ ProLiant Storage System/U-1, RSO/U, and SMART-2/P
Cluster
<%Windows95DRV%>
<%Windows98DRV%>
<%WindowsNT40XDRV%>
Compaq
Compaq ProLiant Cluster/S100 (1500 SMP) w/ Enh ProLiant Storage Sys Mod 1/RSO(Narrow) and SMART-2/P
Cluster
<%Windows95DRV%>
<%Windows98DRV%>
<%WindowsNT40XDRV%>
Compaq
Compaq ProLiant Cluster/S100 (1500 SMP) w/ ProLiant Storage System/U-1, RSO/U, and SMART-2/P
Cluster
<%Windows95DRV%>
<%Windows98DRV%>
<%WindowsNT40XDRV%>
Next >
100
entries...
©1998 Microsoft Corporation. All rights reserved. Terms of Use.
Document: Done

Index

A

B

C

D

E

F

G

H

I

L

M

N

O

P

Q

R

S

T

U

V